ACADEMY CLASS OF 1940

THOSE NAMES IN BOLDFACE INDICATE MEMBERS OF THE CLASS WHO DIED AS A RESULT OF ENEMY ACTION IN WARTIME.

ROBERT IRVING DICE

GEORGE FRANCIS DIXON, JR.

ROBERT RUSSELL DODDERIDGE

ALTON PARKER DONNELL

JOSEPH PATRICK DONOHUE

RAYMOND JOHN DOWNEY

JAMES FRANCIS DOWNING

JAMES GARLAND DUBUISSON

LEO ERWAY DUNHAM, JR.

JOHN PATRICK DWYER

KERMIT ROBERT DYKE

JOHN ROSS EAST, JR.

JOSEPH JACKSON EATON, JR.

DELANO EDGELL

PHILIP LOVELL ELLIOTT

DILL BAYNARD ELLIS

JOHN CHRISTIE EMERY

JOHN ZACHARIAH ENDRESS

GEORGE WASHINGTON ENGLAND, JR.

SANFORD PATRICK ENGLAND

ALBERT DALE EPLEY

FLORIAN JOHN ERSPAMER

CHARLES GILLIES ESAU

CHARLES RICHARD FAIRLAMB

WILLIAM EUGENE FARTHING, JR.

ROBERT JOHN FATE

WALTER JOSEPH FELLENZ

HARLAN BENTON FERRILL

BERNARD AMBROSE FERRY

SYDNEY GILBERT FISHER

EDWARD DUNPHY FITZPATRICK

EDWARD AIKEN FLANDERS

THADDEUS PHILIP FLORYAN

ALFRED JENNINGS FLOYD

LAWRENCE GORDON FORBES

WINSTON CURETON FOWLER

WILLIAM PAYNE FRANCISCO

RICHARD HOBBS FRASER

RICHARD HENRY FREE

HARRY ALBRIGHT FRENCH

CHESTER MOFFET FREUDENDORF

LEE WATSON FRITTER

ARTHUR THEODORE FRONTCZAK

FORD PRIOLEAU FULLER, JR.

LAWRENCE JOSEPH FULLER

DURWARD HENRY GALBREATH

SILVIO EMIL GASPERINI, JR.

ALAN EDWARD GEE

VINCENT EBOL GEPTE

JOHN PAUL GERALD

FRANCIS CLARE GIDEON

WILLIAM JOSEPH GILDART

ALVAN CULLOM GILLEM, II

ROLAND MERRILL GLESZER

RAYMOND HAROLD GOODRICH

SAMUEL McCLURE GOODWIN

THOMAS FREDERICK GORDON

JOHN ANTHONY GRAF, JR.

GILFORD DALTON GREEN

JAMES SCOTT GREENE, JR.

WALTER EUGENE GUNSTER, JR.

CLARENCE EDWARD GUSHURST

DAVID ROGER GUY

WALLACE JAMES HACKETT

BURDETT EUGENE HAESSLY

EDWIN CARROLL HAGGARD

ROLLAND WOODROW HAMELIN

JOSEPH SCHUYLER HARDIN

THOMAS BOWMAN HARGIS, JR.

JOHN STEVENS HARNETT

CHARLES EDMUND HARRISON, JR.

LEONARD LANDON HASEMAN

CHARLES BELLOWS HAZELTINE, JR.

HENRY PATRICK HEID, JR.

LYMAN OSCAR HEIDTKE

WILLIAM ELLIOTT HEINEMANN

EDWARD HENRY HENDRICKSON

JAMES THOMAS HENNESSY

LESTER CECIL HESS

GEORGE COLUMBUS HINES

VICTOR WOODFIN HOBSON, JR.

ELBERT DOTTERER HOFFMAN

THEODORE LOUIS HOFFMANN

WILLIAM NORMAN HOLM

EDWARD FRANKLIN HOOVER, JR.

FRANKLIN WOLFRAM HORTON

WILLIAM FREDERICK HORTON

LLOYD WEBSTER HOUGH

MARK RANSOM HUDSON, JR.

AQUILLA BALLARD HUGHES, JR.

EVAN HARRIS HUMPHREY, JR.

JOSEPH VINCENT IACOBUCCI

MARVIN LEROY JACOBS

BERTIL ANDREW JOHNSON

CARTER BURDEAU JOHNSON

ERNEST BRYANT JONES

WING FOOK JUNG

WILLIAM MYERS KASPER

JOHN JOSEPH KENNEY

RICHARD JOSIAH KENT

WILLIAM PARHAM KEVAN, JR.

ROY HUBERT KINSELL

WILLIAM ROSCOE KINTNER

LAWRENCE RONALD KLAR

MARK CLAIR BAUGHER KLUNK

ROBERT PHINEAS KNAPP, JR.

ARCHIE JOYCE KNIGHT

JOHN RICHARD KNIGHT

RONALD MAURICE KOLDA

FRANCIS EDWARD KRAMER

PAUL HOBART KRAUSS

JAMES FREDERICK KREITZER

NATHAN LOUIS KRISBERG

MICHAEL KUSIV, JR.

THIS BOOK IS DEDICATED TO

ALL MEMBERS OF THE LONG GRAY LINE WHO LOST THEIR LIVES IN AMERICA'S WARS

BY THE CLASS OF 1940 UNITED STATES MILITARY ACADEMY

The Illustrated History of West Point was sponsored and funded by the Class of 1940 as its 50th Anniversary gift to the United States Military Academy.

Most West Point alumni believe that the development of the Military Academy and its graduates has been strongly influenced by the Academy's dramatic natural setting, as well as by the character of its buildings, fortifications, monuments, and trophies. While there have been a number of attempts in the past to portray certain aspects of the setting and the architecture, a serious graphic historic portrayal has always been lacking. Also, there has been little published material available concerning the problems, arguments, and rationale for much of the physical development that is an integral part of the character of West Point.

The setting and the structures have been brought together and unified in this book within the framework of a new basic institutional history of the Military Academy that begins with a consideration of the strategic importance of West Point during the colonial and Revolutionary War periods. Research for this history has unearthed much new and interesting information concerning the founding and continuing development of the United States Military Academy at West Point.

It is the hope of the Class of 1940 that this book will represent a substantial contribution to the body of knowledge concerning the history of the Military Academy within its unique setting; to furthering the ideals and traditions of the Academy; and, through the participation of a publisher of international stature, to bringing the West Point story to the attention of a broad national and international audience.

The Class of 1940 also wishes to honor here the invaluable contribution made to the gift project by our classmate, Major General David S. Parker, United States Army, Retired, the Chairman of the Gift Committee, who died prior to publication of The Illustrated History of West Point.

For the Class of 1940

West Point, New York

June 1990

W.W. Vaughan

Class President

THE ILLUSTRATED
HISTORY OF
WEST
POINT

THE ILLUSTRATED HISTORY OF WEST POINT

By Theodore J. Crackel · Original Photography by Ted Spiegel

Harry N. Abrams, Inc., Publishers, New York in association with The United States Military

Academy Class of 1940 To Commemorate the Fiftieth Anniversary of Its Graduation, 1990

Editor: Adele Westbrook
Designer: Bob McKee
Assistant Designer: John C. Thomas
Photo Editor: John K. Crowley

Library of Congress Cataloging-in-Publication Data
Crackel, Theodore J.
The illustrated history of West Point / Theodore J. Crackel;
photography by Ted Spiegel.
p.   cm.
Includes bibliographical references (p.   ) and index.
ISBN 0–8109–3458–2
1. United States Military Academy—History.
I. Spiegel, Ted.
II. United States Military Academy.
Class of 1940.   III. Title.
U410.L1C68 1991
355'.0071'173—dc20   90—27745

Half-Title Page: Mahan Hall at the United States Military
Academy, West Point, New York.
Title Page: View of Cozzens Hotel near West Point, as shown
in a nineteenth-century painting by John Frederick Kensett.
c. 1863. Oil on canvas, 20 × 34". Courtesy The New-York
Historical Society.

CONTENTS

WEST POINT FOR ALL SEASONS

Aerial view of the United States Military Academy

at West Point in the Hudson Highlands of New York State.

SUMMER

Left: Rappelling is part of cadet field training. Right: Cadets of the three upper classes (third, second, and first), participate in summer training at Camp Buckner, together with troop units of the Active Army.

New cadets enter the Military Academy in June to begin their four-year cadet training program. Here, the "plebes" (fourth class) return to the Academy in mid-August from a Lake Frederick encampment.

FALL *Below: The Superintendent's quarters with the cadet chapel visible in the background. Right: The Homecoming Parade honors previous classes of graduates.*

Left: An encounter with the Army football team can include the firing
of a cannon after points have been scored by the West Point players.
Below: A cadet rides atop an Army Mule at a football game.

WINTER

Left: L'Ecole Polytechnique Monument was presented to the Academy in 1919 by the cadets of the French School as a tribute to the French cadets who took part in the defense of France in 1814.

Far left: Cadets passing Grant Hall as they walk to class on a brisk winter day.

SPRING

The Graduation Parade takes place on the plain and is the final parade for the first class cadet.

Left: When the First Captain says "Class Dismissed" the members of the graduating class fling their white caps into the air. Above: A pair of newlyweds leaves the cadet chapel beneath a canopy of crossed sabers.

THE PURPOSE OF THE UNITED STATES MILITARY ACADEMY

To provide the Nation with leaders of character who serve the common defense.

THE MISSION OF THE UNITED STATES MILITARY ACADEMY

To educate and train the Corps of Cadets so that each graduate shall have the attributes essential to professional growth as an officer of the Regular Army and to inspire each to a lifetime of service to the Nation.

THE OATH TAKEN UPON ENTERING THE ACADEMY

"I, (your name), do solemnly swear that I will support the Constitution of the United States, and bear true allegiance to the National Government; that I will maintain and defend the sovereignty of the United States, paramount to any and all allegiance, sovereignty, or fealty I may owe to any State or country whatsoever; and that I will at all times obey the legal orders of my superior officers, and the Uniform Code of Military Justice."

THE OATH TAKEN UPON BEING COMMISSIONED IN THE ARMY

"I, (your name), having been appointed an officer in the Army of the United States, as indicated above in the grade of Second Lieutenant do solemnly swear (or affirm) that I will support and defend the Constitution of the United States against all enemies, foreign and domestic, that I will bear true faith and allegiance to the same; that I take this obligation freely, without any mental reservation or purpose of evasion; and that I will well and faithfully discharge the duties of the office which I am about to enter; SO HELP ME GOD."

PREFACE

The Illustrated History of West Point is first and foremost the story of the United States Military Academy as an institution. But it is also the story of the people—the officers and cadets—who have made the Academy what it was and is. And, it is the history of West Point as a place—the setting, the land, and the evolution of its striking Tudor-Gothic architecture. *The Illustrated History of West Point* takes an entirely new look at West Point.

Because the story is about West Point, the narrative only rarely ventures beyond the boundaries of the post. When it does, the purpose is to examine issues directly related to the Academy, such as policies and decisions made in Washington that affected the school. Similarly, graduates, individually or collectively, are seldom pursued beyond the gates, and their professional lives are chronicled only in so far as they relate to West Point—those, for example, who returned to the Military Academy as members of the faculty, or as Commandant or Superintendent.

For that reason, it is appropriate to say a word here about the continuing contribution of the Academy's graduates. They have fought with distinction in each of the nation's wars, beginning with the War of 1812, and, since the early days of the Civil War, have provided the Army's senior leadership—Grant, Sherman, Sheridan, Schofield, Hugh Scott, Tasker Bliss, Peyton March, Pershing, MacArthur, Patton, Eisenhower, Bradley, Maxwell Taylor, Creighton Abrams, and H. Norman Schwarzkopf, to name only a few. But their influence has been even more pervasive. They have provided America with leaders in all walks of life—in business, agriculture, the professions, and in government. They built the railroads that made this a continental nation; they have been explorers, professors, bishops, and presidents. And, day in and day out, that contribution is being expanded, as today's graduates make their mark.

The Illustrated History of West Point is essentially a chronological story of West Point's history. A number of themes are followed from beginning to end—cadet and faculty life, institutional governance, curriculum, growth, and expansion. Because of the ebb and flow of many other events and issues, and the discontinuities between war and peace, there is some inevitable overlapping. In some chapters it was necessary to go back and pick up themes that were not fully developed when first mentioned. Conversely, the analysis of some issues has been revisited in more than one chapter. This approach proved essential, given the many currents being followed.

The Illustrated History of West Point follows the evolution of West Point from early settlement to its role as a strategic post of the American Revolution, to its adoption as home of the United States Military Academy, and then through the growth of that Academy. To aid in depicting that evolution and growth, a series of maps was produced especially for this book. These maps focus on the area of the plain and its immediate environs. Beginning with the period immediately following the Revolution, the maps show West Point as it has developed from period to period. Each map shows the major structures that existed in the period depicted—differentiating between those that were constructed during the period, those that persisted throughout the period, and those that existed for a time but were demolished before the end of the period. In order to better portray the changes that took place over time, we have taken some license with the scale of buildings

The United States Military Academy Coat-of-Arms, designed in 1898.

and their depiction, and we have attempted only to show the general shapes of the various buildings. For example, we have chosen to portray all single family quarters as squares, all duplexes, etc., as rectangles, and other buildings in only general outline. Out buildings and other auxiliary structures were usually ignored. This was particularly true in the area below the level of the plain to the northwest—once called Washington Valley—which has traditionally been a service area for the Academy and the balance of the post. In constructing these maps all of the available contemporary maps and related documents were studied in detail and where there were discrepancies they were resolved using the best evidence available—sometimes by a personal inspection of the terrain. The final maps were drawn by a talented and patient illustrator, Andrea Bietzel. I was assisted in the map research by Nancy Loughridge, a colleague at the Papers of the Commanding Generals. West Point cartographer Edward J. Krasnoborski consulted on the project and provided encouragement at every stage.

In the process of researching and writing a work such as this, one accrues more debts of gratitude than can ever adequately be repaid. As a first installment, however, I want to express my thanks to the many individuals on the staff and faculty at West Point who aided me at every turn—and particularly to Lieutenant General Dave R. Palmer, the Superintendent, Brigadier General Roy K. Flint, the Dean, and Brigadier General David A. Bramlett, the Commandant of Cadets, each of whom took time to share with me their own views and to answer my many questions. A special thanks is also due to Colonel Larry Donnithorne of the Superintendent's staff, and to Michael E. Moss, Director of the West Point Museum, both of whom assisted in many ways.

There are also others, without whose help this book simply could not have been written. At the top of that list are Suzanne Christoff, of the USMA Archives, and Judith Sibley and Alan C. Aimone, of the USMA Library Special Collections. All three went far beyond the demands of duty in attending to my research needs. Their ability to ferret out an elusive book or document, or to steer me to a new and critical source, never ceased to gratify and amaze me. Another person who belongs on that list is Dr. Stephen B. Grove, USMA Historian, whose annual reports are models of lucidity and precision. His generosity, and knowledge of the Academy's history, saved me days of effort. My thanks also go to Lieutenant Colonel John K. Robertson for sharing with me a draft of his "A Researcher's Guide to the Occupants of Key Positions at the United States Military Academy and the Lineage of the Academic Departments."

A number of individuals outside West Point also lent important assistance. They include John Slonaker, Dennis Vetock, and Louise Arnold-Friend of the research staff of the U. S. Army Military History Institute at Carlisle Barracks, who supported my research at every turn, and Colonels Rod Paschall, Harold Nelson (now Brigadier General), and Thomas Sweeney, successive Directors of the Institute, as well as Lieutenant Colonel Martin Andresen, the Deputy Director throughout, who opened their facility to me.

I am also indebted to those who consented to speak with me of their own experiences. They include: Brigadier General Elliott Cutler, Brigadier General and Mrs. Sumner Willard, Brigadier General Thomas E. Griess, Mrs. George Lincoln, Major General Chester V. Clifton, and General William C. Westmoreland.

Colonel Roger H. Nye, a former colleague in the Department of History at West Point, and Nancy Loughridge kindly read the entire manuscript. They have, time and again, saved me from error, and supplied suggestions that materially improved the work. Needless to say, the errors or omissions that remain are entirely my own responsibility.

I have a special debt to all those at Harry N. Abrams, Inc., with whom I have worked on this project. Adele Westbrook, senior editor, was part of the process from the book's inception. Her skill and professionalism are apparent on every page, and her patience and cooperation made the experience of writing a pleasant and rewarding one. John K. Crowley, the senior picture editor, was responsible for assembling the extraordinary range of illustrations that grace these pages and add so much life and color to the book. Also, my special thanks go to the designer, Bob McKee, whose talent is evident on every page, as well as to Ted Spiegel, whose marvelous photographs constitute the opening photo essay and enhance the later chapters of the book. (Ted Spiegel would also like to thank Colonel William Wilson, and Major Theodore Russell, as well as the Staff of the Academy Relations Division and the cadets of Company A-1 for all their assistance.)

Finally, I extend my heartfelt thanks to the members of the USMA Class of 1940 who sponsored this project—particularly to those with whom I worked most closely, including Brigadier General Walter Winton and Colonel James Maedler. One other member of that class, Major General David S. Parker, deserves special mention. It was General Parker who conceived and promoted the idea of this book, and then nurtured the effort. General Parker's untimely death, only months before the project was completed, robbed us of a valued friend. His patience and constant good humor were an inestimable help and inspiration to me. In a very real sense, this is General Parker's book.

CHAPTER 1
WEST POINT
BEFORE THE
REVOLUTION

"World renowned, as West Point justly is, there is that in its scenery and associations [which is] more interesting to a poetic or a patriotic mind, than its famed Academy. Its green plain, hidden amidst its mountains; its craggy summits; its rocky barriers; its dark evergreens; its darker waters, flowing on forever; that beautiful view of town and country, seen through the frowning brows of Crow[s] Nest and the Beacon; the quiet vale, where Washington oft bent his steps . . . where the soldiers of the Revolution repose; these forts and ramparts now indistinctly seen, which once guarded these mountain passes; yon ledge of rocks, where [Kosciuszko] once made his little garden; all these and other memorable things, call up whatever is sublime in nature, or noble in history."

Edward D. Mansfield, 1863

The poetic power and strategic importance of the Hudson Highlands is apparent here.

There is an undeniable poetic power in the Highland setting within which West Point reposes, and in the river that West Point commands. It is perhaps derived from the incongruous path which the Hudson has chosen—rising some three hundred miles from the sea in a tiny lake high in the Adirondacks and behaving for much of its course as a river should, then, just above West Point, slicing in an unseemly manner through the granite Highlands to the east, along a narrow, twisting, picturesque gorge.

Or perhaps that power is derived from the ancient granite mountains themselves, through which the Hudson courses and which loom over West Point, framing its landscape. This rock, well over a billion years old, was folded, faulted, and first thrust to the surface some 300 million years ago as the plates of North America and Africa collided. Here, wrote Washington Irving, "gigantic Titans" waged "impious war with heaven" and piled "cliffs on cliffs" and hurled "vast masses of rocks in wild confusion."

Once a part of a chain of mountains not dissimilar to the Alps or Himalayas, these Highlands have been beveled for hundreds of millions of years by erosion and weathering, and finally shaped by the great ice sheets of the glacial age. Acting as enormous graders, smoothing and rounding the northern slopes and summits of the Highlands, the glaciers left the southern flanks that guard West Point irregular and precipitate, and strewn with the loose boulders and debris that gave rise to names such as "Rock Hill" and "Stony Lonesome."

There was a time, before the river breached that granite barrier, when the upper course of the river followed the valley floor to the southwest through Pennsylvania, where the waters joined the Susquehanna and emptied ultimately into the Chesapeake. But, inexorably, the seaward reach of the future great river ate its way backward into the crystalline ridge. Beginning at the heights, it found an ancient fault, following that fault as it plunged toward the lower lands and the sea. Finally, the massive Storm King-Breakneck succumbed, and this waterway, with its shorter run to the sea, soon captured the river in the far valley. The new stream must have followed much the same course as it does today—although its path originally took it to the east of what we know now as Constitution Island.

Then, in the ice age, the levels of the sea dropped, glaciers arose, and the rivers and streams incised channels hundreds of feet deeper than would be possible today. As glaciers extended southward, following the Hudson's course, they gouged a fjord-like channel reaching some 700 feet below the present river level. But, when the glacial ice reached the Highlands it could not fully negotiate the sharp turns where the river followed the geologic faults past West Point, and it carved a new somewhat straighter channel west and south of Constitution Island.

As the glaciers began to wane, some 10,000 years ago, the Hudson carried the glacial water to the sea. The river remained a torrent for hundreds, perhaps thousands of years—the sole exit for the entire Great Lakes watershed, until the glaciers finally disappeared from the St. Lawrence. Then, as the volume of fresh water flowing through the Hudson's channel was finally reduced, its once remarkable granite gorge was filled with hundreds of feet of silt. Ultimately the river became a tidal estuary—a river that, to the marvel of the Indians who were the first to see it, flowed both ways—a river very much as we know it today.

It was the numerous tribes of the Algonquins who initially settled along the banks of the Hudson, for here they found fish and game plentiful, and the soil adequate for small plots for corn. Here, too, they seemingly had found the land, spoken of in a myth retold by uncounted generations, where their wanderings were to cease, a land with a wondrous river that flowed in two directions.

Far left:
Map of the Hudson River region, 1609–1770.

Left:
Henry Hudson's ship, the Half Moon. The Bettmann Archive.

Below:
An Indian village on Manhattan Island prior to Dutch occupation in the seventeenth century. The Bettmann Archive.

These were the Indians who, on a quiet September day in 1609, first saw the small Dutch ship, the *Half Moon,* cautiously approach the mouth of the river. Under the command of an English sea captain, Henry Hudson, the ship had slipped past the sandy hook that guards New York's outer harbor and found an anchorage near Manhattan Island. "It is as pleasant a land as one can tread upon" noted Hudson, and he took aboard a delegation from the local tribe, who brought gifts of green tobacco, yellow maize, and brown loaves of corn bread.

Hudson's first reaction to the land and its people, however, was tempered when a boat and crew sent to explore the river to the north were attacked. One sailor was killed and two others seriously wounded before they could escape to the safety of the ship; still, the report of those who returned prompted optimism. The lands they had seen before being attacked "were as pleasant with grass and flowers and goodly trees as ever they had seen, and very sweet smells came from them."

Hudson and his crew were almost certainly not the first Europeans to see the river that would someday bear this captain's name. That honor might have belonged to some daring Viking, and, if not, almost certainly to one of several other earlier explorers—John Cabot,

Giovanni da Verrazano, or Estera Gomez, among others—whose logs or letters suggest that they came across the mouth of the river without entering it. It was, however, Hudson who first actually explored it.

With the hope that this broad estuary might be a passage to the Pacific, Hudson left Manhattan Island behind and sailed past the pillared twelve-mile wall of the Palisades and through Haverstraw Bay. "The land grew high," reported Robert Juet, one of the ship's officers, as they turned into the channel of the Highlands and were carried onward by a southeasterly wind until they reached what is now West Point.

Here, below the heights that would one day hold Forts Clinton and Putnam, and then a military academy, they lay at anchor through the night. The next morning they negotiated the twisting channel that would later make West Point such a vital position. Beyond the Highlands, the Dutch found the natives again friendly, and they were soon bartering with all who wished to come aboard. Here, on at least one occasion, Hudson himself went ashore. "The natives are a very good people," he noted in his journal, "for when they saw that I would not remain, they supposed that I was afraid of their bows, and taking the arrows they broke them in pieces and threw them into the fire."

Hudson spent more than a week in upper reaches of the river, near present-day Albany, but soon discovered that he could not navigate much farther up the river. He knew now, if he had not already guessed, that this was not the passage to China that had been the object of his expedition and the hope of the Dutch East India Company that had sponsored it. Still, Hudson moved at a leisurely pace, stopping here and there to converse or barter with the local Indians—seeing the pelts the Indians offered, he certainly understood the potential for trade that existed in this land.

On the first day of October, now en route back to the sea, Hudson's ship passed again into the lower reaches of the river where the Indians had been more hostile. Once again, the *Half Moon* and its crew were forced to engage in a running battle before clearing the mouth of the river. A few days later, they hoisted sail and headed home. And thus, wrote Robert Juet, they left "the River into which we had run so faire . . . and steered away East South-east, and South-east by East off into the mayne sea."

Hudson's report to the Dutch East India Company sparked immediate enthusiasm, as it offered the promise of a lucrative fur trade. Within a year the Dutch merchants had sent out a second ship, followed soon by a procession of other vessels. At first, the aim of these voyages was to promote commerce rather than colonization. Shiploads of tobacco and furs, not the establishment of farms and settlements, were the object. But, in 1621, the States-General in Amsterdam chartered the Dutch West India Company with the expectation that it would both "promote trade and profits" and "advance the peopling of fruitful and unsettled parts." The company was empowered to build forts, to establish a government, and to make contracts and alliances. In early 1624, the ship *New Netherlands* sailed for the colony (whose name it would bear) with some thirty families of Walloons. Upon landing, they were scattered in small settlements along the Delaware and Connecticut rivers, on Manhattan Island, and on the upper Hudson at Fort Orange, a trading post established a decade earlier (where the city of Albany now stands). Cornelis Jacobsen May, who had led the group over, became the first Director-General of the colony, and he settled at Fort Orange—a precedent, it would seem, for the later establishment of the state government at Albany.

His replacement, Willem Verhulst, who arrived the next year, chose to reside at the little settlement at the foot of Manhattan. With him came four ships bearing not only more colonists, but the livestock that was essential to the agricultural settlements the colonists hoped to establish. Although the company found it easier to profit from the fur trade, they persisted in the effort to settle the area and, in 1626, sent more colonists and yet another Director-General, Peter Minuit. It was Minuit who purchased Manhattan Island from the Indians, and it was he who established New Amsterdam as a fortified post that would serve as the formal seat of government for the colony.

Despite efforts, however, colonization faltered. It was difficult to persuade worthy farmers and craftsmen to trade a prosperous, safe, and free life in Holland for the wilds and dangers of the Hudson Valley. In 1629, the company responded to the problem by creating the patroon system, which shifted the burden of finding settlers to individual landowners who, in turn, could amass great wealth for their efforts. Grants of substantial estates along the river were made to members of the company, requiring only that, within four years, they settle at least fifty persons on that land. These patroonships were huge plots that might extend up to sixteen miles along one bank of the river (or eight miles along both banks), and as far inland as the settlers could manage to control. Six patroonships were immediately established—two along each of the rivers settled by the Dutch: the Delaware, the Connecticut, and the Hudson. The most important and most successful of these was Rensselaerswyck, which included holdings on both sides of the Hudson near Fort Orange—a vast estate, in all, slightly larger than later-day Rhode Island.

The patroon system that took root in the Hudson Valley, however, was peculiar to that locale. What flourished there was an essentially feudal society where perpetual leaseholds, and not freeholds, were offered in return for a share of everything the land would produce. The patroon reserved to himself a tenth of all grains, fruits, and other crops, and a tenth of all livestock produced. In addition, the tenant was bound to keep up the roads, repair the buildings, cut and deliver firewood, and provide three days' service with his horses and wagon every year. Moreover, the tenant owed the Crown—in the person of the Director-General—an annual quitrent of two bushels of wheat, twenty-five pounds of butter, and two pairs of fowl.

In an important sense this system dictated the kind of settlers that would be responsive to such an offering. In large part those who came to New Amsterdam, and later to New York, to take up leaseholds were of the poorest and meanest sort—whether Walloons, Irish, Swedes, Germans, Danes, or English, they were an illiterate, lawless, hard-drinking, and quarrelsome lot. They squabbled with the Swedes to the south of them on the Delaware, with the English in the Yankee settlements to the north, and with all the neighboring Indians. And, of course, they fought among themselves. As was true of the company they served, their loyalties lay most firmly with profit. They hid their produce to avoid paying the rent, cut wood and sold it illegally, and then lodged complaints against the Director and their patroons whenever any action was taken to stop their activities. They were not an easy group to govern, and the leasehold arrangement proved a source of discontent for generations. For more than two centuries the patroon system shaped the life of the people who lived along the Hudson, and it discouraged many others from settling there.

Still, the Hudson Valley proved a magnet for Europe's disaffected. For those too poor to purchase land, a leasehold that might be obtained for nothing more than a signature was a golden opportunity. More Germans, French Huguenots, and then more English and Dutch came, but material gains often proved elusive. The land was harsh and demanding, the soil often thin and unrewarding, and on the leaseholds, families—who must have hoped for more—found themselves helplessly bound to the land.

The contrast between conditions in the Hudson Valley and in the freeholds of New England was simply too striking to remain unremarked. "The Common People," wrote one New Englander in 1776, "have but little Idea of Liberty—Their Gods are Lords of Manors—One Man in N. England that owns an Acre of Land is better than a Tenant of an Hundred—The other Colonies must fight for them and bring them into the Light of freedom."

Peter Minuit, the third Director, was removed by the Company in 1632, for unduly favoring the patroons in their conflicts with the Company. Unfortunately, the governorship attracted few men of real talent, and the colony as well as the Company suffered. Minuit was replaced by Wouter Van Twiller, a nephew of Van Rensselaer by marriage who was no more inclined to antagonize his powerful in-laws than his predecessor. Moreover, Van Twiller was not above lining his pockets at the expense of the Company. When he was recalled in 1638, the Company sent the even more incompetent William Kieft, a narrow-minded man eager to interfere in minor concerns, but lacking the capacity to conduct the important affairs of the colony. On the one hand, he fixed the hours at which the colonists should go to bed and ordered a curfew at nine o'clock; on the other, he was responsible for the needless and bloody conflicts with the Indians that came close to wrecking the colony.

Kieft was replaced in 1647 by Pieter Stuyvesant, the most picturesque figure and most competent administrator during the entire period of Dutch rule in America. Years before, Stuyvesant had lost a leg in a fight and had replaced it with the wooden peg which became his hallmark. Even today, according to legend, his ghost stumps nightly to and fro along the aisles of St. Mark's Church near the spot where he lies buried.

In some respects Stuyvesant was as narrow and arbitrary as his predecessors, but he was honest and he made an effort to govern effectively. In stark contrast to his predecessors, he dealt more evenhandedly with the Indians, although warfare continued intermittently. Moreover, to his credit, he did not enrich himself significantly at the expense of either the Company, the patroons, or the settlers. That which Stuyvesant could control or influence seemingly prospered; that for which he was dependent on the Company in Amsterdam did not—including measures for the defense of the colony. When the English fleet arrived in 1664, Stuyvesant could do little but fume. Short of all the necessities of war but courage, he was forced to surrender without firing a shot. Though the colony was recaptured and held for a few months by the Dutch in 1673, New Netherlands had irrevocably become New York.

To a certain extent there was little change when the English took possession of New Netherlands. The old patroonships were confirmed as manorial grants from England and new manors were erected. "The lands which I intend shall be first planted," wrote the new governor, Richard Nicolls, shortly after he arrived, "are those upon the west side of Hudson's River" (by which he meant lands that today encompass large portions of Ulster and Orange counties, and West Point). Thus, over the next several decades, vast domains were granted: lands to the south of Rensselaerswyck to Robert Livingston (whose sharp dealings and marriage into the Van Rensselaer family combined to help him amass a vast personal fortune); lands along the lower Hudson to Frederick Philipse, and to Stephen Van Cortlandt; and finally lands on the west bank to Captain John Evans.

England was fortunate in its first representative. Nicolls, who had obtained the surrender from Stuyvesant, displayed all the tact and wisdom of a statesman in his dealings with the Dutch. True, the towns and forts were rechristened—New Amsterdam became New York, Fort Orange became Albany, Esopus became Kingston—but the Dutch were not interfered with in their homes, holdings, or religion. By virtue of his wise policies, his magnetic personality, and his social aplomb, Nicolls seems to have won over most of the Dutch. Entrusted with almost unlimited power, he used it with the utmost discretion and for the good of the province. Unfortunately, Nicolls resigned after just four years and was followed by a succession of lesser, although capable men.

In 1682 Thomas Dongan, son of an Irish Baronet, and a Roman Catholic, was appointed governor. Realizing that feelings against Catholicism were strong in the colony, the appointment was made more palatable by the grant of a somewhat more popular form of

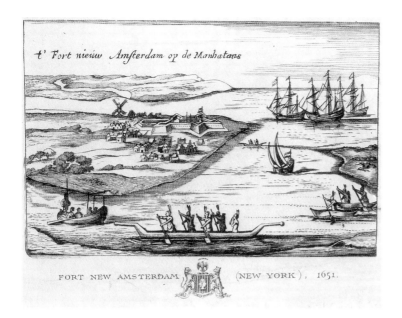

government embodied in a representative Assembly to be chosen by the freeholders. The first such Assembly met in 1683 and passed some fifteen laws, including a Charter of Liberties and Privileges—establishing the principles of popular representation, religious liberty, and the guarantee of those civil liberties that had long been the right of all Englishmen. Unfortunately, by the time these bills were forwarded to England the political tide there had turned—the enactments were disallowed and Dongan was ultimately called home.

Dongan, however, played a role in West Point's history that must be noted. In 1684, not long before he was recalled, Dongan purchased from the Indians a vast tract on the west of the river that included West Point—lands Nicolls had alluded to some twenty years earlier. By chance, this purchase also included a tract of some 4,000 acres that lay just to the north of West Point on either side of Murderers Creek, in the vicinity of present day Cornwall, that had previously been purchased from the Indians and that had been settled by a group of some twenty-five Scottish Presbyterians led by Patrick MacGregorie. Although such duplication was not uncommon in dealings with the Indians, whose concept of land ownership was quite different from that of the settlers, this case was particularly unfortunate because MacGregorie, who had obtained a proper license to purchase the land, had failed to perfect a title. This was an oversight that would later haunt his family and all those who had settled with him, for shortly after MacGregorie's death in 1691 their lands were included in a new patent.

In 1692, Benjamin Fletcher was sent from England as the new governor. His six-year tenure was in most respects unremarkable, but it was Fletcher who, in 1694, conveyed the huge holding on the west bank of the Hudson—the land that Dongan had obtained some ten years earlier, including that which MacGregorie and his friends had purchased—to Captain John Evans under the title of the Lordship and Manor of Fletcherdon. Evans immediately sought to dispossess the MacGregorie heirs and their neighbors, even compelling the unfortunate widow to sell him the house in which she lived. To her and to the others who had originally settled the land, he then granted leaseholds, an action that both bolstered his title and, in keeping them on the land, preserved the settled population—which, as he well knew, was nearly sufficient to satisfy the sole condition of the patent. Evans's heartless methods and temerity were remarkable, even among men such as Robert Livingston—who, it was said, "had pinched an estate out of the poor soldiers' bellies" while serving as purveyor of supplies for the provincial militia.

Evans, however, was soon brought to an accounting. Fletcher's replacement, Richard Coote, arrived with a mandate to correct a number of seeming irregularities in the administration of the colony—in particular the granting of immense tracts of land that had long been the practice in New Amsterdam and now in New York. This, of course, was a sensitive issue. The beneficiaries of the policy had been the most powerful and wealthy men in the colony. A way to divert attention was found, however, when an investigation by the Assembly in 1699 spotlighted Evans and his high-handed tactics in Fletcherdon. On the recommendation of the Assembly, the Crown annulled his grant. In one sense the unfeeling Evans was sacrificed to protect the more influential patroons and the system; in another, he received his just desserts. With his undoing the impetus for reform subsided, and the appointment of the next governor, Edward Hyde Cornbury, in 1702, inaugurated another wave of extravagant grants.

Regardless, the lands of the original Evans patent were now conveyed, for the most part, in smaller tracts—patents of a few hundred or a few thousand acres—beginning in 1701 and continuing through 1775.

The lands that would ultimately constitute the military post at West Point were granted in this way over the years. The first, that which today includes much of the land on the level of the plain and to the north, was patented to Charles Congreve in 1723—a total of 1,463 acres. The next parcel, to the south of Congreve's land and extending essentially to Highland Falls, was granted to Gabriel and William Ludlow in 1731. The third, a small parcel of 332 acres adjoining the first two on the west, was conveyed to John Moore in 1747. These encompassed most of the original post. The balance—the lands added to the post in the later nineteenth century and in the twentieth—were dispensed in other similar parcels in the years through 1775.

The conditions attached to the grant of these smaller patents required that within three years the grantee, or his tenants, would "plant, settle and effectually cultivate at least three acres of land for every fifty acres" of the grant. In addition, the holder paid an annual quitrent of two shillings and six pence per hundred acres, and the Crown reserved for the Royal Navy's use all trees of a diameter of twenty-four inches or greater. Many of the grantees settled the land themselves. But even among those who settled tenants, the troubles that convulsed the east bank of the Hudson were not apparent here.

Some, like John Moore, who had first purchased his West Point property in 1747, were men of wealth who treated the land as a diversion from their occupations in the city, rather than as an investment. In fact, Moore, one of the most prominent citizens of New York, liked the region so much that he purchased the adjacent Congreve grant and combined it with his own. On the latter, in a low, level valley on the banks of the Hudson (later called Washington's Valley) opposite Constitution Island, he built a large summer home. The house was three-storied, and had four chimneys—somewhat pretentious it might seem for this time and place, but the Moores made good use of it. A road behind the house led from the river up the steep hill to a plain that overlooked the Hudson, and thence on to New Windsor. Moore's single tenant, a Dutchman named Daniel Coovert, tilled the acres immediately around the house and on the plain. The lands included, recalled Coovert's granddaughter, "a pretty good sized cornfield" in addition to land on which the cattle were pastured.

The Moore family spent many of their summers there, in the cooler and healthier climes of the Highlands. When John Moore died, his son, Stephen, inherited the property, and it remained for years a family retreat. Upon reaching maturity, Stephen accepted a commission in a British regiment that was posted in Canada. It was not until 1765 that he left the army and retired to his house and lands at West Point. If he made any efforts from that time on to farm the land, he must have abandoned them in short order, for by

1777 the plain was overgrown by scrub pine ten to fifteen feet in height. In any event, in 1775, Stephen broke politically with the other members of his family who were Tories, and left New York for North Carolina, where he served the Patriot cause. Still, throughout the early years of the war, the house on the Hudson was open to the family, and many of them spent a gracious country exile there.

It is likely that the Moores had never reflected on any wartime role their land along the Hudson might play, but its value had been foretold in nearly a century of colonial wars. There was the War of the League of Augsburg, known in America as King William's War (1689–1697). The War of Spanish Succession was known on this side of the Atlantic as Queen Anne's War (1702–1713); the War of Austrian Succession—King George's War (1744–1748); and the French and Indian War (1754–1763). Time and again the Hudson Valley was to be a theater of war in those conflicts. The Indians raided settlements along its banks, the British sailed up the course to invade Canada, and the French moved down it to strike the English colonies. In this, an important pattern was established; the Hudson River-Lake Champlain corridor had become an established north-south highway of war. The defense of the Hudson would define West Point's strategic role and confirm its value in the Revolution that was now at hand.

General John Burgoyne addressing his Indian allies during the French and Indian War, 1754–1763. The Bettmann Archive.

CHAPTER 2
WEST POINT AND THE REVOLUTION 1775-1783

The Capture of the Hessians at Trenton by John Trumbull. 1787–94. Oil on canvas, 21¼ × 31⅛″. Copyright Yale University Art Gallery. Washington's victory at Trenton did nothing to quell his apprehension about the British threat to the Hudson Highlands.

The importance of the Hudson River to the defense of English-speaking North America had been recognized early in the colonial period. Its strategic value during the Revolution was obvious to the British from the very beginning. In its simplest form their strategy called for them to strike north from New York and south from Lake Champlain to seize control of the crossings of the Hudson, and to cut communications between New England and the balance of the colonies. It was commonly thought in Great Britain that if troublesome New England could be isolated, the rest of the colonies would soon come to their senses.

The river's strategic value was just as clear to the Patriots. With the British on the coast, the lines of communication between the rebel forces and regions ran through the Highlands and across the Hudson. These lines of communication were vital and made defense of the river a foregone conclusion. Early in 1775, already concerned that the conflict around Boston would spread, the Provincial Congress of New York warned: "If the enemy persist in their plan of subjugating these States to the yoke of Great Britain, they must, in proportion to their knowledge of the country, be more and more convinced of the necessity of their becoming masters of the Hudson river, which will give them the entire command of the water communication with the Indian nations, effectually prevent all intercourse between the eastern and southern Confederates, divide our strength, and enfeeble every effort for our common preservation and security."

The Continental Congress agreed that the Hudson must be held, but handed the problem back to New York's Assembly. On the thirtieth of May the New Yorkers sent Christopher Tappan and James Clinton to the Highlands to select a site or sites for fortifications and to report their estimates of the cost.

In surveying the region, three principal sites were considered. The first was at the Dunderberg, but here the width of the river weighed against this selection. The next was Anthony's Nose where the river was not only narrow, but the banks on both sides were extremely rugged, particularly the near-vertical 900-foot peak to the east that gave the location its name. The major disadvantage here was that communication with the interior was difficult, particularly so from the high ground on the west overlooking the mouth of Popolopen Creek, where fortifications would have to be built. This would add to the difficulty of construction, but more important, this was a real concern in case the post should need reinforcement while under attack.

The third site, West Point, enjoyed all the advantages offered by the other sites, with few of the disadvantages. But in addition, vessels passing there had to make a sharp, ninety-degree turn to the west, sail a quarter of a mile, then make another right-angle turn to the north as they continued upriver. These bends were the sharpest of any along the Hudson, but they were not the only hazards that a ship had to face at West Point.

The river there was the narrowest in the Highlands and the tidal effects the greatest; at ebb tide the current there was swifter than at any point south of Albany. Moreover, that channel was noted for treacherous winds that could cause the loss of headway, as well as other steering difficulties for any sailing ship trying to negotiate it.

Considering all the possibilities, Tappan and Clinton chose the site at West Point and Martalear's Rock opposite it (soon to become known as Constitution Island). They reported their findings to the New York Assembly on the 10th of June, 1775. But two months passed before anything more was done. It took a warning from General Washington concerning a suspected enemy raid on New York City, to provoke action. Although a false alarm, this red flag caused the New Yorkers to appoint commissioners to undertake the fortifications on the Hudson.

The commissioners obtained the services of Bernard Romans who had studied surveying and cartography, and who had been an official surveyor for the British for a number of years. In one sense this was quite fortunate, for Romans brought not only training but experience to the undertaking. Romans had been with Ethan Allen and Benedict Arnold at Fort Ticonderoga earlier that year, and had helped plan and conduct needed repairs at that important post. In another sense, however, the choice of Romans was unfortunate, for he focused his efforts on fortifying Martalear's Rock and largely ignored West Point proper, the true key to the position.

Romans and the commissioners quickly agreed on a plan. Romans drew an elaborate design calling for a "grand bastion" or principal fort, supported by a series of smaller fortifications. To control the river the plan relied on five blockhouses supported by several additional batteries in the principal fortifications. The entire system of defense was to be placed on Martalear's Rock except for one blockhouse and battery that would be erected at West Point. To Romans the most critical of the fortifications was the central fort, called Fort Constitution—for which the island ever after has been named. It was there that he began work in the fall of 1775. Remnants of these first works—now called Romans's Battery—can still be seen today. By early October, construction material and cannon had begun to arrive on the island, but it was clear that Romans's fortifications would not be completed by winter.

There were a number of military defects in Romans's plan, but the first and most serious was that Constitution Island was dominated by the higher ground across the river. The small blockhouse and battery that was to be placed at West Point would simply have been insufficient to prevent the enemy from taking the heights that overlooked Constitution Island. There they could have placed artillery that would dominate the positions below. Moreover, the artillery on Constitution Island was poorly positioned. Ships sailing north, for example, would be exposed to only a few of the guns until they had passed the crucial first bend in the river and were again underway. The real value of the river's S-turn at West Point was that ships would lose all their headway there as they negotiated the first bend. In Romans's plan the fire of most guns would have been masked as a ship

Constitution Island and its defenses as seen from West Point in this drawing by an unknown artist in 1776. Courtesy Cornell University Library.

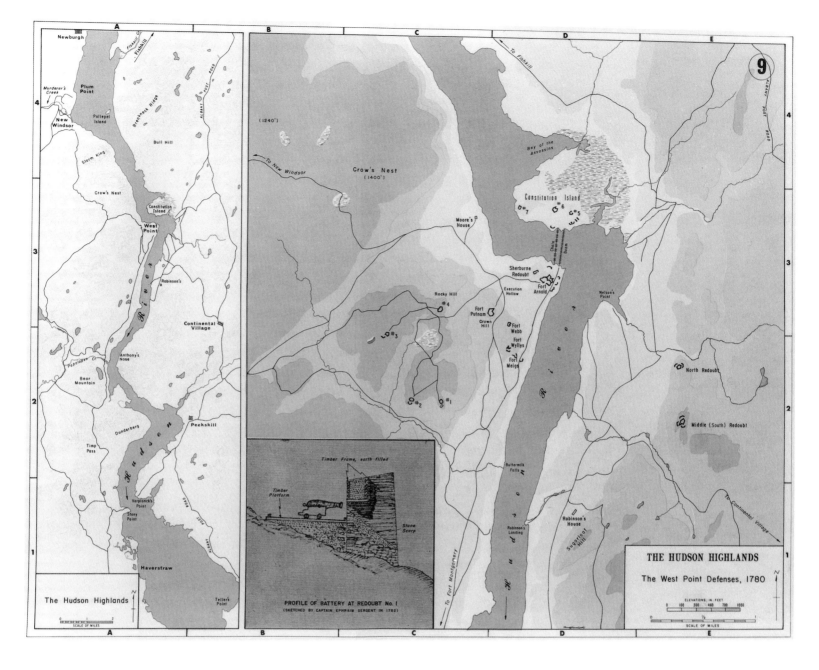

THE HUDSON HIGHLANDS

The West Point Defenses, 1780

Map of the Hudson Highlands showing West Point and its defenses in 1780. From Early American Wars and Military Institutions, *Thomas S. Griess, Series Editor. Copyright © 1986 by Avery Publishing Group.*

approached and entered the turn. Most of the cannoneers in Romans's "grand bastion" would have had a vessel in their sights for only a few moments as it regained speed, racing toward the second and less difficult turn.

These considerations and the lack of progress that season had prompted the commissioners to reconsider fortifying the Popolopen site opposite Anthony's Nose. Indeed, even Romans raised this possibility. By early 1776 the emphasis had shifted from Constitution Island to the Popolopen. There, twin forts were to be constructed on the high ground above both banks of the creek as it entered the Hudson. For that work the commissioners chose a new engineer, Captain William Smith, to replace Romans. From that time until disaster befell these positions in October 1777, the Patriots concentrated their main efforts in defense of the Highlands on the fortifications and water obstacles in this area. The yet uncompleted works at Constitution Island were furnished with a small garrison, but all other construction there stopped.

As might be expected, refocusing the effort prevented any progress for a time, although by April 1776, work was underway at Fort Montgomery, on the north bank of Popolopen Creek. Three months later, in July, when the British occupied New York, even greater urgency was attached to fortifying the site. By autumn, twin forts—Montgomery and Clin-

General George Clinton standing at the fortifications above the Hudson River. The United States Military Academy Library, Special Collections.

ton—had been erected on either side of the deeply ravined Popolopen, and a chain was stretched across the river to obstruct navigation. Because of design and structural weaknesses, however, this chain broke and had to be replaced the following spring by a new, better engineered one.

Washington, quartered at Morristown for the winter of 1776–77, was apprehensive about the defenses being built in the Highlands and expressed particular concern about the overland approaches to the rear of Forts Clinton and Montgomery. But in light of what seemed impossibly rugged terrain to the rear of these forts, nothing was done to secure them from such an attack. Even the delegation that Washington sent to survey the area—including Major General Nathanael Greene, Brigadier Generals Alexander McDougall, Henry Knox, George Clinton, and Anthony Wayne—reported, in May 1777, that "the enemy will not attempt to operate by land" because the terrain was "so exceedingly difficult." Soon, however, Washington's fears were to be realized.

As the Patriots attempted to fortify the Hudson, English officials had adopted an intricate scheme for capturing the vital river valley. If successful, the British would sever New England from the rest of the states and paralyze the American effort. The main invading force was to proceed down the Lake Champlain route from Canada, under the command of an actor-playwright-soldier, General John "Gentleman Johnny" Burgoyne. If needed, General William Howe's troops in New York could advance up the Hudson to meet Burgoyne near Albany. A third, much smaller force would be prepared to attack toward Albany from the west by way of Lake Ontario. As Burgoyne began his move south, however, Howe marshaled the main British Army for an attack on Philadelphia. Washington, who had begun to shift his forces toward the Hudson, hastily retraced his steps and positioned his Army to defend Philadelphia. Defeated in two pitched battles, at Brandywine Creek and at Germantown, Washington abandoned Philadelphia to the British and retired to winter quarters at Valley Forge.

Meanwhile, Burgoyne's southward march to Albany had stalled in front of Saratoga. At that point, General Sir Henry Clinton, who had been left in New York and who had just received reinforcements from England, decided to attack up the Hudson in the hope of relieving the pressure on Burgoyne. Sir Henry devised a sophisticated plan based upon the advice of a Loyalist Colonel, Beverly Robinson, whose home on the Hudson was just below and opposite West Point. The plan called for an attack with three divisions. The first, a diversion, was a feint toward the east bank which would concentrate Rebel units there. Then Clinton would land the balance of his forces at Stony Point, sending them west through the rugged Highlands. Ultimately, he would split this unit, marching one column around Bear Mountain to attack Fort Montgomery from the rear, while the other column would attack Fort Clinton from the south.

On October 5, 1777, General Clinton put this plan into effect, landing a force at Verplanck's Point on the east bank of the Hudson, thus threatening Peekskill and forcing General Israel Putnam to deploy his troops in response. Early the next morning, having deceived Putnam, Clinton went ashore on the west bank at Stony Point, as planned, with the bulk of his forces. Facilitating the deception, a heavy fog shrouded the operation and delayed the discovery of Clinton's real intentions.

Clinton's men, including some 400 Loyalists led by Robinson, then marched into the difficult Highland terrain to take the northernmost fort. The trek led through narrow defiles and up nearly vertical cliffs, but they were unopposed. As the hours passed and the anticipated attack on the east bank never materialized, George Clinton, the new governor of New York, finally understood that the real objective was Fort Montgomery and its opposite number (that had been named in his honor). He quickly appealed to General Putnam for aid and dispatched some light forces to delay the British advance, which he now realized would come from the west. The American force discovered the British behind Fort Montgomery, but it was too late. The Americans were quickly beaten back. The two separate British columns then fixed bayonets and attacked. In less than a half-hour both forts fell.

The next day, October 7, 1777, Sir Henry had the chain across the Hudson cut and sent his representatives in a boat to Constitution Island, under a flag of truce, to request its surrender. There, nervous and undisciplined sentries opened fire on the approaching emissaries. Indignant at this breech of battlefield etiquette, the British returned the following day in twenty-two flatboats loaded with troops and supported by artillery from three galleys. Determined to take the position by storm, they found that the Patriots had retreated the night before. Although they had burned their barracks, the defenders had left in such haste that they had not even spiked the cannon. The British then occupied the island and for a time, at least, control of the river passed into their hands.

Hardly pausing to consolidate his position, Sir Henry continued up the Hudson. He was, however, too late. It was just above Kingston that he learned of Burgoyne's surrender. Clinton, whose forces were not strong enough to hold the Highlands against the victorious General Horatio Gates, feared that he might be cut off from his base in New York, and so he withdrew. He razed the Highland fortifications that he had so recently captured and, on October 20th, retired to New York.

When Patriot forces reoccupied the ruined fortifications they faced the choice of rebuilding or beginning anew elsewhere. Washington's chief engineer in the Highlands, French Lieutenant Colonel Louis de la Radiere, favored refortifying the Fort Montgomery-Fort Clinton area. Israel Putnam, who commanded the region, favored a new start at West Point. To break this deadlock, another commission from the New York Assembly was appointed to assess the problem. That body also recommended fortifying West Point. On January 12, 1778, Putnam, confident that he had the necessary support, announced that the river and the Highlands would be defended at that location. Putnam's decision alone, however, was not enough. Plans for the fortifications were not yet agreed upon, and there were insufficient troops available to undertake the work. Moreover, there was no chain available to seal off the river.

Peter Townsend, of the Sterling Ironworks of Warwick, New York, was asked to forge the new chain but he had not yet been paid for the chain that had been lost at Fort Montgomery and would not fire his forges until the earlier debt had been compensated, at least in part. Finally, an agreement was reached on February 2, 1778. The type of chain that Townsend had built and that Thomas Machin had installed at Fort Montgomery the year before had been considered satisfactory, but the new chain would be even stronger, with links made from iron bar 2-1/4 inches square instead of the 1-1/2 inch bar used in the earlier links.

While the issue of the chain was being resolved, Putnam began to assemble the troops that would be needed. On January 27th, a brigade under Brigadier General Samuel Holden Parsons crossed the ice covering the river and occupied the heights. Wrote Sergeant Simon Giffin, "[we] marched over the Rever on the ise [and] marched back again for thar was no Place to Loge theor on the West side of the Rever." A few men, however, remained on the western bank overnight, and from that day forward, West Point has been continuously occupied by elements of the United States Army. By January 30th, all of the men were able to lodge on the west side of the river. "We mad a hut," wrote Sergeant Giffin, "that 15 of us Lay Prity worm considering the wether being so very cold."

The Patriot plan for guarding the river was uncomplicated: the river would be blocked by a chain and boom stretching from Constitution Island to West Point at a point where any ship, having just negotiated the first turn, would have little momentum as it struck

This illustration, from a mid-eighteenth century Manual of Arms, shows the drill routines prescribed for both the English troops and the colonial militias.

Opposite:
*Kosciuszko's Monument, designed by
John H. Latrobe (who attended the Military Academy but did not graduate).
This statue was erected by the corps of
cadets in 1828 to honor the Polish patriot who fought in the American Revolutionary War.*

them; shore batteries on the west side of the river would both protect the chain and boom, and engage approaching enemy ships. Some of the guns in the fortifications on the plain above the river could also engage the ships, but the primary purpose of these emplacements was to deny the heights to the enemy and, therefore, to protect the rear of the water-level batteries.

In mid-January, Radiere outlined the trace of a new fort on the plateau at West Point, but the difficulties and differences continued. Radiere envisioned a classic Vauban fortress—an extensive, permanent, scientifically-designed fortification that could withstand a prolonged siege. Putnam, the commander of the Highlands, favored a smaller, temporary, field fortification. As Putnam correctly assessed, there was neither sufficient time nor money for anything more elaborate.

As Parsons noted when he took command of West Point in mid-February, this lack of agreement had produced only "perfect chaos." Parsons, however, was undaunted by the problems he faced and quickly determined that his first priority had to be to obtain materials and equipment necessary to build the defenses—whatever they should be. Timber and rock were immediately at hand but he did not have the teams of horses necessary to haul them. These he immediately requisitioned, and within days the teams had arrived and the work began in earnest. Problems remained, but Parsons was not one to idly await their resolution. He lacked money, tools, and equipment, but could use his troops to cut timber and build the fascines (cylindrical bundles of sticks or brushwood) that would be needed to strengthen the earthen parapets. In less than two weeks, over 1,000 pieces of timber had been cut, and 1,000 to 1,500 fascines had been prepared.

The exact nature of the fortifications at West Point, however, had still not been determined. Parsons, like Putnam, was convinced that Radiere's plan was too extensive, but his attempts to convince the Frenchman that the works should better fit the time and money available were no more effective than had been Putnam's. Finally, the Board of War stepped in and ordered that the decision be left to Governor Clinton. He sided with Parsons.

Parsons wasted no more time. The next day, March 12, 1778, he broke ground and began the construction of Fort Arnold and its water-level batteries. When his plan was rebuffed, Radiere left West Point. Parsons now scaled down the scope of the project and moved ahead with plans to construct fortifications of timber, earth, and fascines. Perhaps the new works would not be able to withstand a classic siege with a prolonged pounding by artillery, but, he reasoned, it was better to have a functioning position from which the garrison and militia could fight and maneuver than to have half-finished—and indefensible—fortifications when the British arrived. Moreover, it now appeared that the chain would be emplaced in April and the fortifications needed to protect it had to be ready.

Using every available man, militia and Continental alike, Parsons spurred the garrison on. He understood clearly that the main purpose of Fort Arnold, as he called the new fortification, was to protect the water batteries and chain from attack at the rear. From that he concluded that his first construction priority should be the west and south walls and the southwest bastion. Parsons now moved with energy, and reported to Washington that he hoped to have the key elements of the fort "in some State of Defense" by the end of March. For the first time since the British sojourn up the Hudson the previous October, there were visible signs of progress toward defense of the vital river. Parsons, however, was still short of tools and supplies, finances were precarious, and—most important—he did not yet have the required cannon. In addition, the militia whose enlistments were expiring had yet to be replaced.

Still, Parsons soon found cause for renewed optimism. On March 25th the first guns arrived. In celebration he ordered a salute fired that evening—the first cannonade fired at West Point. Meanwhile, other changes further brightened the picture. General McDou-

gall was sent to take command of the Highlands from the absent (and locally unpopular) Putnam. McDougall's instructions from Washington emphasized the importance of the work and promised needed support. With McDougall came Colonel Tadeusz Kosciuszko, a Polish officer, who had been appointed to supervise construction at West Point in place of Radiere.

McDougall might correctly have complained that the Hudson was still defenseless, but in just a few weeks Parsons had laid a solid foundation upon which the defenses could be built. Although neither the chain nor the fortifications were completed, and the full complement of cannon had not yet arrived, much had been accomplished. Parsons continued to exhort the garrison, and guided by Kosciuszko—with whom he found he could work closely—further progress was made.

Radiere's plan had called for two water-level batteries. Kosciuszko concluded that these would be insufficient and added two more. The first, South Battery, was planted downstream of the battery that already covered the initial approach to the chain. The second, Lanthorn Battery (sometimes called Lantern Battery), was placed on the point at the first bend in the river. Located as it was, Lanthorn Battery could cover the southern approach to the bend, the bend itself, and the chain. Now, with two positions south of the point, one at the point, and the last near the terminus of the chain, any ship attempting to breach the chain would be exposed to a continuous cross fire.

Parsons and Kosciuszko worked well together. Kosciuszko approved of the changes Parsons had already instituted in the size and type of construction of Fort Arnold, and drew new engineering plans to reflect them. Kosciuszko also agreed with Parsons that the surrounding hills presented a potential threat and that, therefore, construction of the south and west walls of the fort should receive priority. Located as Fort Arnold was, with the east face overlooking a cliff that rose more than 100 feet out of the water and with the north side facing similarly difficult terrain, work on these latter two walls could be deferred. Not so with the west and south walls. Averaging nine feet in height, they were to be twenty feet thick at the top of the parapet; a little less thick at the top of the bastion, which would be thirteen feet high. Immediately in front of the walls was a ditch thirty-two feet wide at the top and twenty-four feet across at the bottom. The depth of the ditch was actually determined by the volume of dirt needed to build the walls behind it.

To protect the rear walls of the fort Kosciuszko planned to install eight cannons, positioned in such a way that they would provide a cross fire in front of the walls of the fort to discourage any infantry assault. The gate, located in the western curtain, was also to be protected by guns on each flank. The remainder of Fort Arnold was rather simple in design and would require only a minimum amount of time to construct. The main function of the north and east walls was to provide a stable platform from which the fort's guns could aid the water batteries in denying the river to the enemy. Here, Kosciuszko built only a low parapet of two and a half feet in height and four to six feet across, except for an irregular bastion at the northeast corner, which was to be nine feet high.

The new plan also called for a storehouse, powder magazine, guardhouse, commissary building, well, and a single barracks capable of housing a garrison of 600 men. In the latter, rooms were to be nineteen feet by nineteen feet, containing nine bunk beds, each thirty-six inches wide. With two men assigned to each bed, every room would accommodate thirty-six men. The barracks was built just to the west of Fort Arnold, and soon became known as Long Barracks. The storehouse and commissary were located on the low ground between the point and the Moore House.

The emphasis placed on the sides of Fort Arnold that faced the mountains shows an awareness of the danger of an enemy attack from the rear, and an appreciation of the heights that overlooked the new fort. Both Kosciuszko and Parsons were rightly apprehensive. Less than six months before, the British had seized the forts on the Popolopen

353

A section of the "great chain" that was strung across the Hudson River surrounds a mortar at West Point.

from the rear. Moreover, Kosciuszko had been at Fort Ticonderoga when it was lost to the British. He had warned that if the enemy placed their cannons on nearby Mount Defiance, Ticonderoga would be indefensible, but the commander had paid no attention. When Burgoyne's forces dragged their artillery up those steep slopes to fire down into Ticonderoga the fort was indeed lost.

With construction of the main fortification now underway, Kosciuszko and Parsons turned their attention to the approaches to the new fort. To cover the southerly approach, three smaller fortified positions were constructed along a low ridgeline that rose abruptly from the plain and ran almost due south along the heights adjacent to the river to a point about halfway between Buttermilk Falls and West Point where the ridgeline tapers off. These positions—Forts Meigs, Wyllys, and Webb—were placed so that the first two could fire on any body of troops trying to approach West Point via the river heights. At the same time, Forts Wyllys and Webb could cover a draw to the west of the ridge that leads from the Highlands to the southwest corner of the plain at West Point. Constructed primarily of wood and earth, these fortified positions, with infantry and artillery, provided depth to the overall defenses and denied that ridge to the enemy.

While Parsons and Kosciuszko had been reorganizing the work at West Point, McDougall had been inspecting his new command. His first visit to West Point followed immediately on an investigation into the loss of Forts Montgomery and Clinton. Based upon what he had learned, he approved the works on the ridge to the south of Fort Arnold, and, in addition, immediately ordered a fortification built on the high ground to the west. On April 11th, work began on the latter—Fort Putnam.

The principal purpose of Fort Arnold was to dominate the plain upon which it was built and, thereby, to protect the rear of the water batteries and the chain. Additionally, it would help prevent the enemy from seizing the southern ridgeline upon which Forts Webb, Wyllys, and Meigs were being constructed. Wyllys and Webb could also be supported by cannon fire from Fort Putnam, and Meigs by mortar fire. All in all, this system of fortifications was intended to withstand at least a ten-day siege and hold off the British while the local militia was assembled to relieve them, or until the Continental Army could march to their rescue.

Actually, the militia was expected to perform four major functions in the defense of West Point: first, they were to play a significant role in the construction of the fortifications; second, the militia was expected to furnish a significant portion of the garrison;

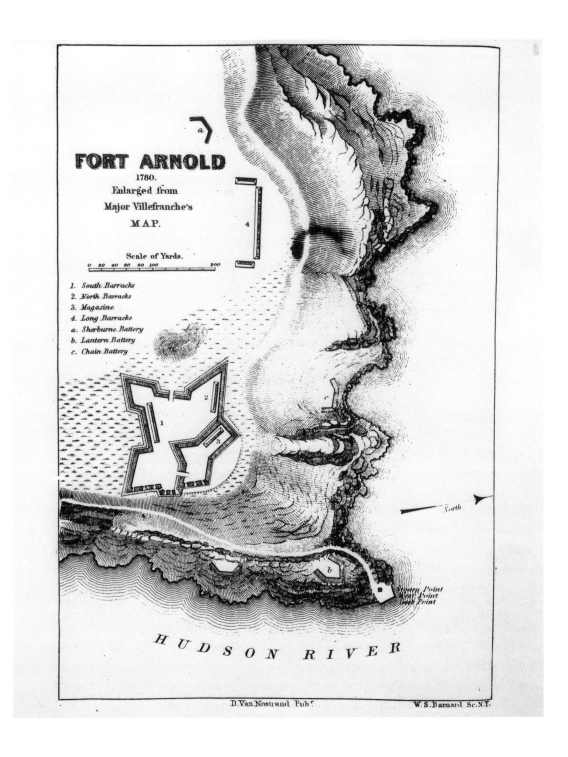

*Fort Arnold in 1780, as enlarged from a
map by Major Villefranche.*

third, the citizen-soldiers would provide the bulk of the garrison's maneuver units, and the outposts and pickets connected with the defense of the post; finally—in the absence of the Continental Army—they would have to raise any siege that the garrison might have to endure.

West Point's primary mission, of course, was to hold the river. The chain and the four water batteries would be the main means of accomplishing that. Fort Arnold would assist by protecting the rear of the batteries and by serving as the magazine for them. In April, when the river began to thaw, the chain was delivered, assembled, and eased across the river. On April 30th it was secured on the far shore, in a small cove on Constitution Island. Thereafter, until 1783, the chain was removed each winter and reinstalled the following spring.

April 1778 had proven to be one of the most productive months in the defensive development of West Point. The river was blocked and the water batteries, as well as Fort Arnold, were in a sufficiently advanced state to be capable of resisting any sudden assault by the enemy. Moreover, the addition of Lanthorn Battery had made the water batteries considerably more effective. At the same time, the works being constructed in the hills behind Fort Arnold would give the post an even better chance of holding out against a British assault until help could arrive. Most of the earlier weaknesses in plans for the overall defense had been eliminated with the changes incorporated by Parsons, Kosciuszko, and General McDougall. Now, only the failure to provide for the defense of the chain's anchor-point on Constitution Island remained as a serious flaw.

Life at West Point settled into an unremitting repetition of fatigue duty as construction continued into the summer. Long hours, and the heat and humidity of summer took their toll in both the rate of construction and in morale. A drunken riot on the 29th of June caused Parsons to temporarily bar the local dram sellers. Parsons, who—despite the excellent results he had achieved—had never been happy with his assignment, now decided to seek a change. Washington's first visit to West Point the next month provided Parsons with the opportunity to request reassignment. The general obliged him and appointed a new post commander, Colonel William Malcom.

Malcom found much yet to be done, although Kosciuszko assured him that—with sufficient manpower—the works could be completed in a short time. The new commander tightened discipline and exhorted the available workers to double their efforts. Stone masons were sought to face and strengthen the fortifications, and Kosciuszko began construction of the bombproof magazine inside Fort Arnold. Workers were in such demand, however, that Malcom even accepted Governor Clinton's offer to use Tories from New York's overcrowded jails as forced labor.

In late August, Washington ordered his Chief Engineer, General Duportail, to examine the works at West Point and to report his findings. This report, even if critical of some details of Kosciuszko's works, was generally favorable. The additions that Duportail proposed were "inconsiderable," he noted, although he did strongly encourage the construction of fortified positions covering the eastern terminus of the chain on Constitution Island. After due consideration, Washington approved Kosciuszko's plan, but added the works on Constitution Island that Duportail had recommended.

By autumn, life at West Point began to settle into a somewhat less demanding routine. The men lived either in huts laid out in two long rows on the plain or in the two-story Long Barracks which had been constructed that summer. Years later, this structure would become the first cadet barracks of the Military Academy.

A less demanding routine, however, did not mean that laxity was countenanced. The post commander enforced strict discipline in all things. When the laundry women began to inflate their prices, he imposed a ceiling on their charges. When some of the men resisted using the latrines that had been dug, again he acted. "The necessary [is] to be covered every evening . . . and every man in garrison [is] ordered to make use of them only—if any dirty fellow is detected [violating] this so necessary a regulation, he shall be ignominiously punished."

Still, there were respites from duty and fatigue. Military balls were held, and young women from the local settlements were invited. "The Dutch Girls are generally pretty well looking and entertaining," wrote one Continental soldier, "but have large ankles." These girls, he continued, were "fond of Dancing, Riding in Slays etc, for which they have become famous."

The spring of 1779 began uneventfully enough and, as navigation became possible on the river, the chain was once more installed. Construction on the fortifications had slowed for lack of materials, and also because of maintenance demands on the existing fortifications—which, being of a temporary nature, were now beginning to deteriorate.

Anthony Wayne achieved an important victory in 1779 when his Light Infantry recaptured Stony Point, discouraging any further British offensive moves up the Hudson River.

Meanwhile, in New York City, Sir Henry Clinton began to look north. He hoped to force Washington into a decisive battle by seizing or at least threatening West Point. This scheme, however, depended upon reinforcements from Europe, which Sir Henry expected momentarily. Confident that these troops were only days away, he launched his first attack at Stony Point and Verplanck's Point—the two ends of the critical King's Ferry. Initially, the plan was successful. On May 31st Sir Henry occupied Stony Point and cut one of the main Patriot lines of communication across the river. But then his plan hit a snag—the expected troops from Europe failed to arrive. Washington now reinforced the Highlands. Lacking reinforcements, and with the Continental Army in the vicinity of West Point, any further British advance up the Hudson was blocked. When Washington surmised that the British were not strong enough to continue their advance, he ordered Stony Point retaken. This task was assigned to Brigadier General Anthony Wayne. With the help of Baron Frederick von Steuben at West Point, Wayne carefully trained his forces. On July 16th, in a brilliantly executed attack, "Mad" Anthony Wayne's Light Infantry recaptured the position.

During the balance of the spring and summer of 1779 the fortifications at West Point were expanded to their fullest—although construction on these works continued into 1780. Thereafter, until the end of the war, the engineering effort would be confined to improvements and maintenance to keep the works in serviceable condition. The earlier decision to build only temporary field fortifications, rather than the more expensive and time-consuming permanent works, now resulted in a constant struggle to maintain the facilities. It explains the constant complaint of inspectors who always seemed to find the works in a state of decay and decline.

This last expansion of the complex of fortification began in the spring of 1779. Kosciuszko had previously submitted plans for a redoubt on the high ground west of Fort Putnam. Now, he called for a series of redoubts along the ridges immediately to the south and west of that position, forming an outer ring of defensive positions that would further protect Fort Putnam and West Point against any attack from the west.

The outer ring of redoubts on the west side of the river was complemented by the construction of additional works on the east bank. First was a redoubt on Constitution Island that responded to Washington's concerns. Built roughly in the center of the island,

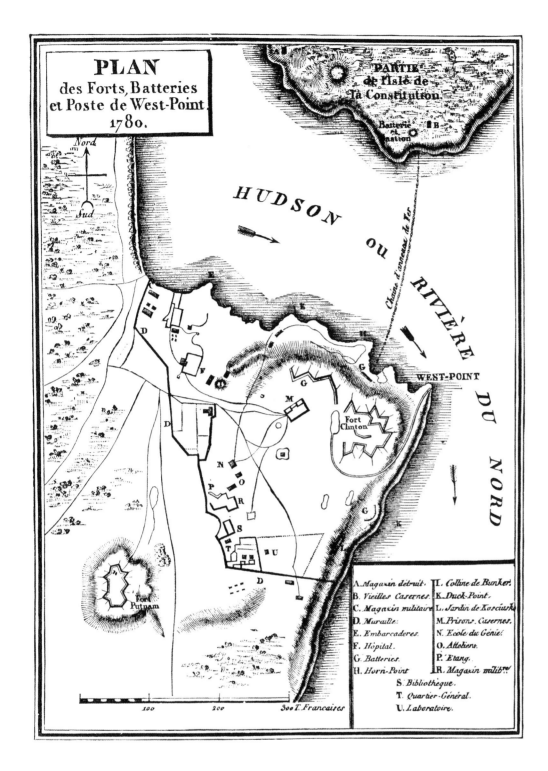

A French map of 1780 showing West Point and the position of the "great chain" across the Hudson River. It is possible that this map was drawn as part of a plan proposed by Duportail to establish a school of engineering at West Point—note the buildings designed "school of engineering" ("N") and "library" ("S"). The location of "N" coincides with that of the later Academy building. The structure marked "S" seems never to have been built.

it could block an attack on the chain from the east. In addition, three redoubts on the east shore were constructed on the ridges east and south, completing an outer ring of protection for the main works and chain on both sides of the river.

With most of West Point's fortifications completed or under construction by mid-1779, it was time to evaluate and scrutinize the post's capabilities. In late August, General Duportail conducted another inspection and prepared a lengthy report. The basic aim of any attack, he concluded, would be the destruction of the chain. Washington's chief engineer weighed several methods by which the British might try to achieve that end and concluded that only bombproof shelters to better protect the troops were now needed. These, Duportail believed, would assure "the defense of this mountain, as much as it is necessary to do it, in view of the number of troops the enemy can sacrifice to the attack of West Point."

In addition to the fortifications constructed during these years, a number of other structures were completed at West Point. In Washington's Valley—near the Moore House—there were warehouses and a hospital. On the plain there was Long Barracks (which survived until a fire destroyed it in 1826), and along the base of the high ground that sprang out of the plain, a number of smaller buildings that included a laboratory in which gunpowder was manufactured or refined, the headquarters, and scattered officers' quarters, mostly frame structures. Many of these buildings survived the war. One such—a two-story structure about the size of a country schoolhouse—became the first classroom of the Military Academy created some years later under President Thomas Jefferson.

There is no evidence of any permanent or regular school at West Point during these years. It is possible, however, that some training was given to the troops of engineers assigned to units there—that was the case at numerous other posts. Some more formal, yet short-lived schools, were established. An ordnance school, for example, was begun at Carlisle, Pennsylvania, early in the war to train officers in the art of manufacturing and repairing both artillery and ammunition. Later, during the winter of 1778–79, General Henry Knox, with the artillery regiments at Pluckemin, New Jersey, established an artillery school "where lectures are read in tactics and gunnery." There is no record of any such school at West Point during the years of the Revolution—certainly there is no reference to one in official papers, or in personal letters, diaries, or memoirs. Moreover, the demands of first constructing and then maintaining the fortifications at West Point undoubtedly left little time or energy for any other endeavors.

"The "Black Year" of 1780 began at West Point with one of the worst blizzards ever known in the Hudson Valley—a bad omen, as the rest of the year was to prove. It is said that the temperature dropped so rapidly that boats froze fast in the river and their occupants had to return to shore as best they could across the ice. The soldiers at West Point, gripped by the sub-zero temperature, huddled behind closed doors as the howling wind swept away the tents of those still encamped on the plain. That storm lasted for three days, during which the garrison struggled simply to survive. Given the extreme cold, heating fires were a necessity, but also a danger. Men trying to keep warm sometimes built their fires too high, or did not tend them carefully; buildings were burned on the plain and bombproof shelters in the redoubts were set ablaze. Finally, on the 5th of January, the snow and cold abated somewhat, but the winter continued to be colder than usual—the worst of the war.

The weather and a shortage of rations fostered discontent as well as misery among the troops. Not long after the storm abated roughly a hundred men from the 4th Massachusetts Brigade mutinied and set off for home with their arms. Although orders were issued to bring them back dead or alive, the mutineers, when captured, received comparatively lenient punishment—most were ultimately pardoned, although some thought to be the ringleaders received up to one hundred lashes.

The warmer weather in the spring and then the summer brought with it the task of rebuilding and repairing the damage the weather and the fires had caused. The passing months also brought a succession of new commanders, including—in August—Benedict Arnold.

Arnold was no newcomer to the Hudson as a theater of the war. Three times before he had fought along the Hudson-Champlain corridor: at Fort Ticonderoga; en route to Montreal; and at Saratoga. By this time, however, the once heroic patriot was planning treason. He knew well the strategic value of West Point, and long before arriving at the post had concocted a plan to surrender it to the British—thus hastening the end of the war and helping to ensure a British victory.

A view of West Point drawn by the engineer, Major L'Enfant, in 1780. From History of West Point by Captain Edward C. Boynton. The United States Military Academy Archives. Photo: Philip Pocock.

The seeds of this treason had been sown in Philadelphia during the late winter of 1779, and had progressed through a year of intermittent negotiation with Sir Henry Clinton in New York. Unable to conclude a satisfactory agreement, however, Arnold finally took a new tack and began to scheme to win command of West Point, a prize the British could hardly resist. His scheme worked. On June 15th, Arnold, using an assumed name, wrote to Major John André (Arnold's contact at Clinton's Headquarters), indicating that he expected to assume command at West Point in the very near future. The next day he visited West Point and once again sent a letter to the British. It was surprising, he said, that "a Post of so much importance should be so totally neglected." Rocky Hill, which commanded the outer fortifications, was "defenseless from the back," he said, adding, "[you] may land three miles below and have a good road to bring up heavy Cannon to Rocky Hill." Arnold's letter was carefully phrased. Although the works were "well executed," he wrote, they were "wretchedly planned"—implying that the post could be seized even if at full strength, providing the British knew its weaknesses and had assistance from within.

By August 1780, when Arnold took command at West Point, the deal had been struck. If the post, its arms, its stores, and its garrison should be handed over, the "sum even of 20,000 pounds" was to be paid to Arnold. With his ultimate escape in mind he chose to live in the Robinson House, opposite and downstream from West Point. He also made arrangements for Peggy, his young wife, and their infant son to join him there.

At West Point, Arnold busied himself, showing all the indications of a commander intent upon improving the defense of the post. Still, upon closer inspection, his activities actually promoted the decay of the existing fortifications and the delay of further works by focusing efforts and energies elsewhere. He directed the repair of certain buildings, but—at the same time—he increased the number of guards, thereby *decreasing* the number of laborers available.

On the night of September 21st, after a year-and-a-half of secret correspondence, Arnold and André met for the first time, at Verplanck's Point. Precisely what passed between them during that meeting is not certain, but Arnold did give André several papers pertaining to the defenses of West Point, and their conversation ran on so long that approaching daylight made it impossible for André to return to the British ship *Vulture*, which had brought him to the rendezvous.

Arnold then made arrangements for André to be escorted back to the British lines and he provided a pass that should have seen André safely through. The Briton shed his scarlet uniform jacket, replaced it with a civilian coat, and set out in the late afternoon with an escort provided by Arnold. The pair was stopped late in the day by a detachment of militia, whereupon the local commander told them that it was too dangerous to continue after dark and suggested that they remain with the militia for the night.

This illustration of Major André about to be captured by American militiamen appeared in Harper's Weekly *on October 2, 1880, one hundred years after the event.*

The next day, André's party was on the road again before daylight, but after breakfast his escort informed him that he would have to cover the last fifteen miles to White Plains on his own. This was a no-man's-land in which bandits operated freely, while wearing the uniforms of the militia of both sides. His escort having departed, André struck out alone, but when he heard a report that rebel horsemen had been seen on the road ahead, he turned west toward Tarrytown. At about ten o'clock, as he approached a bridge just above that town, he was halted by three militiamen. Expecting to encounter only Loyalists in that area, André revealed that he was British. When he learned that the militia were Patriots instead, André produced the pass that Arnold had signed, but to no avail. When a search revealed the papers dealing with West Point in his boot, his fate was sealed. He would ultimately be hanged as a spy.

André's captors, perhaps motivated more by the hope of reward than by patriotism, delivered their prize to Lieutenant Colonel John Jameson at North Castle, who sent off a message to Arnold explaining the circumstances of André's capture. At the same time, however, he sent the papers concerning the defense of West Point to General Washington.

Arnold was more fortunate than André. The evidence revealing Arnold's treachery reached Washington only after the traitor had been warned and had escaped—although not a moment too soon. Washington, who was actually en route to Arnold's headquarters at Robinson House, was always just ahead of couriers dispatched to bring him the news. Word of Washington's imminent arrival reached Arnold just minutes after he learned that André had been captured, and that word of the affair had been sent on to the commander-in-chief. Arnold departed a mere thirty minutes before Washington's arrival, but even then, the latter still had not learned of the attempted treachery. By the time Washington knew the truth, Arnold was safely aboard the *Vulture*.

Washington, having missed Arnold at his headquarters, proceeded to tour West Point, expecting to find the commander there. He was alarmed by what he saw: half-empty magazines, shoddy barracks, crumbling parapets, and a sinking chain. Once the general had received the evidence of Arnold's perfidy, these deficiencies loomed even larger. As his aide, Alexander Hamilton, warned, "Arnold has made such dispositions with the garrison as may tempt the enemy in its present weakness to make the stroke this night."

It would be prudent, Hamilton advised the commander-in-chief, "to be providing against it." Washington had come to the same conclusion and immediately began deploying his forces to foil any possible attempt by Clinton's troops to seize West Point. Washington now personally assumed responsibility for the Highlands, and riders dashed in all directions to spread the alert and issue his orders.

For some hours the troops at West Point remained entirely unaware of these events. In fact, a celebration of sorts took place on the plain that evening, where one of the officers provided a fireworks display. It was not until about eleven o'clock that the post received Washington's warning. Immediately, the garrison was roused, and by two o'clock in the morning the forts and redoubts were fully manned. The troops spent the next several days on alert. Water casks were filled, provisions distributed, and all available troops were marshaled to man the defenses.

The alert lasted for five days, and even for some time afterward a heavy guard was continued and detachments were positioned south along the river at the site of old Fort Montgomery and at the cove above Buttermilk Falls (now Highland Falls) to insure early warning of any attack.

Soon the state of alarm subsided and a calm settled over West Point. Once again, the theater of war shifted away from the Hudson. And henceforth, Fort Arnold would be known as Fort Clinton.

In the spring of 1781, Washington had hoped to retake New York—but to be successful this would have required the help of the French. Ultimately, however, the opportunity to cooperate with both the French Army and fleet against the British came not at New York against Sir Henry Clinton, but at Yorktown, in Virginia, against Lord Charles Cornwallis. In June 1781, Washington began to move southward toward the crucial battle that would end the war.

After the brief period of concern following Arnold's attempted treachery, West Point had been largely stripped of troops, since Washington's main Army lay between the river fortress and Sir Henry Clinton's forces in New York. As one officer put it, West Point was left "under the care of ingovernable and undisciplined militia." In addition, the shift of forces to the south now drew away most of the troops that had been interposed between West Point and the British in New York, and the proper garrisoning of the post once more became a critical factor. But Washington was determined not to make the same mistake he had made in 1777. He would not leave the Highlands as completely vulnerable to the British in New York as it had been before. This time, Washington left behind a considerable force—seventeen New England regiments, a legion of horse, a regiment of artillery, and as many of the state troops and militia as could be retained in service.

Still, General Alexander McDougall, again commander of the region that included West Point, complained loudly about the number and quality of soldiers he was being sent. His complaints multiplied when Washington sent him the Corps of Invalids.

"The bringing forward the Corps of Invalids from Philadelphia and Boston," Washington wrote, "was a matter of necessity and not choice; we must therefore submit to some inconveniences and put them to duties of the lightest kind." Washington felt compassion for this wretched regiment, whose ranks were filled with soldiers who had survived both the rigors of battle wounds and the even more perilous subsequent treatments by eighteenth-century surgeons. To a degree, he held himself responsible for them, and before they were ordered to march to West Point he wrote to their colonel, Lewis Nicola, directing him to pay the greatest attention "to the convenience and accommodation of this body of veterans, both on their march and in quarters." The trek would have its reward, however, for they might benefit from "the pleasant and healthy situation of [West Point] which is remarkable for the salubrity of its air." Moreover, he added, they would benefit

Alexander Hamilton, depicted here in an engraving made from a miniature by Archibald Robertson, was a proponent of the idea that the United States should have a military academy.

from "the accommodations of a stationary post." And of course, there was "the importance of trusting its defence to a body of tried men." "All," Washington concluded, "point out very forcibly the propriety of employing your Corps as a part of the garrison."

The Corps of Invalids had been created by act of Congress in June 1777: eight companies, each authorized five officers, eleven non-commissioned officers, four musicians, and one hundred men—all of whom had wounds that had made them unfit for more active service. The Corps had been employed at light garrison duties, and as guards at magazines and arsenals. It had small detachments at Boston, Rutland, Easton, Trenton, Fishkill, and West Point; a larger contingent was stationed in Philadelphia, which was also their headquarters. In addition to their regular duties, officers of the Corps were to assist with recruiting in the neighborhoods where they were stationed, and to train newly appointed junior officers prior to their being assigned to the marching regiments. To this end, one day's pay each month was to be withheld from the officers of the Corps for the purpose of "purchasing a Regimental Library of the most approved Authors on Tactics and the Petite Guere," although there is no evidence that these deductions or purchases were ever made. In fact, there is little to suggest that the Invalids devoted any effort to instructing new officers, or even to preparing their own officers for that role. The Corps seems to have been fully occupied with its garrison and guard duties.

The consolidation of the Corps of Invalids at posts in the vicinity of West Point was largely complete by late July, and Colonel Nicola established his headquarters at nearby Fishkill. "A number of these unfortunate men," wrote Colonel John Lamb, Chief of Artillery at West Point, "are capable of doing no duty but eating their rations." But, he conceded, "it is no doubt a piece of refined policy to bring these maimed men from a distant post, to present them to our soldiery, who have sagacity enough to infer, that after losing eyes, hands and feet, in the public service that their patriotic sufferings will be amply rewarded." To the local garrisons, however, the Invalid Corps was simply a burden. Just a year later the War Office noted the "miserable state" in which the Corps existed, "the very great expense" which attended it, and "the very little service received from it." Benjamin Lincoln, then Secretary at War, suggested to the Congress that the "really meritorious and debilitated officers and men" should be provided for in another manner.

Some chroniclers of the Military Academy have suggested that the officers of the Invalid Corps created a school for engineers that was a precursor to the later Military Academy. There is no evidence to suggest that any such school ever existed at West Point. Though there was a small detachment of Invalids at West Point before the main body arrived, there is no indication that they provided any instruction—even the informal sort occasionally available at some other posts.

With the departure of Washington and the main body of the Army, life at West Point settled back into a tedious routine. "Time rather hangs heavily," wrote one officer. One day was much like another. Drummers mounted the parapet of Fort Clinton at eight-thirty sharp in the morning and beat "The Pioneers' March," which called the men to work on the fortifications. "Roast Beef" signaled an hour's lunch, and then the drums recalled the men to work. Later "Retreat" and then "Tattoo" ended the day's labor. So passed the days until the end of October, when the rumor of victory over Cornwallis energized the camp. The story's confirmation sent the men into a violent, joyous celebration. Among the officers, General McDougall led the festivities; like the men in the lower ranks, they drank, shouted, sang, and danced with abandon in a celebration that lasted three days.

In the spring of 1782, with peace only a formality away, Washington brought the Continental Army back to the Hudson Highlands and established his headquarters at Newburgh, just above West Point. That winter the troops were housed at the sprawling New Windsor Cantonment and at sites all around West Point.

While the Continental Army waited for the war to end officially, there was time to relax and celebrate. One occasion, in particular, presented itself—the birthday of Louis Joseph, the dauphin, or heir apparent to the King of France. This was certainly the grandest celebration held at West Point during the war. But it was more than a salute to the French dauphin, it represented an expression of Patriot appreciation and gratitude—Washington's in particular—for French support during the Revolution.

For the occasion, a grand pavilion two hundred and twenty feet in length and eighty feet wide was built, supported by one hundred and eighteen pillars made of tree trunks. The whole was covered with the boughs or branches of trees, and decorated with evergreens and garlands of flowers. It is reported that five hundred gentlemen and ladies took part in the magnificent festival. Thirteen toasts were announced, each by the firing of thirteen cannon, a military band played, and Washington himself led the dancing at the ball that evening. The highlight for the guests and the troops who were encamped encircling the post on both sides of the river, was "a general *feu de joie*" itself announced by thirteen cannon, in which thousands of troops discharged their arms into the air. This was "immediately followed," we are told, "by three shouts of acclamation and benediction for the dauphin, by the united voices of the whole army on all sides." It was, however, also a celebration of their own Patriot victory and, even more to the point, of the anticipated disbanding of the Army—to be followed by the return of the men to their homes and families.

The colonnade that was constructed at West Point in 1782 for the celebration of the birthday of Louis Joseph, the heir apparent to the King of France. From History of West Point *by Captain Edward C. Boynton. U.S.M.A. Archives. Photo: Philip Pocock.*

CHAPTER 3
THE FOUNDING OF THE MILITARY ACADEMY 1784-1801

In December 1783, after General Washington had delivered his farewell address and resigned his commission, General Henry Knox took command of the remnants of the Army, most of which were stationed in the vicinity of West Point. Knox retained command until June 1784 when the Army was largely disbanded. Only eighty officers and men were retained—twenty-five at Fort Pitt, and fifty-five at West Point—all under the command of brevet Major John Doughty, who was the senior remaining officer of the United States Army.

The winter of 1784–85 was another cold season, and once again the men suffered as the bitter winter winds swept down the ice-covered Hudson. But, when the weather improved, there was more than enough work to keep the small detachment busy. As soon as the sun came out, they labored to preserve the stores of powder, drying it and repacking it in new kegs. When that was not possible, there were hundreds of cartridge boxes that required mending and oiling, and thousands of small arms that needed repair.

In 1785, after the Army had been expanded by levying the militias of several states, Major George Fleming took command of West Point. Under Fleming the old arms, powder, and camp equipage of the army were preserved and stored, or condemned and sold, as rapidly as circumstances permitted. The committee on the War Department reported in 1788 that about five thousand arms had been repaired at West Point and were now ready for service. About ten thousand more awaited repair, they reported, but, as a matter of economic necessity, the work was "going on at that post on a small scale." There were also, at West Point, a large number of cannon and mortars. Although these were generally fit for service, their carriages or platforms—left over from the recent war—were now defective, thus rendering the artillery largely useless. The immense quantities of powder stored in the magazines at West Point, however, were reported to be in "excellent order." Great attention had been paid to the powder, which was aired, cleaned, proved, and repacked regularly. The structures there, however, were a different story; built of "wood and materials unseasoned," they were "going fast to decay."

The fortifications were also decaying. Fort Clinton, the committee reported, had "been Slightly built for a temporary purpose" and had "decayed in such a manner" that unless "substantially repaired" it would "soon become a heap of rubbish." In fact, the decay had progressed so far that the redoubts had been stripped of their artillery in 1787, at which time a large number of guns had been sold for old iron. The committee estimated that at least $10,000 would be required to repair the fortifications, redoubts, and buildings at West Point—an amount they knew was beyond the financial capability of the young nation. Moreover, this sum did not include the cost of purchasing the land itself.

In late 1779, Stephen Moore, who owned the land upon which the fortifications and facilities of West Point had been built, had presented a petition to the Continental Con-

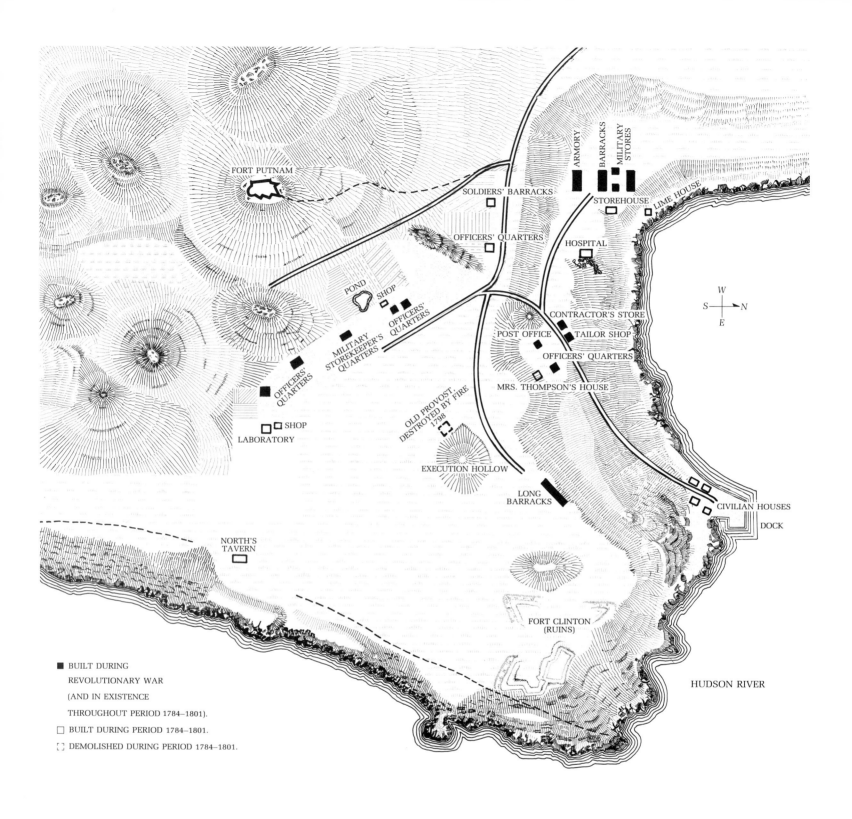

FORT PUTNAM

SOLDIERS' BARRACKS

OFFICERS' QUARTERS

POND   SHOP

MILITARY
STOREKEEPER'S
QUARTERS

OFFICERS'
QUARTERS

OFFICERS'
QUARTERS

SHOP
LABORATORY

OLD PROVOST,
DESTROYED BY FIRE
1798

EXECUTION HOLLOW

NORTH'S
TAVERN

LONG
BARRACKS

ARMORY
BARRACKS
MILITARY
STORES

STOREHOUSE   LIME HOUSE

HOSPITAL

CONTRACTOR'S STORE

POST OFFICE   TAILOR SHOP

OFFICERS' QUARTERS

MRS. THOMPSON'S HOUSE

W
S ——+—— N
E

CIVILIAN HOUSES

DOCK

FORT CLINTON
(RUINS)

HUDSON RIVER

■ BUILT DURING
REVOLUTIONARY WAR
(AND IN EXISTENCE
THROUGHOUT PERIOD 1784–1801).

□ BUILT DURING PERIOD 1784–1801.

⸢⸥ DEMOLISHED DURING PERIOD 1784–1801.

Map of West Point, 1784–1801.

gress asking payment for damages to his property, as well as compensation for the wood and timber that had been used to build barracks and fortifications. In December 1779, Congress had ordered the Quartermaster General to estimate the damages due Moore. His report had concluded that Moore was owed $292,000 in Continental script. On February 7, 1780 the Congress had issued an order to the Treasury in favor of Moore for $10,000, and also a draft on the governor of North Carolina for an additional $30,000—both to be made as partial payments toward satisfaction of the larger estimate of damages.

In July 1783, Moore petitioned for the balance due him on the earlier estimate of damages, and for the value of the additional wood and timber taken in the years since the last payment. In addition, he requested that a reasonable annual rent be established and paid. In September the committee considering his request proposed that a new estimate of damages and a fair annual rental be determined by a commission of three persons—one chosen by the Superintendent of Finance, one by Moore, and the third by the first two. The committee also suggested the outright purchase of the land and proposed that the Secretary at War should "report to the Congress the quantity and limits of the land which may be proper to purchase." The commission revised the estimate of damages downward to 2,227 Pounds, and established the rent at $437 per year. The rent apparently was paid, but nothing further was done to satisfy the balance of the debt.

In June 1786, Moore again asked for payment of the balance due to him, and once again the committee appointed to reexamine his claim recommended that the Board of Treasury pay it—"in such way as the State of Finances will best admit." The finances of the young nation, however, did not admit an immediate payment, and again the claim languished.

Congress, nonetheless, continued to consider the purchase of West Point and ordered a report by Henry Knox, now the Secretary at War, concerning the military value of the post. Knox was unequivocal: "In case of an invasion of any of the middle or eastern states by a marine power the possession of Hudson's River would be an object of the highest importance as well to the invader as to the United States." West Point, he continued, was "of the most decisive importance to the defense of the said river."

West Point offered the following advantages, Knox reported: the narrowness of the river at that point; the "peculiar bend or turn of the river" there; the high banks on both sides of the river; the "demonstrated practicability" of fixing a chain at that point; and the difficulty of investing the fortifications that overlooked the river batteries and the chain. "A regular siege of West Point properly garrisoned and furnished," he concluded, "would require a large army, vast war-like apparatus and much time." This would allow the militia of the States in the vicinity adequate time to "draw forth their utmost force" for West Point's relief.

Knox went on to note that, although some might regard West Point as an interior post, "the reverse is a fact, as may be proved by a slight consideration of the facility with which it can be approached by water." Vessels coming in from the sea which arrived at Sandy Hook in the evening, could reach West Point before the next morning, for the river could easily be navigated at night. West Point, he concluded, was vital "and as such ought to be guarded at the common expense of the Union with at least one company of troops." This cost would be small, he argued, in contrast to the "humiliating and distressing consequences" of allowing Great Britain or any other marine power to find the post defenseless. "Your Secretary," he concluded, "being convinced of the importance of retaining West Point as a military post until the United States shall possess a navy," strongly recommended its purchase.

On August 3, 1786, the Congress approved the purchase of West Point and authorized the Board of Treasury to negotiate an equitable price with Moore. Again, however, the effort came to naught. In 1788, the committee on the War Department reported that "owing to the absence of the said proprietor" the purchase has not yet been effected. Then, in the turmoil that surrounded the adoption of the new Constitution and the change in form of government, the issue once more faded from sight.

In May 1790, Stephen Moore approached the new government and asked its representatives for compensation. The petition was referred to Alexander Hamilton, the new Secretary of the Treasury, who submitted his report on June 10th. Hamilton quoted Knox's 1786 report at length and added that he, too, was convinced that the land should be purchased. Hamilton put forth two reasons for this belief—in addition to the strategic value of the land. First, "where the public safety requires the permanent occupancy of the property of an individual for the public use" purchase was the most equitable solution. Second, outright purchase was more economical in the long run.

The new Congress acted with dispatch. A bill was introduced on June 15th, authorizing the President to purchase Moore's land. It was agreed to by both houses before the end of the month, and signed by President Washington on July 5, 1790. The price was fixed at $11,085. On September 10, 1790, Stephen and Griselda (Grisey) Moore, his wife, signed the deed transferring West Point to the government of the United States of America.

During the years following 1784, the garrison had generally consisted of a single, under-strength company whose primary task had been the security and servicing of the stores there. But in 1794, when the Corps of Artillerists and Engineers was created, it was head-quartered at West Point.

Timothy Pickering, who had succeeded Henry Knox as Secretary of War in January 1795, took a special interest in the progress of the new Corps of Artillerists and Engineers. Under his watchful eye, training was begun—with both field pieces and the heavier sea coast artillery. This was initiated in the summer of 1795 under the supervision of two foreign officers, Majors Louis Tousard and John Jacob Ulrich Rivardi. Pickering, as he left office in January 1796, reported to the Congress:

> The corps of artillerists and engineers appear to be an important establishment. To become skilful in either branch of their profession will require long attention, study and practice; and because they can now acquire the knowledge of these arts advantageously only from the foreign officers who have been appointed with a special reference to this object, it will be important to keep the corps together for the present, as far as the necessary actual service will permit. Its principal station may then become a school for the purpose mentioned. To render this school more complete, provision is wanting for a geographical engineer and draughtsman.

But this was not in any sense to be a permanent military academy. What Pickering proposed—and what he put into place—was a temporary school that would train the officers of the new Corps in the essential skills they would require. To that end, three of the five field grade officers he appointed were foreign officers with training in engineering and artillery: Lieutenant Colonel Stephen Rochefontaine, and Majors Tousard and Rivardi. He also hired and sent to West Point two "temporary engineers"—also foreign officers—as additional instructors. Rochefontaine, a French professional soldier and veteran of the American Revolution, was appointed to command the new Corps—the bulk of which had been assembled temporarily at West Point. Only Majors Henry Burbeck and Constance Freeman were American born, but Burbeck and his battalion were assigned to the western frontier, and Freeman was regularly detached on other duty. Although American officers might chafe at serving under foreign officers, Pickering was convinced that this was the best available solution.

Rochefontaine arrived at West Point on January 10, 1796, and assumed command from Major Tousard. He was well aware of Pickering's desires for the Corps and as soon as the instructors (the "temporary engineers") arrived he began classes for the officers. Instruction was conducted in a room of the former provost prison, one of the few brick structures built there, which had been converted to an officer barracks. During the balance of the winter, classes were scheduled six days a week from eleven A.M. to noon, and from four to five P.M. In the morning, the instructors explained the different principles of fortifications and guided studies in texts provided. In the afternoon, the officers drew plans of fortifications based on the morning's instruction. In the evening, Mr. Warren, one of the "temporary engineers," was available to demonstrate the principles of drawing to those who needed this instruction. In March, when milder weather allowed company drill to

Timothy Pickering. The Bettmann Archive.

be resumed, the schedule of classes was reduced to three mornings per week—Tuesday, Thursday, and Saturday.

Unfortunately, Rochefontaine's effort to train his officers was marred by his own poor relations with them. He had been at West Point barely a month when the officers of the Corps drafted a letter of complaint against him to the new Secretary of War, James McHenry. The cause, in part at least, was the difference between Rochefontaine's stern manner and that of the more lenient Tousard, who had been in command at West Point since the Corps was formed the year before. The officers resented Rochefontaine's "wishes to innovate," as well as what they believed were his efforts to "render the duty hard and disagreeable"—referring, of course, to the daily classes which he insisted they attend. (Moreover, Rochefontaine believed, Tousard was disappointed at the former's selection to command the Corps and had secretly worked to turn the officers against him.)

This program of training largely came to an end in April, barely two months after it had begun, when the officers' barracks (in which classes were held) was burned. (A few years later, accounts of the incident suggested that the fire had been the work of the disgruntled officers, but there is no hint or suggestion that this was the case in the contemporary reports.) "The want of a proper place to meet with the gentlemen upon theoretical instruction Since the Destruction of the officer Barrack," Rochefontaine wrote, "has led me to Exercise oftener in the Field upon Manoeuvers of Field pieces and Infantry." Although he sought new quarters for the classroom, instruction was conducted only infrequently from that date onward.

Not long after the fire, Rochefontaine's relations with the officers had deteriorated so badly that he became embroiled in a duel with one of them, Lieutenant William Wilson. The underlying factor in this was the general dissatisfaction noted above, but the proximate cause was an epithet Wilson hurled at Rochefontaine which was followed shortly

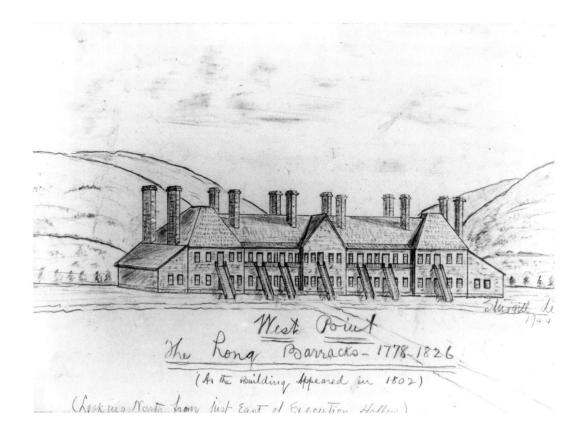

Long Barracks as it appeared in 1802.
Drawing by Colonel Walter Sturgill.
U.S.M.A. Photo: Philip Pocock.

by an altercation in which the colonel struck the young officer with the hilt of his sword. Rochefontaine related the story of what followed:

> The agreement after we met was, that in order to avoid the formality of a Duel, we should settle the dispute by a Rencontre with two loaded pistols each and a Sword. The fires were to be given at pleasure and the distance be such as it Suited the two adversaries. The first fire went off almost at the same time on both sides. My second pistol went off unaware and I remained against my antagonist who had yet a Loaded pistol against me. He came up to me within three steps and misfired. It is a general rule in such occasions to lose the chance when the pistol has not gone off, yet my adversary cocked up and missed his fire a second time. In order to prevent his firing a third time, I fell on him to try to prevent him from cocking his piece, but he did it notwithstanding, and his pistol missed fire again, the muzzle touching my breast. The two witnesses came up then and separated us.

Unfortunately, this result satisfied neither Wilson nor the other officers, who then publicly denounced Rochefontaine. "The mind of the officers" was "so completely set against" him, Rochefontaine complained, that he could hardly function. Although a United States citizen "I am still looked upon as a stranger," he lamented. "It may be to the general advantage," he concluded, "to place a man drawn out of the U.S. at the head of a Corps officered by American Gentlemen."

Rochefontaine remained at West Point until he was discharged in 1798, but his effort to train the officers was abandoned. Two of the three battalions of Artillerists and Engineers were reassigned in the summer and fall of 1796—three companies were detached to the westward and southward, and five others were sent to the sea coast. Pickering concisely summarized the result of Rochefontaine's efforts: "The officers have made very little improvement." Moreover, he noted, "we have been totally disappointed in our expectation of finding instructors in the Foreign officers appointed to command." The problem was "the disgust conceived by the captains and subalterns of the corps against their field officers, especially Rochefontaine."

Just outside the boundaries of the post was a grog shop opened in 1796 by Thomas North. Here the soldiers gathered off duty and drank. North was no man to encourage moderation so his establishment gave rise to frequent disorder in the garrison. It also caused friction with many of the local lads, who also gathered there. They had "a hostile disposition towards the Soldiery" noted Captain William Steele, who—in 1800—commanded the only artillery company remaining at West Point. "There is scarcely a public day of any sort that they don't assemble [at North's], and endeavor to raise a disturbance with the Soldiers," he wrote.

In April, Steele placed North's premises off limits, and ordered guard patrols to enforce his order. On July 4, 1800, a particularly large crowd had gathered at North's and when the Captain sent a patrol to check for soldiers among them, the guards were disarmed and beaten. Word spread quickly among the garrison and, before Steele could gain control, his men had stormed the establishment. Those inside retreated upstairs and from there held off the troops with the weapons they had taken from the patrol.

When Steele had regained control of his men he formed them up in front of North's place and ordered the surrender of those within. When, at first, they refused, Steele ordered an artillery piece brought forward. He leveled it at the front door. That prompted those inside to reconsider. They surrendered forthwith.

In 1800, the physical facilities at West Point were not remarkably different from those found there at the conclusion of the Revolution. The provost prison—built during the last years of the war and then converted into an officers' billet—had burned. The wartime soldiers' huts had largely disappeared and some smaller barracks had been converted to other uses. Otherwise, little had changed. Long Barracks still stood on the north edge of the plain near the ruins of Fort Clinton. There were the ordnance storehouses and hospital below the plain, by the river. On the level of the plain there remained the headquarters, the quartermaster's storehouse and office, the laboratory, and some scattered quarters for the officers.

Some historians have mistakenly attempted to establish a link between the school Rochefontaine briefly conducted and the later United States Military Academy. The best evidence to the contrary is that immediate contemporaries did not see any such ties. Washington's last annual message, in December 1796, made a cogent case for the establishment of a military academy, without reference to the on-again, off-again school at West Point. "However pacific the general policy of a nation may be, it ought never to be without an adequate stock of military knowledge. . . . [F]or this purpose an academy where a regular course of instruction is given is an obvious expedient." Later, in 1799, and again in 1800, when more formal military academies were recommended, the proposals made no reference to expanding on the training that had been attempted in the Corps of Artillerists and Engineers. That was not the model upon which they hoped to build, for it had been nothing more than a temporary expedient—and an ineffectual one at that.

The idea of establishing a military academy dates back much further—to the beginning of the struggle for American independence. As early as November 1775, John Adams had recognized that somehow "we must make our young geniuses perfect masters of the Art of War in every branch." He inquired, of Knox, asking the names of those officers who had a knowledge of "the Theory and Practice of Fortification and Gunnery," and "what books are best upon these subjects?" "The officers of the army in General," Knox replied, "are exceedingly deficient in the Books upon the military art which does not arise from their disinclination to read but the impossibility of procuring the books in America." He especially recommended Marshall Saxe's *Memoirs Upon the Art of War*. "I do not know of any book that would be of more service to our Young Army [than] this," Knox wrote, but listed for Adams a number of other titles which he also recommended. Adams replied, "I could wish that the public would be at the expense not only of new editions of these authors but of establishing academies for the education of young gentlemen in every branch of the military art."

In September 1776, in the midst of recriminations concerning the defeat at Long Island, Knox joined Adams in calling for a military school. "Military academies must be Initiated at any expense," Knox warned. Without some such "radical Cure" from Congress, the army will continue to get "the same unmeaning puppies for officers with which she had been curs'd," Knox complained. The visit to Washington's encampment of a committee of the Continental Congress gave him another opportunity to promote the idea. At the conclusion of that visit, Knox supplied the committee with detailed "hints for the improvement of the Artillery," advocating the establishment of a military academy "to be nearly on the same plan as that of Woolwich . . . a place to which our enemies are indebted for the superiority of their artillery." The committee, in turn, called for the establishment of an academy to be collocated with a continental laboratory or ordnance facility. The ordnance school founded at Carlisle, Pennsylvania, shortly thereafter was a response to that initiative. This establishment operated for nearly two years, from 1777

Major General Baron (von) Steuben recommended the establishment of an American military academy in 1783. The Bettmann Archive.

through 1779, but it was hardly the academy that Knox had envisioned. While in operation, the laboratory's school focused its efforts almost wholly on the fabrication and repair of weapons.

Adams, in the meantime, assured Knox of his support for the creation of a military school and asked him to provide a plan. At the same time he revealed that he had moved to appoint a committee to consider such a plan. The creation of the Invalid Corps, however, was as close as the Continental Congress came to a broader "school" to train the Army's officers. In theory, it was (among other things) to serve as a "School for propagating military knowledge and discipline." In reality, however, it was far from that, and never served the ends of military education for which it had been created.

Clearly, during the nation's war for independence, there was a recognition of a need for professional military education, and several proposals were advanced. However, the efforts in that direction were, at best, temporary and imperfect expedients.

At the close of the war—as the new nation began to consider the nature of its peace establishment—there was another brief revival of interest in military academies. Benjamin Lincoln, the Secretary at War for the Continental Congress, submitted a plan in March 1783 that included provisions for five magazines or arsenals: one each at Springfield, Massachusetts; at West Point; at Carlisle; at New London, Virginia; and at Camden, South Carolina. At each, he added, "a military academy should be established and suitable buildings be erected to accommodate the pupils." Also at each, "officers of abilities and information" should "superintend the instruction of the scholars in the mathematics and such other branches of education" that would be required "to form a perfect engineer—artillerist—dragoon and Infantry officer."

Congress then appointed a committee to study the requirements of a peacetime military establishment. Alexander Hamilton, who chaired the committee, sought Washington's views. The general, in turn, solicited the opinions of a number of trusted officers, including Generals Steuben, Knox, Heath and Huntington, as well as Colonels Pickering and Gouvion. Each of these men incorporated in his recommendation a provision for one or more military academies. Gouvion and Pickering, on the one hand, called for more narrow technical schools to prepare officers for artillery and engineers. Knox, Heath and Huntington, on the other hand, envisioned a somewhat broader academy (or set of academies) that would prepare officers for all branches of service, even for the militia.

Steuben at first declined to respond at length to Washington, though he did suggest "the establishment of military academies and manufactures for the United States is a matter of great consequence." But Steuben was already in the process of providing his detailed recommendation directly to Benjamin Lincoln, the Secretary at War. In that plan he proposed a broadly based, three-year program of study for up to 120 young men—eighty cadets of infantry, twenty of cavalry, and twenty of artillery and engineers.

Although Washington considered carefully the counsel he had received, his ultimate recommendations were much more modest than those of his advisors. After noting that Steuben's recommendations must already have been laid before the committee, he concluded that he would be satisfied, for the present, if provision was made "for instructing a certain number of young gentlemen in the Art of War particularly in all those branches of service which belong to the Artillery and Engineering Departments."

Hamilton, in the committee report, concluded that Lincoln's proposal for three armories and academies would be too expensive. "The benefits of such institutions," he remarked, "rarely compensate for the expense." In any case, he wrote, "such institutions can only be the object of future consideration." Hamilton did, however, follow Washington in proposing training and instruction for the artillerists and engineers at the post where they were stationed. In 1784 the Congress was so divided, however, that nothing

West Point in 1789 as painted by Colonel Walter Sturgill. U.S.M.A. Photo: Philip Pocock.

came of any of the proposals for a peacetime establishment. In the face of this inability to create a peacetime force, the army was virtually disbanded.

With the adoption of the new Constitution in 1789 a truly federal military force finally came into being. Still, this force was modest. While Congress struggled to define the nature of the new military establishment—particularly measures to effectively regulate the militia, that Army, under the leadership of first Josiah Harmar, and then Arthur St. Clair, sustained a succession of humiliating defeats at the hands of the Indians in the Northwest. Of a force of some fourteen hundred (the majority of whom were raw recruits and militia—"poorly armed, poorly supplied, utterly untrained and without discipline"), St. Clair contrived to lose almost seven hundred, or half his strength, in a single disaster.

Anthony Wayne, selected the next year by Washington to command the new Legion of the United States, took special pains to drill his new command and to organize an effective supply service. These efforts yielded complete victory over the Indians at Fallen Timbers in the summer of 1794. Wayne had shown that a few months of training implemented by a competent commander could accomplish much.

There remained, however, the problem of training officers, particularly in the technical branches of artillery and engineers. At a Cabinet meeting in November 1793, which Washington called to discuss the contents of his fifth annual address, the issue of a military academy arose. Hamilton and Knox favored the proposal but Thomas Jefferson opposed it on the grounds that the Constitution did not specifically authorize such an institution. Washington chose to leave the issue to Congress, suggesting only that officers needed "an opportunity for the study of those branches of the military art which can scarcely ever be attained by practice alone." Congress heeded this advice when it created the new Corps of Artillerists and Engineers in 1794; it also authorized two cadets for each of the sixteen companies and the purchase of books, instruments, and apparatus necessary for their training.

Despite the early interest that had been shown in a military academy, little of substance was done to create one until 1798. Then Alexander Hamilton, nominal head of the New Army which had been created that year in response to the threat of war with France, again began to promote the idea. In July, he asked General Louis Le Begue Duportail, the former Chief of Engineers of the Revolutionary Army, for his thoughts on the establishment of such a school. "This," Hamilton wrote "is an object I have extremely at heart." Duportail's plan reached Hamilton late in the year and was then submitted to the War Department.

By that time James McHenry, Secretary of War, had also taken up the cause, but he was inclined toward a plan that had been submitted by Louis Tousard—a proposal for the "Formation of a School of Artillerists and Engineers." Tousard suggested that an academy be created and located at one of the established arsenals and foundries. He favored either Carlisle, Pennsylvania, or Springfield, Massachusetts. The director of the new school, he proposed, should be a field grade officer, assisted by two captains who would teach artillery tactics. In addition there would be a professor of mathematics and a professor of drawing, each of whom would instruct in the practical application of these subjects. Classes in mathematics and drawing would be held on Monday, Wednesday, and Friday mornings; artillery practice was scheduled for Tuesday and Thursday afternoons. On Thursday mornings the director of the academy would lecture on the science of fortifications. It was a simple and straightforward plan that appealed to McHenry. To the Secretary of War, this school would be the training ground for a body of qualified artillery and engineer officers.

By late spring 1799, McHenry had convinced President John Adams—who had first addressed this subject some twenty years earlier—that a military academy should be established immediately. By July, he could report to the President that "measures are in progress," for he had submitted a long letter to the Committee of Defence that echoed Tousard's proposal. Congress, however, did not act upon it.

That fall, Hamilton again turned his attention to the subject. "A regular Military Academy," he wrote James Wilkinson, was "indispensable." He promised that during the upcoming session of Congress the subject would command his "best exertions." In November 1799, he submitted a new plan to the Secretary of War, with a proposal to organize an academy consisting of five schools. The first was to be the Fundamental School. All entrants, except those "who by previous instruction elsewhere may have been acquainted with some or all the branches taught," would complete two years of basic instruction there. They would study "arithmetic, algebra, geometry, the laws of motion, mechanics, geography, topography and surveying, and the designing of structures and landscapes." A cadet's education after the Fundamental School would depend upon the branch of the military that he was destined to join. Those anticipating duty with the Corps of Artillerists and Engineers would be expected to devote an additional two years to the study of advanced mathematics and mechanics, the theory of gunnery and ordnance topics, as well as fortifications and engineering. There was also to be a school for infantry and one for cavalry. And those scheduled for the naval service would be enrolled for two years at a naval academy—to study astronomy, navigation, seamanship, and naval architecture.

Hamilton also provided for rotation through the academy of various members of the Active Army, both commissioned and non-commissioned officers, for regular periods of further training. The staff for his proposed academy was to consist of six directors and eighteen faculty members, suggesting a student body of about two hundred cadets. The administration's proposal prepared by McHenry and submitted to Congress by Adams on January 14, 1800, followed Hamilton's plan closely. The most important deviation was a streamlining by McHenry of Hamilton's infantry and cavalry schools into a single institution. Later, however, sensing that the proposal was in trouble, McHenry submitted a supplement to the bill, suggesting that only the Fundamental School (with its fifty cadets) and the School of the Artillerists and Engineers (also with fifty cadets) were needed at that time. McHenry also sought estimates of the cost of establishing such an institution from prominent engineers and architects—estimates that ranged from $39,000 to $80,000. The latter figure was an estimate submitted by B. Henry Latrobe, who had prepared a plan and sketches of a large, classically adorned structure that could house this academy.

But, in an era of deteriorating domestic affairs and general dislocation of public matters, the academy bill lay unattended with the military affairs committee until McHenry personally interceded with Harrison Gray Otis, the chairman. "I consider the measure of the last [greatest] importance," he said, "as it respects character, efficiency, utility and economy in every part and portion of our system of defense . . . I ask for it your protection." Under normal circumstances the bill would have been in good hands, for Otis was a respected and well-connected member of Congress. These, however, were not normal times. Not only were fundamental party rivalries threatening to erupt into broader conflict, but all the branches of government were traumatized as well by the upcoming transfer of the government from Philadelphia to the new capital of Washington, in the equally new District of Columbia.

Otis, however, did manage to get the bill through committee and presented it to the House of Representatives in March. But the political current was running strongly against the project. Republican attacks against the Federalist military establishment, which they believed to be a threat to their political existence, and thereby to the nation, were gaining breadth and vigor. Even more importantly, the Adams Federalists, growing weary of Hamilton's domination, were beginning to lend support to the Republicans.

As an early warning of the difficulties to come, the military academy bill was attacked on its first reading, and once again it languished. Otis, who had been asked by McHenry to manage the bill, left Philadelphia in late March and did not return to his seat until Congress met in the new term in Washington late that year. Without his support, and without the votes of the Adams Federalists (which he might have delivered), the bill died—the victim of both Republican concerns about a partisan Federalist military establishment and a growing split in the Federalist party. In fact, the vote, sixty-four to twenty-three, said more about the political infighting of the times than it did about the strength of opposition to the idea of a military academy.

As bleak as prospects appeared for a military academy in early 1800, they took a turn for the better that summer. Hamilton continued to promote the issue—in July he wrote the new Secretary of War, Samuel Dexter, that it was "an object of primary importance" which should "be zealously pursued." Dexter, however, needed no prodding. He was already considering ways of circumventing congressional footdragging and opposition. Artillery and Engineer cadets (presumably to have been groomed in their units to fill vacancies opening in the junior officer ranks) had been provided for in 1794. In addition, in 1798, the Congress had authorized "teachers of the arts and sciences" for each of the regiments. By the time he received Hamilton's letter, the new Secretary had formulated a plan of his own and was ready to have it copied for transmittal to the President.

Dexter proposed using the existing authority to appoint cadets and instructors for the regiments, but to assemble them on a permanent basis at West Point, where several companies of artillerists and engineers were routinely stationed. This plan needed no further congressional approval—beyond later annual funding. "I am very ready," Adams answered, "to appoint both cadets and teachers"; and he then launched into a catalogue of specific instructions. Dexter was to "take the earliest measures" to obtain the books, instruments, and apparatus that would be necessary and that were provided for by law. He was also to make inquiries "for proper characters" for teachers. The Secretary had recommended that they begin with two teachers of mathematics and an engineer, and Adams concurred. The President proposed Captain William A. Barron as a teacher. Barron, who had been commissioned a few months earlier in the Second Regiment of Artillerists and Engineers, had previously taught mathematics. Dexter suggested, as the engineer, a Frenchman, Jean Xavier Bureaux de Pusy, who had been proposed by Hamilton. But Adams rejected the Frenchman. "I have an invincible aversion to the appointment of foreigners, if it can be avoided," recalling the recent unpleasant experience with Rochefontaine. It "mortifies the honest pride of our officers," he concluded, "and damps their ardor and ambition."

Adams's response had barely reached Dexter when the Secretary fired back more details. In anticipation, he had already begun to consider potential instructors. But the only name he could yet add to Barron's was that of the engineer, Jean Foncin, an associate of de Pusy's. Adams, in response, agreed to appoint Foncin, but not ahead of Barron. "If you can find another American mathematician better than Barron, it is well," wrote Adams, "if not, we will appoint him first teacher." He suggested, nevertheless, that Dexter should continue to inquire about American mathematicians. The upcoming fall election soon diverted Adams's attention, but Dexter continued his search for acceptable faculty. In August, he began to make inquiries about Jonathan Williams. Williams was not a teacher, but was well read in mathematics, the sciences, and natural philosophy. He was also not a soldier—despite brief periods of service with the Pennsylvania militia during the Whiskey and Fries's Rebellions—but his translation of two French military texts suggested more familiarity with these subjects than most officers could boast. In September, Dexter offered Williams a commission as a major, but revealed neither his plans for a military academy nor the role Williams might play there. The latter declined in hopes of obtaining a civil appointment, but did agree to have the works on artillery and fortifications, that he had translated, published for use by the War Department.

Adams's loss of the election in November ended all hope that the administration would be able to see the project through to maturity. What is more, a fire gutted the War Department's offices, bringing work there, on all matters, to a halt. "All the papers in my office [have] been destroyed," wrote Dexter, as he began the slow process of restoring some measure of order to the day-to-day routine. Finally, for the President, the tragic death of a son dampened any remaining enthusiasm he might have had for affairs of state.

Still, during the early months of 1801, Dexter turned his attention once more to the effort, although it must have been clear that little could come to fruition before the Adams administration left office. He renewed the offer of a commission to Williams and this time was somewhat more direct about his plans. This time Williams accepted. "I have been indefatigable," he wrote, "in brushing up all my former mathematical knowledge and adding to the stock." In addition, Williams wrote, he had begun to gather a personal library on military engineering and had started work on a program of lectures on subjects he thought essential to the young men he soon hoped to be instructing.

On his last full day in office, Adams filled the vacancies in the cadet ranks. But this, in the midst of an orgy of appointments made during the last days of the administration, was an act of political expediency—if not spite—rather than an effort to revive the earlier plans for an academy with which his administration had for so long been involved.

Adams departed Washington on March 4, 1801, only hours before the inauguration, and left the fate of the military school in the hands of a new administration which, past actions being the guide, seemed likely to reverse any progress that had been made. By all indications, proponents of the school should have expected little. In Washington's cabinet, in 1793, Jefferson had argued that proposals to create a military school were

Major Jonathan Williams became the first Superintendent of the Military Academy in 1801. This portrait is by Thomas Sully. West Point Museum Collections, United States Military Academy.

unconstitutional. More recently, in 1800, an academy bill had been vigorously attacked by the same Republicans who now controlled the Executive branch and dominated the Congress.

Contrary to all expectations, however, the new administration acted quickly to establish the school, and did so with an energy and facility that had been lacking in Adams, McHenry, and Dexter. The first notice of their intentions came on April 11, barely a month after the new administration had taken office, when Secretary of War Henry Dearborn offered the position of teacher of mathematics to George Baron, an Englishman who was at the time residing in New York. Dearborn outlined the duties, salary, and benefits, and indicated that "West-Point on the Hudson, will probably be the position for the school." (Baron, a civilian who had earlier taught at the Royal Military Academy at Woolwich, is not to be confused with the American, Captain William Amhurst Barron, whom Adams had favored, and who was, in 1802, ordered to West Point by the new administration, to teach mathematics there.) Four days after offering to hire Baron, Dearborn notified the commander at West Point of the plans "to establish a military school" there.

At the same time, the administration selected a military officer to superintend the new school—Jonathan Williams, who had recently been commissioned by Adams with this role in mind. Williams was a nephew of Benjamin Franklin, and for a time had been secretary to the old sage in Paris. He was a lay scientist and an officer of the American Philosophical Society. Jefferson had been acquainted with him in both capacities for a number of years. They had corresponded both in reference to Society business and scientific endeavors. Williams was a moderate Federalist, but if Jefferson harbored any concerns about his politics or loyalty, Williams made every effort to dispel them. In a solicitous letter to the new President, just after the inauguration, Williams took pains to assure him that his recent appointment to the Army by Adams had no political basis. Dearborn ordered Williams to Washington in April, and after a brief interview offered him the appointment as Inspector of Fortifications. Williams at first declined, but when it became clear that in this role he would head the new military school at West Point, he changed his mind.

Within another month the overall plan had taken shape: a Superintendent had been selected, curriculum considerations had been addressed, measures were underway to engage a qualified faculty, and facilities were ordered for students and staff alike.

In May, the facilities at West Point were surveyed and plans made to prepare the buildings for use as a permanent school. Lieutenant Colonel Louis Tousard, newly appointed Inspector of Artillery, reported that $1,500 would suffice to prepare a mathematics room, a drawing room, quarters for the cadets, two mess rooms, and quarters for the officers, teachers, and surgeon, as well as their families. Dearborn ordered work to proceed immediately: "No expense must be ignored that shall be actually necessary to render the . . . buildings comfortable outside painting [which] should be attended to on the score of economy." Major John Lillie, who took command of the post in June, supervised the repairs. His young daughter, Mary Ann, was amused when he had the seats painted green. But green paint was what was on hand, and economy dictated its use. On July 2, 1801, less than four months after the administration had taken office, Dearborn ordered the cadets to West Point.

Dearborn and Jefferson had moved with a purpose and alacrity that suggests that the new Academy was viewed as part of some larger plan—as, in fact, it was. Jefferson had recognized the need for an adequate regular military establishment, but he feared the mischief a Federalist officer corps might cause. Congressional sanction of the Academy was an element of the Military Peace Establishment Act of 1802 with which Jefferson initiated a political and social reform of the military establishment as a whole. That bill allowed Jefferson to discharge the most vociferous of his opponents in the Army and created new opportunities for Republican appointments at the lower levels. The institution at West Point on the Hudson provided one more means to further Jefferson's reformation of the Army, for it would soon admit, and train, the sons of the country's sturdy Republican stock.

It is interesting that the new administration had been able to move so much more effectively in establishing the school than had the previous administration. To begin with, of course, they built on the foundation created by Adams and Dexter. But the real answer is bound up in the motive that impelled them to take these actions. There had been more than a decade of debate over the role—even the necessity—of a regular military establishment in American society. After having once suggested that the powers of the Constitution would not authorize the establishment of a Military Academy, it might have seemed strange that Jefferson would then move so purposefully to create one.

Jefferson's creation of the Military Academy has, until recently, seemed to be a paradox. This was a "Hamiltonian institution created by Jefferson," wrote one historian. It was "a curious turn of the wheel," or an "ironical" affair, wrote others—that Jefferson should create a military school. When obliged to account for Jefferson's motive in creating the Military Academy, most fell back on one or both of two related themes. This was a national academy that emphasized science instead of the classics; or a school that was intended to provide trained engineers—military and civil—for the new nation. "[Jefferson] was eager," wrote Stephen E. Ambrose, "to found a national institution that would eliminate the classics, add the sciences, and produce graduates who would use their knowledge for the benefit of society. Within this framework Jefferson realized that a military academy had the best chance of success." Dumas Malone argued that Jefferson was "little concerned about the professional training of army officers in time of peace, [but that] he fully recognized the usefulness of engineers in peace or war and valued the infant Academy chiefly for its potential scientific contribution." Some authors have placed more emphasis on the military nature of the school. Others have stressed the peaceful benefits it produced—particularly from the engineers it trained.

More recent reexaminations of Jefferson's relations with the Army, including my own *Mr. Jefferson's Army*, have shown these earlier efforts to rationalize Jefferson's founding of the Military Academy to be unpersuasive. Jefferson simply did not consider the Military Academy at West Point to be a key institution of scientific learning—although no doubt he would have liked to have seen one established. Similarly, formal engineering training was neither the sole nor the primary goal of the Academy. In fact, an engineering curriculum (beyond the construction of rudimentary field fortifications) was not even introduced until a decade after Jefferson left office. If Jefferson had intended West Point to be an important element of a national scientific school, it seems certain that he would have chosen differently in terms of student body, faculty, and curriculum.

The extent of scientific training conducted at the Military Academy in its early years is easy to exaggerate. At times, in fact, the administration seemed to resist efforts to include any emphasis on science beyond the practical necessities of officership. For example, when Williams requested new books he was put off by Dearborn with the excuse that scientific thought was changing so rapidly that these texts would soon be useless. Also, as will be seen, the early faculty could be better characterized as laymen with interests in science and mathematics than as professional scientists such as were beginning to appear on the faculties of the nation's better colleges. The early curriculum at West Point clearly showed the very limited extent of either scientific or engineering instruction. In 1802, and for several years thereafter, while other institutions were offering higher mathematics, astronomy, natural philosophy, and chemistry as a matter of course, the Military Academy offered only the rudiments of mathematics and military fortification. Moreover, they made no pretext of doing otherwise. The mathematics text—C.H. Hutton's *Mathematics*—was so basic that it was widely used in primary schools. In many ways, the curriculum at West Point was more like that of a secondary or even an elementary school than a college—and for good reason. Some cadets, upon arrival, could neither read nor write; a larger number had only the most rudimentary skills in either arithmetic or grammar. By administration design, instruction was to impart only the most basic, practical knowledge needed by army officers of that day—sufficient mathematics and practical skills to lay artillery correctly, to construct simple fortifications, and to make rudimentary maps. Jonathan Williams, the Superintendent, had loftier goals but found them consistently frustrated. He argued "that mere mathematics would not make either an artillerist or an engineer." But, although French and drawing were soon added to the curriculum, the administration resisted all efforts to alter the basic nature of the school. It was not until the eve of the War of 1812 that the direction of the school began to change, and not until after Sylvanus Thayer became Superintendent in 1817 that West Point began to offer more than the rudiments of engineering.

At "the elementary school at West Point," reported a graduate of 1806, cadets "so fortunate as to render themselves serviceable either in the artillery or engineers" must have done so by "their own industry, and not in the education received by them at West Point, which was barely sufficient to excite a desire for military inquiries and of military pursuits."

The administration obviously envisioned the new Academy at West Point as something more than a school for engineers. In point of fact, the cadets appointed by Jefferson were

almost uniformly given artillery rather than engineer warrants. From among the best of these, a few were later chosen to be engineers, but the school graduated men into all the branches. The newly-commissioned graduates were assigned where they were needed—or possibly, where they were qualified to serve. Of the fifty commissioned during Jefferson's two terms, fourteen were made engineers, twenty-seven were sent to the artillery, eight to the infantry, and one to the dragoons. (One additional cadet was graduated, but not offered a commission.)

As recent scholarship has demonstrated, the efforts to explain Jefferson's founding of the Military Academy at West Point as a manifestation of his enlightened interest in science or engineering simply cannot be made to square with the evidence. Rather, the founding of the Military Academy needs to be seen as part of a more comprehensive Jeffersonian plan for the military establishment. It was no coincidence that the formal sanction he sought for the Academy was contained in the first broad program of military reform. The Army had to be made compatible with the views of the new administration. The creation of the Military Academy is no paradox when viewed as part of a broader political concern: the necessity to create and safeguard a new, Republican regime.

Jefferson's announcement to Nathaniel Macon of a "chaste reformation" of the military establishment came just two days after the first formal report indicating the contemplated establishment of a Military Academy. That juxtaposition was hardly coincidental. The Academy was to be an integral part of Jefferson's effort to Republicanize the Army. The President's new school would prepare loyal young Republicans for commissioned service in his reformed Army.

At West Point, where the first handful of cadets had been Adams appointees, the change was immediately noticeable. Joseph Gardner Swift, one of the Adams cadets, reported that after the new administration had come into power, "appointments to military office were made from families of prominent Democrats [Jeffersonian Republicans] and of less Educated Persons than had been heretofore appointed." Drawn from Republican families and trained under officers carefully selected for the task, these young men, it was hoped, would form an officer corps that would be thoroughly attached to the republican principles they were sworn to defend.

Dearborn and the President were diligent in their efforts to select cadets from within the country's Republican ranks. Applicants whose recommendations came from Federalist sponsors stood little chance of nomination; recommendation by a High Federalist meant almost certain rejection. The political affiliation of Academy applicants (or of their families) was a common and important subject of mention in letters of recommendation. The files of the very early years are fragmentary, but those that exist are indicative. "His father . . . is a Republican and I am informed the young man is also . . ." reported one correspondent. "He is . . . of reputable parentage, the family have all be[en] considered as thoroughly attached to republican principles," wrote another. You will not take exception to "his moral character, his education [or] his political creed," reported still another. These young men were all offered cadet warrants, though not all accepted them.

The failure to obtain an appointment was equally subjected to political interpretation. One such applicant noted that he published a Republican newspaper in New York State and that he had always been "attached to the principles of republicanism and your administration." When his letter met with silence he complained that "perhaps I may be suspected in my politics." The circumstances supported his conclusion. His paper had once backed a candidate who (in the factional disputes within the Republican party of New York) had earned administration displeasure by allying himself with some Federalist elements. The young editor was convinced that his secondhand indiscretion had disqualified him in the President's eyes. "I was always a friend of his administration," he again pleaded, but the appeal fell on deaf ears. The young man's brother, apparently not tainted by family associations, received an appointment straightaway.

Jefferson knew from the beginning that it would be easier to create vacancies in the Army—his "chaste reformation" of the Army through the Military Peace Establishment Act of 1802 had done just that—than it would be to fill them with qualified men of Republican persuasion. Federalists, on the average richer and more likely to have obtained an education, held the upper hand. "The children of illustrious families," wrote John Adams, "have generally greater advantages of education . . . than those of meaner ones, or even those in middle life." How was Jefferson to create a Republican Army if Republican sons were unprepared for officership?

To break the upper-class monopoly in the officer corps something had to be done to break the upper-class monopoly in education. If the commissioned ranks were to become accessible to all classes of citizens, if the aristocracy of wealth and birth in the Army was to be replaced with the aristocracy of virtue and talent, if men were to be included who lacked the advantages that wealth and position offered, then education and training would have to be provided that would equip them to lead. The new establishment of Republicanism in the Army necessitated the Academy that Jefferson created at West Point. His new military school would train men from the Republican stock of the country for positions of leadership in the new Army. For many it would provide the education they could not otherwise acquire. It was a key component of his new military establishment, and its creation was the conscious, purposeful act of an eminently and consistently political man. West Point would provide Republican sons with the fundamental skills they needed to serve as officers in Mr. Jefferson's Army.

CHAPTER 4
THE EARLY YEARS
1801-1817

By the time George Baron, the new instructor, arrived at West Point in late July of 1801, preparations for the new Academy were well under way. In May, the Secretary of War, Henry Dearborn, had ordered that quarters be readied for the Inspector of Artillery, the Inspector of Engineers, an instructor of mathematics, and up to thirty cadets. The post, which had recently quartered three of the Army's four artillery battalions, was more than adequate to accommodate the new school.

Facilities at West Point in 1801 had changed little in the decades since the Revolution. The building chosen as the Academy was one of those—a small, two-story frame building about the size of a country schoolhouse, constructed sometime before 1780. It had variously served as the post headquarters, as an officers' billet, and may also have been used during the Revolution as an occasional classroom for the artillerymen stationed there. This building, situated on the western periphery of the plain, was used both for recitations and chapel until 1815. (Sylvanus Thayer lived in the structure from 1817 until the Superintendent's new quarters were completed in 1820; the older building was razed not long after.) The most prominent structure on the plain was the decaying Long Barracks, located just west of Fort Clinton's ruins. After being refurbished in 1806, it served for a decade as a cadet barracks. Scattered about the western and southern edge of the plain, on either side of the Academy, the officers' quarters nestled against the steep slopes that reached up nearly 400 feet to the recently refurbished Fort Putnam. On the flats below the plain, near the river, were the ordnance storehouses, a small hospital, and a collection of smaller structures. Virtually all of these structures dated from the Revolution.

In July 1801, the cadets received their orders from Dearborn to report to West Point. By the end of September, the dozen thus far appointed had arrived and classes began. Baron initiated their instruction using Charles Hutton's *Mathematics*, a text that he had brought with him. Hutton was a former colleague of Baron's at the British Army's school at Woolwich; his book soon became the Academy's basic mathematics text, and remained so until 1823. Classes in mathematics—the only regular subject—began at eight o'clock each morning, and continued until noon. Each lesson was demonstrated at the blackboard and accompanied by a lecture from Mr. Baron concerning its application. The afternoons were variously occupied in military exercises or field sports.

Trouble arose for Baron almost at once. The junior officers at the post, who were also expected to attend the classes, refused to do so. One of these, Lieutenant William Wilson, whose altercation with Lieutenant Colonel Stephen Rochefontaine just a few years earlier over this same issue has been noted, was most likely the source of the trouble again. But Dearborn assured Baron of his support. "If the Subalterns persist in their contumacy," he wrote, "their ignorance of the duties of an officer, and their culpable want of ambition shall be noticed in an exemplary manner."

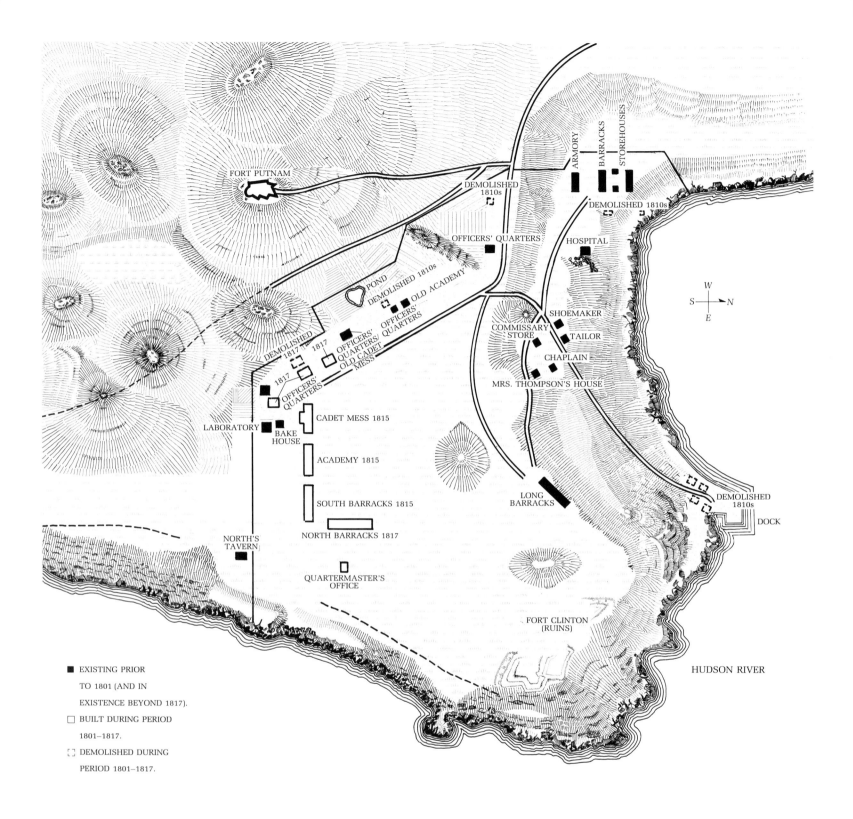

Map of West Point, 1801–1817.

When Wilson and Lieutenant Lewis Howard took a cadet, Joseph Gardner Swift, into their mess, Baron objected. He did not want the officers' arrogance and lack of discipline to infect the cadets, who, until then, had evidenced "good conduct," as well as "diligence and rapid improvement." Wilson, however, persuaded Swift to resist the order. In response, Baron pronounced Swift "a mutinous young rascal." But, when Swift attempted to avenge this insult, the instructor fled to the Academy with the young cadet in close pursuit. Baron bolted the door in Swift's face and, from the window of the upper story, he berated the cadet with coarse epithets which were returned in kind.

"You may confidentially rely on my aid in support of your authority," Dearborn again assured Baron, and then advised Swift to apologize or be dismissed. Wilson again coun-

Within the map:

FORT PUTNAM

DEMOLISHED 1810s

ARMORY
BARRACKS
STOREHOUSES

DEMOLISHED 1810s

OFFICERS' QUARTERS

HOSPITAL

W
S — N
E

POND
DEMOLISHED 1810s
OLD ACADEMY

SHOEMAKER

COMMISSARY STORE
TAILOR

DEMOLISHED 1817
1817
OFFICERS' QUARTERS
OFFICERS' QUARTERS
OLD CADET MESS

CHAPLAIN

MRS. THOMPSON'S HOUSE

1817
OFFICERS' QUARTERS

LABORATORY
BAKE HOUSE

CADET MESS 1815

ACADEMY 1815

SOUTH BARRACKS 1815

LONG BARRACKS

DEMOLISHED 1810s

DOCK

NORTH'S TAVERN

NORTH BARRACKS 1817

QUARTERMASTER'S OFFICE

FORT CLINTON (RUINS)

HUDSON RIVER

■ EXISTING PRIOR TO 1801 (AND IN EXISTENCE BEYOND 1817).

□ BUILT DURING PERIOD 1801–1817.

⌐⌐ DEMOLISHED DURING PERIOD 1801–1817.

seled Swift to stand his ground. "The officers of the post deemed Mr. Baron's conduct to be so ungentlemanly and irritating," Swift recorded, "that an apology could not be made to him." Baron again sought the help of the Secretary of War, who now decided to transfer the troops then stationed at West Point and to replace the officers with "some more judicious characters."

Baron finally lost the Secretary's support when the officers brought charges against him. His conduct, they alleged, was unbecoming one of his position and responsibility: he degraded the officers to the enlisted soldiers, abused his wife and children, and made a "habit of collecting many Citizens of the lowest rank and the most depraved characters at his house."

Baron was placed under arrest in November and instruction came to a halt. This was how matters stood when Major Jonathan Williams, the new Superintendent, arrived in mid-December. Williams heard the charges against Baron and reported to the Secretary of War that the instructor should be encouraged to resign. Dearborn concurred, but when Baron refused, the Secretary dismissed him.

Williams took over the teaching responsibilities upon Baron's departure, but reminded the Secretary of War that a regular professor should be appointed as soon as possible, stating his preference for a military man. That, he noted, "would ensure perfect harmony, and answer the ends of the institution." While waiting for this to be resolved he modified the curriculum that Baron had established, adding geometry to the arithmetic and algebra already being taught.

In March 1802, instruction again came to a halt when Williams became ill. He took an extended leave in order to recover, retiring for a time with his family to their home in Elizabeth, New Jersey.

Any disappointment that might have been felt at the suspension of classes in March, however, was dispelled by news of the passage of the Military Peace Establishment Act of 1802, which confirmed, in statute, Jefferson's creation of the new school. Formulated by the administration and introduced in December 1801, it passed the Congress and was signed into law by Jefferson on March 16, 1802—the date celebrated ever since as that of the Academy's founding.

Interior view of Old Fort Putnam at West Point. Anne S.K. Brown Military Collection, Brown University Library.

INTERIOR VIEW OF OLD FORT PUTNAM, AT WEST POINT, NEW YORK.

The provisions of the act which created the Academy were carefully drawn to allow the President exceptional powers over the new Corps of Engineers which was to constitute his new Military Academy. The division of the Artillerists and Engineers into separate branches had been proposed by the previous administration in 1800, but Jefferson and Dearborn saw a particular advantage in this arrangement and effected the change. The officers of this new engineer corps were all to be appointed by the President, and in this way would be peculiarly beholden to him. Moreover, in creating this corps, Jefferson was not bound by the traditional system of promotion by seniority; instead he could choose whomever he wished with regard only to ability and to compatibility with the new regime. This corps, more than any other, belonged to Jefferson.

The dismissal of Baron had forced the administration to renew its search for an acceptable faculty. In their earlier deliberations, Dearborn and Jefferson had taken great care to avoid the selection of men with strong Federalist leanings. Nonetheless, the same shortage of qualified Republicans that had prompted the school in the first place now made it necessary to cast an especially broad net. Although Baron was a Republican, Jefferson found that he could not avoid choosing some instructors who were moderate Federalists—"Republican Federalists" he called them. Williams was one of these. More staunch Federalists, however, were not even considered. It would have been unthinkable to select any strongly anti-administration role models for the young men. The administration rejected all who were tainted by loyalties to the Hamiltonian faction.

To replace the civilian George Baron, Dearborn proposed a military officer with a very similar last name, Captain William Amhurst Barron. This Barron, like Williams, was a moderate Federalist and had earlier been John Adams's choice to head the mathematics instruction. He was a Harvard graduate and had tutored there. Although the officer was unknown to Williams, his credentials were impressive and, more importantly, he had served with the Artillerists and Engineers since his appointment by Adams in 1800. The new Superintendent assured Dearborn that "a Teacher belonging to the Corps, would tend to harmonize with the students and the officers of the Garrison." Barron was named an assistant professor of mathematics and ordered to West Point.

Having secured legislation to establish the Academy as a permanent fixture in the military establishment, the administration immediately sought a second mathematics instructor. Jared Mansfield came to the attention of the administration through the efforts of Abraham Baldwin, a Republican Senator from Georgia. Baldwin, formerly from Connecticut, had once been a student of Mansfield's and had been associated with him in Republican political circles there. But Mansfield had more to recommend him than mere politics. He had taught mathematics at Yale, and in 1801 had published a book, *Essays Mathematical and Physical,* which included a chapter on the "Theory of Gunnery," discussing the physics of projectiles. When Baldwin sent a copy of the book to Jefferson, the President ordered several additional copies and asked the Georgia Senator to inquire as to Mansfield's interest in teaching at the new military school. When Mansfield indicated a willingness to serve, he was appointed to the new Corps of Engineers and, in May 1802, was ordered to "repair with convenient dispatch to the post of West Point."

In the spring of 1802, as he regained his health, Williams began once again to organize the affairs of the fledgling Academy. As he soon discovered, however, everything came under the watchful eye of the administration in Washington. Every change or addition was closely scrutinized. In February, when he had attempted to introduce practical geometry into the curriculum, he had been thwarted by the absence of mathematical drawing instruments. Williams immediately ordered twelve sets of the instruments and then put Dearborn on notice that it would "soon be necessary to have a good drawing Master." It had also been necessary to order the surveying and mapping instruments required for both field work and practical exercises. But the wheels of government procurement moved slowly, and in the spring he found it necessary to renew these requisitions; to them he added a request for one hundred copies of his own translation of Scheel's work on Artillery. "I will consult the President, and will write you an answer," replied the Secretary of War to this request. A few weeks later the promised answer arrived. "You will observe the notes made by the President on the margin of your list," wrote Dearborn, who then instructed Williams to procure those items that had been approved.

Captain Barron arrived at West Point in the late spring—while Williams was still convalescing at his New Jersey home. But, based on the latter's written instructions, Barron initiated classes again in June. As he had done himself the winter before, Williams now directed Barron to "proceed to theoretical and then to practical geometry, before the students acquire the higher parts of algebra; it would . . . be a loss of time to wait until a student becomes a perfect algebraist, before he is even a theoretical geometrician." When he returned to West Point in July, Williams was impressed by Barron. He reported to Dearborn that the Captain was presiding over the daily duties of the Academy and that he "anticipated much Satisfaction in my dealing with him."

Mansfield arrived in August and he immediately joined in the instruction of cadets. Williams lectured occasionally on the construction of fortifications, and from time to time other engineer officers were available to assist, but the burden of presenting instruction fell to Barron and Mansfield. With an additional instructor available, classroom hours were extended, now beginning each morning (except Sunday) at nine o'clock and continuing until two o'clock. Four afternoons each week, from four o'clock until sunset, the cadets met for field exercises. There, they learned to measure heights and distances and the other skills, including drawing, necessary to make a military map.

Williams retained the Hutton text that George Baron had introduced at the Academy, but both the text and the necessary mathematical instruments were in short supply. When more were requested, Williams also submitted a list of other books and instruments that were needed. In July 1802, that first list was reviewed and approved by Dearborn and Jefferson, and the latter suggested some additional titles. Given this success, Williams submitted a second list to Dearborn with an explanatory note: "Considering the infant state of the Institution you will probably think the list too extensive, but if you will please to take into view the important national Establishment to which I hope it will in one time increase, you will doubtless consider it rather below than above what a proper apparatus ought to be." This second list, however, was less favorably received. The first list, with the President's additions, constitutes the first known purchases for—and the origin of—the new Academy's library: Bezont's *Cours de Mathematiques a l'usage de l'artellerie* (four volumes) and the companion set *Cours de Mathematiques a l'usage de la Marine* (six volumes); also selected volumes of the *Encyclopedie Methodique*—particularly the multi-volume *Dictionnaire methodique* on *Art Militaire, Arts & Metiers, Equitation, L'Escrime, Geographie, Marine,* and *Mathematiques* which Jefferson had recommended. Dearborn sent along other titles from time to time, and the library was further enlarged by the purchase of books from Williams, Swift, and Wadsworth.

I regret to see "so few Students," Williams wrote as the fall of 1802 approached: "it would give me great pleasure to have my full number of cadets [forty], composed of intelligent young men with a proper degree of Rudimental knowledge." Williams was pleased with his assignment to direct the new Academy, but was not at all satisfied with the progress he had yet made. "In all your conversations with the Secretary," he reminded Captain Decidus Wadsworth, one of his engineers, "you will never . . . lose sight of our leading star, which is not a little mathematical School but a great national establishment to turn out characters which in the course of time shall equal any in Europe." Wadsworth, however, warned Williams that the time was wrong to press the administration for additional faculty. "The moment is not yet arrived for us to ask for them with a tolerable Prospect of Success," he argued. But a month later, when Barron reported a conversation with Dearborn in which the latter seemed inclined to aid the Academy, Williams fired off a "digest report" on the needs of the Academy and the Corps of Engineers—in particular noting the necessity for teachers of drawing and French.

Officers' quarters at West Point seem always to have been in short supply, and their assignment was a contentious issue from the very beginning. For years, officers lived in the scattered quarters that had housed their predecessors in regiments of artillerists and engineers. Many of these structures survived from the period of the Revolution.

Lieutenant Colonel Lewis Tousard, the Inspector of Artillery, arrived in September 1801, some months ahead of Williams. Dearborn had earlier directed that houses be prepared for both, but Tousard, the senior, got the largest and finest residence (relatively speaking). When Williams arrived he had to accept a smaller and less desirable one just off the plain to the northwest, overlooking the ordnance warehouses and the river below. Disappointed, Williams approached Dearborn about having that house renovated; the latter replied that, although he could have repairs made, "it may be proper to mention to you in confidence that Col. Tousard will probably go out of service." The administration's Army bill, which formally established the Military Academy at West Point—and which was then under consideration by the Congress—also provided for a substantial reduction in the number of officers. This reduction was designed to allow Jefferson and Dearborn to rid the Army of many of the more vociferous Federalist opponents of the new Republican regime. Tousard, who was closely identified with the Hamiltonian faction, was one of those slated to go as soon as the bill became law. His quarters would then become available for Williams.

The bachelor officers were quartered wherever space allowed. These quarters, described by a visiting French officer as "little houses, irregularly built," were nonetheless, he said, better than the barracks available to French officers. Here, the bachelors organized themselves into informal messes. Lieutenants William Wilson and Lewis Howard formed the self-styled "artillery mess," while Lieutenants James Wilson and Alexander Macomb made a similar but separate arrangement.

The cadets likewise organized their own messes and accommodated themselves as best they could, but, reported one, they "were not comfortably lodged." Some of the structures being used to house the cadets, Williams reported, needed to be pulled down. Long Barracks, he suggested, which was then being used for the troops on post, could accommodate both troops and cadets if renovated. The two wings of that building would suffice for the cadets; the main section could be reserved for the artillery company usually assigned there. He suggested that, with plaster and a few other repairs, sixteen good cadet rooms could be furnished, at least temporarily.

As 1802 drew to a close, the officers and cadets faced the unpleasant prospect of another winter at West Point in the poorly-heated frame buildings. Williams asked the Secretary of War to allow winter vacations that would "commence annually on the 1st day of December and terminate on the 15th day of March following." Dearborn concurred and this practice continued until 1817, by which time new buildings more suitable for winter occupancy had been constructed.

Despite some problems, Williams had cause for satisfaction as the first term of operation came to an end, including, on the 12th of October 1802, the first graduation of cadets from the Academy. Cadets Joseph Gardner Swift, Simon Levy, and Walter Armistead were

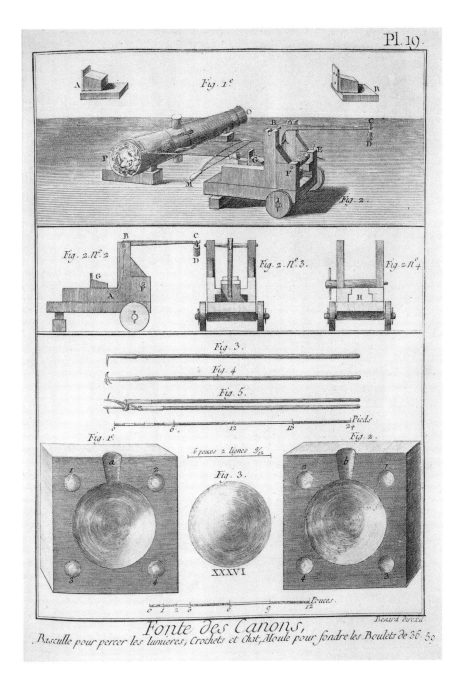

A page from the Encyclopedie Methodique, Volume 24, Arts et Metiers Mechaniques, Planches, c. 1783. U.S.M.A. Library, Special Collections. Photo: Philip Pocock.

examined in arithmetic, algebra, geometry, trigonometry, and the elements of fortifications. They all passed, and the first two were appointed Second Lieutenants of Engineers, thus becoming the first graduates of the Military Academy. Armistead chose to remain at his studies for a few more months before accepting a commission.

Williams's relations with the administration had, in most respects, been quite happy. For example, his request for a teacher of French and of drawing had met with quick administration approval and was presented to Congress early in the next session; in February 1803 the bill passed and was signed. Williams was cautioned against recommending "intemperate men, foreigners, or men far advanced in years." But he found it impossible to meet all these criteria, and the choice was eventually made in favor of Francis D. Masson, a Frenchman, who was appointed to fill both positions. In September 1808, Christian E. Zoeller was appointed teacher of drawing, but Masson retained his position as teacher of French until his resignation in 1812.

A significant event in the fall of 1803 was Williams's creation of a national society to promote the study of the military sciences. In November, he assembled the officers of the Corps of Engineers and laid out his plan for an organization that would stimulate the collection and dissemination of useful military knowledge, particularly in those areas not then supported by public funds. The name "The United States Military Philosophical Society" was adopted—indicating the extent to which this new organization was modeled on the American Philosophical Society of which Williams had been an active member and officer. Williams was elected president, and Wadsworth vice-president.

Not everyone was as enthusiastic about the new organization as Williams. Wadsworth, the second ranking engineer officer, confided to Williams that he had feared the new organization was superfluous or could even be dangerous to the prospects of the corps. "The organization of the Corps of Engineers, if the Act of Congress be attended to, did of itself constitute us a *military Philosophical or rather Scientific Society*," Wadsworth noted: the Corps being stationed at West Point, and its control of the military school there "shew that it was the Intention of Congress to give us opportunity and the Means of Improvement in military Sciences." In promoting the interests of the new Society, he feared the officers "might be suspected of wishing to change our Corps into something different from what was originally contemplated."

However, Williams's success in obtaining Jefferson's patronage of the organization had "diminished somewhat" Wadsworth's apprehension. "Independent of [the President's patronage]," he wrote, "I see no particular Advantage or necessity of" the association. With that patronage, however, he conceded, "I foresee many eminent Advantages to us as Individuals and as officers resulting therefrom." With that he pledged his support and accepted the office which had been offered. Under Williams's active direction the society soon embraced, as members, "nearly every distinguished gentleman in the navy and Union, and several in Europe." In 1807 the membership stood at about 200, including Thomas Jefferson, James Madison, James Monroe, John Quincy Adams, John Marshall, Benjamin Latrobe, and Charles Cotesworth Pinckney.

If the advance of military science had been Williams's only motivation in founding this new Society, Wadsworth would have been justified in questioning its necessity. But there was more to it than that. A clue to that added motive may be found in the report of a chance meeting at Albany between Williams and Alexander Hamilton just days before Williams offered his plan for the Society. The two men conversed at length, reported Swift, who was accompanying Williams. "General Hamilton, Colonel Williams and General [Philip] Schuyler discussed the subject of the Military Academy, the colonel giving his ideas and purposes to encourage an enlargement of the present plan; General Hamilton approved." This meeting and the support he received for his plans may have suggested to Williams the desirability—even the necessity—of creating an organization that would encourage and harness broad support for the continued growth of the new Academy.

The society, however, offered little to its general membership, and seldom met outside West Point—an objection raised by Timothy Pickering, who rejected an invitation to join. However, in 1808, when Williams was pressing the administration to transfer the Academy to the capital, he arranged a meeting of the society at the War Department in Washington. Although the meeting was well attended, Williams failed to generate adequate support for his long-sought relocation of the Academy.

In essence, the United States Military Philosophical Society was little more than a tool of its founder, Jonathan Williams, and its fate was bound up with his own. When Williams resigned from the Army in 1803, the society floundered. He revived it in 1805 upon his return, but when he resigned permanently, in 1812, it was disbanded within a year.

For Williams, all his efforts were focused upon two issues that dominated the years of his superintendence—the relocation of the Academy, and its command by engineers. Removing the Academy to Washington was Williams's consuming desire. From the beginning, Dearborn encouraged him in the belief that the President favored the move, but reminded him that Congress, having designated West Point as the site of the Academy in 1802, would now have to act to change it. In many respects, Williams's failure to more firmly establish the Academy at West Point during his tenure as Superintendent was due to his desire to see it moved to Washington. Williams, in 1808, described the Academy as "like a foundling, barely existing among the mountains," but his concern was less that it was a "foundling" than that it still existed "among the mountains." He was reluctant, throughout his tenure, to do anything that might foreclose a relocation, and so failed to initiate the buildings and improvements that the Academy so obviously needed to make it a permanent fixture.

The second issue, command at West Point, had first become a problem in September 1802 in a dispute between Captain George Izard, who commanded the artillery company stationed at the post, and the recently-promoted Lieutenant Colonel Jonathan Williams of the Engineers, the Superintendent of the Academy there. Dearborn had earlier decreed that the commander of troops should have no control over "matters relating to the academy," while the officer superintending the Academy should have no "command of the troops of the garrison." Problems arose, naturally, in areas not so clearly delineated. The most immediate cause of friction was the requisition of supplies, which, Williams found, had to be made through the artillery captain. If Izard disapproved the issue, as he sometimes did, he was in effect controlling affairs of the Academy. The real issue, however, was one of principle—of whether or not engineer officers could command other troops. Williams complained, "in effect, [by losing] controul over my requisitions, the Commanding officer of the Engineers, whatever be his nominal Rank, may become inferior even to a Subaltern."

This issue was never resolved to Williams's satisfaction, and was to become a continuing source of irritation. "We still keep up personal appearances," wrote Williams, but he was humiliated by the arrangement. "It is not in the power of man to be consistent if he is to have *command* as a Lieut. Col. under the *controul* of a Captain." In December 1802, Williams asked Dearborn to reconsider the issue, with particular attention to the situation at West Point. The Secretary ignored his request, so in March of the next year Williams and Wadsworth drew up a set of demands—"points" which they "determined to be essential to their existence as Officers of the Corps." The first and most important was that engineer officers would have the same military authority as officers of the other corps. Of most immediate concern was the specific situation at West Point, which was "appropriated to the Corps of Engineers," and therefore ought to be commanded by an engineer (as long as the engineer was senior to other officers at the post). Once again, Dearborn simply ignored the issue.

In June, when confronted directly, Dearborn's response was negative, and Williams submitted his resignation. The Secretary asked him to reconsider, but warned: "No change however can take place, in the principles earlier established to the command contended for." Williams was unmoved, and his resignation was accepted.

Dearborn explained the position of the administration to Wadsworth, now the senior engineer. "It is the wish of the Executive," Dearborn wrote, "that the Gentlemen who have received appointments in the Corps of Engineers should devote their Time and Attention exclusively to the Theory and Practice of their Profession. By this means," he added, "we may avoid the unpleasant Necessity of employing Foreigners as Engineers."

The departure of Williams and his family from West Point broke up "our principal social circle," wrote Swift. "Colonel Williams had been the friend and adviser of every one of us." The social life at West Point was restricted, at best; cut off, as they were, from other society, they were left to their own devices. This was particularly so in the winter when ice closed the river, although in that season their number was sometimes enlarged. Often, the officers of the Corps of Engineers spent the worst of the winter months at West Point. There, despite the harsh weather, they enjoyed their revelries with old friends. But, beginning in the early spring these officers would depart to supervise the construction of fortifications along the coast. Such seasonal losses were keenly felt—permanent losses even more so.

The different social origins of the officers and their wives sometimes caused difficulties. Not long after arriving at West Point Elizabeth Mansfield reported that, although the other wives were polite, they were "used to living in high style." They exhibited "a set of manners very different from our acquaintances in New Haven," she wrote a friend. "I see them seldom; tho I have been treated by them with the greatest attention. You know I was never no hand at visiting and I visit less now than ever." In a short time, however, such distinctions lessened.

The loss of Williams and his family was compounded just a few months later when Jared Mansfield accepted the appointment as Surveyor General and moved to Cincinnati, Ohio. "Mrs. Mansfield," Swift recalled, "was a very intelligent lady, and her conversation not only agreeable but instructive to the young gentlemen who found a welcome at her residence."

Upon Williams's resignation, command of the Corps of Engineers and the superintendency of the Military Academy devolved upon the next senior officer of the corps, Major Decius Wadsworth. Until the spring of 1804, however, Wadsworth was heavily engaged in directing the extensive harbor fortification program then in progress along the Atlantic seaboard, and found it difficult to spare much time to supervise Academy affairs. The result was that actual control at West Point was left largely in the hands of the senior engineer officer, Captain Barron.

By the spring of 1804, the staff of the Academy was reduced to only Barron and Masson, with the occasional assistance of Macomb, Swift, or Levy—Barron conducting instruction in mathematics and fortifications during the morning hours, and Masson teaching French and drawing in the afternoons. Wadsworth returned to West Point in the late spring of 1804. He assisted when he could, but he was frequently ordered away on inspections, and in the fall, ill health caused him to take an extended leave of absence. In effect, Barron remained in charge of the Academy—with unfortunate results. "Never was West Point so in want of you as at this moment," wrote Macomb to Williams in October 1804. "Everything is going to ruin; morals & knowledge thrive little & courts martial & flogging prevails. The military academy instead of being the seat of knowledge & the place of application is fast turning into that of ignorance & idleness." Wadsworth's resignation early the next year left Barron in full command, and the decline at West Point continued.

Barron seemed to have difficulties on every front. There were charges of irregularities in his accounts, and allegations that he had neglected his duties at the Academy. His fellow officers complained that he "has become so strongly infected with the pride of Command, as to believe that He is competent to form, govern & instruct a Corps." Moreover, there were rumors that Barron, a bachelor, kept a woman in his quarters.

All of this caused Williams to reconsider his earlier resignation. Moreover, word from every side encouraged his return. Macomb had circulated a petition among members of the Corps asking that Williams be prevailed upon to return. "It has been hinted by the President," Macomb wrote Williams, "that your return to the service would be very pleasing to him." In fact, the administration had kept the lieutenant colonelcy open in just such a hope.

General James Wilkinson, the Army's commanding general and a long-time friend of Williams, strongly encouraged a reconsideration. Wilkinson, in fact, wrote three separate letters to Williams—all dated March 29th. "I am authorized by the Secretary of War," began the first, "to inform you that, if agreeable to you, the President will reappoint you to the Command of the Corps of Engineers." Dearborn, however, had attached a condition: "You are not to interfere with the discipline, Police, or Command of the Troops of the Line, but by [the President's] orders to which alone you are to be subject." In his second letter, Wilkinson took pains to point out that "your right of Command is held in trust by the President, & will be conferred when it may be deemed convenient to the Public Service—in the meantime you are subject to his orders only." This accommodation did not foreclose the prospect of command, as had earlier been the case, but made little additional concession to Williams. Still, this was as far as the administration would go. "If nothing else will do," Wilkinson advised, "silence your Military Sense, look forward to a change for the better, & in the interval avail yourself of a *little sinecure.*" In the last letter, which Wilkinson marked "confidential," he nurtured Williams's long-standing dream of relocating the Academy. "It is determined to remove the Corps from West Point," he revealed, "& you may, I am persuaded, regulate its Permanent fixture. The President prefers this place [Washington] & it is the most proper—but the Expense & the shew are objections. Baltimore, Fredreck Town, & Harpers ferry have been spoken of."

Thus encouraged, Williams acquiesced and rejoined the Corps on the terms offered. But, before returning to West Point, Williams met in Washington with Dearborn to discuss affairs of the Academy and the Corps of Engineers at large. For the most part this discussion was unremarkable, but in a private conversation the Secretary informed Williams of persistent rumors that Captain Barron was keeping a woman in his quarters. An explanation was required.

When he returned to West Point, Williams learned immediately that the Secretary's information concerning Barron had been correct. But Williams's first impression allayed his suspicions; the young woman, Sarah Dobbs, Williams reported, was "of a very decent appearance & deportment." Still, he called Barron to his quarters and "in a very candid manner stated the suspicions that such an appearance had excited." Barron insisted that Dobbs was only his housekeeper and a strictly virtuous young woman. "On the honor of a Gentleman and a Soldier," he proclaimed, "(except for dress & external open appearance) he knew not the sex of the person in question." Williams was inclined to accept Barron's explanation and to let the matter rest. Shortly afterwards, however, when others at West Point openly questioned the virtue of the woman, Barron charged them with slander and demanded a formal hearing on the matter.

Testimony before the Court of Inquiry revealed that Sarah Dobbs and a second young woman, Margaret (Peggy) Gee, the housekeeper for another officer at West Point, had "committed every degree of prostitution" with young men of the post. Moreover, Barron's housekeeper, Dobbs, had even carried on illicit liaisons with cadets in her room in Barron's quarters. One cadet, in fact, had crawled through the wrong window and was discovered by the Major half in and half out of his parlor. Barron threw a spitting box at the head of this unfortunate lad and then gave chase, but the cadet escaped. Both Dobbs and Gee—each about sixteen years of age and daughters of local families—were expelled from the post and barred from ever returning.

Barron professed no knowledge concerning the activities of these young women and Williams, "in order to preserve [the former's] reputation from the stain of suspicion," destroyed the records of the inquiry. "Barron loves solitude," Williams had written Swift earlier that year, "and at West Point he must this year have enjoyed it in supreme degree." Williams, of course, was referring to the harsh winter they had just endured and had no inkling of just why Barron might have sought and valued his seclusion.

"I have endeavored to put the academy on the best footing its present means would permit," Williams reported to Dearborn, some weeks after his return to duty in April 1805. That included a new daily schedule that added an hour of drill, led by the adjutant, Lieutenant Macomb, before breakfast, and two hours of study in quarters each afternoon. This was followed either by some period of recreation—for which sports were recommended—or by practical exercises in gunnery, surveying, or engineering. He also sought and obtained permission to establish a central cadet mess. "Both pay & rations," he informed Dearborn, "are swallowed up in food" in the separate messes. "They have nothing left for clothing," he noted. A single mess, managed by a steward, would operate on "little if anything more than the present Rations," and leave the cadets with the means to clothe themselves. This would not only end the frequent calls on the War Department for special considerations, but would provide meals that were "regulated in quantity & quality."

With Dearborn's approval a general mess was established in August. The facility chosen was the large quarters, just south of the Academy building, that had been occupied by Captain George Fleming, the military storekeeper at West Point, who was relocated to the valley nearer his storehouses. The mess was supervised by Barron who, despite the recent rumors of scandal linking him and his housekeeper, had been promoted to Major. A baker named Morrison, who had supplied the post with bread, was engaged as Mess Steward. The building was a large structure which contained, in addition to the kitchen and mess room, separate quarters for Morrison and his family, as well as for Major Barron. The size of the structure may be judged by the fact that each set of living quarters contained a parlor, bedroom, kitchen, and dining room. Although the mess operated without significant complaint from the cadets who ate there, it was abandoned in late 1806 because of the growing disaffection with Barron. Thereafter, the cadets were assigned to board in small messes arranged with local families—an arrangement that continued until 1813 when a central mess was again organized in the same facility.

Williams had less success in obtaining musicians. Music, he believed, would "take off the monotony & give a spur to the Military Spirit." A drum and fife were essential, he told Dearborn, and a band was highly desirable—so much so that Williams volunteered to find the instruments, if only musicians could be furnished. To that argument the Secretary turned a deaf ear.

In June 1805, before moving his own family back to West Point, Williams again raised the issue of relocating the Academy. If this move was imminent, he told Dearborn, he would not relocate his family. He would raise no objection, he said, if the decision was made to move the school to Washington, "but if any other place be thought of" he hoped to be allowed to "freely express all proper Sentiments." Dearborn responded that he "was persuaded that whenever a new site for the Academy is established" it would be Washington, but he could offer no assurances as to when that might be.

Williams's desire to relocate the Academy was, in part, motivated by his (and his wife's) fondness for city life and society. It also reflected his conviction that the Academy would fare better if it were located under the eye of Congress and the administration. But his zeal in this regard was not matched by that of his subordinates. By 1806 most had come to regard West Point as the permanent home of the Military Academy. Barron, for example, sketched out an extensive building program which included a new academic hall, a new mess hall, and a new laboratory. He also proposed the extensive renovation of the old Revolutionary War "Long Barracks." This "commodious tenement," wrote Barron, was now more than adequate to accommodate all who were attached to the Academy. In addition, Barron noted the need for a number of ancillary items: apparatus for the laboratory and for engineering, a complete military library, a clock and bell, and a morning gun.

Williams, however, continued to hold out hope that the Academy would be moved to Washington, and he wished to do nothing that would jeopardize that possibility. Expenditures on the scale that Barron had recommended would almost certainly tend to fix the location. Therefore, he wrote Dearborn in May 1806 that he considered "West Point as a temporary Station for the Corps of Engineers & Military Academy." Short term expedients, therefore, were all that he would recommend: repairs to make the first floor of the Academy building suitable for temporary use; and minor renovations of the old barracks to accommodate the cadets. He also renewed his request of the year before for musicians, or even a band.

Dearborn approved the temporary measures, ordering Fleming to proceed with the required repairs of the barracks and the Academy, and also to the various officers' quarters. The Secretary added the mandate that "no greater expense would be laid out upon them than is absolutely necessary to render them comfortable."

The issue of the permanent location of the Military Academy aside, Williams could have taken justifiable pride in many of the developments at West Point. The buildings were being put in order, if only for temporary use; and the Academy had graduated fifteen cadets in 1806—more than in all the previous years combined.

Late in the year, however, Williams, who had been absent much of the year supervising the construction of fortifications, received new and distressing reports concerning Barron's conduct at West Point. In November, Macomb wrote that he had just been informed of "a thousand things which have happened & do happen at West Point in your absence." He reported that "Gees of *notorious fame* were the companions of your second officer and that those who were by your orders expelled from the Point were not only permitted to return but to take a seat at your second officer's table." Williams was furious. "I shall . . . pursue the same steps I took relative to a former professor of Mathematics also named Baron who was disgracefully discharged," he wrote Macomb in return. Still, it was a matter that required some discretion. "This affair is a delicate & a very painful one," he wrote Dearborn. "There is a disgrace in publicity that [for the sake of the institution] I wish it were possible to avoid."

In January 1807, when Barron was faced with the charges that had been made against him, he admitted that he had been foolish to allow Peggy Gee to return and, sometimes, to remain for months, but he continued to insist that, otherwise, he was innocent. This time, however, his protestations were not enough. Barron was linked, by the testimony of a number of officers and cadets, not only to Gee—and Dobbs before her—but also to a number of women of questionable reputation whom he had allowed to frequent West Point. At first, Barron demanded a formal inquiry, but, in March, when faced with the

Joseph G. Swift was the first graduate of the Academy and became its Superintendent in 1812. This portrait is by Thomas Sully. West Point Museum Collections, U.S.M.A.

Opposite:
Thomas Jefferson by Gilbert Stuart. c. 1805–07. Oil on canvas, 48³/₄ × 39³/₄". Collection Bowdoin College Museum of Art.

evidence arrayed against him, he agreed to resign and thus put an end to the matter. The mess steward, Morrison, and his family, who were also implicated in the affair, were likewise required to leave West Point. After that, the general military mess which they had operated was closed.

Barron's position was filled by Ferdinand R. Hassler, who had been appointed in February 1807, anticipating Barron's imminent departure. Hassler, a Swiss mathematician, had an excellent reputation and was a valuable addition to the staff. When increased demands on the engineers prevented Williams from effectively overseeing affairs at West Point, he ordered Captain Joseph Gardner Swift to West Point. Under Swift's direction the Academy ran smoothly during 1807. In part this reflected Williams's advice to Swift. The "leading principle" he told the young officer was to require "a gentlemanlike deportment towards" the professors by all concerned, and "in this particular," he cautioned Swift, "the example of the commanding officer has more influence than any orders whatever."

Of course, not everything went so well and the example of the commanding officer did not penetrate to all members of the West Point community. An altercation in one of the new separate messes, between a cadet and an enlisted waiter, initiated a series of difficulties. The culprit, it turned out, was Cadet Samuel Rathbone, who struck the waiter repeatedly for failing to obey his order. For this inappropriate behavior Rathbone incurred the ire of his fellow cadets, who decided to punish the man by denying him all social intercourse—"sending him to Coventry." Any cadet who did not comply was threatened with similar silence. Williams objected. "Putting any one into Coventry is merely not speaking to him except so far as duty requires," he explained. "This is done in armies only in cases where there is some personal disgrace of Character or Conduct, which renders a Man unworthy of Society, although not of a nature to be cognizable by Law." This case, Williams insisted, was covered by martial law and should be handled accordingly. Under this circumstance he would not allow "self erected Censors" to prevail. "Nothing of that kind shall ever be permitted on this Ground," he added, and forced the cadets to relent.

The threat of war with England in 1807–08 and the subsequent expansion of the Army produced an unexpected opportunity for Williams to renew his call for an enlargement of the Academy—and again to argue for its transfer to Washington. In fact, the President intimated to him that both would be welcomed. Williams submitted his plan in draft form to Jefferson and incorporated, in the final proposal, the suggestions of both the President and Dearborn. "It never can be supposed," he argued, that members of the Corps of Engineers were, axiomatically, "efficient elementary teachers." Instead, he proposed adding three permanent professorships that could be drawn either from the corps or from among civilian academics: a professor of natural and experimental philosophy; a professor of mathematics; and a professor of the art of engineering. In addition, the proposal added a total of five assistant professors and teachers who would usually be drawn from among the engineer officers. Also, he proposed occasional instruction in architecture, chemistry, and mineralogy to be provided by visiting civilian professors, and training in riding and swordsmanship to be conducted by a part-time instructor. Assured that the move to Washington would be approved, he also recommended an appropriation "for the proper building, apparatus, library, &c." This, he argued, "being once well done" would "not [be] subject to repetition."

In spite of a strong endorsement by the President, Congress provided no augmentation of the Corps of Engineers, no provision for permanent professors at the Military Academy, no appropriation for new facilities, and no action on the request to move the school to the capital. They did, however, enlarge the number of cadets authorized from 44 to 200. With the expansion of the Army, the administration had requested that cadets be ap-

pointed for each of the added artillery companies, including the new light artillery. The Congress went further and authorized cadets in all branches—artillery, cavalry and infantry, for a total of 156 new cadets.

In fact, the growth that was authorized at the Academy had little to do with plans and proposals that had been formulated at West Point. Rather, it reflected a response to the nation's growing troubles with England. Still, in a significant sense, the addition of cadets to all the branches of the Army was an endorsement of the Academy that Williams had nurtured.

But neither Williams nor the administration was pleased with this result. On the one hand, Williams's plans to expand the Academy and relocate it had been rejected. On the other, Dearborn had not asked for cadets of infantry and cavalry, and after they were authorized, he did not appoint any. He summed up the administration's concern at the beginning of the next session of the Congress, in December 1808; they had appointed the artillery cadets but "no other appointments of Cadets can with propriety be made until the site for the Academy is established and provision made for the reception of the additional number" now authorized. The administration then resubmitted Williams's proposals, but to no avail.

In the years that immediately followed, these proposals were resubmitted regularly by Jefferson and then by Madison—with similar results. Congress showed little interest in augmenting the Academy, and no willingness to agree on any other location for the school, although many were proposed. It was not until the country began to move toward war in 1812 that any positive congressional action was forthcoming. Even then, it was the emergency that provoked long overdue reform, and the lack of agreement concerning any alternative site that permanently fixed the Academy at West Point.

In April 1808, Williams had been required to assume personal direction of the construction of the harbor defenses of New York City. Although close enough to ensure general control over events at West Point, he left Lieutenant Alden Partridge in day-to-day charge of the Academy and the thirty-five cadets who reported for duty at the commencement of the new term. Partridge, an 1806 graduate, had originally been retained at West Point as an assistant professor of mathematics; this new arrangement continued for several years. This period also saw other shifts in the faculty. Christian Zoeller was appointed in 1808 as a teacher of drawing, freeing Francis Masson (who had been teaching both French and drawing) to add instruction in military engineering. In 1809, the mathematics instructor Ferdinand Hassler resigned, leaving the teaching load largely to Partridge. The management of the Academy was further complicated in 1810, when Zoeller also resigned, and Masson went abroad to study—leaving his brother Florimond to assume his duties.

By 1809, Williams was beginning to tire of the constant strain imposed upon him by his multiple duties and by his repeated contests with the administration and the Congress. He unburdened himself to Jared Mansfield, beginning with his old complaint: "The military academy is at present in a miserable state resulting from an Absurd Condition in its original creation 'that it shall be stationed at West Point'." "My zeal is almost burnt out," he told Mansfield, "and without the fuel of public patronage it will certainly be extinguished."

Williams had enjoyed the steady patronage of Dearborn and Jefferson, but his relationship with William Eustis and James Madison proved less satisfactory. Eustis was a Revolutionary War veteran, but he had been a surgeon—sometimes attached to General Washington's personal staff—and not a line officer. Although he had been elected to the House of Representatives in 1800 and 1802, he brought little useful experience and minimal talent to the post of Secretary of War. His appointment by a southern President said more about the conjunction of his Republican politics and Massachusetts roots than any special competence for the job. To Williams's particular chagrin, Eustis had no interest in relocating the Academy. Said Williams, "it seems to have been incompatible with his ideas of self-dignity to receive advice."

Eustis has often been portrayed as hostile to the Military Academy—and he does seem almost to have destroyed it—still, there was an ambivalence in his decisions that belied outright hostility. Rather, his actions revealed a lack of policy direction admixed with indecision and incompetence. At one moment he would seemingly attack the Academy, the next, he would act in its behalf. In 1809 Eustis ordered troops of the line to West Point, crowding the cadets out of their barracks and reducing the civilian faculty. Just months later he was attempting to persuade Mansfield to return to West Point to teach—emphasizing the "importance of the institution." The next year he established new regulations requiring that before appointment cadets should have a solid background in reading, writing and in mathematics, and then, just a month later, dictated that all cadets serve an apprenticeship as privates in their companies before being considered for commissions. Although he was soon persuaded to reverse the latter decision, it reinforced the general conviction that his intentions were malevolent.

In November 1810, he reassured Williams of continued administration support for the institution, and then, within six months, ordered almost the entire corps of cadets away from West Point. After that, the Academy lay dormant for well over a year (from mid-1811 to early 1813), and for a time had neither cadets nor faculty. Yet, as if to confound the critics, Eustis and the administration were all the while actively supporting a plan to augment the school along the lines laid out by Williams in 1808. And, in June 1812, they succeeded.

This on-again, off-again support (or hostility) frustrated Williams and all the Academy's supporters. "I totally despair," he wrote in 1810, "of any alteration that will raise the Academy to that state which the honor of the nation and the advantage of the Army indispensably require." Even the augmentation of the Academy in 1812 could not rouse his spirits, for it had failed his primary objective—moving the Academy to Washington. Nor did the administration's efforts encourage his trust in or respect for Eustis. There are, he wrote Swift, "many reasons I have to detest the domination of William Eustis." He would not, said Williams, be obliged "to respect a man for whom I cannot have a shade of respect," nor would he receive "orders founded in ignorance, and dictated with petulance." Williams tendered his resignation in July 1812 and the administration accepted it. Eustis was forced out not long after.

President Madison appointed Joseph Gardner Swift, who had risen to be Williams's second in command, to the vacant colonelcy in engineers. In 1802, Swift had been the first graduate of the Military Academy and had spent the intervening years supervising the construction of harbor defense fortifications and as an occasional teacher of mathematics at the Academy. Now, despite being actively engaged in the field throughout the second war with England, he displayed a strong interest in reviving the school. The vehicle was "An Act Making Further Provision for the Corps of Engineers," that had been signed into law by Madison on April 29, 1812. In many respects this act provided everything that the men of West Point had been seeking, and more—save, of course, the move to Washington that had been championed by Williams. In addition to the teachers of French and drawing already provided for, the act authorized a professor of natural and experimental philosophy, a professor of mathematics, and a professor of the art of engineering. Moreover, assistant professors were provided for each subject. The act further provided that cadets would thereafter be appointed "in the service of the United States." No longer would they be appointed as members of a specific regiment. Moreover, the cadets were to be organized into companies of non-commissioned officers and privates

Alden Partridge, who had joined the faculty upon his graduation from the Academy in 1807, and who had been made Superintendent in 1815, was popular with cadets, but not with the other instructors. West Point Museum Collections, U.S.M.A.

with officers from the Corps of Engineers for the purpose of military instruction. They were to be encamped at least three months each summer. They were to be between the ages of fifteen and twenty upon admission and were to be well-versed in reading, writing, and arithmetic. Each was to be given a degree upon completion and then commissioned "in any Corps, according to the duties he may be judged competent to perform." Finally, the act provided an appropriation of $25,000 for buildings, academic and engineering apparatus, and a library.

In the latter months of 1812, despite the initiation of hostilities with the British, the first concrete steps were taken to reactivate the Academy. Before he left office, Eustis approved preliminary plans and contracts for a new barracks, mess hall, and academy building, and approved the recruiting of a new faculty. Eustis departed in late fall of 1812 and James Monroe became acting Secretary of War. (Monroe, who was then the Secretary of State served, for a short time, in both capacities.) John Armstrong arrived to assume the post in January 1813.

Swift reported to Monroe in December 1812 that "some of the Academic Staff, officers, and cadets are appointed" and that he intended to "commence the Military Academy prior to the 1st April 1813." Andrew Ellicott, a former astronomer of the United States, accepted the professorship of mathematics, and Partridge was made professor of engi-

TO CAP.ᵗ ALDEN PARTRIDGE,
OF THE MILITARY INSTITUTE,
NORWICH VERMONT.

This plate is most respectfully dedicated by Huddy & Duval.

neering. In addition, Zoeller was reappointed as drawing instructor, and Florimond Masson, who had earlier substituted for his brother, was now appointed in his own right as instructor of the French language. Swift also persuaded Jared Mansfield to return to the Academy to occupy the chair of professor of natural and experimental philosophy. Mansfield accepted but repeatedly postponed his arrival. He did not finally report until August 1814—and then only under the threat of dismissal.

As Swift had promised, the school began to function again with the spring term of 1813. "I find [the Academy] in as good condition as could be expected after laying dormant so long," Swift reported to John Armstrong in July.

Swift was not altogether satisfied with the organization of the Academy, nor with the changes that Williams had sought and that the Congress had finally authorized. In 1808 he had made his own recommendations to Williams and in many respects they went well beyond those of his superior. In addition to the mathematics, natural philosophy and engineering that Williams had sought—and which the Congress had provided in 1812—he recommended instruction in ancient and modern history, in geography, in morality, and, on a different plane, in fencing and dance.

In formulating this earlier plan, Swift had been motivated by the belief that Army officers had to be more than narrowly trained military technicians. His own experience had convinced him that officers had to work closely with civil authorities—national, state, and local—and that these officials generally represented the best-educated and most socially active segments of the population. Swift had come from a respected New England family and was at ease in any company, but not all cadets enjoyed this advantage. That was particularly true of many of Jefferson's Republican sons.

In 1813, Swift moved to incorporate his own ideas into the growing curriculum. He secured the assignment of Reverend Adam Empire as both chaplain and acting professor of geography, history and ethics, and then, the next year, obtained the services of Pierre Thomas as swordmaster.

For the most part, however, his efforts ran afoul of both the demands of the ongoing war with England, and the inclinations of Captain Alden Partridge, who was nominal head of the Academy during Swift's frequent, extended absences—just as he had been earlier under Williams. Qualified officers were needed immediately to meet the needs of an expanding Army. The War Department demanded that as soon as "a tolerable knowledge of books indicate the fitness of a young man for an Ensigncy and Lieutenancy" his name be transmitted to them, and that he be commissioned. In any case, Partridge proved more interested in drilling the cadets than in providing classroom instruction. By the end of July 1814—barely a year after the Military Academy had returned to full opera-

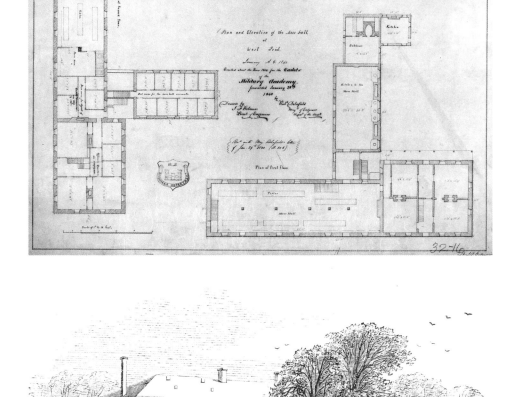

Plan and elevation of the mess hall at West Point (1815), as drawn in 1840. National Archives and Records Administration, Cartographic and Architectural Branch.

A view of the 1815 mess hall. Built of stone and stucco, it was demolished in 1852. From History of West Point by Captain Edward C. Boynton. U.S.M.A. Archives. Photo: Philip Pocock.

tion—thirty cadets had been commissioned. The course of study implied in the law of 1812 and expanded upon by Swift was set aside before it had even been put into practice.

A contract for the construction of the new buildings had been signed in the fall of 1812 with builder Jacob Halsey and mason Thomas J. Woodruff. Final approval from the War Department, however, was delayed repeatedly as the war went from bad to worse in 1812 and 1813. Construction was finally ordered to begin at West Point in the spring of 1814.

In the meantime, the old Long Barracks had once more been renovated and 100 of the 160 cadets then at the Academy were billeted there. The balance were quartered in other locations around the post. Classes, which had long since outgrown the original frame Academy, were held wherever space could be found—sometimes in the professor's quarters.

The new barracks and mess hall were ready to receive cadets by the spring of 1815, and the Academy building was finished later the same year. All three buildings were constructed of rough gray granite with slate roofs. The three-story barracks was a long, narrow building with modest wings at each end. Its central element contained forty-eight small, two-man rooms for the cadets, while the wings at each end featured small suites generally used by the bachelor officers. This building, soon known as South Barracks, was located on the southern boundary of the plain.

The mess hall, or refractory, was located on the same line as South Barracks, near the southwest corner of the plain. It was a two-story building with mess rooms on both floors, a kitchen, and quarters for the steward. The mess hall was enlarged in 1823, when a larger kitchen was added to the rear of the original structure, with rooms on the second floor of the addition for the staff of the mess.

The two-story Academy was located between South Barracks and the mess hall and on the same line as the two previous structures. On the first floor were the engineering room, the chapel, and the chemistry laboratory. Above them were the Adjutant's Office, the library, and the philosophical department. These three buildings established the continuing tradition of bounding the plain on the south with the Academy's major edifices.

In December 1815, Swift reported to Monroe that the buildings had been completed and that the Academy now needed a second barrack. In addition, he reported, they required new quarters for the Superintendent, the professors, and the other married officers—a total of six new sets of quarters. He also suggested a chapel and a new hospital. Swift's request for an additional barrack was approved the next year, as was a request for three sets of quarters, but the balance of the proposed construction, including the chapel and new hospital, was postponed.

Quarters for the officers at West Point were in such short supply during the early years that families were usually required to share houses—a custom that was perpetuated by the construction, beginning in 1819, of duplex structures (referred to as "doubles") which soon became the norm. The arrival of new officers precipitated crises of greater or lesser proportions as arrangements had to be made to house them. When Jared Mansfield arrived with his family in 1814, they were assigned to share a set of quarters with Dr. Samuel Walsh, the post surgeon. Dr. Walsh had earlier been instructed to clear the south part of the house, but, having guests, had not done so. When notified that the Mansfields had arrived, he rushed to the dock and told the professor that "he was sorry," but that he could not admit them just then, "as he had company, & could not spare any part of the house." When Mansfield insisted, Walsh angrily relented but heaped abuse on the professor, his family, and his servants. That ill-treatment continued for several days, until Mansfield threatened to have the surgeon arrested.

The first new officers' quarters were located along the west edge of the plain, on a line roughly perpendicular to that of the barrack, Academy, and mess hall. Contracts for the first three sets were made with John Forsyth of Newburgh in January 1817 and the quarters were completed late that year. The Superintendent's house and others were added

The 1815 Academy building housed the academic departments and the library. From History of West Point *by Captain Edward C. Boynton. U.S.M.A. Archives. Photo: Philip Pocock.*

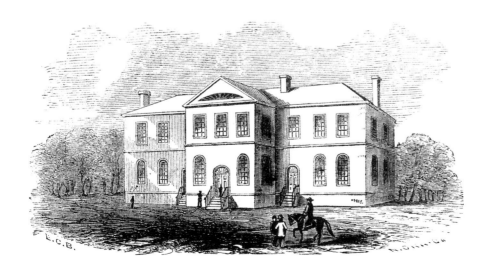

just a few years later on the same line. The new quarters—two-story brick structures with eleven finished rooms—were "commodious and pleasant," wrote Elizabeth Mansfield. She complained, however, that the kitchen was located in the basement and often smoked intolerably, filling "every part of the house." She also complained of losing the view afforded by her old quarters. "I should prefer keeping this [her old quarters] and having it put in repair," she wrote before moving; the old quarters looked north up the Hudson, through the ancient gap the river had etched between the massive Storm King and Breakneck. "You can have no idea," she wrote, "of the beauty and grandeur of the scenery as you view it from this house in the summer." Still, she moved.

The second barrack, somewhat larger than the first, was erected in 1817. It was located to the north and at a right angle to the earlier barrack, and extended out into the plain. This structure, known as North Barracks, was designed by Claude Crozet, who joined the faculty in late 1816. It was four stories high, provided forty large, four-man rooms, and was constructed of the same rough gray stone as the earlier buildings. The mason was Thomas Woodruff, who had worked on the previous buildings; the carpenter was John Morse of New York City. The two barracks provided sufficient billeting for the entire corps of cadets for more than thirty years. These "public edifices" were "without any pretension to architectural embellishment, but solid and substantial," reported the London *Quarterly Journal*. Notably, it was the aging Long Barracks that most pleased the eye of that critic; although "entirely destitute of ornament," that wooden structure, he opined, had "more architectural beauty of form than any other building on the Point."

From 1807 to 1815, Lieutenant (and then Captain) Alden Partridge had provided what continuity there was in the administration of the Academy. As the senior engineer officer at West Point he had assumed command during the frequent absences of the Superintendent—who at that time was also the Chief of Engineers. Having joined the faculty upon his graduation in 1806, Partridge had spent his whole Army career at West Point.

Although he had held the title of professor of engineering since 1812, Partridge had little interest in purely academic affairs, preferring instead the more narrowly military subjects. "He was passionately fond of drilling," recalled one graduate, but he made even this interesting by "forming diminutive armies and fighting over renowned battles." These were "always accompanied by an intelligible and interesting lecture" showing "how fields were won." Although a rigid disciplinarian, and sometimes prone to favoritism, he was popular with the cadets.

But, Partridge could not get along with his faculty colleagues. While acting in command at West Point and then as Superintendent, he was jealous of his prerogatives and grew first to resent being subordinated to anyone but the Chief Engineer, and finally to resent even that authority over him. Still, his accomplishments at West Point were not insignificant. Under his immediate supervision the school had struggled along beneath a burden of barely adequate appropriations, as well as wholly inadequate facilities and staff. By 1815, such problems had largely been overcome, and Partridge was convinced that these successes at the Academy were due largely to his efforts.

Partridge soon embarked on a campaign to make himself *de jure* what Jonathan Williams had been *de facto*—the unquestioned master and guiding force of the Academy. Partridge began, in late 1814, by drafting new regulations for the administration of the Academy—regulations that would put him firmly in charge. Then, in early January 1815, without Swift's knowledge or permission, he carried the draft regulations to Washington, and received the approval of the Secretary of War, James Monroe (who had once again assumed that office). There were four key provisions of the new regulations. First, a permanent Superintendent would report directly to the Secretary of War. Second, the Chief Engineer's authority and responsibilities relative to the Military Academy were restricted to the point where he became little more than an inspector for the Secretary of War. Third, the Superintendent was empowered to determine when cadets were prepared for commissions, and which corps they should join. Finally, the authority of the Superintendent was to be unchallenged at West Point—even upon the assignment there of a more senior officer.

At West Point the reaction to Partridge's efforts was as immediate as it was predictable. Even while Partridge was seeking Monroe's approval of his new proposals, his colleagues at West Point were penning a joint letter to the Secretary denouncing the Captain. They complained that he had failed to follow the practices prescribed in the act of 1812 either in examining new cadets prior to accepting them, or in recommending those further along for commissions. He had made the process dependent upon "favor, or friendship," not qualification, they complained. These objections, of course, were red herrings. The real issue was that the faculty wanted the power to influence events, and refused to be wholly left out of the decision-making process.

When Swift also objected to Partridge's action—and to Monroe's failure to consult with him—the Secretary suspended the new regulations "until General Swift's opinion can be known." Although in general agreement with the proposals Partridge had made, Swift was emphatically opposed to those aspects of the regulations that stripped away his authority. "The Military Academy shall be under my control," he wrote Ellicott, "or I will have nothing to do with it."

Partridge, when he heard of Swift's opposition, assured the general that he had not intended to cause friction, but strongly reasserted his own case. "I think Sir that the experience acquired in more than six years constant duty in it, and performing the duties of Superintendent for more than five years, ought to afford me data tolerably accurate to ascertain what will be for its advantage."

Swift, however, prevailed and the new regulations were amended restoring the Chief Engineer's responsibility for, and authority over, the permanent Superintendent. The amended regulations were approved February 21, 1815, and, on the basis of these regulations, Partridge was appointed Superintendent.

Partridge's elevation to the superintendency did little, of course, to eliminate friction with the faculty. "You must come and reside here," wrote Ellicott to Swift, arguing that "in my opinion it is necessary both for the reputation of this institution, and the welfare of our country." Partridge was "almost unrivalled in the management of Cadets," Ellicott admitted, but strongly intimated that his authority should be confined to that area.

Opposition to Partridge at West Point was led by Mansfield, who chafed under Partridge's close supervision. "Mr. Ellicott & myself have had the mortification daily of receiving visits from the Superintendent" complained Mansfield. They were "inspected, watched & looked in with an eye of suspicion" which was calculated "to bring us into contempt with our pupils," said Mansfield. "The object of all this," he alleged, "is nothing more nor less than the usurpation of all power & authority, & patronage, to the Mil[i-tary] Commander."

Mansfield, and to a lesser degree Ellicott, kept up a steady stream of complaints to members of Congress, the Secretary of War, and the President. By early 1816, the cumulative effect of this criticism was beginning to tell in Washington. In February, President Madison informed Swift that he wanted Partridge's resignation. Swift, however, argued that such precipitous action would be unfair. When the issue was again raised by Secretary of War William H. Crawford, who had replaced Monroe, Swift argued that there were few officers qualified for the duty—and none who would voluntarily take the post. For a time, the matter was allowed to drop.

By late 1816, however, the administration had reached a final decision to remove Partridge. Swift, who had been his champion, was no longer consulted on this issue. In

Portrait of President James Monroe by Thomas Sully. West Point Museum Collections, U.S.M.A. Photo: Philip Pocock.

September, French mathematician Claude Crozet, a graduate of the Polytechnique School in Paris, was appointed to fill the professorship of engineering which Partridge had vacated in assuming the superintendency. In November, Captain Sylvanus Thayer, who was in France inspecting the French military establishment and schools, was informed that he "had been designated by President Madison to be permanent Superintendent of the academy and that he was to return in the Spring of 1817 to assume that duty." Thayer, then thirty–one years old, had graduated from the Military Academy at West Point in 1808 and had served for two years as an assistant professor of mathematics. During the recent war, he had made a name for himself as an engineer by his successful planning and execution of the defense of Norfolk, Virginia.

At West Point, where the officers were unaware of the administrations's maneuvering, the lines between Partridge and the academic staff became ever more sharply drawn during the winter of 1816–17. Only Swift's decision to take quarters at West Point kept the situation there in check. Partridge was seemingly blind to everything but his own desire to rule. He wholly misunderstood the cause of the opposition to him, and completely misjudged its extent. In an effort to right matters he repeatedly sought to increase his own control over affairs at the Academy—a course that only made matters worse. He could not understand the position or the attitude of the faculty, and complained frequently to Swift of being thwarted by them. He could see no remedy but greater authority for himself, and new and more stringent regulations for the governance of the school.

During the spring, as the situation further deteriorated, Swift departed for Washington to attend the inauguration of James Monroe. Swift had great respect for the new President. Monroe has "done more for the Corps than ever has been done before put all together from 1802 to 1814," he had written just a few year earlier. But in Washington, Swift discovered that, in recent months, he had not been consulted on many key decisions concerning West Point; Monroe, he learned, had personally decided many issues. "Major Thayer may be ordered to West Point for the purpose of Superintending," Swift was now informed—the first he had known of Thayer's candidacy for the post. In addition, he discovered, the new President intended to visit and inspect West Point on an upcoming swing through the northeast. While there, Monroe intended to make "such arrangements as may be proper for its future government." In the meantime, Swift was instructed, "no other alterations will be made in relation to it." Swift's continued support of Partridge had seemingly cost him the confidence of the new administration.

Monroe stayed at West Point for three days, during which time he was introduced to the faculty and officers of the Academy, and received orally and in writing their complaints against Partridge. Mansfield discussed the problem at length with the President, and with apparent effect; Monroe ordered that a court-martial examine the charges brought against Partridge. In the face of the administration's clear determination to oust Partridge, Swift was now forced to withdraw his patronage.

Partridge was to be replaced by Thayer upon the latter's arrival at West Point. No one, however, informed Partridge, and that oversight would cause unnecessary misunderstanding and bitterness.

CHAPTER 5
SYLVANUS THAYER: FATHER OF THE MILITARY ACADEMY 1817-1833

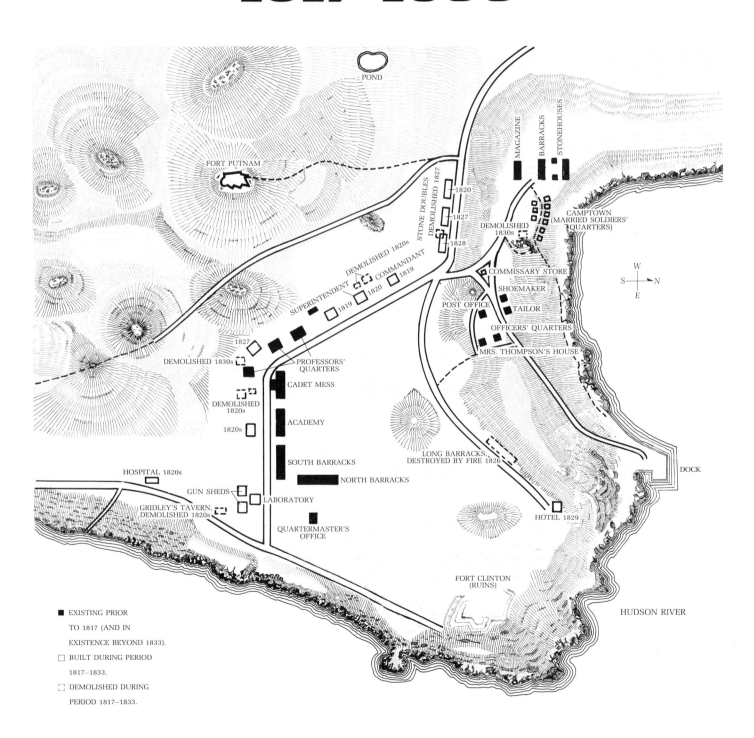

POND

FORT PUTNAM

MAGAZINE
BARRACKS
STONEHOUSES

STONE DOUBLES
DEMOLISHED 1827

1820

1827

1828

CAMPTOWN
(MARRIED SOLDIERS'
QUARTERS)

DEMOLISHED
1830s

DEMOLISHED 1820s
SUPERINTENDENT   COMMANDANT
1820   1819

COMMISSARY STORE

SHOEMAKER

1819

POST OFFICE   TAILOR

OFFICERS' QUARTERS

1827

DEMOLISHED 1830s

PROFESSORS'
QUARTERS

MRS. THOMPSON'S HOUSE

DEMOLISHED
1820s

CADET MESS

1820s

ACADEMY

SOUTH BARRACKS

LONG BARRACKS,
DESTROYED BY FIRE 1826

DOCK

HOSPITAL 1820s

GUN SHEDS

NORTH BARRACKS

LABORATORY

GRIDLEY'S TAVERN,
DEMOLISHED 1820s

QUARTERMASTER'S
OFFICE

HOTEL 1829

W
S · N
E

FORT CLINTON
(RUINS)

HUDSON RIVER

■ EXISTING PRIOR
TO 1817 (AND IN
EXISTENCE BEYOND 1833).

□ BUILT DURING PERIOD
1817–1833.

⌐⌐ DEMOLISHED DURING
PERIOD 1817–1833.

Sylvanus Thayer arrived at West Point on July 28, 1817, and presented the orders placing him in command. The disbelieving Partridge departed on leave but he refused to accept dismissal from the post. He reappeared on August 28th, and the cadets, who by now had returned to West Point after a summer leave, welcomed him enthusiastically. A small group, who were waiting idly by the landing when he arrived, rushed to meet him, and escorted him noisily up the hill. There, more cadets crowded around Partridge and wildly cheered his return.

Partridge immediately sought out Thayer and asked to be allowed to use his former quarters, but Thayer refused—the house had been cleaned and assigned to Captain David D. Douglass, assistant professor of mathematics, who had already moved in. The next morning Partridge renewed his lodging request, arguing that—by virtue of his rank—the quarters belonged to him. Again Thayer refused. Partridge then wrote out an order and handed it to Thayer. "Captain Partridge having returned to West Point," it read, "in conformity with the law establishing the Military Academy, taking upon himself for the present, the Command and Superintendence of the Institution as Senior Officer of the Engineers present." Thayer chose not to argue the point, but merely observed that he would not resign and that if Partridge assumed command "he should consider the responsibility as taken from himself."

Partridge then ordered the corps paraded. He listened with delight as the cadets cheered the order announcing his resumption of command. In his quarters, Thayer wrote out a brief report of the affair to Swift (who was in New York), mailed it, and went straight to the wharf. He hailed the first sloop heading for the city.

Partridge's usurpation ended two days later when Swift's aide-de-camp arrived at West Point with orders restoring Thayer to full command. The next day Swift arrived at West Point, placed Partridge under arrest, and ordered him to Governor's Island in New York harbor. Partridge, however, tarried at West Point another five days, using as an excuse the difficulty of collecting his furniture and papers. When he did depart, on the evening of September 10th, the cadets escorted him to the dock, shouting and cheering. Right behind them marched the post band who, against Thayer's explicit instructions, joined in giving Partridge a rousing send-off.

At Partridge's court-martial, which was presided over by General Winfield Scott, the former Superintendent was found guilty of disobedience to orders and of mutiny. He was sentenced to be cashiered but, in light of the "zeal and perseverance" which he had brought to "his professional duties," the court recommended to President Monroe that the punishment be remitted. The President accepted the recommendation for clemency, and directed that Partridge report to Swift for reassignment. Partridge, however, was too

Opposite:
Map of West Point, 1817–1833.

Sylvanus Thayer *by Robert W. Weir, c. 1844. Oil on canvas, 66 × 45". West Point Museum Collections. U.S.M.A.*

The larger plate to the right of the uniformed figure is a metal ornament used on the leather dress caps in 1815. (These were the first "fried eggs," as they are now called.) The uniform shown here was adopted in the 1820s.

embittered to comply. He chose to resign instead and, throughout the rest of his life, was relentless in his attacks on Thayer and the Academy.

Thayer, upon first assuming command at West Point at the end of July 1817, had been instructed by the administration to work closely with the faculty—Monroe, on his recent visit, had spent several days listening to their complaints about Partridge's failure to consult with them. Based on the faculty's advice, Thayer was to submit recommendations to the Secretary of War concerning the division of cadets into classes, the courses of study each class should pursue, the texts which should be employed, and the number of assistant professors required.

The stipulation that Thayer had to obtain the faculty's concurrence in the recommendations he sent forward marks the true inception of the academic board as it has existed until only recently—empowered *de jure* or *de facto* with the authority to establish the Academy's course of instruction. Although Congress had specified in 1812 that the "Academical Staff" should confer degrees upon cadets who had completed their classes and should identify those who should receive commissions, the board had not functioned in either capacity. Partridge had ignored that provision of the law and had done as he saw fit—graduating and presenting for commissions whomever he chose, whenever he chose. In 1819, Thayer proposed that the academic board should be responsible to "fix and improve the system of studies." The War Department approved, despite the objections of some in Washington that this would allow professors "to prescribe their own duties" and could lead "to the caprices of novelty and abuses of routine."

Thayer, in obedience to his instructions, drafted a memorandum asking each professor to sketch out a program for his department, "specifying the branches to be taught, the time required for each, and the books which shall serve as guides." The faculty, in late 1817, included Jared Mansfield, professor of natural and experimental philosophy; Andrew Ellicott, professor of mathematics; Claude Crozet, professor of engineering; Christian Zoeller, teacher of drawing; and Claudius Berard, teacher of French. In addition, Thayer soon detailed Second Lieutenant George Gardiner as instructor of infantry tactics and soldierly discipline, and made him responsible for the interior police and administration of the Academy.

In his memorandum to the faculty, Thayer outlined a rough daily routine for the school: "principal studies" from eight o'clock in the morning to twelve-thirty or one o'clock in the afternoon, followed by French and drawing from two to four o'clock. In addition, he advised them that, in the future, cadets would be admitted to the Academy only once each year, and that they would be arranged into regular classes and advanced to the next higher class only after successful submission to general examinations. He concluded on a reassuring note. "I have thus given you the outlines of my hasty and desultory reflection on some of the means of better organizing the instruction of this institution," Thayer advised the faculty. But he had done so, he said, "not with an idea that the opinions here advanced are the most correct, but with the view to invite a discussion of the subject and to elicit your opinion thereon. This business is new to me and I rely with pleasure on the superior judgment of the learned professors." Thayer's diplomatic approach to the faculty stood in stark contrast to that of Partridge's.

Within a month, Thayer had consolidated the reports of the various members of the faculty and had prepared a new plan of study for the Academy. This was forwarded to Washington and quickly approved both by General Swift, the Chief of Engineers, and by the Secretary of War.

The first step in instituting this program was a general examination of the cadets. The results were revealing; a number of cadets had made little, if any, progress in their studies, although some had been at the Academy under Partridge for several years. A number

of others were judged incapable of completing the course satisfactorily, and twenty-one were recommended for removal. These, Thayer wrote, "are deficient in natural abilities and all are destitute of those qualities which would encourage a belief that they could be advanced through the four years' course of study. The public money would be wasted, therefore, by retaining them here any longer."

To those that remained, Thayer drove home the point that neglect of studies would no longer be tolerated: "When it shall appear," he warned, "that any cadet has been habitually inattentive to his studies, he will be struck from the rolls of the military academy." He then ordered the faculty to prepare weekly reports on the progress of their classes—noting in particular those cadets who had neglected their lessons or who had not made suitable progress. "[I] have dismissed some Cadets, suspended others, and shall persevere," wrote Thayer, "until I produce that state of Military discipline which is as indispensable in an institution of this nature as in a regular Army." In support of Thayer, General Swift informed the cadets bluntly that "implicit obedience was their only course" in response to the new regime, and he directed Thayer "to dismiss from the institution with promptness any offender."

Instruction began again at the conclusion of the examinations in accordance with the curriculum Thayer and the faculty had devised. But difficulties were encountered almost immediately when Professor Crozet found that the cadets had not been taught descriptive geometry and, therefore, were not yet ready for the formal engineering program he had prepared. Immediate adjustments to the program were required. After quick consultations with Thayer and the academic board, Crozet revised his course to include instruction in that new branch of mathematics. "We now see Crozet with his blackboard before him, chalk in hand, an animated intellectual face, about to teach his class a new science, without a textbook," wrote Edward Mansfield, son of Professor Jared Mansfield. "With extreme difficulty he makes himself understood [in English]. With extreme difficulty his class comprehends that two planes at right angles with one another are to be understood on the same surface of the blackboard, on which are represented two different projections of the same object. But at last it is done. The professor labors with inexhaustible patience and the pupils are pleased to receive into their minds new ideas."

In December 1817, Thayer ordered another round of examinations, and was pleased with the results. "The examination was highly satisfactory," he wrote John C. Calhoun, the new Secretary of War, "except that many were found deficient in the French language,"—a situation he attributed to the need for an additional instructor, a position he had already been authorized to fill, and for which he was seeking candidates.

Above left:
While Thayer was in France (1816–17), he had purchased over 1,000 volumes for the Military Academy library. The collection has been restored and, as can be noted in this photograph, the books have been gilt stamped as had been done originally, at Thayer's request, when he acquired the books. U.S.M.A. Library, Special Collections. Photo: Philip Pocock.

Above right:
The restored Thayer Collection in the present Academy library includes classical works by Buffon, Lagrange, Lalande, and Laplace. It is considered one of the finest collections of early books on military art, science, and engineering in the country. U.S.M.A. Library, Special Collections. Photo: Philip Pocock.

Jared Mansfield by Thomas Sully. c. 1828. Oil on canvas, 29 × 24". West Point Museum Collections, U.S.M.A.

Claude Crozet by J. Carroll Beckwith. n.d. Oil on canvas, 31½ × 25". West Point Museum Collections, U.S.M.A.

John C. Calhoun, Secretary of War. U.S.M.A. Library, Special Collections. Photo: Philip Pocock.

The new Superintendent had ingratiated himself with the faculty, but to the cadets he remained "a most mysterious personage." In his early years as Superintendent, Thayer was not at all popular with the cadets—especially with those who had been at West Point under Partridge. "We had seen Capt. Partridge everywhere and on all occasions," wrote one graduate, but "Thayer we never saw." They complained incessantly about the discipline, and challenged his system whenever the occasion allowed—but to no avail. There were even personal affronts. Once, when Thayer was offering advice to a graduating cadet about his choice of corps—engineer, artillery, cavalry, or infantry—the young man cut him off, saying, "Major Thayer, when I want your advice I'll ask you for it!"

The lack of discipline among the cadets was one of Thayer's primary concerns. At first, he attributed it to the lingering influence of Partridge, and then, in later years, to lack of support from the Adams and Jackson administrations.

When he faced a seeming mutiny of the corps of cadets in 1818—orchestrated by the same cadets who had so joyfully welcomed Partridge back to the post the year before—he expressed an opinion that their rebelliousness was due to "erroneous and unmilitary impressions of the cadets imbibed at an inauspicious period of the Institution."

The affair, however, had less to do with discipline itself than with how that discipline was being administered. The central figure was Captain John Bliss, whom Thayer had made instructor of tactics. His duties included both the tactical training of the cadets and the maintenance of discipline. In fact, it was Bliss's reputation as a strict disciplinarian that had impressed Thayer. Unfortunately, his heavy-handed methods were not well suited to disciplining the high-spirited, bright, and articulate cadets, and predictably, he became a focal point for their wrath.

The issue came to a head on November 22, 1818, when, during a parade, one cadet deliberately marched out of step, and repeatedly ignored Bliss's injunctions to correct himself. The captain flew into a rage, stepped into the ranks, and "violently seized by the collar, shook, jerked, and publicly damned" the offender.

That night, in the barracks, the cadets elected a committee of five to present their grievances to Thayer. He met briefly with the committee and explained firmly that though they had the right to make complaints as individuals they had no right to band together to present a petition. He then dismissed them without receiving their petition. When the committee persisted, drew up new charges, and again confronted Thayer, he placed the five under arrest and then ordered them off the post. "[Their] first object," wrote the Superintendent, "was to remove Captain Bliss . . . and even dared to threaten me with rebellion, in case of a noncompliance with their wishes."

The young men took their case to the War Department and to Congress, but received no satisfaction. After a year's suspension, President Monroe ordered them reinstated. Thayer, however, refused to allow them to attend classes, and their classmates graduated without them. Embittered, the five cadets resigned as a body and went back to Congress in a last, vain effort to prosecute their case. A court of inquiry upheld Thayer's action, and a congressional investigation came to a similar conclusion, finding that the cadets had been both "wrong and mutinous." As for Captain Bliss, Calhoun concluded that he "does not appear to possess sufficient command of his temper" and ordered him transferred.

Thayer had been quick to blame Partridge's influence for these problems, and on the surface he seemed to have had some justification. Four of the five agitators had been Partridge cadets, and one, at least, Thomas Ragland, had been a Partridge favorite. Moreover, other Partridge cadets had supported the five, including Cadet Andrew Jackson Donelson, who was encouraged in his actions by the uncle (the future president) for whom he had been named. Bliss was replaced as Commandant of Cadets by Captain John R. Bell, and he, in turn, by Major William J. Worth, who served from 1820 to 1828, but the effort to instill discipline did not slacken. To better deal with the problem, Thayer issued a new set of 200 regulations which more fully defined and circumscribed cadet life. Among other things, the new regulations forbade cadets to: go beyond the walls of West Point; be absent from their rooms without permission; cook in their quarters; play cards; miss or misbehave at Sunday service; scuffle, duel, or issue a challenge; write or publish a newspaper article concerning the Academy; write directly to the Secretary of War; ask for, or receive money from relatives or friends; wear civilian clothes; organize any society or hold meetings without permission; or take more than one newspaper or periodical without permission. "Gentlemen must learn it is only their province to listen and obey," said Thayer.

Cadet discontent smoldered and then exploded again one winter night in December 1821. The cry, "Fire!" sent the cadets scrambling from their beds to man the primitive post pumper. The mess hall was ablaze, and before the flames were extinguished, most of the roof was destroyed. Only after the fire had been contained was it discovered that a loaded cannon had been dragged from the artillery park while attention was focused on the fire, and had been aimed at the Superintendent's quarters. Serious injury and damage had been avoided only because the slow match, or fuse, had burned out before it reached the main powder charge. The culprits were never identified.

This incident only strengthened Thayer's resolve to enforce discipline. He secured the assignment of two additional tactical officers, Lieutenants Zebina J. D. Kinsley and Henry W. Griswold, moved them into the North and South Barracks, and charged them (and the cadet officers) with the responsibility for reporting cadets who disobeyed the regulations. Cadets reported on their "skin list" would report to the Commandant of Cadets each day in his office. The cadets, as gentlemen and men of honor, were expected to answer truthfully any and all direct questions concerning the reports. Where doubt existed, all a cadet had to do was deny the accusation and the report was forthwith canceled. As a result, lengthy judicial procedures were largely done away with. Although some guilty parties may have thus evaded punishment, the process worked because it appealed to a profound sense of honor in which both officers and cadets took particular pride. It was, in effect, the genesis of the Academy's venerated honor system. The punishment for those found guilty was the issuance of demerits which had to be "walked off" on guard duty in the company area.

Thayer's early belief that the lack of discipline among cadets stemmed from the leniencies of the Partridge era proved less valid, however, when discipline did not improve as the last of the so-called Partridge cadets departed West Point. Thayer's most important weapon in his battle for discipline was dismissal, but that weapon was blunted when so many were returned to the Academy by the President or Secretary of War because of the "youth" of the offender, or because the young man's previous conduct had shown no "vicious traits." In 1825, Thayer instituted another disciplinary device, the cumulative total of demerits—a measure that would highlight the repeated misconduct of those he might wish to dismiss. Thereafter, the number of demerits given a cadet each year would play a part in computing his class standing, and soon Thayer obtained approval to dismiss cadets who accumulated more than 200 demerits in any academic year.

After a drunken and near riotous Fourth of July celebration in 1825, Thayer decreed that there would be no more alcohol served to cadets on the post for any reason. (Cadets had previously been allowed to have wine at the annual Independence Day dinner they gave for the officers on the post—an infraction of his rules which, up until then, Thayer had chosen to ignore by leaving the post that day.)

Discontent with Thayer's heavy-handed discipline grew throughout the next year, reaching an explosive climax in the "Egg-Nog Riot" on Christmas Eve of 1826. The trouble began when Cadet Jefferson Davis and a number of other Southerners invited the corps to join them in partaking of some holiday eggnog. Davis, who left the party to round

Cadets 1813–21, 1821–32.

Cadet uniforms of 1813–21 and 1821–32. The Bettmann Archive.

up more revelers, learned that one of the tactical officers, Captain Hitchcock, intended to break up the affair. Davis rushed back to the room where the libation was being served, shouting, "Put away that grog, boys. Old Hitch is coming—." Old Hitch, however, had already arrived, and he immediately placed Davis under arrest, ordering him to his room. Davis obeyed, but when the captain ordered the balance of the group to disperse, one cadet pulled a sword and chased the officer back to his quarters in the barracks. Hitchcock returned shortly with reinforcements, but the tactical officers were met by a barrage of stove wood, stair railings, and chair backs—anything that could be broken up. One cadet, Walter Guion, seized a pistol and attempted to shoot Hitchcock, but fortunately the weapon misfired. Then Guion and others primed their muskets, and vowed to defend themselves to the death. Cooler heads prevailed and the affair finally ended without further injury. But, before it was over, North Barracks had been almost completely wrecked. Nineteen cadets, including Guion, were finally dismissed, but Davis, who had honored his arrest, was spared.

Thayer was never able to achieve the level of discipline to which he aspired. His efforts brought him repeatedly into conflict with the cadets, as well as with the administration, which he often saw as undermining his actions by returning cadets to the Academy whom he had dismissed. Still, he was unbending in his efforts. Thayer was by nature aloof and even cold in his official dealings, yet he was scrupulously fair, honest, and even handed. He was always the gentleman; discipline was dispensed with kindness—there was no meanness in him. But these were qualities that cadets often came to admire in him only after they had left the Academy. His colleagues found a warmth in him that was seldom evident to the cadets. "With all his strictness and apparent coldness on duty," Professor Albert Church later recounted, "he had a heart as big as breast could hold."

Cadet life was not all regulations and harsh discipline, although it was a spartan life at best. The cadet rooms were generally crowded. There was hardly room enough to spread out the narrow mattresses on which the cadets slept, for in those days they had no bedsteads. The rooms in both barracks were ventilated only by the doors and windows and a large fireplace—before which many a late-night meal was illicitly prepared. The South Barracks, in particular, was very cold in the winter. Cadets, at their studies there, were often obliged to sit at their tables before the fire with blankets at their backs, scorching on one side and freezing on the other. Those in North Barracks fared somewhat better, but even here the fireplaces provided the only source of heat.

To prevent danger from fires, each room was furnished with a large sheet-iron fender, which it was the duty of the last person leaving the room to place before the fire. Fires

Below left:

The Thompson house, as it was photographed in 1870. The Thompsons moved into this house in 1838. It was one of the few structures to survive the years of the Revolutionary War and originally had been the military storekeeper's quarters. From 1808 to 1878 Thompsons provided meals for a small number of privileged cadets. U.S.M.A. Library, Special Collections. Photo: Philip Pocock.

Below right:

North's or Gridley's tavern provided cadets with both illicit meals and liquid refreshment. U.S.M.A. Library, Special Collections. Photo: Philip Pocock.

from neglect of this regulation were frequent, although speedily extinguished by a quick-acting cadet bucket brigade.

The cadet mess or "cadet commons," as it was sometimes called, had been reestablished in 1813 under Isaac Partridge (an uncle of Captain Partridge), in the old storekeeper's quarters. It was moved into the new mess hall when that building was completed in 1815. About that same time, however, complaints of nepotism and profiteering led to the dismissal of the senior Partridge. Robert Nichols then took over the position and ran the mess successfully until he died, two years later. Thereafter it was operated by a succession of contractors who were awarded the business upon submission of the lowest bids. In 1821, William Cozzens won the contract and continued for several years in that role. Cozzens served the cadets very adequate, though plain meals—some even pronounced it excellent fare. He was known particularly for the quality and quantity of bread and butter he offered. "Give young men plenty of first-rate bread, butter and potatoes," he was heard to say, "and they will require little meat, and never complain of that."

A few fortunate cadets were allowed to board with Mrs. Alexander Thompson. Her husband had been the military storekeeper at West Point beginning in 1806, and when he died in 1809, the widow and her three daughters were allowed to remain in their quarters just below the level of the plain on the road to the dock. At that time there was no organized mess and many cadets boarded with local families, including that of Widow Thompson. When the central mess was reorganized in 1813, Mrs. Thompson asked that she be allowed to continue boarding cadets, as it was her family's only means of support. Partridge, the Superintendent, agreed. (That permission was continued by successive Superintendents until the death of the last surviving daughter in 1878.) A place at the Thompsons' table soon became an envied honor, which was granted to a dozen cadets annually. Not only was the fare at the Thompsons' excellent and vastly more varied than at the mess hall, but there was no requirement to march to and from meals, nor to bolt down one's food. Here cadets enjoyed the comforts and observances of a private family at a table at which Mrs. Thompson or one or more of her daughters was always present.

Other cadets who wished to escape the plainness of the mess hall diet might—although strictly forbidden to do so—visit the public house located just steps away from the southern boundary of the post and barracks. This establishment, first operated by Thomas North and then, after 1819, by Oliver Gridley, was situated just beyond the woodyard at the rear of the barracks and was easily reached through well-concealed openings in the plank fence that marked the post boundary there. "Scarcely a night passed," one graduate recalled, "in which one or more parties [of cadets] did not enjoy" the hospitality there. North's—or Gridley's—was so close, in fact, that when a cadet was found absent from his room by an inspector, his roommate could simply slip through the fence and warn

Above left:
Benny Havens's tavern was located just south of the Academy in the town that would later become known as Highland Falls. When Gridley's closed in 1824, Benny Havens's establishment—although off limits—became a favorite source of nourishment, both solid and liquid for many cadets. U.S.M.A. Archives.

Above right:
A section of the mural in the contemporary Officers' Club at West Point that depicts cadets making their way to Benny Havens. U.S.M.A. Archives.

the offender. The errant lad could return to the barracks, report to the inspector within the authorized ten minutes, and then, if he dared, go back and resume his supper. But supper was not all that these innkeepers served to the cadets, and during the first eight years of Thayer's regime most of the cadets in search of liquid nourishment found it at this abode.

Thayer did everything in his power to stop these visits. He sent tactical officers again and again to Gridley's and made life extremely uncomfortable for the owner. So much so, in fact, that less than a year after Gridley had purchased the property, he agreed to sell it to the government. This was exactly what Thayer wanted, but, after having convinced Gridley, he was unable to secure the appropriation necessary to complete this deal. Gridley continued in business until 1824, when the government finally purchased and took possession of the property. Old Grid's establishment was made over into a cadet hospital. As a bonus, the government gained historic Fort Putnam, which was situated on the farm, and the spectacular view that it commanded. Gridley, who was glad enough at first to be done with Thayer's harassment, soon came to believe that he had sold too cheaply and complained about the loss for the rest of his life.

Gridley's loss proved to be Benny Havens's gain. Havens had once lived on the post, near the dock, and had, at times, boarded cadets. But when Gridley's closed, he was operating a tavern just below Buttermilk Falls—in the town known today as Highland Falls—a mile or two south of the barracks. With Gridley's gone, Benny Havens's establishment acquired a new and loyal clientele. Some went for Benny's buckwheat cakes, oysters, and roast turkey, but those who had tried suppers both there and at Gridley's, insisted that "Old Grid" had provided the better fare. Still, Benny had other claims to fame, including his "hot flip"—eggs, well beaten, sweetened and spiced, in ale, the whole then heated by plunging a red-hot iron or "flip dog" into it. Done properly—as Havens could do it—this brew had a delicious caramel-like flavor. To these attractions Benny added the bonus of his Irish wit, quite liberal credit, and a willingness to barter for almost anything a cadet might bring from the barracks. Havens "was the sole congenial soul in the entire God-forsaken place," noted Edgar Allen Poe, who attended the Academy (1830–31) without graduating.

Benny Havens enjoyed a monopoly of this business for years, and it made him famous. In 1838, an army doctor, Lucius O'Brien, while visiting a friend at West Point, became so fond of the establishment that he composed some verses honoring it and its proprietor. Sung to the tune of "The Wearin' o' the Green," it soon became known as "Benny Havens, Oh!":

> Come, fill your glasses, fellows, and stand up in a row,
> To singing sentimentally, we're going for to go;
> In the army there's sobriety, promotions very slow
> So we'll sing our reminiscences of Benny Havens, oh!
> Oh! Benny Havens, oh!—oh! Benny Havens, oh!
> So we'll sing our reminiscences of Benny Havens oh!

Over the years, other bards have added verses commemorating events in the lives of West Point, its cadets and its graduates—the number now exceeds sixty.

Not all the cadets were inclined to spend their free moments at Grid's or Benny Havens. Some spent their leisure time hiking and climbing thorough the scenic highlands that surround West Point. Some formed musical clubs and provided entertainments. Others, more academically inclined, formed literary and debating societies. The *Amosophic Society* was organized in 1816 and merged, in 1823, with the *Philomathean Society*. The next year this recent amalgam merged with another newly formed club, the *Ciceronian Soci-*

The West Point Hotel (1829–1932) had
sixty-four rooms and was situated on
the edge of the plain. U.S.M.A. Ar-
chives.

ety, creating the *Dialectic Society* (1824)—a cadet association that continues today to be active at the Academy. These societies were organized for "improvement in debate, composition, and recitation," and offered cadets a welcome relief from the tedium of day-to-day life. Membership often included as many as twenty percent of the corps of cadets. Thayer and the faculty encouraged these clubs and usually provided meeting rooms—often one of the section rooms on the first floor of North Barracks—in which the societies' sometimes extensive libraries and collections could be maintained.

As early as 1820 the board of visitors noted the need for a suitable hotel at West Point. The following year, when Cozzens took over the mess hall, he added to its operation (as far as space would allow) an officers' mess and rooms for visitors to the post. The expansion of the mess hall in 1823 made more space available, but in 1824, when the government purchased and closed Gridley's—which had provided some lodgings—even that larger facility was strained. "The floors of the parlours . . . are literally covered with the beds of the strangers that crowd here," wrote one guest. The demand for facilities to accommodate visitors continued to grow and in 1829 Thayer received approval to construct a hotel—a stone structure some 50 by 60 feet, containing sixty-four rooms—to be paid for from the proceeds of the sale of wood cut from public lands. William Cozzens was the first to operate the new West Point Hotel—as it came to be known—and continued to manage it for a number of years.

Throughout the early- and mid-1820s, the officers had messed "very pleasantly" at Cozzens's, but in the autumn of 1829, when he took over the new hotel, he announced that he could no longer afford to keep up the mess, without an increase of price. When the officers rebelled at this, the mess was broken up and the officers were left to their own devices. Some had their meals prepared in the basement of the Old South Barracks and took them in their rooms, others went down to Mrs. Kinsley's to board. However, after some unsuccessful agitation in 1832 to obtain a separate officers' mess, most of the officers gravitated back to Cozzens and took their meals at the new hotel.

As noted earlier, when President Monroe had visited West Point in the summer of 1817, he had listened at length to the faculty objections to Partridge, but he had also been bombarded with complaints about the officers' housing. Thayer's first instructions from the War Department, after arriving at West Point, directed him not only to coordinate a new program of instruction, but also to investigate the problem of housing. Aside from three new houses for professors that were just being completed, the hodgepodge of existing quarters for the faculty was inadequate and badly in need of repairs. Thayer immediately asked the Secretary of War to station a quartermaster at West Point and to furnish

View of Cozzens Hotel near West Point,
*as shown here in a nineteenth-century
painting by John Frederick Kensett. c.
1863. Oil on canvas, 20 × 34". Courtesy
The New-York Historical Society.*

Opposite above:
*The Superintendent's house was com-
pleted in 1820. Various additions have
been made to the original structure
since then.*

Opposite below:
*The Commandant's quarters, built in
1819, is the oldest set of quarters in existence today at West Point.*

him with enough funds to make the most urgently needed repairs. He was quick to add, however, that repairs alone would never solve the deficiencies in housing. In December 1817, he requested funds for new quarters for the Superintendent and for three other new structures—two brick houses for professors and a stone duplex for teachers with families. At the same time, he surveyed the other needs of the post and requested funds for a new hospital and monies to enlarge the kitchen of the recently completed mess hall. To support his housing request Thayer drew up a report "designating the number and size of the apartments assigned to officers at West Point or occupied by them; together with information as to the number of rooms which . . . should be assigned to officers stationed there." That report was submitted in January 1818. "A reference to past expenditures for the repair of these Quarters will prove the expediency of replacing them by new & *perma-nent* buildings," he wrote, adding that he believed each professor should be provided a two-story house "40 by 27 feet" (at a cost of about $4,000 each) and that "every two teachers or assistant-Professors having families" should get a similar house. The unmarried officers, he noted, were adequately accommodated in the new barracks.

After due consideration, his report and request for new housing was approved, but it was not until the spring of 1819 that the contracts were let. The two brick professors' quarters on either side of the yet-unfinished Superintendent's quarters were completed in early November 1819. The set to the north was occupied first by Captain Bell (1819–20) and then by Major William J. Worth (1820–29), followed by the successive Commandants of Cadets. It is still the quarters of the Commandant, and the oldest set of quarters at West Point today. The Superintendent's house, just to the south, was finished the next year, in 1820. The three new brick structures were located on, and extended northward from, the line of quarters begun in 1817. The stone doubles were located to the west of the old quarters that had for a long period been occupied by the Mansfields—on a site, it is said, which once held Revolutionary War barracks.

In 1826, Thayer asked for another set of brick quarters for the professor of chemistry, and for two more stone doubles. When appropriations fell short of what was needed to complete all of these immediately, he stretched the project out, beginning all three but completing only two in 1827—the last, one of the stone doubles, was finished the next year. The three stone doubles—remodeled and enlarged repeatedly over the years and long since known as "Professors Row"—have housed most of the Academy's most influential department heads. The brick professors' houses of this era (except the quarters for the Superintendent and Commandant) were demolished in the first decade of the twentieth century to make way for new barracks.

In 1830, Thayer gained approval to construct a new hospital. That two-story structure was completed in 1834; wings on either side of the central wards provided quarters for the surgeon and, for a time, some of the bachelor officers. In 1833, Thayer proposed a combined academic building and "exercise hall," and a new chapel. Although the academic building was approved, nothing further was done on either project until after his departure.

Thayer also installed running water in many of the buildings on post by drawing from a mountainside reservoir through iron pipes, and considered, but rejected the notion of lighting the Academy with gas and heating it centrally by steam. His purchase of the Gridley property had not only rid him of old Grid's troublesome establishment, but had also provided room to the south for the Academy to expand without encroaching on the plain—the borders of which he lined with trees.

The growth of the faculty under Thayer meant an enlarged social circle. "We have an addition to our society of several families," noted Elizabeth Mansfield in March 1818. "Among them are ten young Ladies" whose presence, she reported, had made it a gay winter. There were "regular assemblies, occasional balls, tea parties, sleighing parties, &c." And, there were lessons for the ladies in music, French, and drawing. Among the officers—particularly the married officers whose larger quarters made substantial gatherings possible—there were many parties to which, in this compact society, all were invited. Of necessity, the entertainments were plain and inexpensive. The dancing consisted mainly of quadrilles, Spanish dances, and an occasional waltz, but the evening always ended with a Virginia reel. Card playing had been another favorite pastime among army officers and wives, but when Thayer announced the ban on card playing among cadets, he strongly suggested that "all officers and families of this post" would, in the future, "exclude card playing from their social parties."

Thayer, although a bachelor, also entertained regularly—hosting "delightful" dinner parties and, occasionally, a chess party. His years in France had made him something of a gourmet and a wine connoisseur, and he kept a first-rate wine cellar in the Superintendent's quarters. Thayer's entertainment of the many distinguished visitors who were drawn to West Point revealed a cultivated and urbane nature. He was perfectly at home with men of all callings, foreign and domestic—soldiers, statesmen, lawyers, physicians, divines, historians, poets, scientists, and merchants. "In expressing his ideas," wrote Thomas J. Cram, "his voice was low, distinct and very impressive; and when he spoke all present would listen with rapt attention." And yet he had a way of drawing out the best from each person with whom he spoke, making everyone feel comfortable in his presence.

The officers at West Point also entertained and, in turn, were entertained by both the old Hudson River families and the newly rich, whose fine homes began to spring up along the river's banks. One of these was the wealthy and hospitable Gouverneur Kemble who had built his mansion directly across from West Point, at Cold Spring. On Saturday nights Kemble held regular dinner parties—usually affairs for men only—at which Thayer and the other officers were frequently guests. There they met and mingled with some of the brightest and most powerful men in America, including George Bancroft, Edward Everett, Hugh S. Legare, Washington Irving, Martin Van Buren, and many others.

For some years prior to Thayer's arrival, the better cadets had been drafted into the role of assistant instructors. For the cadets it meant extra privileges and freedom from many of the more mundane aspects of cadet life. Thayer objected to the practice and, although he was unable to avoid it altogether, he did manage to have a number of young officers assigned as assistant instructors. Frequently, newly commissioned officers would simply be retained at West Point after graduation; others were called back to the Academy after only a year or two with their regiments. With time on their hands, these young officers organized literary societies similiar to those they had known during their cadet years. They "took great pains" in preparing their presentations, wrote Albert Church, and the weekly meetings "were of great interest and profit." Occasionally, the clubs would open their meetings to all of the officers and ladies of the post, adding yet another dimension to the routine of daily life.

In the interest of better instruction and daily recitation, the classes at the Military Academy had been divided into small sections at least since the reorganization of the school under Swift in 1812. After the examinations in January 1818, however, the academic board adopted a "method of organizing the sections, according to the graduation of talent." This, they said, would "give sufficient scope to young men of genius," while insuring that the slower cadets would also cover the essential material. Sectioning by demonstrated talent was, in itself, a simple matter, but the modification of the course of studies to accommodate the difference in sections was another matter. The academic board spent the balance of the spring studying the problem. The result was a concept of instruction geared to the capacities of the students; all received the most essential knowledge and the better sections went progressively deeper into the subject.

The twin pillars of the academic program were French and mathematics—mathematics was the basis for training in engineering, and French was, at that time, the language of the advanced texts. In a cadet's freshman (or Fourth Class) year, his studies were limited to these two subjects—the mathematics including algebra, geometry, and trigonometry. In the sophomore (or Third Class) year, drawing was added to the French and mathematics, which that year included analytical and descriptive geometry. Having completed this foundation, cadets moved on to the more technical sciences during their last two years. Second Class cadets studied natural and experimental philosophy (physics), chemistry (beginning in 1822), and topographical drawing. Finally, in the First Class year, cadets arrived at the course toward which the whole curriculum had been aiming: engineering—to which was added instruction on the science of war, a smattering of rhetoric, and an introduction to the moral and political sciences.

Once this program had been installed—and validated by the performance of cadets in their public examinations—both Thayer and the board resisted efforts to alter it. The board, whose primary function was the establishment and maintenance of the curriculum, was reluctant to make changes and grew ever more so over time. The power of the board to resist even Thayer's efforts to institute change was clearly evident as early as September 1823 when the Superintendent proposed that they should "detach the subject of Grand Tactics, in the course of instruction, from the Department of Engineering and impose the duty on the Instructor of Tactics." The initial discussion of the proposal went on "for some time" but the board reached no decision and postponed further discussion until its next meeting, at which time the subject was further postponed and never reintroduced. The strength of the academic board derived first from its charter in Academy regulations, which placed the curriculum squarely in its hands, and also from the three essential rules of its operation: first, all decisions were to be made by a majority of the members present; second, no decision or opinion was to be divulged until regularly promulgated by the Superintendent; and, finally, no individual comments or opinions were to be divulged on any occasion. Whatever their internal differences and conflicts, the board spoke with one voice to the outside world.

There was one important exception to the academic board's ability to deflect change from the outside during these years. The Academy was essentially forced to add courses in civil engineering to that which had been an almost wholly military engineering pro-

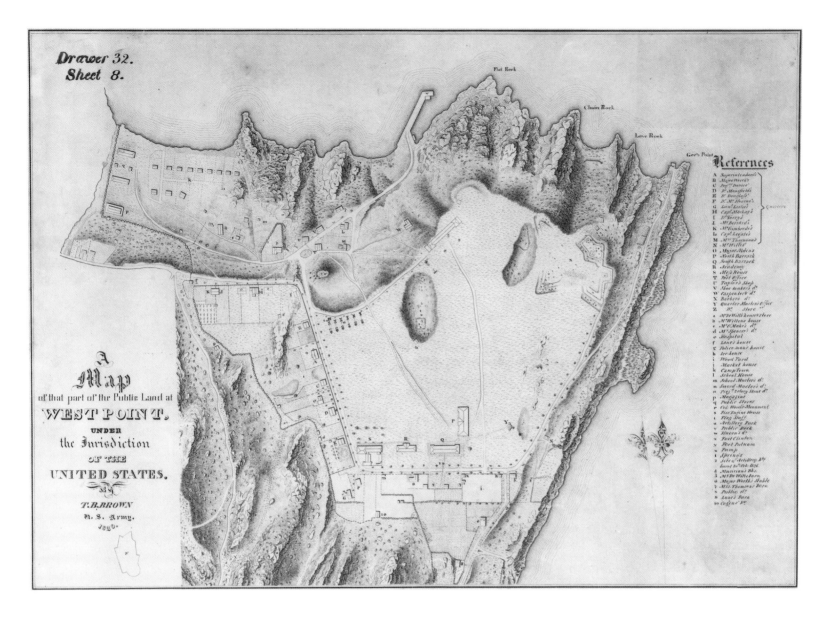

A map of the public land at West Point under the jurisdiction of the United States in 1826, by T.D. Brown, United States Army. The National Archives and Records Administration, Cartographic and Architectural Branch.

gram. In this case, the impetus for change lay largely outside the Academy. A growing interest in internal improvements in Washington and across the country made the introduction of civil engineering inescapable—despite resistance from Thayer and the academic board.

Momentum had been building since 1818. In 1821, Rufus King, who served that year on the board of visitors, proposed including civil engineering in the course of instruction at West Point. "If instead of confining the studies to mere military mathematics," he wrote, "the branch of civil engineering were taught, greater public benefits would be derived from this Academy." Wars and combats would be infrequent, King pointed out, "but the science, which may be employed in constructing canals, roads & bridges, is always in demand, and those who possess the same would meet with constant and profitable employment." Still, neither Thayer, nor Crozet, professor of engineering, nor other members of the academic board made any move to broaden the engineering program. When Crozet left West Point for the University of Virginia in 1823, the curriculum he was teaching still focused exclusively on the military arts—essentially the same course he had been teaching since 1819, encompassing "permanent and field fortifications" and their "appendages," and "the different modes of attacking and defending fortified places."

Even though Thayer, in 1823, had observed that if, at any time, some of the graduates were not needed in the military ranks, "they might be usefully employed as Civil Engineers either in the service of the General Government or of the States," he meant only that there could be some natural transfer between the civil and military branches of the subject, and made no suggestion that the course then taught at West Point be broadened. As late as 1825, he was still arguing against the introduction of "any new studies" into the Academy's curriculum. "Those who are not satisfied with the existing course of studies," he asserted, "have not reflected upon the nature and object of the Institution and have not considered that this is a special school designed solely for the purpose of a *military* education."

David E. Douglass assumed the chair of engineering in 1823, just as the national debate on internal improvements took on renewed vigor with the introduction of the General Survey Bill. The issue was a heated one, but by year's end the mood in Congress was clearly in favor of an increased role for the federal government—and the Army. Events outside West Point were beginning to exert an irresistible force on the course of studies. The bill, as it began to take final shape, would empower the President "to cause the necessary surveys, plans and estimates to be made of the routes of such roads and canals as he may deem of national importance in a commercial or military point of view, or necessary to the transportation of the public mails." This legislation directed the use of military engineers and considerably increased federal participation in internal improvements.

At West Point, the debate over this bill was watched with concern and anticipation. Changes in the curriculum at the Academy would be essential if the mission and role of the Army was broadened. At the end of January 1824, the academic board directed Douglass to review his course. Early the next month the internal improvements bill was passed. Douglass, who was immediately appointed to the Army's new Board of Engineering for Internal Improvements, rushed to prepare a trial course in civil engineering and introduced it that spring to the top section of his engineering class. In June, he examined this section separately on the subject. "When we consider the rising demand in our country for civil engineers," the 1824 board of visitors reported, in response, "we must admit that the full endowment of this branch of study would be a great national economy." Beginning that fall, Douglass introduced the course to the entire class.

With congressional prodding, the Academy had responded. But the Congress was not finished and, the next year (1825), posted another clear message when it considered sending some of the cadets to Europe to improve their knowledge of civil engineering. Douglass responded by suggesting that he should be sent to Europe instead; he could then, he argued, introduce what he learned into his new course at West Point. In the end, neither Douglass nor the cadets were sent, but in 1827, Douglass renewed his request and augmented his supporting argument. The Academy badly needed a textbook in civil engineering, he pointed out, and promised that—if he were allowed fifteen to eighteen months abroad—he would complete one fitted precisely to the requirements of the institution. Again he was disappointed, for his assistant, Dennis Hart Mahan, was sent to Europe instead. Douglass had to content himself with self-study and the experience he could gain in private engineering engagements. Nonetheless, he began to introduce changes into the civil engineering course that progressively broadened it—adding material on roads, bridges, and inland navigation. Successive boards of visitors endorsed the changes, and in 1830 they noted with satisfaction that "a large portion of the cadets are destined to act as civil engineers." The cadets had come to a similar conclusion, but were possibly less sanguine about the pace of change. In 1829, they formed the *American Association for the Promotion of Science, Literature, and the Arts* for the purpose of improving their knowledge of civil engineering. The civil engineering program continued to be expanded throughout the next decade, adding topics as contemporary interests dictated, including railroad construction, tunneling, and the creation of artificial harbors.

Despite the academic board's apparent reluctance to introduce the new program, the Military Academy did move more rapidly than any other school in the nation in responding to the need for civil engineers. It was the first school of civil engineering and the leading center of such instruction until the Civil War. When Congress directed the use of Army officers as civil engineers, it changed the curriculum for the cadets and affected their perspective as to possible careers after graduation. As West Point historian Sidney Forman put it: "Successive national administrations simply called upon the men and the institution they could command to solve the problem at hand, men and an institution whose training and skills were applicable and adaptable to the age of improvements."

Thayer had welcomed public scrutiny of the Academy and its cadets as a means of building public support for the school. He approved summer marches to Hudson, New York, in 1819; to Philadelphia in 1820; to Boston in 1821 (where the cadets paid a call on former president John Adams); and to Goshen, New York, in 1822. The cadets proved popular with the people wherever they went and the widespread publicity they received was almost universally favorable. Thayer's revitalization of the board of visitors served the same purpose. The board was invited to look into details of academic activity and the physical plant, and to report its findings to the Secretary of War. Distinguished educators, men of science, leading officers of the Army, the Navy, the militia, and members of Congress—often men who had previously expressed hostility toward the Academy—were invited to West Point as members of these boards. Thayer believed that criticism of the school arose largely from a lack of information or from prejudice, both of which could be resolved by personal contact and observation. As a substantiation of this remedy, it should be noted that the boards' reports usually contained high praise of the Academy and its programs. Under the benevolent influence of the beauty of the Hudson Highlands in June, coupled with the spectacle of martial music and dress parades, competently-held examinations, erect and correct cadets, the suave and gracious hospitality of the Superintendent, as well as the enthusiasm of the majority of their colleagues, even opponents were won over to at least a toleration of the institution, while those who had been lukewarm often became the Academy's firm defenders.

Thayer, during his first eight years as Superintendent at West Point, had enjoyed the full patronage of both President James Monroe and Secretary of War John C. Calhoun. Seldom had either man questioned Thayer's efforts. On the contrary, when Congress cut the size of the Army in 1821, and considered abolishing the Academy, the administration swiftly came to its defense. "In the present condition of the world," Calhoun told them, military science could not be "neglected with impunity." The Academy, Monroe added, "forms the basis, in regard to science, on which the military establishment rests."

The years from 1826 to 1833, however, were marked first by decreasing support and finally by the rise of active hostility in Washington. In the last years of John Quincy Adams's presidency, the process of government was so consumed by controversy and torn by the realignment of political factions that Thayer had no success in focusing the attention of the administration on the needs of the Academy. In the summer of 1827, he went to Washington to seek the aid of President Adams personally. Thayer confided in the President his concerns about "the moral condition of the institution," noting in particular "a habit of drinking [that] had become very prevalent among [cadets]." Something had to be done to restore discipline! Thayer laid out a new set of regulations and asked for the President's approval. Adams, however, deferred judgment, and Thayer's effort proved fruitless.

*West Point Military Academy in 1828 as
depicted by George Catlin. West Point
Museum Collections, U.S.M.A.*

In the election of 1828, a tidal wave of votes submerged Adams and swept Andrew
Jackson into the presidency. Neither the new President nor his Secretaries of War, John
Eaton (1829–31) and Lewis Cass (1831–36), were well disposed toward Thayer. They
were particularly unsympathetic to his attempts at maintaining the level of discipline he
favored. Jacksonians looked upon the Military Academy as a haven for sons of the privileged. Moreover, they believed that it provided the sole avenue of entry into the officer
corps, denying the regular citizen access and producing an increasingly aristocratic body.

Jackson's own attitude toward West Point was somewhat more ambiguous. He once
described it as "the best school in the world," but he clearly disapproved of Thayer's
dismissal of cadets for what he considered to be mere boyish pranks. Thayer, he believed,
was unbending and autocratic. Moreover, Jackson's military career had been confined
almost entirely to the command of volunteers. In his experience, the regular establishment that West Point now fostered had sometimes seemed almost as great an obstacle as
the enemy itself.

Some historians have attributed Jackson's hostility to Thayer to some mistreatment by
the Superintendent of Jackson's nephew, Andrew J. Donelson, who had supported the
Partridge mutineers. Donelson was an aide to Jackson both before and after his attendance
at the Military Academy and he corresponded extensively with his uncle. Upon Jackson's
election to the presidency, Donelson became his private secretary. Obviously, Donelson
had ample opportunity to influence Jackson against Thayer, but there is no persuasive
evidence that he did so. In fact, from the correspondence between Donelson and Thayer,
one could conclude that their relationship was quite cordial. Others have blamed the
President's prejudice on George Wurtz Hughes, who was dismissed by Thayer in 1827
only a few days before graduation for brawling with one of the tactical officers. Hughes
supposedly went to Washington and devoted himself to poisoning Jackson's mind against
Thayer. Whatever the cause, Jackson's antipathy toward Thayer increased.

As soon as the cadets discovered that appeals to Washington brought dramatic reprieves, even from judgments of courts-martial, discipline declined even further. Rein-
statements followed so rapidly upon dismissals that Thayer was driven to sending cases
that required extreme discipline directly to the War Department for action. Earlier admin-

Cadet captain uniform c. 1818–39 and cadet corporal uniform c. 1839–53. Drawn by Dick S. Von Schriltz. Copyright K/S Historical Publications, 1969. Anne S.K. Brown Military Collection, Brown University.

Andrew Jackson thought highly of the Academy, but he frustrated Thayer's efforts to maintain discipline. The Bettmann Archive.

istrations had occasionally reinstated cadets, but in the first two years of Jackson's first term seven of sixteen cadets sentenced to dismissal were reinstated. Bitterly, Thayer complained that the President "is in the habit of dispensing with the most important regulations of the Academy in favor of his friends." The chances of success if one approached Jackson, he calculated, were "three to one" in the cadet's favor.

In 1830, Thayer's troubles were compounded by attacks upon the Military Academy from other quarters. First came a broadside from Alden Partridge, who published an attack on the Academy entitled *The Military Academy at West Point Unmasked: or Corruption and Military Despotism Exposed.* The book was composed of three appeals: first to the Congress; next to the President; and, finally, to the American people—each warning that West Point was spawning a "military aristocracy."

At about the same time, in the House of Representatives, the Academy came under attack as a repository for the sons of the rich and influential who would monopolize the offices of the Army. The most outspoken opponent was Davy Crockett of Tennessee, who proposed abolishing the Academy entirely. Still, few in Congress actually stood with Crockett in his opposition to the Academy, and Partridge's bitter, but transparent, attack did not attract many followers. The fact was that the Academy had a carefully-cultivated base of support in Congress. (For example, since 1826 the Academy had annually sought recommendations for potential candidates from each congressman.) These attacks thus proved more of an annoyance than a serious threat. Nonetheless, this congressional support was of little help to Thayer in his personal dealings with Jackson.

With Jackson's reelection in 1832, Thayer concluded that they must have a showdown. The ease with which cadets could gain reprieves from Jackson was causing a growing laxness in discipline. He discussed the problem with Ethan Allen Hitchcock, the Commandant of Cadets. "We agreed," recalled Hitchcock, "that the evil influence was spreading. [Colonel Thayer] noticing it chiefly in the growing neglect of study, while I observed it principally in the tendency to disorder." They decided that, given Jackson's apparent hostility to Thayer, Hitchcock should go to Washington and seek a personal interview with the President. On the 24th of November, Hitchcock met with Jackson, but the results only confirmed their worst expectations. "Sylvanus Thayer," Jackson raged, "is a tyrant!

The autocrat of all the Russias couldn't exercise more power." Nothing Hitchcock could say would alter the President's opinion.

Thayer suspected as much and, even before Hitchcock returned from Washington, he wrote to Cass, the Secretary of War: "I am led to believe that there is something at this institution which does not altogether meet with the President's approbation, but I am at a loss to conjecture whether the dissatisfaction, if such really exists, relates to persons or things." Thayer could have had little doubt as to the real state of affairs, but his letter left the administration ample latitude in which to propose a solution, if they desired to do so. Hitchcock's report of his interview with the President, however, left no doubt that Jackson's antipathy was directed toward Thayer personally. Cass's response to his letter, although solicitous, did nothing to change that view. In January, Thayer put the administration to the final test by offering his resignation as Superintendent and asking to be reassigned to other duty. Although the administration delayed in responding, his resignation was ultimately accepted with no attempt to persuade him to change his mind. Thayer would be reassigned after the upcoming June examinations.

Even though Thayer lost his personal battle with Jackson, he was successful in a larger sense; the system he had installed at West Point endured. Certainly, many elements of that system had been conceived under Swift, such as the annual boards of visitors, the four-year curriculum, the semi-annual examinations, and the small sections and daily recitations. Yet it was Thayer who had vitalized and adapted the system and, even more, it was Thayer who had made it work. "He had brought order out of chaos," wrote historian James Morrison, "no trifling achievement considering the muddle he had inherited from Alden Partridge." For his efforts Thayer has become known as the "Father of the Military Academy."

But Thayer's legacy went far beyond the system itself, for he embodied what was to become known as "The Spirit of West Point." In every aspect of his person he represented to the cadets rigid, impartial justice, uncompromising honor, impeccable honesty, literal, unquestioning obedience to orders, and towering intellect. "His comprehensive mind embraced principles and details more strongly than any man I ever knew," wrote one graduate. "His object was to make [cadets] gentlemen and soldiers. And he illustrated in his person the great object he sought to accomplish."

In addition, Thayer's influence was perpetuated by his students, who dominated the school until long after the Civil War. Alexander Macomb, for many years the Chief of Engineers, had advised him that "for the sake of harmony" at West Point, professors should be selected from among those who had graduated and taught there—men "who would advance the interests of the institution and conform willingly to its discipline." As the opportunities arose, Thayer willingly complied, and in doing so filled the faculty with men of his own mold and making.

In 1827, the resignation of Dr. John Toorey as acting professor of chemistry had given Thayer the opportunity to appoint Lieutenant W. F. Hopkins, an 1825 graduate, to that post. Mansfield's resignation the next year left vacant the highest-paid professorship at the Academy. (Professors' compensation was still controlled by the law of 1812, which gave the professor of natural and experimental philosophy the pay and emoluments of a lieutenant colonel, while the other professors were paid as majors.) There was, therefore, keen interest in the position. Douglass, who had been Mansfield's assistant for five years before accepting the chair of mathematics and then engineering, wanted the position and he had a strong claim to it. He had been at the Academy longer than any other member of the faculty, and had served as secretary of the academic board since its inception. Thayer, however, chose Lieutenant Edward H. Courtenay, who had graduated at the head of his class in 1821. Courtenay had served three years at the Academy as an assistant

Dennis Hart Mahan *by Robert W. Weir.*
n.d. Oil on canvas, 31 × 26". West Point
Museum Collections, U.S.M.A.

Colonel Sylvanus Thayer's Office (re-
stored) in the Superintendent's quarters
at West Point. U.S.M.A. Archives.

professor (first assisting Mansfield in natural philosophy and then Douglass in engineering), and was then assigned as assistant to the Chief Engineer in Washington. Courtenay assumed his duties as head of experimental philosophy on September 1, 1828 and was officially confirmed by the Senate early the next year.

David Douglass, disappointed by his failure to gain the more prestigious and lucrative assignment to which he felt he was entitled, resigned eighteen months later. To replace him Thayer chose Dennis Hart Mahan, a graduate of the class of 1824. Mahan had been retained at the Academy, first as an assistant professor of mathematics and then, in 1825, as principal assistant to Douglass in engineering. In 1827, since his health was poor, he had been sent to Europe to recover, as well as to study military and civil engineering.

In the midst of these changes in the academic staff, Thayer also chose a new Commandant of Cadets. Major William J. Worth, who had been appointed in 1820, requested relief from the assignment and return to his regiment in 1828. He suggested as his replacement, Captain Ethan Allen Hitchcock, who had been his assistant. Hitchcock, only months before, had been relieved of his assignment at West Point at his own request, but when offered the commandantcy, he returned. He reported back in March 1829, and remained throughout the balance of Thayer's tenure.

By 1830 there were new men in charge of the Departments of Chemistry, Natural and Experimental Philosophy, and Engineering, and a new Commandant of Cadets. Further changes later in the decade would only more firmly entrench the Thayer influence.

The examination of 1833 was among Thayer's last official acts, and in an ironic sense, it typified his administration of the school. The classes performed handsomely—particularly the graduating class of 1833. They did so well, in fact, that Joel Poinsett, the president of the board of visitors, admitted that they were the best examinations he had ever

heard, but wondered aloud how the class as a whole could have done so well without knowing beforehand the subjects upon which they would be examined. That remark was overheard by a member of the faculty who reported it to Thayer.

Thayer was incensed, and he would not allow this last insult to pass. He immediately ordered Mahan to prepare a full synopsis of the subjects in his whole engineering course. The class was then ordered back to the examination room, where Thayer explained that Poinsett's remark forced him to take the unusual step of reexamining the entire group. Poinsett objected and attempted to apologize—insisting that his remark was intended as a compliment—but Thayer would not be dissuaded. The injury done to the Academy and to the class, he insisted, could be repaired only by a thorough reexamination.

"The examination was resumed and continued with the deepest interest," recalled one of those who was reexamined, "each member of the class feeling that an appeal was made to his honor as well as his pride." When this examination was completed "the highest compliments" were extended to the class by Poinsett and by the other members of the board. The class, the Academy, and Thayer had been vindicated.

A few days later, on July 1st, the class graduated. Afterward, every member came to Thayer's office to shake his hand and say a personal farewell. That evening Thayer strolled down to the dock and stood with the small group of officers who often gathered on pleasant summer evenings to await the night boat to New York. They watched and chatted casually as the boat docked and off-loaded a few passengers and some cargo. Then, as the whistle sounded the ship's departure, Thayer turned to his companions and extended his hand, saying "Good-bye, gentlemen." He then stepped aboard the boat, leaving the officers on the dock in shocked silence. After sixteen years, Sylvanus Thayer had bade farewell to West Point.

CHAPTER 6

GROWTH, WAR, AND FULFILLMENT 1833-1865

"Your own late domicile," Dennis Hart Mahan wrote Sylvanus Thayer in late 1833, "is gradually putting off its bachelor habit, by such additions as single gentlemen do not always think of." The community at West Point was adjusting to a new Superintendent, Major Rene E. DeRussy, and the quarters, which had known only the bachelor, Thayer, was being shaped according to the wishes of Mrs. DeRussy.

"Everything wears an unsettled aspect," Mahan continued. And well it might. Thayer's inability to get along with the Jackson administration had meant that a number of matters had simply been held in abeyance—both in Washington and at West Point—until a new Superintendent was in place. Barely a month after arriving, DeRussy forwarded to the War Department the plan for a chapel which had "been under consideration" at West Point for some time. "The details are not yet drawn," DeRussy noted, but he forwarded the general plan since he was "anxious to begin the building immediately." Similarly, no plans had yet been drawn for an academic building originally proposed by Thayer, approved in Washington, and already partially funded. This structure was to provide an enclosed area for drill and exercises, a floor of section rooms, and additional quarters for the bachelor officers.

DeRussy attempted to shed the aura of aloof dignity in which Thayer had wrapped the superintendency. He regularly invited cadets to his home for tea, where they conversed as equals with him, his charming wife, and other members of the faculty. And, he encouraged other officers to do the same. DeRussy had graduated from West Point in 1812. Although he had known Thayer during his cadet years at West Point, both as fellow cadet and as an instructor, DeRussy was hardly a "Thayer man." He was much more in sympathy with Jackson's conviction that Thayer's rigid discipline bordered on the tyrannical and that this was the real source of cadet misbehavior.

An example of this new attitude was DeRussy's attendance at the ball held at the end of the summer encampment in 1833. The new Superintendent, wrote one cadet, was "dancing and waltzing away as young as any of us." "It occurred to me," the young gentleman noted, "that it would be rather difficult to find Colonel Thayer lowering his dignity so far as to go to a cadet's ball, much less dance at it."

DeRussy, however, found the cadets more easily won over than the faculty. Mahan, already emerging as the school's dominant figure, wrote Thayer, "We are going on here *tant bien que mal*, but I am sorry to say with an overproportion of the latter."

Among the few accomplishments of DeRussy's superintendency was the completion of the chapel (1836) and construction of the new academic and exercise hall (1838). The chapel, a simple, rectangular Greek temple form, was typical of structures then being built in the Greek Revival Style. To this was added impressive Doric columns and a portico. DeRussy's original proposal was to place the chapel on Trophy Point just west of the hotel that had been built a few years earlier, but that was overruled, probably because of the distance from the barracks and other structures. The interior was adorned

Opposite:
The diploma that was presented to Cadet James Duncan in 1834 upon his graduation from the United States Military Academy. U.S.M.A. Library, Special Collections. Photo: Philip Pocock.

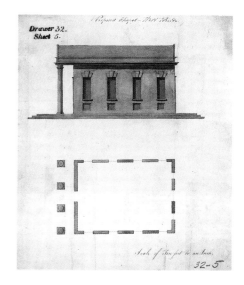

Drawing of a proposed chapel at West Point. This was not the chapel that was eventually built. National Archives and Records Administration Cartographic and Architectural Branch.

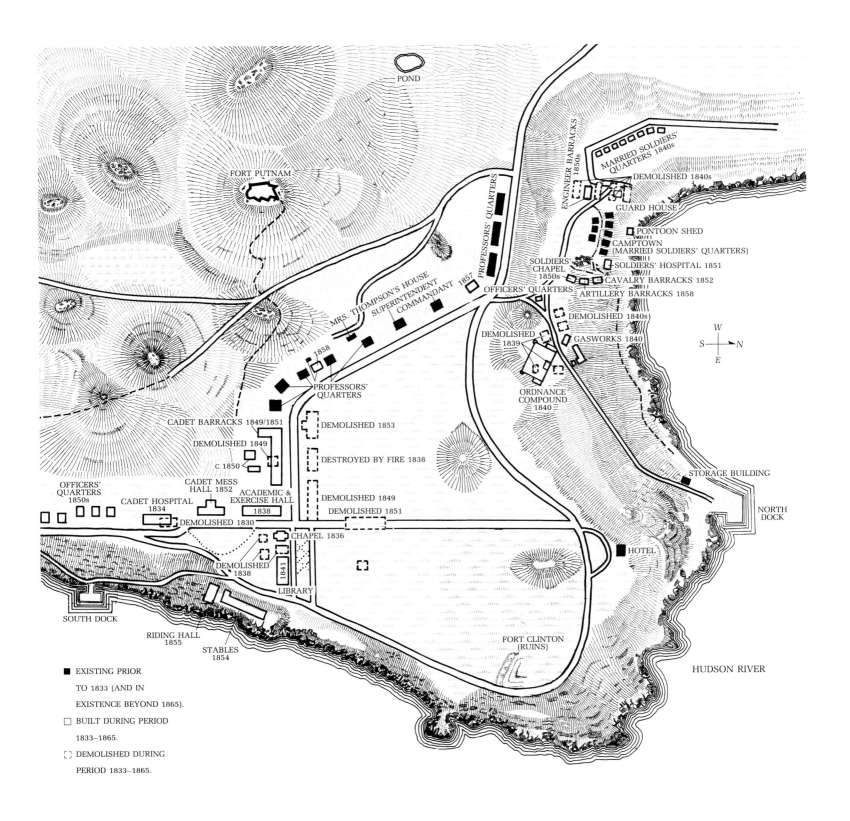

POND

FORT PUTNAM

MARRIED SOLDIERS' QUARTERS 1840s

ENGINEER BARRACKS 1850s

DEMOLISHED 1840s

GUARD HOUSE

PONTOON SHED

CAMPTOWN (MARRIED SOLDIERS' QUARTERS)

SOLDIERS' HOSPITAL 1851

SOLDIERS' CHAPEL 1850s

CAVALRY BARRACKS 1852

ARTILLERY BARRACKS 1858

PROFESSORS' QUARTERS

MRS. THOMPSON'S HOUSE

SUPERINTENDENT

COMMANDANT 1857

OFFICERS' QUARTERS

DEMOLISHED 1840s

DEMOLISHED 1839

GASWORKS 1840

W N S E

1858

ORDNANCE COMPOUND 1840

PROFESSORS' QUARTERS

CADET BARRACKS 1849/1851

DEMOLISHED 1853

DEMOLISHED 1849

DESTROYED BY FIRE 1838

STORAGE BUILDING

C. 1850

CADET MESS HALL 1852

ACADEMIC & EXERCISE HALL

OFFICERS' QUARTERS 1850s

CADET HOSPITAL 1834

1838

DEMOLISHED 1849

DEMOLISHED 1851

NORTH DOCK

DEMOLISHED 1830

CHAPEL 1836

DEMOLISHED 1838

HOTEL

1841

LIBRARY

SOUTH DOCK

RIDING HALL 1855

STABLES 1854

FORT CLINTON (RUINS)

HUDSON RIVER

■ EXISTING PRIOR TO 1833 (AND IN EXISTENCE BEYOND 1865).

□ BUILT DURING PERIOD 1833–1865.

⌐⌐ DEMOLISHED DURING PERIOD 1833–1865.

Map of West Point, 1833–1865.

with a large mural that was painted over the altar by Professor Robert W. Weir, head of the Department of Drawing (1834–76). In his years at West Point, Weir established himself as one of the important American painters of the century. (His "Landing of the Pilgrims" hangs in the rotunda of the Capitol in Washington, D.C.) Constructed of marble, the chapel remained essentially unaltered until 1910, when it was moved to the West Point cemetery where it stands today—the oldest public building at West Point.

The new academic building, roughly 75 by 275 feet, was constructed of stone and stucco. A three-story building, it featured a hipped roof and round-arched openings on the first floor that hinted at an Italian Renaissance influence, but the east front, opposite the chapel, was adorned with a two-story portico supported by six Doric columns similar to those of the chapel—giving the whole a rather nondescript appearance. It was the largest building yet constructed at West Point.

In only one other area did DeRussy make any notable progress, and that was in his relations with President Andrew Jackson. The new Superintendent was able to convince the administration that restoring cadets who had been dismissed for disciplinary reasons was counterproductive. "I had hoped that a lenient system of administration would be found sufficient for the government of the Military Academy," wrote the President to the cadets, "but I have been disappointed and it is now time to be more rigorous in enforcing its discipline." Henceforth, cadets who did not "demean [conduct or behave] themselves as they are required to do by the regulations" would suffer the "prescribed punishments" without reprieve.

Discipline, however, did not improve. The cadets' celebration of the New Year on January 1, 1837 was a case in point. Six of them dragged the reveille gun into the narrow area between the North and South Barracks and fired it. "The effect was great," wrote one of the participants, "only four windows on the west side of N. Barracks escaped having their eyes put out." They then hoisted the gun to the fourth floor of that barracks and attempted to fire another salute to the New Year. Fortunately, this effort failed and then more levelheaded leaders took command of the situation. Discipline in the corps of cadets had seemingly collapsed under DeRussy.

Though DeRussy had been more satisfactory to President Jackson than Thayer had been, he did not impress the new President, Martin Van Buren, who took office in March 1837. Van Buren had known Thayer for some years through Gouverneur Kemble's Saturday night soirees and admired the officer, his methods, and the school he had nurtured. DeRussy proved less satisfactory and Van Buren soon ordered his Secretary of War, Joel Poinsett, to find a new Superintendent. Poinsett, too, knew Thayer; he had been the president of the board of visitors for whom Thayer had reexamined the graduating class in

Cadets' summer encampment on the plain in 1835. The West Point Hotel, built in 1829, can be seen on the left. Lithograph by Seth Eastman. West Point Museum Collections, U.S.M.A.

Robert W. Weir *by David Huntington. c.*
1874. Oil on canvas, 30 × 25″. West
Point Museum Collections, U.S.M.A.
Photo: Philip Pocock.

Richard Delafield *by Charles C. Curran.*
c. 1910. Oil on canvas, 34 × 27″. Na-
tional Portrait Gallery, Smithsonian In-
stitution. Gift of Mr. Albert Delafield.

1833. However, instead of remembering that incident unfavorably, Poinsett admired Thayer for it, and was determined to reappoint him. Thayer, however, resisted so stubbornly that the Secretary finally agreed to look elsewhere, but he did exact a promise from Thayer that the latter would serve if no other suitable officer could be found. Thayer undoubtedly felt that his return would only precipitate renewed barrages from the Jacksonians—a prospect that might endanger the Academy.

The search for a new Superintendent went on for over a year, and in the meantime DeRussy stewed. "I long to resign the reins of this complicated and arduous Command into more able hands," he wrote Gouverneur Kemble, "and God knows, I will never envy the lot of the one selected for the Service; I have *seen* and *felt* enough of the difficulties attending the Superintendence of this Institution to be satisfied that nothing gratifying can grow out of it."

On February 19, 1838, a fire that heavily damaged the 1815 Academy building roused him from his lethargy. That structure had housed the engineering, chemistry, and natural philosophy departments, as well as the post headquarters, and the library. The fire destroyed much of the building and wholly undermined its structural integrity. The records of the post headquarters were completely burned, but the apparatus of the various departments and most of the books in the library had been saved.

Poinsett immediately instructed DeRussy to draw up plans and estimates for the required rebuilding and to determine what temporary measures would be necessary until permanent buildings could be constructed. The Superintendent responded that plans and estimates would be forwarded as soon as possible, but advised the administration that he planned to ask for two new buildings: the first for a library and natural philosophy instruction, and a second to house the chemistry classroom and laboratories. In the meantime, he proposed locating the library and all the academic departments in the new academic building just completed. "By next September all the Academic Exercises will commence in that Spacious Building," he wrote. The necessary renovations were rushed through and the academic departments did move into the new structure, although the library remained at the hotel where the books had been placed when they were rescued from the fire.

A month later, DeRussy forwarded to Washington the preliminary plans and estimates of costs for the new buildings he proposed. In appearance the new designs copied many of the features of the academic building that had just been completed. The structure to house the library and the natural philosophy department was to be a two-story structure with the library in one wing and classrooms in the other. The chemistry building was to be a small, one-story structure with a lecture room, laboratory, and recitation rooms for both chemistry and mineralogy. Both buildings featured low hip-roofs largely hidden behind railings all around, and arched openings on the first floor. The proposed buildings had a somewhat Italianate appearance—harmonizing well with the new academic building. DeRussy recommended locating the buildings to the rear of the destroyed Academy building, on line with the north faces of the new academic building and the chapel.

The administration approved DeRussy's plans but he was replaced in September 1838 and the actual construction was left to his successor.

The administration's choice to succeed DeRussy was Major Richard Delafield, who had graduated in 1818 at the head of his class. His had been the first class examined under Thayer. Unlike many of his classmates, Delafield had been won over by Thayer and his methods. He was an energetic officer with a large nose and a bustling manner. From the breadth of his activities during the first month of his superintendency, it is clear that he arrived with a mandate from the administration to restore order and direction. He possessed "clearsightedness [and] promptitude," wrote Dennis Hart Mahan, professor of en-

The old cadet chapel was built in 1836 and served the cadets and members of the post until 1910. During these years it occupied a site near the library, but when it was necessary to make way for new academic buildings it was removed stone by stone and rebuilt in its present location in the post cemetery. U.S.M.A. Archives.

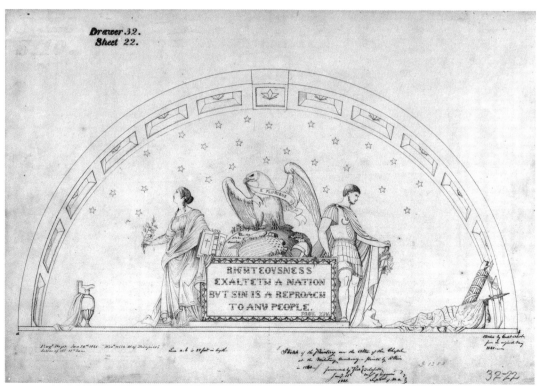

A sketch of the painting by Robert W. Weir called Peace and War that hangs over the altar of the old cadet chapel. This drawing was done by Cadet J.W. Abert in 1840. National Archives and Records Administration, Cartographic and Architectural Branch.

gineering, to Secretary of War Joel Poinsett, "and a determination to examine everything with his own eyes."

Not since the arrival of Thayer had a Superintendent shown so much energy. He reviewed the board of visitor reports beginning in 1820, and immersed himself in a quick review of the professional subjects being taught at the Academy. To the academic board, Delafield recommended the addition of geography and history, and suggested dropping the second year of French. And, he studied the plans which DeRussy had presented for the new library and the chemistry department.

Drawing was considered an essential element in the cadet's educational program. This drawing of Hercules Killing the Centaur was done in 1838 by Cadet William Tecumseh Sherman. West Point Museum Collections, U.S.M.A.

This evocative portrait of Alfred Sully (class of 1841) as a cadet was painted by his father in two days. Alfred Sully by Thomas Sully. c. 1839. Oil on canvas, 24 × 20″. Private Collection. Photo: Jim Strong, Inc., New York.

A small fire in North Barracks gave him an opportunity to call attention to the need for new barracks. "So inappropriately are these buildings [North and South Barracks] located and arranged for their safety, as well as that of the occupants," he wrote Charles Gratiot, the engineer chief, "that I shall bring the whole subject of buildings before the Department before commencing any new ones under existing appropriations." He would devise "an entire system" that would be "suited to the wants of the institution," he promised—a system "that when adopted shall not be departed from." He could not, he said, "reconcile it to my views of the best interest of the institution to commence the buildings of the Library, Philosophical, Chemical and Mineralogical Departments until some such System has been adopted." At the same time he wrote to Thayer who, in reply, admonished him "not to move a finger till a general plan for the entire new system shall have been matured & adopted."

Of even more immediate impact, Delafield set about restoring discipline. He clamped down hard on those who frequented Benny Havens's congenial establishment and forbade civilians in the area to sell either food or liquor to the cadets. He punished infractions of the regulations with a heavy hand, and ended DeRussy's practice of permitting students to attend officers' parties.

Not surprisingly, most cadets disliked Delafield, for he failed to administer his tough discipline with the same compassion that had mitigated the harshness of Thayer's rule. In addition, he was not popular with the other members of the garrison—nor did his popularity increase with time. When Delafield departed "there was many a dry eye at the dock," it was reported. To most cadets and officers he was perceived as mean and vindictive; his better side was seldom apparent.

Yet, Delafield did have a better side; he did sometimes show genuine concern and compassion for the cadets, and he was open to new ideas, particularly when they might benefit cadets. John Tidball claimed that Delafield saved him from dismissal upon learning that the charges against him had been made by an unfair and spiteful tactical officer. Delafield also acted in the cadets' behalf in other ways, and was not afraid to break with tradition. He lengthened the period between parade and supper, thus allowing cadets more time to bathe. And, he opened the library to cadets "all time when not on duty." He believed that it was irksome to cadets "to be confined in quarters the whole afternoon without employment." Of course, it did not escape him that at the library "they may innocently amuse, if not advantageously instruct themselves" and thereby reduce "the temptation to violation of the Regulations."

Delafield broke with tradition in other ways too. He replaced the side-button trousers which the cadets wore with flyfronts, much to the embarrassment of the ladies on post. Mrs. Delafield reportedly told her husband that "cadets thus dressed should not come in person to the house." Despite the protests of the wives, this style soon became regulation at West Point and throughout the Army.

Unquestionably, however, Delafield's greatest contribution came through his influence upon the physical development and growth of West Point. In November 1838 he appointed a board of three officers, Professors William H. C. Bartlett and Dennis Hart Mahan, and Captain Charles F. Smith, "to draw up a general design and project for the buildings [that were] becoming so necessary." During the early months of Delafield's administration it was the replacement of the destroyed old Academy building and the creation of a general plan to guide all future development that most occupied his time and energy. To assist them, Delafield and the board engaged the services of Isaiah Rogers, an architect from New York City. Rogers, who was noted for his work in Greek Revival architecture, had earlier designed the Astor House, a New York hotel, and was, at the time, supervising construction of the New York Merchants Exchange, one of his most significant works.

View of the Highlands and the Hudson River from West Point. Lithograph by Charles Parsons after Benjamin Bellows Grant Stone. c. 1859. 18 × 24". West Point Museum Collections, U.S.M.A.

Delafield's architectural board made its report in February, and recommended that—in addition to replacing the old Academy building which had burned down—both the North and South Barracks should also be replaced. The board also recommended relocating the buildings. "The present location of the barracks," they reported, "deprives the Institution of nearly, if not quite, one third of the plane [sic] for military manoeuvers."

Rogers's first designs reflected the Greek Revival style with which he was most closely associated. Delafield was dismayed: "They are in *no manner* suited to our wants, or the discipline of the corps—and would cost ½ a million. I cannot think of submitting them, being in principle worse than the existing buildings altho *very* elegant." Instead, encouraged by the interest Secretary of War Poinsett was taking in the project, Delafield provided his own "rough designs made in haste, of the first study for Barracks for Cadets." The next day he also sent a copy of these same sketches to Rogers, pointing out that they "combine the useful and desirable properties not heretofore named to you."

Disappointed with the Rogers's plans, a second architect, Frederick Diaper, was engaged. Diaper, who had been born and educated in London, and was most noted locally for his Italianate residences in the city, probably came to the attention of those at West Point because of his design of "Beverwyck," a home he was then building for William Paterson van Rennsselaer of Albany. Drawing on his English heritage and training, Diaper's first plan for the barracks, which he submitted in the spring, was in the "Gothic or Elizabethan" style.

Delafield was so taken by Diaper's Tudor-Gothic designs that subsequently no other style of architecture received any serious consideration. On June 3, 1839, in a long report to Joseph G. Totten, the newly appointed Chief Engineer, he summarized the work that had been done to date. Enclosed with the report were the plans for the barracks and library which had been submitted by the architects. Of the plans for the barracks only Diaper's work pleased him, though even with it he found serious problems in the details. "Another design after this style of Architecture has presented itself to my mind," he noted, however, and promised to submit his own drawings "at the time of asking approval."

Of the plans submitted by the architects for the library and the natural philosophy department, none were acceptable, Delafield reported. As a result he offered his own design which he recommended for approval—a Tudor-Gothic plan that clearly reflected Diaper's influence. Delafield's plan met with the immediate favor of both Totten and Poinsett in Washington, and after some minor modifications by federal architect Captain Robert Mills of the corps of engineers, it was formally approved.

Delafield's preference for the Tudor-Gothic, over the Classical Revival architecture that was then the accepted style in federal buildings, derived from the interplay between the architectural style and West Point's unique environment. Diaper's Tudor-Gothic was "not only pleasing to the eye," Delafield noted, "but suited to the scenery." A later generation of architects, following the same motif, would confirm this conjunction of style and setting with designs whose massive vertical walls seemed to spring from the rock itself—suggesting a unity there in the natural and the man-made.

Of course, the choice of the Tudor-Gothic had a historic logic that could hardly have escaped him. The origin of the Tudor influence was essentially military; in medieval England, where it had developed, the petty conflicts of the times usually centered around the homes of the warring barons. These homes therefore took on the character of forts possessing serrations called battlements along the tops of the walls, as well as corner towers, sally ports, moats, and narrow windows—all features contributing to the structure's defensive strength. Later, under the influence of a Gothic revival, these once functional features became merely decorative. By the last years of the eighteenth century, scores of massive country homes and public buildings with battlements and turrets sug-

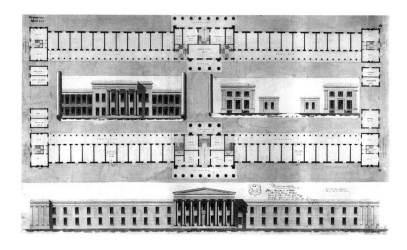

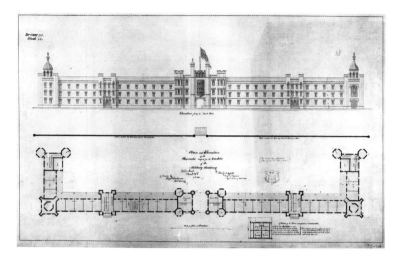

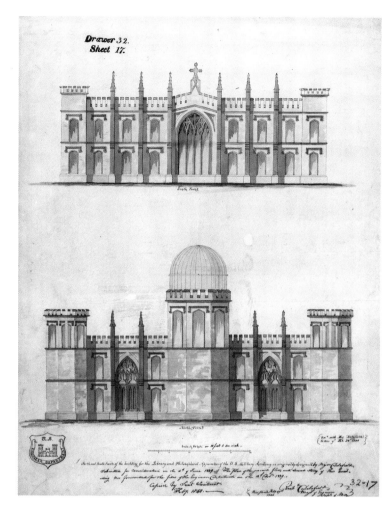

gestive of castles were being built in England. "The medieval Gothic is the most militant architecture of the modern Western world," wrote Professor Charles W. Larned, who guided a later era of reconstruction at West Point, "and this has been combined with the Tudor style—which has come through Oxford to embody academic education—in such a manner as to present an imposing and massive military ensemble which blends into the academic by gradual transition."

Delafield's general plan called not only for a radical departure in architectural style, but also in the placement of buildings. In line with the board's observation that the present location of the buildings was ill-conceived, Delafield recommended situating the new barracks and other future buildings along the eastern edge of the plain—on the bluffs overlooking the river, to the south of Fort Clinton. The proposed new barracks should be "placed on the Bank of the River and as near the Academic Halls as can be to economize the time of passing" between them. The new library was to be on one flank of the barracks—on the river side of the chapel, on the same line as the chapel and the new academic and exercise hall. A new mess hall was to be positioned "on the opposite flank" of the barracks—just south of Fort Clinton. Further, Delafield's plan called for that dilapidated fort to be restored and to be used as an ordnance and artillery compound. Totten, the Chief Engineer, visited West Point and inspected the sites proposed. He approved the location of the library, but deferred a decision on that portion of the general plan that placed future buildings along the eastern or river-side of the plain. The plan to renovate old Fort Clinton was rejected out of hand.

The new library was begun in 1839 following the Tudor-Gothic lines proposed by Delafield. It was completed in 1841. The east wing contained the library of about 20,000 volumes; in the west wing, on the first floor, were the offices of the Superintendent, the

Above upper left:
Plan of barracks for the cadets, as designed by the architect, Isaiah Rogers. c. 1839. National Archives and Records Administration, Cartographic and Architectural Branch.

Above lower left:
Delafield's 1840 plan and elevation of barracks for the cadets (as drawn by Captain Eastman) followed Diaper's design closely. National Archives and Records Administration, Cartographic and Architectural Branch.

Above right:
North and south fronts of the building for the library and philosophical apparatus, as originally designed by Major Delafield. National Archives and Records Administration, Cartographic and Architectural Branch.

Below left:
Plan, section, and elevation of the library, as drawn by Cadet E.G. Beckwith under the direction of Professor D.H. Mahan in 1841, as part of cadet exercises in drawing class. U.S.M.A. Library, Special Collections. Photo: Philip Pocock.

Below upper right:
Plan of the library, as drawn by Major Delafield in 1839. U.S.M.A. Library, Special Collections. Photo: Philip Pocock.

Below lower right:
It was the 1838 destruction by fire of this 1815 Academy building that prompted the round of construction undertaken by DeRussy and Delafield. National Archives and Records Administration, Cartographic and Architectural Branch.

adjutant and the treasurer and, above them, the lecture hall and apparatus of the natural philosophy department. Construction of the library on the approved site necessitated tearing down two buildings that had housed the ordnance shop and laboratory. A new ordnance compound with three stone buildings and a large yard enclosed by a stone wall, all similar in design and material to the Tudor-Gothic library, was constructed on a site approved by Totten just beyond and below the northern boundary of the plain, on a flat area that was then occupied by three small buildings—the post office, the Thompsons' house, and a set of officers' quarters. When these three structures were razed the Thompsons (and the small cadet mess they continued to operate) were moved into the old storekeeper's quarters that sat slightly behind the line of brick professors' quarters. Construction on the compound began in 1839 and was completed early the next year.

Delafield began immediately to seek approval and funding for new barracks, but it was not until 1843 that he succeeded. This was a period of renewed attacks on West Point and that may account for some of the delay. "You see by the notice I sent you," wrote Cadet William Dutton to a friend, "that great efforts have been made to abolish the Academy. But so far from proving successful—a 'bill' *has passed both houses* to build a new barracks . . . that will cost at least 150,000 dollars." Dutton assumed, correctly it seems, that the willingness of Congress to approve such large expenditures was a sure sign that the institution at West Point was in no serious danger.

Later the same year, with that appropriation in hand, a board of engineer officers met at the Military Academy to study the plans for the barracks and to consider the school's other requirements. They approved the Tudor-Gothic style Delafield favored and the barracks plan which is generally attributed to him—although in his design there is a clear debt owed to Diaper. The board, however, recommended disapproval of Delafield's scheme to locate the Academy's future buildings along the eastern perimeter of the plain. The board suggested instead that they be placed on the line of new buildings—the aca-

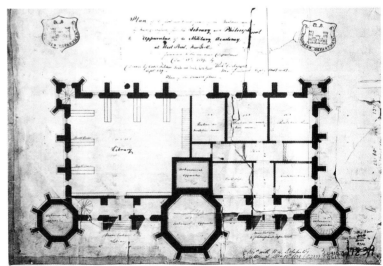

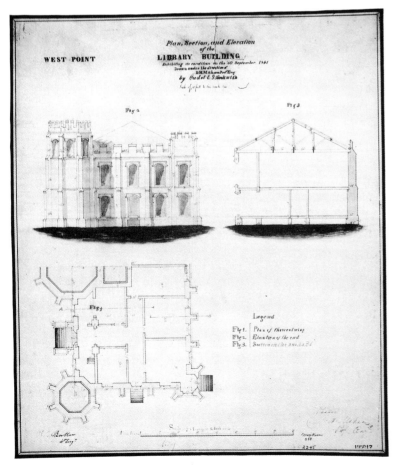

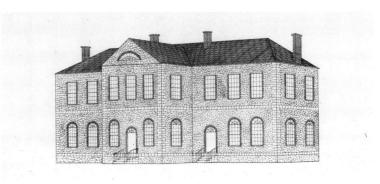

demic building, the chapel, and the library—that had recently been established along the south boundary of the plain. Delafield protested the board's action, but Poinsett approved their recommendations. It was the spring of 1845, only months before Delafield departed, that construction of the barracks finally began.

Delafield's West Point was becoming a "great stone castle," as one cadet put it, and such it would remain. "It is not desirable that any scheme should attempt to sweep the field clean and destroy architectural associations made honorable by generations of great men," wrote Larned, in 1901, as a massive new wave of construction was being considered. "It is of the highest importance," he continued, "to preserve intact the structural sentiment which gives character and individuality to the Academy."

The political attacks on the Academy that had begun early in Thayer's superintendency continued periodically into the 1840s. They centered on two issues: West Point's monopoly on Army commissions, and the large number of graduates who resigned their commissions. This clamor became so loud in 1838 that, when Congress authorized new regiments, it specified that some officers were to be drawn from civilian circles. The same year, there was legislation passed that lengthened to four years the active service required of Academy graduates. In 1843, when the Academy was again accused of being the breeding ground for an aristocratic officer corps, the institution began to collect data concerning the status of parents of each cadet. With that information in hand, friends of the Academy were able to respond that of 194 cadets at West Point the vast majority (156) came from families in moderate circumstances, while twenty-six came from homes of reduced means, and six came from families that were considered indigent. Only six came from wealthy families.

In truth, the Academy had never been in serious danger from these attacks. The institution had many friends, and even its sometime critics often voted for West Point whenever its existence seemed threatened. Since 1828, when Secretary of War James Barbour began the practice of seeking nominations for appointments from each member of the House of Representatives, Congressmen had come to value the opportunity to "appoint" cadets to the Academy. In 1843, Congress formalized this arrangement by authorizing House members to have one cadet each at the Academy and to name candidates whenever vacancies occurred in their district. Even in the absence of a more worthy rationale, this gave members a strong motive for defending the Academy against its enemies.

Captain Henry Brewerton, who had graduated from the Academy in 1819, succeeded Delafield on August 15, 1845. Brewerton's appointment as Superintendent generally coincided with the beginning of a period of growth and fulfillment at the Military Academy that commenced with the cessation of Jacksonian attacks and the conclusion of the Mexican War (in which West Point's sons had served with such clear distinction), and ended with the Civil War that was to make West Pointers famous throughout the world. Certainly, the period from the late 1840s through the end of the next decade was one during which the Congress was more favorable to the Academy than at any time previously. In this atmosphere, Brewerton did much to add to the convenience of life at West Point. He graded the surface of the plain, built the south wharf and the road leading to it, and enlarged the water supply. In 1850, he persuaded a telegraph company to run a line from New York and to establish an office at West Point. Of even more importance, he continued Delafield's general program of construction.

Brewerton assigned Captain Frederick A. Smith, instructor in practical engineering, to oversee the construction of the barracks. The west half of the barracks was completed and occupied in 1849, after which South Barracks was torn down. The east section of the new barracks and the central sally port was completed in 1851 under the supervision of Captain George Washington Cullum. The occupation of the final section of the new structure was followed by the demolition of North Barracks. Other new buildings followed in quick succession, a mess hall (1852), stables (1854), and a riding hall (1855).

From 1829, when the arrangement was dissolved by which Cozzens had provided meals for the officers in rooms at the west end of the cadet mess, until the fall of 1841, when Lieutenant Irwin McDowell was assigned to West Point, no sustained effort had been made to establish an officers' mess. McDowell, however, "was full of the mess question." After graduating in 1838 he had been assigned to the northern frontier where his regiment "came under the influence" of the British regiments opposite them. There his regiment formed the 1st Artillery Mess. It was "a very modest affair compared with those" which it emulated, McDowell noted, still "the mess life . . . had a great charm for me." When he arrived at West Point he immediately began to promote the same kind of formal mess he had known in his regiment. He had little immediate success, making only one convert, Lieutenant Alexander Shiras. That conversion, however, was a critical one because Shiras occupied a two-story brick house immediately behind the mess hall—one of those completed in 1817. His quarters provided adequate space in which to organize and operate a small mess, but, as McDowell put it, "we could not well set up a mess table on two legs only." To solve this problem, McDowell, the Academy's adjutant, arranged the immediate assignment to West Point of Lieutenant Henry Wayne, a former classmate also from the 1st Artillery, who was as much an enthusiast for a mess as McDowell.

Henry Brewerton by Daniel Huntington. c. 1874. Oil on canvas, 35 × 30″. West Point Museum Collections, U.S.M.A.

Upon Wayne's arrival, the mess was launched, being officially established on December 20, 1841 at the quarters of Shiras and McDowell. To purchase the necessary mess fixtures they levied an initiation fee of one-third of a month's pay—married officers (who would not take their meals there) to pay half that rate. And, in keeping with the mess traditions they copied, they prescribed that "the dinner costume of the Mess shall be the full uniform prescribed by the General Regulations of the Army with the exception of the sword, sword belt and cap." This meant that at dinner the members appeared in their swallowtail coats with their high-standing collars, gold lace, and epaulets—with a red sash at the waist. Delafield, the Superintendent, attempted to promote the mess by offering to purchase, with the Post Fund, "a complete service of plate" if the majority of the young officers would join. Still the officers demurred. "There was a decided hostility to the mess in the beginning," McDowell recalled. One reason for this, McDowell suggested, was that the officers resented the initiation fee, fearing that they might not stay long enough at West Point to benefit from their investment. Yet another "very potent cause" of early disaffection was pointed out by Professor Henry Kendrick who joined the mess in 1844. Kendrick insisted that the requirement that members should dine in full dress uniform was the principal objection to the mess. The evidence, however, suggests that it was the officers' dislike of McDowell or Delafield or both that caused them to withhold their support. McDowell believed that the Superintendent was the problem; he had been at odds with the single officers for some time over the issue of quarters assigned to them. But, it is just as likely that it was McDowell himself who was the problem, for in promoting the mess he had antagonized many of the single officers. "I was enthusiastic, & perhaps I was not judicious, or did not take my measures sufficiently with reference to the fact that others did not see the question as I saw it," he later admitted. In 1844, an influx of new officers to the Academy brought several new members to the mess, including Kendrick and Delafield. The next year, however, just days after the departure of McDowell and Delafield, a flood of new members joined, including a number who had earlier refused.

With the increase in 1844 to nearly a dozen resident members, the West Point Army Mess, as it was now known, outgrew its original small quarters and was allowed to move into rooms in the west end of the cadet mess. At the same time, the membership petitioned for a separate, new mess building to be located along the line of brick officers' quarters. Though agreeing in principle that a mess facility should be provided, the Chief of Engineers and Secretary of War did not approve of locating it in the midst of family housing. Totten suggested several alternatives, including special provision for the officers' mess in the proposed new cadet mess. That suggestion proved most agreeable to the members and, in 1852, large and elegant rooms, designed specifically for the mess, were provided in the new mess hall. In that building, on the floor above the mess, the officers were also permitted to establish a Billiards Club. Many of the married officers who had not joined the officers' mess were drawn to this club, although, in 1859, the two organizations merged.

After 1845 the mess became the center of social activity for the bachelor officers. They ate, drank, and entertained there. They took their seats at the mess table according to their military rank—the senior officer present sitting at the head of the table. No discussion of the affairs of the Military Academy was allowed at the table "before the removal of the cloth." No card playing was allowed in the mess parlor, and dogs were not permitted in any of the mess rooms. Ladies were admitted only on special occasions. Visiting officers were extended the "civilities of the Mess," and their first meal—as well as a bottle of wine of their choice—was paid for by the resident members. Here, they feted the new Superintendents, the new families on post, and the newly-wedded officers and their wives.

Of course, there were other activities for the officers, including a Shakespeare club and a chess club. But, just as the officers' mess was the focal point of their social life, the Napoleon Club was the center of their intellectual activity. Professor Mahan was president and he assigned the Napoleonic campaigns to be discussed by each member. Officers were allowed six weeks to prepare the papers and, finding ample authorities at the library, in both French and English, they worked diligently on them. When he was Superintendent, Robert E. Lee gave the club a room in the academic building. Under Mahan's close supervision, the walls were painted with large maps of the theaters of Napoleon's campaigns in Spain, Italy, and Germany. Here, the officers submitted their analyses of these campaigns to Mahan and their colleagues for review and discussion. Here, also, officers would sometimes take cadets to a lecture on a key battle or campaign.

These outlets for the energies of the young bachelor officers stationed at West Point were all the more important due to the inadequacy of the quarters usually assigned them. Quarters for the single officers had been included in the plans for South Barracks, but as the number of instructors grew, these accommodations became insufficient. Thayer had planned quarters for the surgeon and a number of bachelors in the wings of the cadet hospital that were completed in 1830. The surgeon and his family occupied one wing and the unmarried officers the other. In 1834, however, the single officers were turned out of these rooms to accommodate a married assistant surgeon. Still, relief did seem to be in sight; planning was already under way for the academic and exercise building, in which the whole upper story was intended to provide billeting for the single officers. They scarcely had settled into these quarters in 1838, however, when the 1815 Academy building was destroyed in a fire and their rooms were needed to replace the lost academic facilities. The single officers were once more forced out, as their quarters were transformed into a drawing academy and additional section rooms.

Delafield, who inherited this problem, did what he could to accommodate the unmarried officers, but he could not keep them happy. Finally, exasperated with one officer's complaints, the Superintendent pointed out that, if the officer wished to be reassigned, he "apprehended no difficulty whatever . . . in finding an officer to succeed" him. Henry Brewerton, who replaced Delafield in 1845, had more compassion. "It has been my desire

Below left:
Map of the Territory of New Mexico in 1846–47, drawn by Lieutenants J.W. Abert and W.G. Peck, both of whom were graduates of the United States Military Academy. The belt and buckle shown were worn by Topographic Engineers. West Point Museum Collections, U.S.M.A.

Below right:
Plan and elevation of proposed officers' quarters, as designed and drawn under the direction of Colonel Robert E. Lee, U.S. Corps of Engineers. National Archives and Records Administration, Cartographic and Architectural Branch.

and study to make this class of officer as comfortable as possible in respect to quarters," he wrote Totten, "well knowing that this has been a source of discontent heretofore, and that we could not expect to retain officers of merit at the Academy . . . unless this cause of complaint was to some extent removed." Brewerton made available to the single officers "some 20 or 30 fine rooms in the new barracks for Cadets," he reported, in addition to two former professors' quarters.

Not everyone agreed that the bachelors were well served when billeted in the cadet barracks. Officers should be "free from the disagreeable contact of cadets and the noise and disturbance to which they are continuously exposed in the barracks," wrote Captain George Cullum. Brevet Colonel Robert E. Lee (who replaced Brewerton) agreed, and he proposed constructing a building specifically for the unmarried officers. Early in 1854, he submitted handsome designs for such a structure, which were approved. However, Lee departed before more could be done. John G. Barnard, who followed Lee, was less sympathetic and put a halt to the project. "I feel myself some doubt about the expediency of erecting" the quarters for the unmarried officers, he wrote Totten, shortly after arriving, for "it adds nothing to the accommodation of married officers." He favored "the multiplication of cottages" for families, rather than the new bachelors' quarters. "So long as the Corps of Cadets is not increased," he argued, "the unmarried officers . . . [can] find quarters in the barracks."

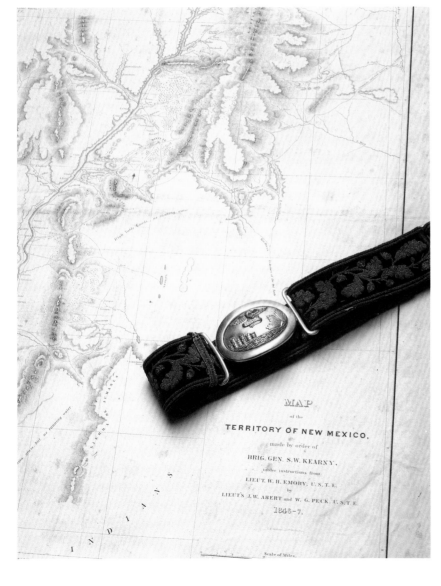

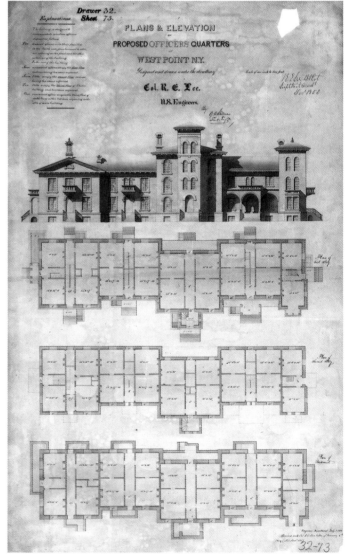

Robert E. Lee, who had succeeded to the superintendency on September 1, 1852, was the son of a Revolutionary War hero and a descendant of one of Virginia's first families. He had graduated from West Point second in his class in 1829 and had gone on to serve with great distinction in the Corps of Engineers. Lee had compiled an outstanding record during the Mexican War and was considered by many to be the most promising officer in the Army.

George Washington Custis Lee, the new Superintendent's oldest son, was a cadet when the senior Lee arrived, as was his nephew, Fitzhugh Lee, son of Robert's brother, Smith Lee. The new Superintendent, as a consequence, took a particular interest in the cadets, although he showed no partiality to his son or nephew. He invited cadets for informal visits on Sunday afternoons, to small dinner parties, and to more formal holiday affairs. On occasion, the Lees would use George Washington's silverware, thus honoring cadets and officers alike.

Lee was a man of dignity and grace, strikingly handsome, quiet, and patient. Wrote one cadet, "by his generous, manly and consistent conduct he has won the respect and esteem of every Cadet in the Corps." Lee was extraordinarily lenient with the cadets: some who ran away and returned a few days later were given another chance; one who lied to the officer of the day was forgiven when he confessed and convinced Lee that he had learned his lesson. By nature, Lee was not a disciplinarian, and could not bring himself to become one. He simply could not understand why cadets would not obey the regulations. He himself had completed his four years at West Point without a single demerit. One day, while riding with his younger son Robert, they came upon three cadets far off limits. Catching sight of Lee, the cadets jumped a fence and disappeared into the woods. Lee

The earliest known portrait of Robert E. Lee in the dress uniform of a Lieutenant in the U.S. Corps of Engineers, at the age of thirty-one. This painting was done in 1838 by William E. West. Courtesy of Washington and Lee University.

Cover for the "Song of the Graduates" in 1852 that was drawn by Cadet James Abbott McNeill Whistler. Anne S.K. Brown Military Collection, Brown University Library.

simply remarked: "I wish boys would do what is right. It would be so much easier for all parties."

The lax discipline of the period ideally suited one cadet, James Abbot McNeill Whistler, who entered the Academy in 1851, following in the footsteps of his father, George Washington Whistler, who had graduated in 1819 and had been an assistant teacher of drawing at the Military Academy from 1821 to 1822. The younger Whistler was to became one of the country's best-known artists, and even then, he was usually first in Professor Weir's drawing class. His fun-loving nature, however, sometimes got the better of him. On one occasion, while studying engineering drawing, he embellished a bridge by adding three young boys lounging on the structure. Reprimanded for having placed the boys on the bridge, Whistler made the drawing again, this time putting the boys on the river bank below the bridge. Reprimanded a second time and told to do away with the boys, he again drew the bridge, this time placing three small gravestones on the bank. His sarcastic wit, his habit of studying only that which interested him, and his tendency to ignore his military duties repeatedly got him into trouble. During an examination in chemistry, Whistler was asked to discuss silicon. "I am required to discuss the subject of silicon. Silicon is a gas—" he began. "That will do, Mr. Whistler," said the examiner, ordering him back to his seat. He failed chemistry and was dismissed. In later years, Whistler, who always retained an affection for West Point, would often say, "If silicon was a gas, I would be a major general today."

Cadet life at the Military Academy had changed little in the days since Thayer had departed. Until at least 1849, cadets occupied the same barracks, and, until 1852, ate in the same mess hall. The size of the corps of cadets had changed little from year to year—it usually numbered about 200. In 1846, cadet William Dutton described the "order" which dictated the arrangement of his barracks room. Except for the iron bedsteads, that had been introduced by Delafield (cadets who chose them paid a charge of twenty cents each month to defray the cost of purchasing them), the order could just as well have been dated any time in the previous quarter century. "Bedstead—against door; Trunks—under iron bedsteads; Lamps—clean on mantel; Dress Caps—Neatly arranged behind door; Looking Glass—between washstand & door; Books—neatly arranged on shelf farthest from door; Broom—Hanging behind door; Drawing books—under shelf farthest from door; Muskets—in gun rack and locks sprung; Bayonets in scabbards; Accoutrements—Hanging over musket; Sabres, Cutlasses & swords—hanging over muskets; Candle Box (for scrubbing utensils)—against wall under shelf nearest door & fire place; clothes—neatly hung on pegs over bedsteads; Mattress & Blankets neatly folded; Orderly Board—over mantel; chairs—when not in use under tables; Orderlies of rooms are held responsible for the observance of the above mentioned arrangement."

In 1847, in response to complaints about the poor physical conditioning of cadets, Henry Brewerton, the Superintendent, suggested organizing cricket clubs as a "means of healthful and manly exercise" during the months "when drill was suspended." Cricket, he pointed out, was "much in vogue in the British service" and was "highly conductive to physical development." But the cadets preferred football (a form of soccer). "It is amusing," wrote one, "to hear them complaining at drill of being almost tired to death, & then as soon as drill is dismissed their fatigue passes off & they all turn out & kick foot ball until parade. As soon, however, as they put on their belts for parade they suddenly become tired again, which lasts until after supper when they rest themselves by kicking the ball as hard as they can until call to quarters."

Messing arrangements were also not much changed, although contracting out had been replaced by the hire of a purveyor whose salary was independent of the number of cadets he fed. The purveyor was required to furnish a plain, but substantial soldier's regimen. For breakfast there was "the remains of the meat of the former day's dinner, cut up with potato with considerable gravy," bread, butter, and coffee. At dinner the fare was roast beef, veal, or mutton, boiled potatoes, and bread—green vegetables and sweets were almost unknown at the mess. At tea, the evening meal, there was bread, butter, and tea or coffee, supplemented occasionally by cornbread and molasses. The menu changed daily, but was repeated each week. For years, the main complaints had been that cadets were forced to wolf down their meals in order to finish on time, and that the food was boring. Now, under the purveyor system, the quality of rations also began to slip. When Jefferson Davis brought a congressionally appointed commission to West Point in 1860, they heard a chorus of complaints about the food. These, in turn, were followed by some quick, if not wholly effectual, remedies. "They have caused an improvement in our mess hall fare until it now presents a respectable appearance," reported Cadet Tully McCrea, shortly thereafter. "If the cleanliness only equalled the quality," he added, "I would be satisfied. But I see no change in that respect. Last night my coffee tasted so plainly of soapsuds that had not been rinsed from my cup that I could not drink it."

Life in the classroom, too, remained little changed. Once the section entered the recitation room the teacher would call upon a cadet who "immediately rises from his seat, arms himself with a piece of chalk and sponge," and would take his place in front of the blackboard. "Thus armed, and standing in the position of a Soldier, the subject which he is required to demonstrate is announced to him." The cadet then faced about "toward the board and, while some other one is demonstrating, performs the necessary work." In turn, each cadet would be required to demonstrate or explain his work.

The culmination of this academic work was a series of examinations in January and June. Failure in any subject was tantamount to dismissal. Cadets in the upper sections

CADET LIFE AT WEST POINT.—Sketched by Theodore R. Davis.—[See Page 426.]

Various scenes of cadet life at West Point are depicted in these drawings from Harper's Weekly, including a scene at the bottom in the center, show ing an examination before the board of visitors in the 1850s. U.S.M.A. Library, Special Collections. Photo: Philip Pocock.

usually had little to fear, but those of the lowest section—the "Immortals"—suffered considerable anxiety. During the examination, each cadet would be called upon in turn to discuss one of the more important subjects of the course. Shortly before the examination, the instructor in each section would list the subjects to be examined on separate bits of paper, shake them up in a hat, and then draw them out one at a time, recording the subject chosen on a roster of his students opposite each name in succession. For the "Immortals," getting an advance look at this list might mean the difference between a career as a civilian and a career as a soldier. This prompted a rather peculiar distortion of the code of honor by which, as gentlemen, they lived. While the corps would think it dishonorable to lie, or worse, to steal—including copying from another cadet's blackboard

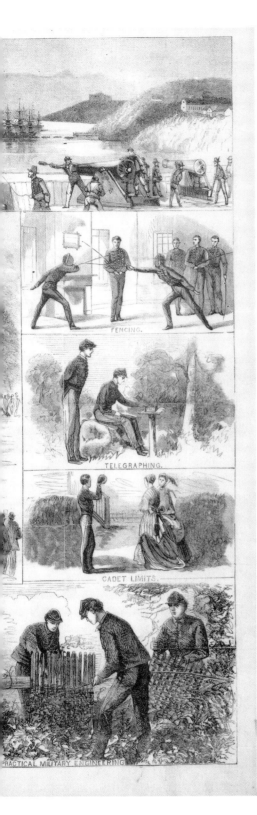

during a recitation or an examination—they seem to have adjudged that there was nothing wrong with an attempt to acquire the examination in advance. Faculty members, particularly the younger officers, often seem to have winked at the practice—while, at the same time, they did all in their power to defeat the efforts. Cadets would bribe their way past servants, steal into an instructor's house in the wee hours of the morning, and even enter offices through ventilator shafts to gain access to the lists. They were known to defeat locks and even to disassemble desks (and reassemble them when done) to copy these examinations. "You may think that is not altogether honest," one cadet admitted to his sweetheart after having recounted the escapade of another, but he insisted that the end justified the means.

Cadets could temporarily escape the harsh routine of the barracks and the section-room by several approved means: the debating and literary societies, informal sports, hiking, reading, and occasional organized entertainments. In addition, some engaged in unauthorized enterprises such as "running it" to Benny Havens, or to Garrison's Landing across the river, or even into New York City. Drinking or even possessing alcohol, visiting local taverns, or departing the post under any guise were offenses that risked dismissal, but this did not deter the more adventurous. Members of the opposite sex were yet another reason cadets strayed beyond the limits; more than once they brought young trollops to

the post and even into the barracks. This too, of course, invited almost certain dismissal if the offending cadets were caught.

The Dialectic Society was the sole authorized debating society almost immediately after its founding in 1824. It met on Saturday nights to read and critique members' papers and to debate topics which had been approved by the Superintendent. Over the years, these included: "Does the United States owe a greater debt to Thomas Jefferson or Alexander Hamilton?"; "Should capital punishment be abolished?"; "Ought females to receive a first-rate education?"; "Should nations go to war to preserve the balance of power?"; "Whether universal suffrage should be allowed?"; and "Has a state the right to secede from the union?". Only once did the Superintendent veto a topic; in 1843, Delafield re-

William H.C. Bartlett *by Robert W. Weir. c. 1871. Oil on canvas, 30 × 25". West Point Museum Collections, U.S.M.A.*

Alexander H. Bowman *by George C. Eichbaum. c. 1875. Oil on canvas, 30 × 25". West Point Museum Collections, U.S.M.A.*

fused to let the society debate the question: "Has a state under any circumstance the right to nullify an act of Congress?" There were also unauthorized groups, such as the Independent Roysterers Club, that were secretly organized "to promote social intercourse" among its membership. The Roysterers were most active from 1840 to 1842. This group thrived on raucous but largely innocuous revelry in North Barracks, and an occasional illicit foray to Buttermilk Falls. Though associations of this genre were generally limited in membership and short lived, the Military Academy was seldom without one.

Except for Christmas and New Year's—which were celebrated by suspension of classes for the day and a feast in the mess hall—Saturday nights were the only time cadets were allowed to attend entertainments. In the main, such activities included Dialectic Society productions, plays put on by the cadets, band concerts, and shows provided by an occasional touring troupe.

Possibly the greatest change in the life of cadets during this period came with the introduction of horses and riding lessons. In 1839, Secretary of War Poinsett overrode the opposition of the academic board and ordered that equitation be added to the program. To preclude foot-dragging on the part of the board he dispatched a sergeant, five dragoons, and twelve horses to West Point. Most cadets, once they had become proficient, enjoyed riding, but not everyone was enthusiastic about the new activity. More than a few faced the prospect with nothing more than grim determination, experience having taught them that the horse was likely to get the better of each encounter. One cadet got a measure of revenge, but was written up for "cruel and inhumane treatment of a dumb animal, i.e., he kicked his horse." In his defense he simply noted, "The horse kicked me first." But, for Ulysses S. Grant, a middling student otherwise, riding provided a chance to excel. He had grown up around horses—"horses seemed to understand him," his mother had said—and he was the most daring horseman at the Academy. Cadets often went to the riding hall just to watch him. "It was as good as any circus to see Grant ride," recalled a classmate. Once, before the board of visitors and a large crowd of spectators, he demonstrated his ability to handle his mount. The riding-master had one of the dragoons hold a pole parallel with the ground but at arms' length above his head—one end resting against the wall. He then signaled Grant, on York, his favorite mount, to jump it. The pair cleared the pole, and landed "with a tremendous thud," amidst a din of applause. To satisfy the crowd, Grant and York repeated the feat three more times.

During the early years of this period, West Point's academic board under the leadership of Dennis Hart Mahan (class of 1824), professor of engineering, 1830–71, chose two of the best of Thayer's disciples to head its departments: William H. C. Bartlett (class of 1826), professor of natural and experimental philosophy, 1834–71; and Albert E. Church (class of 1828), professor of mathematics, 1837–78. (Professors were appointed at the pleasure of the President, but were seldom removed; most stayed for years.) These men, with Mahan, were the nucleus of West Point's intellectual vigor. But there were others, too, who would play important roles at West Point in these years who had also come under Thayer's influence: Jacob W. Bailey (class of 1832) and Henry L. Kendrick (class of 1835), professors of chemistry, 1835–57 and 1857–80 respectively; and, of course, the Superintendents from 1838 to 1866—Delafield (class of 1818), Brewerton (class of 1819), Lee (class of 1829), Barnard (class of 1833), Alexander H. Bowman (class of 1825), and George W. Cullum. (The only Superintendents of this period who were not Thayer men were P. G. T. Beauregard, class of 1838, who served as Superintendent just five days in 1861, and Zealous B. Tower, class of 1841, who served only two months in 1864.)

Thayer's influence was pervasive, but it was Mahan who was the reigning spirit. It was Mahan who defended West Point in the press, Mahan who acted as confidential advisor to prominent public figures, and Mahan who exploited those connections to protect what he perceived to be the best interests of the Academy. Even more significantly, it was Mahan who guided the academic board for four decades and led it in its battles with the Superintendents who passed through West Point, and with the Army's hierarchy in Washington.

Mahan had a brilliant scientific mind—his *Course of Civil Engineering* was the leading text on the subject for decades—but he was more, he was the nation's leading war theorist. To his official title, professor of civil and military engineering, Mahan often added the words "and of the Art of War." His brief text *Advanced Guard, Outpost and Detachment Service of Troops with the Essential Principles of Strategy,* commonly known as *Outposts,* guided the military thought of two generations of America's professional soldiers. Still, his personality prevented him from winning the affection of cadets, for he was aloof and relentlessly demanding.

William H. C. Bartlett's interests were much narrower than Mahan's. As professor of natural and experimental philosophy, he concentrated on his own field, especially mechanics and astronomy, without venturing into other academic areas. But there, he achieved distinction. His *Elements of Analytical Mechanics,* first published in 1853, went through nine editions and was widely used in American colleges.

Bartlett, unlike Mahan, was a favorite of the cadets, for he went out of his way to interest them in the subject he was teaching—sometimes assembling the entire class in the lecture hall to demonstrate a point with the laboratory apparatus. Moreover, he had a flair for skillful questioning that could lead students to see his subject from a whole new perspective. "It was always easy to see he was able," wrote one former student, "but it was on such exceptional occasions that we knew he was great."

Albert E. Church, professor of mathematics, gained scholarly recognition with a widely used series of mathematical texts. He resembled Bartlett in his devotion to a single academic discipline, but he lacked his colleague's ability to stimulate his students' interest. Church was kindly and patient with students who sought his help, but he was not a dynamic classroom teacher. To cadets he seemed, as one put it, "an old mathematical cinder, bereft of all natural feeling." This may have been due, in part, to the fact that so many academic deficiencies occurred in the subject he taught. A sonnet, by an anonymous cadet, lamented the difficulty in which so many found themselves in Church's course:

Of all the girls I ever knew,
The one I've most neglected,
Is Called Miss "Anna Lytical,"
For her I've least respected.

Oh! Anna! Anna Lytical
I'll never love you more
For you, I fear, will cause my fall,
And make me leave the Corps.

Albert E. Church *by Daniel Huntington. c. 1875. Oil on canvas, 30 × 25". West Point Museum Collections, U.S.M.A.*

When questioned about the disproportionate percentage of academic failures in mathematics, Church's response was to suggest that cadets should devote more time to his subject. To accomplish this, he recommended eliminating some of the non-scientific subjects from the curriculum. Since the mathematics program—which dominated the first two years of the curriculum—supported both engineering and natural philosophy, Church could count on both Mahan and Bartlett to join him on the academic board in resisting outside attempts to modify his program. In this, they were always successful.

Though the academic board was presided over by the Superintendent, its decisions were made by majority vote. The board, which had come to fruition during the Thayer era, was the most powerful entity at West Point. And, in matters over which the board had primacy, Mahan, Bartlett, and Church usually had their way. These three men set the intellectual tone for the Academy. Throughout this period, the board enjoyed a large degree of autonomy in governing the institution; they designed instructional programs, selected texts, and passed on curriculum changes. And, they examined cadets, determined order of merit standing, recommended graduates for branches of the Army, and decided whether students found deficient at the semiannual examinations should be allowed a second chance.

But the academic board did more: it acted as a buffer between the academic program at West Point and those outsiders who tried to effect change. Only once, between 1838 and 1854, were board members defeated on a major matter—in 1839 they had been forced by the Secretary of War to introduce riding. In a hierarchical organization such as the Army (where obedience to the orders of superiors in the chain of command was ingrained) the academic board provided a means of resisting unwanted change. The board could usually "study" an issue until it simply disappeared; it would postpone action while one committee and then another weighed every aspect of the problem—until the troublesome Superintendents or Secretary of War let the matter slip or moved on. Upon the rare occasions when that strategy failed, it was often able to frustrate the implementation of changes board members found odious. And when it could not, it was usually able to outlast its foe and ultimately reverse the decision. Although there might be internal strife, the board stood united as an unyielding bulwark against outsiders. It provided a mechanism by which essential institutional stability was maintained. Without it, each new Superintendent or Secretary of War could have whipsawed the program as he saw fit.

The academic board was repeatedly called upon to defend the scientific orientation of the curriculum and the heavy emphasis placed on mathematics. One of the first cases occurred when a board of officers (headed by Winfield Scott) was convened in 1843 to study the Academy. They took issue with what they considered undue stress on these subjects, and called for an increase in practical military training. The academic board responded that all officers needed a basic knowledge of mathematics, science, and engineering, and that mathematical training developed mental discipline. Moreover, they pointed out, only the upper sections went beyond the scope of courses taught in civilian colleges. "One of the most important objects of the Academy," the academic board argued, was to provide "a thorough course of mental as well as military discipline." And this, they argued, was best accomplished through "a strict sense of mathematical and philosophical study." The ideal vehicle to attain this was the course, as they taught it—"the result of the experience of many years." "The officer whose mind has been thus disciplined," they argued, could serve effectively "in whatever station the interests of the service may place him." This argument, which was repeated whenever the curriculum came under attack, always seemed to disarm the critics.

Lieutenant General Winfield Scott. 1862. U.S.M.A. Library, Special Collections. Photo: Philip Pocock.

Proposals for curriculum change or revision—whether generated externally or internally—were the issues that most concerned the academic board. The regulations specified that no more than ten hours daily be devoted to academics, including both classroom time and study periods, and each department fully utilized every minute of its allocation. Meals, formations, and other duties occupied much of the remaining time, leaving cadets with barely two hours for recreation. Because that schedule was so crowded, a new course could only be introduced by shortening or eliminating an existing one. Even a slight modification of the curriculum required painstaking study, planning, and interdepartmental haggling. The sheer complexity of making a change often militated against it.

The first major alteration in the curriculum occurred in 1854 during Robert E. Lee's superintendence. For several years the boards of visitors had been recommending the addition of courses in the humanities and an increase in military training. In Washington, Totten, the Chief of Engineers, became a champion of this idea. Despite the academic board's insistence that there was no time available in the curriculum for these subjects, the campaign for change continued. The only way to include new courses, the academic board reported, would be to extend the course from four to five years. This, they were certain, would be as unpalatable to those in Washington as it was at West Point. But they did not reckon with Totten's determination. Finally, in 1854, he gained the support of Secretary of War Jefferson Davis. To the chagrin of all at West Point, Davis ordered the academic board to inaugurate a five-year course. In this case, Mahan and the board could not resist. To ensure that the reforms were carried out as intended, Davis's implementing directive specified that none of the additional time would be allocated to engineering, natural philosophy, French, drawing or chemistry. Instead, the increase would be devoted to adding new courses in Spanish, history, geography, and military law, and in augmenting existing programs in English and military training. It was the most significant defeat the academic board had ever suffered—although the last act had yet to be written.

In 1858, the academic board petitioned a new Secretary of War, John B. Floyd, for a return to the old system. They argued that not only was the five-year program intellectually exhausting for the cadets, but it also diverted the students' time and attention from vital scientific subjects. As far as the majority of the academic board was concerned, West Point should abandon the humanities, reduce military training to its pre-1854 status, and return to its old preserves: mathematics, science, and engineering. At first, Floyd backed the board and ordered the reinstatement of the four-year program, but later he reversed himself. Finally, the five-year program was abolished in 1861, at the outbreak of the war. At the war's end its two main supporters had been removed—Totten had died, and Davis was discredited. The program was never reestablished. The newly-added courses were either dropped quietly or dramatically scaled back. The academic board had simply outlasted its opponents.

Another issue had arisen in the spring of 1855, when Lee accepted a transfer to cavalry in order to gain a promotion. The law required that the Superintendent be from the Corps of Engineers; thus Lee would have to be replaced. Jefferson Davis, the Secretary of War, neither wanted to deny Lee the promotion (which he was unlikely to receive for several years in the engineers) nor to see West Point lose him. There was, however, no immediate recourse—although later that year, Davis recommended that the superintendency be opened to officers of all branches of service. Opposition was raised throughout the engi-

West Point from the plain, showing the barracks, the chapel, and the library, c. 1855. West Point Museum Collections, U.S.M.A.

View of the United States Military Academy at West Point in 1857. U.S.M.A. Library, Special Collections. Photo: Philip Pocock.

neer corps and the proposal was defeated. Davis, however, renewed this effort with more success in 1860.

Engineer Captain John G. Barnard relieved Lee on April 1, 1855. In Barnard's case, the requirement that the Superintendent be an engineer had the peculiar effect of placing him over the more senior Major William H. T. Walker, an infantry officer and the Commandant of Cadets. An act of Congress the next year solved the problem by giving the temporary rank of colonel and lieutenant colonel to the Superintendent and Commandant of Cadets respectively. Barnard's tenure as Superintendent was brief—lasting less than a year and a half—and generally uneventful. In September 1856, Richard Delafield was sent back to West Point and once again assumed command.

When Delafield returned to the post on the Hudson, he immediately undertook a thorough review of the Academy's operation—much as he had at the beginning of his first tour. "He is a pretty keen old fellow, who has poked his long nose into everything you can think of since he has been here," wrote Cadet Henry du Pont. But Delafield was a strict disciplinarian and, after the lax years of Lee and Barnard, his efforts to restore discipline aroused considerable animosity. Moreover, his manner of sarcastic reprimand further embittered cadets. "He is arbitrary—a hypocritical and deceitful man," wrote one. "I have concluded that he is insane," wrote another.

Delafield's task was complicated by the temper of the times. The issues that had begun to divide the nation and would lead to civil war were as evident at the Military Academy as elsewhere. Although there was some tendency toward unity at the Academy, due to the nature of the school as a national institution, it was not possible to suppress all of the sectional biases that the cadets brought with them. "I have had the good fortune to make many friends among [southerners] both here and at College and I find in them almost everything you would wish in a gentleman," wrote a cadet to a recently graduated comrade. But then he added, "You have observed, however, as well as myself, at West Point rather too much of sectional feeling on some occasions." The cadets reflected the feelings that were current in their home communities, and correspondence with family, hometown newspapers, and furloughs kept that localist spirit alive.

Sectional feelings were not only brought to West Point, they were also injected into life there by the events and debates of the times. The reaction to John Brown's raid on Harper's Ferry in October 1859, showed that quite clearly. The news of Brown's raid, and of his trial and subsequent execution, was followed with intense interest and furious debate at the Military Academy. "In each scene of the tragedy West Point was deeply engrossed," recalled Morris Schaff.

Delafield kept a tight rein on that debate. He kept a particularly close eye on the activities of the Dialectic Society. Delafield had had earlier run-ins with that organization concerning such issues. In 1838, there had been "an animated discussion" concerning "the justice of lynch law." That debate had "got very warm" and "came very near merging into the discussion of abolition." Sectional aspects of the log-cabin and hard-cider presidential campaign of 1840 had also been reflected in the Dialectic Society debates when the cadets asked, "Ought the South to prefer William Henry Harrison to Martin Van Buren at the coming Presidential Election." In fact, the Dialectic Society had become so much an agency of division that, in September 1842, the academic board complained that the society had "given rise to improper feelings" and recommended its "dissolution . . . as soon as circumstances will permit." The next spring, when the society proposed to debate the question: "Has a state under any circumstances the right to nullify an act of Congress?", Delafield intervened, forbade the topic, and effectively disbanded the organization. When Superintendent Henry Brewerton replaced Delafield, in 1845, he was asked by the cadets to revive the organization and he did so, but with the explicit warning that the organization must be "governed by wholesome rules, and the discussion of subjects [must be] confined within proper limits." The society's subsequent restraint appears to have kept them out of trouble with the Academy's leadership, but at a certain cost. Unable to take on the central issues of the times, the society was nearly moribund by the late 1850s.

John Brown at his arraignment before the federal court at Charleston, S.C. for his raid on Harper's Ferry. Drawing by James E. Taylor. The Bettmann Archive.

To Dr. Thomas Featherstonhaugh. with Compliments. James E. Taylor. John Brown arraigned before the court at Charleston.

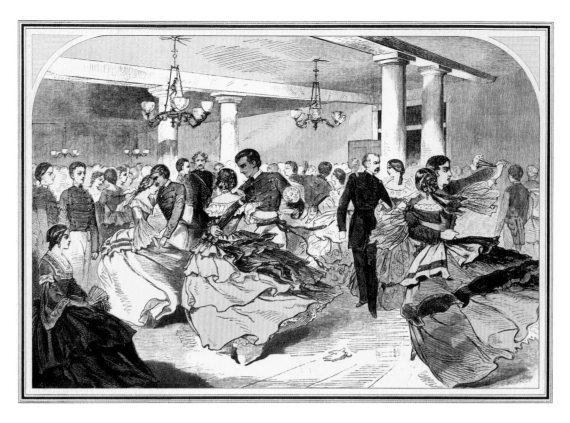

A Cadet Hop at West Point *by Winslow Homer. c. 1859. Anne S.K. Brown Military Collection, Brown University.*

Until the mid-fifties, sectional sentiment at West Point had only occasionally erupted into open hostility. From that time onward, however, sectional feelings grew steadily more intense and overt. Fights between Northerners and Southerners became commonplace. In the summer of 1856, Dodson Ramseur of North Carolina wrote home that he was looking forward with pleasure to punishing severely any miserable abolitionists in the new plebe class. Emory Upton, who entered the Academy that summer, had previously been a student at Oberlin College in Ohio, a radical school that admitted both women and blacks. Upton, a staunch abolitionist, was the object of much attention from the Southern upperclassmen. In 1859, Ramseur's roommate, Wade Hampton Gibbes, of South Carolina, made an offensive remark concerning Upton's supposed intimacies with Negro girls at Oberlin. Upton demanded an apology, Gibbes refused to give one, and Upton challenged him to a duel. They met that night with swords. As a crowd of cadets gathered on the first floor of the barracks the two went upstairs into a darkened room. When the affair was finished, Upton had received a cut on the face—a scar he would carry the rest of his life.

As the national crisis approached, even the strongest ties of friendship at West Point became strained. A mounting bitterness seeped into the corps from every side. The political parties, harried and divided by slavery, had named their candidates. Lincoln was the Republican standard-bearer, and the remnants of the Whig Party, (out of which the Republicans had grown), nominated John Bell of Tennessee. The splintered Democrats nominated Stephen A. Douglas of Illinois, and Southern radicals, seceding from the party, nominated John Breckinridge of Kentucky. In October 1860, a month ahead of the election, a group of Southern cadets decided to hold a straw vote at West Point. "A better scheme to embroil the corps and to precipitate hostilities between individuals could not have been devised," wrote Schaff. When Lincoln received 64 votes the Southerners promptly appointed tellers for each division to interrogate cadets personally and discover the names of "the Black Republican Abolitionists" in the corps who had voted for him. The interrogations produced violent confrontations. Fistfights broke out everywhere.

The intransigence of the Southern cadets only intensified with the actual election of Lincoln on November 6, 1860. On the 9th, South Carolina called a Secession Convention,

and, at West Point, on the 19th, Henry S. Farley of South Carolina handed in his resignation—the first member of the corps of cadets to withdraw in response to Southern secession. Before the end of the year, he was joined by most of the other South Carolina cadets, three others from Mississippi, and two from Alabama. Two other cadets resigned in January 1861, four more in February, and another four in March. A few officers also departed—the leave-takings sometimes turning into mournful occasions.

On January 23, 1861, Delafield was relieved by Captain Pierre G. T. Beauregard. Beauregard, of Louisiana, had been appointed in late December 1860, during the closing days of John B. Floyd's term as Secretary of War. Joseph Totten, long time Chief of Engineers, had nominated Beauregard in an attempt to thwart Jefferson Davis's renewed effort to open the superintendency to officers of all branches of the Army. Beauregard had a reputation for brilliance as an engineer and, equally important, many well-placed political connections. The combination, Totten hoped, would make it embarrassing, if not impossible, for Davis and his allies to oppose his nomination—thereby undercutting Davis's effort.

Beauregard, however, was relieved of his new command just five days after he assumed it. The new Secretary of War, Joseph Holt, was informed that Beauregard planned to resign as soon as his home state of Louisiana left the union. Holt fully understood the devastating impact of having a sitting Superintendent resign to join the rebellious South. Holt immediately ordered Delafield to reassume command at West Point, and, on January 28th, the old Superintendent once again took up the now familiar reins. He remained in command until March 1, when he was relieved for the last time by Major Alexander H. Bowman.

On April 12, 1861, less than three months after having been relieved at West Point, Colonel P. T. G. Beauregard, CSA, ordered the Confederate shore batteries in Charleston Harbor to open fire on Fort Sumter—the opening salvos of the War Between the States. The next day, the officers, professors, and cadets at West Point were ordered to take a new oath of allegiance. Those who refused were dismissed. By April 22nd, only those from the Southern states who intended to stay with the Union remained at the Academy. Of

Above left:
Many notable Europeans have visited the Academy, including the Prince of Wales in 1860, as seen in these illustrations from Harper's Weekly. U.S.M.A. Library, Special Collections. Photo: Philip Pocock.

Above right:
In 1861, symbolic of the division that would occur throughout the country during the Civil War, Colonel Beauregard, former Superintendent of West Point, fired upon Major Anderson, former Artillery instructor at the Academy, who was stationed at Fort Sumter. Woodcut. The Bettmann Archive.

the 278 cadets at West Point on November 1, 1860, eighty-six had been appointed from the Southern states. Of these, sixty-five were discharged, dismissed, or resigned for causes connected with secession.

On May 6th, the first class (now in their fifth year at the Academy) was ordered to Washington, D.C. They were commissioned and immediately assigned to units of the growing Union Army. They did not even have a formal graduation ceremony. The new first class, which had already spent nearly four years at West Point, immediately petitioned that they, too, be allowed to take the field. In June, their petition was granted. They were hastily examined and graduated, and ordered to the capital. As soon as they were commissioned, they were assigned to train the "three month" regiments then encamped around Washington.

At the outbreak of hostilities, the Military Academy immediately reverted to the more familiar four-year curriculum. The fourth class undertook mathematics and French, along with some English and geography. The third class continued the study of mathematics and French, as well as drawing and riding. The second classmen had courses in natural and experimental philosophy, chemistry, drawing and riding. The first class studied military and civil engineering, the science of war, ethics, law, mineralogy and geology. In addition, military science was taught in each of the four years. It was a curriculum that was remarkably similar to that of a decade—even two decades—earlier, and it remained fairly stable throughout the war.

Other features of the Academy's operation were thrown into turmoil. Early in the conflict, the officer personnel of the academic and tactical staffs were in constant flux. In 1861 alone, thirteen officers applied for and received orders for service in the field. The Superintendent, Alexander Bowman, complained in September that instruction in artillery and cavalry had to be totally suspended because of the lack of officers, horses, and guns. As the war progressed, the able-bodied officers were replaced by those who were paroled or disabled, or by appointees from civil life, but these substitutes were not always properly qualified. Some fell short of the intellectual requirements, while others, whose wounds were slow to heal, were physically unable to fully carry out their duties. The turnover rate among these instructors was high and extended absences were frequent. This often necessitated a return to the unsatisfactory expedient of employing cadets as teachers. It was not until the last months of the war, in 1865, that a sufficient number of qualified officers became available to restore a measure of stability.

Despite these difficulties, academic studies were continued without interruption throughout the war—except for one brief period during the New York City draft riots in the summer of 1863. At that time, the Superintendent was ordered to dispatch a detachment of several officers and fifty-nine men to the city to help restore order—essentially the entire regular force at West Point. This left the cannon and powder magazines at the Academy unprotected at a time when rumors were rampant that the New York mob intended to march up the Hudson and seize the material. These fears, though baseless, caused the staff at West Point some anxious moments; ball cartridges were issued to cadets, guards were posted, and pickets with field guns were established at the South and North Docks and Gee's Point. This vigilance was maintained for several days.

Although far from the front, each campaign and battle of the war was followed with close attention at West Point. Spirits rose and fell with the fortunes of war. In the early years of the war, the President's calls for days of fasting and prayer were observed solemnly, but, as fortunes changed, the days of victory were a cause for thanksgiving and rejoicing. In the fall of 1864, one-hundred gun salutes were fired in honor of the victories at Mobile Bay and Atlanta, and in December of that year a salute of thirty-six guns was ordered in honor of "General Sherman's gift to the nation of the city of Savannah."

Cadets at West Point in 1863. U.S.M.A. Archives.

Major Zealous B. Tower became Superintendent in July, 1864, replacing Alexander Bowman. Tower had been first in his graduating class in 1841 and afterwards had stayed on to teach at the Academy. One of Tower's former students, General Ulysses S. Grant, had only recently been made Commanding General of the United States Army. Interest in Grant, therefore, was high, and stories of Grant's high jinks as a cadet enjoyed great currency.

One story involved both Grant and Tower. Cadet Franklin Gardner (who later became a major general in the Confederate Army) had brought into Tower's engineering class a huge heirloom watch, some four inches in diameter. It was being passed from hand to hand when Tower arrived. It was Grant who found himself with the watch at that point and he hastily stuffed it under his coat, which he carefully buttoned down. A few moments later, Tower sent four cadets, including Grant, to the board to work out problems. Grant finished his figuring, put down his chalk and, on Tower's instruction, began to explain what he had done. Suddenly the old watch in his coat began striking the hour—*bong, bong, bong*. Lieutenant Tower first thought the noise was coming from the hall and closed the door, but the *bongs* only got louder. Now, furious at some obvious cadet prank, Tower began hunting under desks and in closets for the source of the disturbance. While the rest of his class struggled to maintain their composure, Grant calmly continued his mathematical recitation. Eventually Grant out-talked the alarm and sat down. Only years later did Tower learn the origin of the clangor.

The wartime Superintendents, Alexander H. Bowman, Zealous B. Tower, and George W. Cullum, were faced with numerous challenges, but none more troublesome than the criticism repeatedly leveled at West Point because of the large number of cadets and graduates who had deserted the Union. To make matters worse, one of the main critics was Secretary of War Simon Cameron. In his 1861 annual report, he singled out the militia and volunteers for praise, and then attacked the Military Academy. Its graduates were bound "by more than ordinary obligations of honor to remain faithful to their flag," Cameron argued. He blamed the defections on the disciplinary system at West Point which, he insisted, failed to distinguish between immorality and simple violations of regulations. He argued that it encouraged cadets to substitute "habit for conscience." A number of Radical Republicans in Congress joined Cameron in his attacks on the Academy. Early Union defeats and McClellan's lack of aggressiveness, some charged, stemmed as much from lukewarm patriotism as from incompetence. Others simply echoed the old Jacksonian complaints: there was an aristocratic tone in the Regular Army; and there was discrimination which regulars, in particular West Point graduates, practiced against militia and volunteer officers.

The champions of West Point won a critical battle in 1863 when they defeated a Radical Republican effort in Congress to abolish the Military Academy by killing its appropriation. By then, however, the improving fortunes of the Union forces under Grant, William

A Pic-Nic on the Hudson by Thomas Prichard Rossiter, c. 1863. Oil on canvas, 29 × 45". The Julia L. Butterfield Memorial Library, Cold Spring-on-Hudson, New York. Included in the painting are Professor Robert W. Weir, Miss Louisa Weir, Miss Cora Weir, and General Truman Seymour.

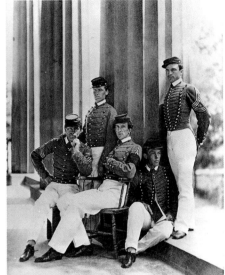

Above left:
Cadets assemble behind the old bar-racks in 1863. Culver Pictures.

Above right:
Cadets of the class of 1863. U.S.M.A. Archives.

T. Sherman, George H. Thomas and other graduates (coupled with the less than sterling performances of non-West Pointers such as Benjamin F. Butler, John C. Fremont, and Daniel E. Sickles) had reduced the impact of the anti-West Point attacks. Moreover, it did not escape anyone's attention that the successes of the South had largely been engineered by West Point graduates. Even the final victory in 1865, however, did not completely silence the voices of hostility and suspicion, or prevent new criticism after the war.

Still, West Point had much of which to be proud. West Point graduates, taken as a group, acquitted themselves valiantly in combat, just as they had earlier in Mexico and against the Indians. But there was a difference in the Civil War. Prior to 1861, no graduate had attained the rank of general officer in the line of the Army. In this war, graduates of the United States Military Academy had stepped forward and had led the armies of both the North and the South. At the conclusion of the struggle, all of the forces in the field on both sides were commanded by graduates; nearly all the corps, and a majority of the divisions. Every important battle of the conflict had been commanded by a graduate on one or both sides—generally both. Of the sixty most critical battles or campaigns, all but six were commanded on both sides by West Point graduates. Of the exceptions, a graduate commanded one side in every case, and was victorious on all but one occasion. Equally significant, it was almost exclusively Academy graduates who performed the Herculean logistical feats that had sustained the largest armies the world had ever known—that, in fact, had made a new modern form of warfare possible.

This outcome served to validate the approach the Academy had employed since Thayer had taken the helm, and for many years it nurtured the institution in the belief that this was the approach that would best secure the future. For better or for worse, the Academy, for years to come, would bask in the glory of the accomplishments of its graduates in that titanic struggle between the North and South.

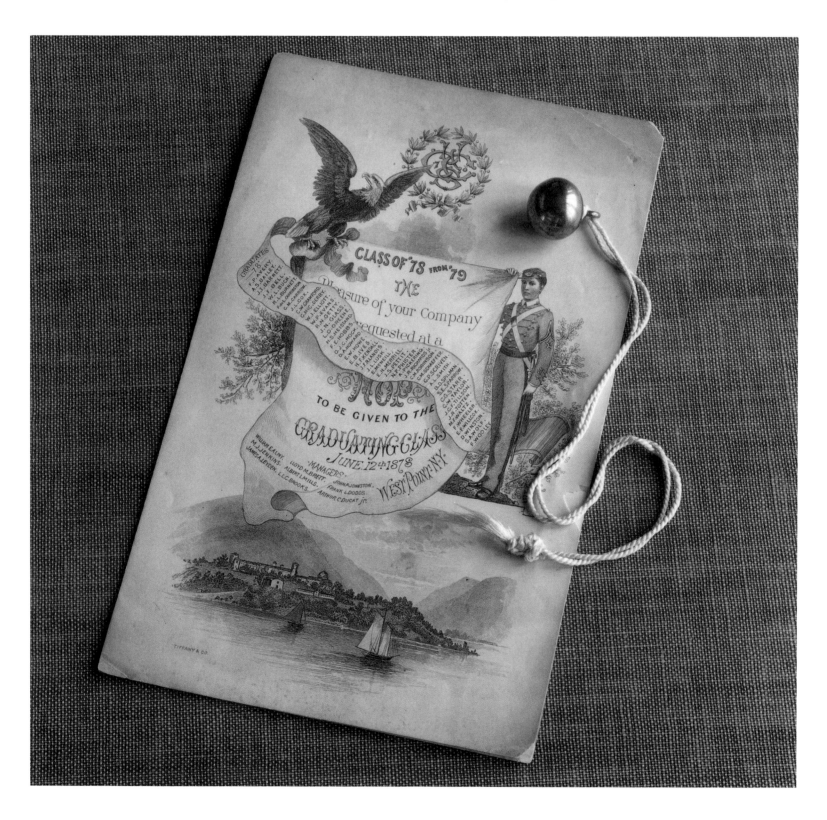

During the winter of 1865–66, a small group of second classmen conceived the idea of forming their own billiards club—an illicit one, of course, for no such thing was permitted by the regulations. The very idea of such an undertaking would have been unthinkable only a year before, but now the war was over and a new standard of behavior seemed acceptable. In searching the barracks for a safe location, the cadets discovered a small auxiliary coal room hidden behind the huge coal bunkers in the cellar under "C" company. They bought the silence of the furnace tender, ordered a table from New York, and set about emptying and cleaning their new club room. They boarded up the window and filled the opening with tanbark to deaden the sound of the balls. They installed a stove, a card table, a half-dozen chairs, four kerosene lamps with reflectors, a supply of pictures on the walls, a stock of pipes and tobacco, a keg of cider, a barrel of crackers, and a whole cheese—everything needed to furnish a first-class billiards room.

The table was shipped to a willing individual in the town of Garrison, and then, one night, transported across the ice and cautiously up to the barracks where it was carefully and quietly carried to the newly decorated club room.

The secret was well kept for two or three months, until a voucher from the manufacturer came to the attention of the Academy's treasurer. Obviously the cadets had purchased a billiard table! But where had they put it? The officers conducted several searches through the barracks, through the attic among the timbers and cobwebs, and through the washrooms in the basement of the barracks—but not the coal bunkers which were still piled high. They even went so far as to search some of the houses in the vicinity of the barracks. The members of the club were so careful that their visits to the billiards room continued to go undetected. Meanwhile, the club was in full operation and the membership had grown to about thirty.

The table was little used during the summer, but in the fall and early winter the club members (now first classmen), once again availed themselves of its privileges. Late one night in November, however, two officers who were returning from the mess spied some cadets stealing into the 6th division. Anticipating that they might discover the phantom billiard table, the officers followed the unwary cadets into the basement hall and watched them disappear into the coal bins. A door opened and a flood of light filled the passage. The click of balls confirmed the officers' suspicions. The officers held a whispered consultation. Should they break in immediately, or wait and burst in with the other officers the next night? They decided to wait.

The officers' discovery had in turn been observed, however, and their conversation overheard. Upon learning of their narrow escape, the club members decided to yield in style. The room was put in order, the balls spotted on the table, and a note was left for the officers. Early the next evening, the lamps were lit and the room abandoned for the last time. When the officers arrived they found the neat and brilliantly-lit room, as well as the billiard table they had so long sought. But try as they might, the authorities could

find no further clue as to the club's membership, and the matter was allowed to drop. The table was placed in the Commandant's quarters, where it stood for years.

Billiards and other temporary diversions aside, cadets in the post-war era lived in much the same way as had their predecessors. The barracks built in 1851 had coal-fired boilers that provided steam heat. (The steam pipes inadvertently provided the cadets with a useful means of signaling the approach of an inspecting officer.) In time, gas lighting was added and running water was installed in the basements to provide water for the boilers, though there were still neither baths nor toilets in the barracks. Baths, lavatories, and commodes were in a long low building at the rear of the barracks known as the "cadet sinks." Cadets who did not bathe at least once a week were reported and punished. Clothes were washed twice a week at a central laundry, and cadets who did not turn in laundry also drew demerits.

Punishment still meant walking guard tours or "extras" on the "area." This entailed marching back and forth in a prescribed area behind the barracks in full uniform with the rifle at shoulder arms. Some spent hour after hour walking the area with nothing but the gloomy stone walls and fellow sufferers to gaze upon.

Of course, time did bring some changes. Since 1808 the Thompsons—the widow and then her daughters—had provided meals for about a dozen select cadets who enjoyed not only the excellent food and the opportunity to linger over it, but also the homelike atmosphere of the Thompson household. In 1878, with the death of Miss Amelia Thompson, the eldest and last surviving Thompson daughter, this small, exclusive mess was closed. The Thompson house—known earlier as the military storekeeper's house, and the last of the Revolutionary War structures on post—was razed shortly thereafter.

In the years soon after the war, it became the custom of the first class to celebrate the arrival of the year in which they would graduate. The New Year's Eve celebration of 1876 was a particularly raucous affair. While some cadets sang songs at the top of their lungs, others rolled cannonballs along the floor of the barracks piazzas, and others set off firecrackers. They continued this racket until dispersed by the appearance of the tactical officers. In 1877 the tactical officers were ready to act and put a halt to the celebration almost before it began. The next year the class learned that the tactical officers were again organizing in advance to stymie their New Year's revelry. The officers were so confident of success that some had promised to give their lady friends an opportunity to see the midnight celebration, and then to witness their dexterity in dispersing the celebrants.

The class decided, therefore, that no one would engage in the usual fun, and when midnight arrived the area was quiet and deserted. A few days later the class circulated a rhyme dedicated "to the Officers and Ladies who attended the Surprise Party given by the Class of '78, not in the area":

> For many days the class of Seventy-Eight,
>
> Discussed if it were best to celebrate,
>
> With usual noise and customary din,
>
> The hour on which their final year's begin,
>
> But since the Supt. has held such pleasant sway,
>
> And don't enjoy such acts of foolish play,
>
> 'Twas well decided by the thoughtful class,
>
> To cease from noise, and let the old year pass.

Two years later the "success" of an elaborately planned New Year's celebration of the class of 1880—and the aftermath—brought an end to such affairs. Just an hour before midnight, when the barracks sentries were removed, the plan was put into action. Small detachments were silently dispatched to man the reveille gun and the guns of the siege battery at Trophy Point, and others were sent to man a gun that had been secretly placed on the roof of the barracks; the balance were given fireworks that had been smuggled onto the post. At the last minute, the ground floor doors of the barracks were locked from the inside. All was still, then the chapel bell signaled midnight. Before the second chime could sound, the cannons were fired as if one. The tactical officers, who were celebrating at the mess, came rushing toward the barracks, but were met by a barrage of roman candles, rockets, and firecrackers. In the confusion, the cadets who had manned the guns returned and were admitted to the barracks. By the time the "tacs" could gain entry to the barracks and assume control, all the members of the corps were "asleep" in their bunks—except the cadet officers, who were found bound and gagged. In response, John Schofield, the Superintendent, confined the entire corps to cadet limits (the immediate area of the academic buildings, barracks, and mess hall), prohibited cadets from visiting

Graduation Day at West Point - the Cavalry Charge *by R.F. Zogbaum. 1886. From Harper's Weekly. U.S.M.A. Library, Special Collections. Photo: Philip Pocock.*

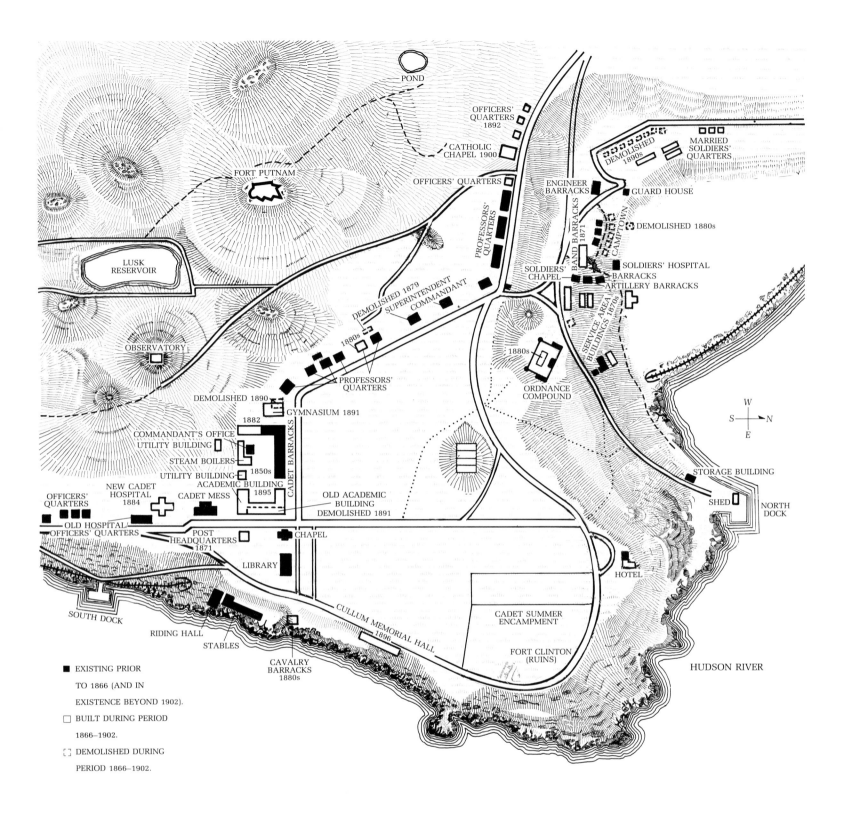

POND

OFFICERS'
QUARTERS
1892

CATHOLIC
CHAPEL 1900

MARRIED
SOLDIERS'
QUARTERS

DEMOLISHED
1890s

OFFICERS' QUARTERS

ENGINEER
BARRACKS

GUARD HOUSE

FORT PUTNAM

PROFESSORS'
QUARTERS

BAND BARRACKS
1871

CAMPTOWN

DEMOLISHED 1880s

SOLDIERS'
CHAPEL

SOLDIERS' HOSPITAL

LUSK
RESERVOIR

DEMOLISHED 1879

SUPERINTENDENT

COMMANDANT

BARRACKS

ARTILLERY BARRACKS

SERVICE AREA
BUILDINGS 1870s

1880s

1880s

OBSERVATORY

PROFESSORS'
QUARTERS

1880s

ORDNANCE
COMPOUND

DEMOLISHED 1890

GYMNASIUM 1891

1882

COMMANDANT'S OFFICE

UTILITY BUILDING

STEAM BOILERS

UTILITY BUILDING

1850s

NEW CADET
HOSPITAL
1884

ACADEMIC BUILDING
1895

CADET BARRACKS

OLD ACADEMIC
BUILDING
DEMOLISHED 1891

STORAGE BUILDING

SHED

NORTH
DOCK

OFFICERS'
QUARTERS

CADET MESS

OLD HOSPITAL/
OFFICERS' QUARTERS

POST
HEADQUARTERS
1871

CHAPEL

LIBRARY

HOTEL

W

S ← → N

E

SOUTH DOCK

RIDING HALL

STABLES

CAVALRY
BARRACKS
1880s

CULLUM MEMORIAL HALL
1896

CADET SUMMER
ENCAMPMENT

FORT CLINTON
(RUINS)

HUDSON RIVER

■ EXISTING PRIOR
TO 1866 (AND IN
EXISTENCE BEYOND 1902).

□ BUILT DURING PERIOD
1866–1902.

⸙ DEMOLISHED DURING
PERIOD 1866–1902.

Map of West Point, 1866–1902.

the officers' quarters, and ordered additional officers into the barracks to ensure that discipline was maintained.

In the wake of this demonstration, the class of 1881 forwent the observance of the New Year and, with the permission of the Superintendent, sponsored an entertainment just one hundred nights before graduation—a particular treat, since one of their number had convinced Samuel Clemens, the humorist better known as Mark Twain, to attend the festivities and address the cadets. This event evolved into what quickly became known as the "Hundredth Night Show." In songs, skits, poems, and readings the cadets poked fun at themselves, the officers and even the Superintendent. The show was soon taken over by the Dialectic Society, which has continued the production to this day.

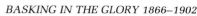

Cullum Hall was built in 1897–99 by the firm of McKim, Mead, and White, in a Neoclassical style, with Beaux-Arts influences visible in various details and decorations.

For the first few years, the show was held in the Dialectic Society hall in the barracks above the sally port. But it became so popular that it was soon necessary to move it to the mess hall, where the entire corps and the officers and their wives could attend. Its popularity, of course, derived from its pointed wit and humor. In 1898, however, the cadets went too far in their sharp satire of Commandant of Cadets Otto L. Hein's efforts to eradicate hazing. "The very considerable licence permitted cadets" in entertainments, reported Hein, had been "curtailed." In the future "all reference, either in disapprobation or praise, to commissioned officers on duty at the Academy or elsewhere" was prohibited. Hein was so displeased with the Dialectic Society's performance that for a time he took away their meeting hall in the barracks and converted it to a cadet lounge.

In the last years of the Civil War, and during those immediately following, discipline had again grown lax at West Point. To a certain degree, this was because the officers who returned to the Academy at this time were not inclined to enforce regulations that often appeared petty in light of their recent wartime experiences. But this laxity also reflected the attitudes or capabilities of the Superintendents. Lieutenant Colonel George W. Cullum—who had long served as Henry Halleck's chief of staff, and who had been shunted to West Point in 1864 when Halleck was replaced by General Grant—was unable or unwilling to overcome the reluctance of his officers to enforce discipline. Cullum left little mark as Superintendent, and is better known for his *Biographical Register of the Officers and Graduates of the United States Military Academy,* or his work on behalf of the Association of Graduates, or his bequest that built a memorial hall (1897–99) named in his honor. Cullum was followed, in 1866, by an even more ineffectual officer, Colonel Thomas Gamble Pitcher. Clearly, the wartime requirements in the field for the most capable officers had proven, as John Schofield later noted, "prejudicial to the interests of the Military Academy." A difficulty, he added, that had "continued some time after the close of the war." Pitcher, an infantry officer, was the first non-engineer chosen to superintend the United States Military Academy under provisions of the Act of July 13, 1866 which provided that the Superintendent might be chosen from any branch of the service. His selection seems to have been made to demonstrate the imprudence of this provision of the Act. Pitcher had little to recommend him for the position, and added nothing to his reputation while at West Point. He had graduated fortieth of forty-one in the class of 1845 and had subsequently enjoyed a generally undistinguished career. Following Pitcher's

Thomas G. Pitcher *by Daniel Huntington. c. 1874. Oil on canvas, 30 × 25″. West Point Museum Collections, U.S.M.A.*

William Tecumseh Sherman *by G.P.A. Healy. c. 1865. Oil on canvas, 61⅝ × 38″. West Point Museum Collections, U.S.M.A.*

Thomas H. Ruger *by Daniel Huntington. n.d. Oil on canvas, 30 × 25″. West Point Museum Collections, U.S.M.A.*

reassignment from West Point in 1871, he became Governor of the Soldiers' Home in Washington, D.C., and remained there until he retired in 1878. Under Pitcher, discipline suffered so markedly that, in 1871, even the board of visitors remarked on its decline.

The most striking manifestation of the tendency toward lax discipline at West Point was the dramatic increase in hazing that occurred at this time. Hazing, in more innocent forms, had long been a feature of West Point life. It began as mere devilment. "When at first us new Cadets stood post [guard]," wrote William Davidson Frazer, who had come to West Point in 1830, "the old cadets used to come round at nights and try to fool us in trying to cross our post, and to frighten us at night." This occasional annoying of the plebes, however, led in only a few years to a well-entrenched system of hazing, which had become common practice by the mid-1830s. William Tecumseh Sherman recalled that he had been "broken in by a course of hazing" when he arrived at West Point in 1836. By the time of the Civil War, hazing was thought a custom of the Academy. Still, hazing as it was practiced before 1860 was largely limited to the period of the summer encampment and consisted primarily of harmless pranks.

During the Civil War, however, hazing assumed a more sinister aspect. Now, throughout the year, upperclassmen forced plebes to do exhausting physical exercises that sometimes resulted in serious injuries; or to eat or drink unpalatable foods or beverages; or, in any number of ways, to humiliate themselves. This change was concomitant with, if not precipitated by, the practice (begun under Cullum) of segregating the plebes for some weeks in the barracks when they first arrived—a period that soon became known as Beast Barracks. No longer were plebes introduced directly into the corps during the encampment, as had previously been the custom. The ostensible purpose of this new practice was for a few upper classmen to teach the new cadets saluting, marching, and other basics of military life at the Academy. Instead it introduced a form of "official hazing" in which upperclassmen attempted to drive all sense of self-importance from the plebes and to teach them unquestioning and instant obedience. Day and night they were harassed, called "Beast," "Animal," "Thing," or "Mr. Dumbjohn." They were braced, double-timed, and ordered to do impossible tasks. Heads back, chests out, stomachs in—they were constantly ordered about, berated and harassed. This official setting apart of the plebes by the administration at West Point led almost automatically to their continued isolation from the other cadets when they left Beast Barracks. Now they did not become a real part of the corps—were not "recognized" by the upperclassmen—until they became third classmen.

As a result of the lax discipline, hazing in Beast Barracks soon was completely out of hand. Cullum, unable to curtail the practice in any other way, threatened to hold a court of inquiry. Instead, the third class, to which the hazers in question belonged, took a voluntary pledge to abstain from committing such offenses in the future. But, in 1867, hazing once more broke out. Pitcher, who had replaced Cullum, was similarly unable to stop it until he was finally instructed to extract an oath of obedience from the cadets. In the spring of 1868, and again in 1869, all members of the plebe class—just months before they became third classmen—were required to swear that they would not interfere with, harass, molest, or injure any entering cadets, and that they would not demand menial services of any sort from the new plebes, or even accept voluntary services from them.

In 1871, President Grant personally selected Colonel Thomas Howard Ruger to succeed Pitcher as Superintendent. Ruger was a good choice. He had graduated high in his class in 1854, and had a brilliant record in the Civil War as a division commander. More to the point, Grant knew him to be a strict disciplinarian. When the father of a cadet whom Ruger had disciplined for misconduct sought to have the new Superintendent transferred, alleging that he was too strict, Grant simply sent the letter to Ruger with the remark: "It may amuse you—do with it as you please."

"The present 'Supe,' who is a most rigid martinet, has instituted a good many reforms and tightened all the loose 'screws'," wrote Cadet Tasker Bliss in 1872. Ruger was particularly tough on hazers. When Cadet Hugh Scott was caught hazing a plebe, he was turned back a year. A few months later, when Scott rescued a fellow cadet from drowning, his classmates hoped that the Superintendent would grant a reprieve. Ruger, however, was unbending.

Not all upperclassmen approved of hazing, but to oppose it openly was to risk retaliation from other members of the corps. When, in 1875, Cadet Charles Robinson found a new cadet doing menial service for a member of the first class he reported it. To cadets, this act—reporting a cadet for an offense committed by so many—was unprecedented. Fellow cadets were expected to overlook such offenses. Robinson was severely censured by the other cadets. Clandestine meetings were held and Robinson was "cut" or silenced by both the first class and his own yearling, or third, class. When Ruger learned of this he immediately reduced the cadet officers (first classmen) to the ranks and put much of the class under arrest. Still, Robinson was "cut" by most of his own classmates for his last three years at West Point. Though he was made a cadet lieutenant his first-class year, the cumulative pressure of the course and the cut were ultimately too much for him. He was found deficient in academics at the end of his last year and was dismissed.

Schofield, who replaced Ruger in 1876, addressed the corps concerning hazing in the strongest terms. Hazing, he told them, was "essentially criminal," moreover, it was a "vicious and illegal indulgence." Schofield, who in his own day had been known as the worst prankster in the corps, sharply criticized the newer practices. He found particularly offensive the new custom of addressing the new cadets with insulting names and epithets. In his day, he told them, a cadet called "beast" or worse, "would have done his best to kill his assailant on the spot." Moreover, he added, "Anyone who would have addressed another in such words would have been denounced and cut even by his own class."

Efforts to stamp out hazing proved fruitless. For one thing, the practice was concealed by a code of silence among the cadets. As Robinson had learned, upperclassmen simply did not report each other. Plebes kept silent for fear that life would be made even more miserable for them if they reported hazing. Moreover, the plebes often did not resist because they felt that withstanding the hazing proved their manhood and thus elevated them in the eyes of their peers—when questioned, they would answer that they simply could not identify their assailants. Douglas MacArthur, who had been a particular target of upperclassmen in 1899, was questioned on this point by a congressional committee investigating hazing. MacArthur was asked: "Was it too dark for you to recognize the faces of your hazers?" He responded: "I do not think it would have been if I had looked at them." "But," he added, "it is generally customary for fourth classmen not to look at those people who are hazing them."

Almost the only cadets who could be disciplined for hazing were those caught in the act by the tactical officers or faculty. These young men were often dismissed—but they were reinstated almost as often. They would address their appeals to sympathetic members of Congress (often Academy graduates) who believed that dismissal was too harsh for what were often viewed as no more than boyish pranks. Schofield called on Congress and the administration to consider the long-term impact of the practice. Said Schofield, "Let it once be understood that boys can be disobedient and get Congress and the President to support them—then disband West Point. It will be West Point no longer." But Schofield's warning went unheeded.

By the mid-1890s, hazing had become so firmly entrenched that Commandant of Cadets O. L. Hein inaugurated new, more stringent measures. But his efforts to break up what he called a "pernicious system of underground hazing" that had come to be "akin to torture in some cases," had no lasting impact. The case of Cadet Oscar L. Booz, in 1900,

John M. Scholfield. This photograph is from the 1877 Class Album. U.S.M.A. Library, Special Collections. Photo: Philip Pocock.

Monument to Major General John Sedgwick, who was killed in 1864 during the Civil War, but whose name has been preserved in this statue, cast from the cannon of his corps and dedicated in 1868.

demonstrated this. Booz had run afoul of an upperclassman and had been called out to fight. A third classman of approximately the same height and weight as Booz was designated by the class fight committee to restore the honor of their class. When Booz caught a solid blow to his solar plexus, he went down and refused to resume the fight. Plebes and upperclassmen alike pronounced him a coward. Booz then became the target of a systematic hazing campaign, one feature of which was forcing him to drink a particularly large dose of tabasco sauce with every meal. Soon his throat was so badly inflamed that he could tolerate few beverages except water. Booz ultimately resigned and, within a year, he died of tuberculosis of the larynx. His family charged that the hazing had caused his death. A congressional investigation followed and, although it concluded that the tabasco sauce was not responsible for his death, it directed strong criticism at West Point and at the practice of hazing. Congressional investigators found that the fertile minds of the upper classmen had devised more than one hundred methods of annoying and harassing plebes. This investigation was followed by legislation on March 2, 1901 that forbade hazing.

Into this atmosphere of widespread hazing, in 1870, came the first black cadets. Although they were not hazed in the traditional sense, the social climate among the cadets ensured that the black cadets would be subjected to scorn and maltreatment during the whole of their stay at West Point. Between 1870 and 1889, twenty-three blacks were nominated to the Academy. Of these, twelve were admitted, but only three graduated—Henry O. Flip-

The various uniforms that were worn by cadets in 1888 are on display here. U.S.M.A. Archives.

per in 1877, John H. Alexander in 1887, and Charles Young in 1889. Flipper was dismissed from the service in 1882, but went on to become a successful mining engineer in the West and in Mexico; Alexander died on duty as a second lieutenant in 1894; and Young, who attained the rank of colonel, was retired in 1917 for disability. Young, in 1889, was the last black of that era to attend the Military Academy. Beyond West Point, times were changing; the Jim Crow laws, which were enacted throughout the South, had repercussions across the country. No other black cadet was admitted to West Point until after World War I, and no more were graduated until 1936.

As early as 1865, Benjamin F. Butler of Massachusetts had reportedly been seeking a young black man to accept an appointment to West Point, but he was unable to identify a willing candidate who had all the requisite qualities—the intellect, the physical ability, and the psychological makeup that would enable him to cope with the insults, taunts,

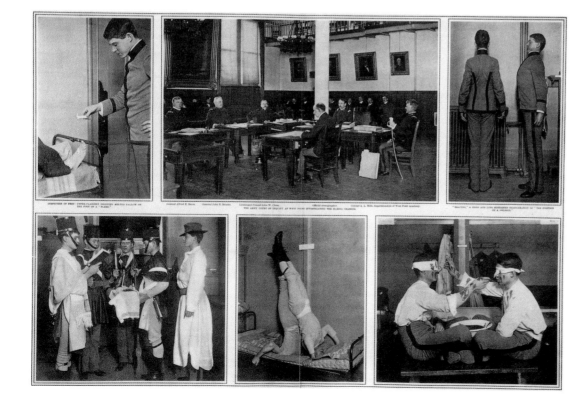

These are the first known photographs of the controversial practice of hazing that "plebes" had to endure at West Point. This page is from a 1902 issue of Leslie's Weekly. U.S.M.A. Archives.

Henry O. Flipper, the first black graduate of the United States Military Academy in 1877. U.S.M.A. Archives.

and social exclusion he was sure to experience. Five years later, in 1870, James Webster Smith, of South Carolina, became the first black to be admitted to the Academy. He was ostracized by the white cadets from the beginning; they refused to room with him and even objected to sitting at the same table in the mess hall. Smith's first year was plagued by trouble and fights which resulted in his being turned back one year. After that, Smith seems to have struck an accommodation with the other cadets—although one that featured the frequent exchange of slurs. He struggled through four years at West Point, but in 1874 was found deficient in natural philosophy and dismissed.

Henry Flipper entered West Point in 1873 and roomed with Smith for one year. Where Smith had resented and fought openly against the social ostracism, Flipper took the opposite approach. Flipper was involved in none of the exchanges of insults or blows that had characterized Smith's years. Still, although he seemed to have gained their grudging respect, he was as completely ostracized by the cadets as Smith had been.

Flipper was philosophical about the behavior of the other cadets, and tried to rationalize their conduct. It is clear, however, that it required all his strength and self-control to endure the unrelenting pressure of cadet prejudice. The majority, he believed, would have preferred to treat him "with proper politeness." They were gentlemen, he insisted, and would "treat others as it becomes a gentleman to do." The fact that they would not associate, nor speak to him other than officially, he attributed to some control or power that the lower social elements held over them. In Flipper's view this latter group came from "the very lowest classes of our population." They were "uncouth and rough in appearance," and had "little or no idea of courtesy." They used "the very worst language" and were, by Flipper's assessment, "much inferior to the average Negro." The control this class exercised surprised him. "It seems to rule the corps by fear," he wrote. "Indeed I know there are many who would associate, who would treat me as a brother cadet, were they not held in constant dread of this class." To some degree, this optimistic view may have been fostered by his experience with the officers at the Academy who, he said, had treated him "with uniform courtesy and impartiality."

In a bittersweet sense, Flipper's faith may have been justified, for when he graduated he was accorded a round of applause, in which his classmates joined heartily. Released by graduation from the restraint of the lower class, they were no longer hesitant to speak or to congratulate him, or to shake his hand. "All signs of ostracism were gone. All felt as if I were worthy of some regard, and did not fail to extend it to me," he wrote.

In 1878, a year after his graduation, Flipper published an account of his experiences at West Point and outlined the philosophy that had allowed him to endure. According to Flipper, the black man's immediate need in 1878 was not continued agitation or legislation for social equality, but rather the fullest self-development of his mental and moral potential. Flipper's views on gradualism, agitation, and social equality were strikingly similar to the ideas that Booker T. Washington would embrace some seventeen years later.

The most unfortunate of the black cadets at West Point was Johnson Chestnut Whittaker, who entered the Academy in 1876. He roomed with Flipper his first year and tried to follow his example of meeting ostracism with silence. However, Whittaker clashed with one of the unwritten rules of the Academy—when a white cadet struck him he did not fight back, but rather reported the cadet who had hit him. The pressure of the added torment he now suffered took its toll. One morning, in 1880, he was found in his room, bound to his bed, bruised and cut, and smeared with blood. Initially the authorities accepted Whittaker's story that he had been attacked by several masked men, but, as the investigation progressed, they came to doubt him. In the end they concluded that he himself was responsible and that the assault had been feigned as a way to divert attention from his academic difficulties.

The court of inquiry in session while hearing testimony in the case of Johnson C. Whittaker. Anne S.K. Brown Military Collection, Brown University Library.

After more than two years of investigations and trials, which thrust Whittaker and West Point into the national spotlight, he was convicted of perjuring himself and of other acts unbecoming an officer or cadet. Despite the fact that these proceedings were disapproved by President Chester A. Arthur, Whittaker was dismissed from the Academy because of an academic deficiency. From this judgment there was no reprieve.

A year later, in 1883, John H. Alexander joined the corps, followed the next year by Charles Young—the second and third black cadets to graduate. Both proceeded through the Academy, attracting as little attention to themselves as possible, and leaving little more of a record there than any other cadets. Alexander graduated in 1887, thirty-second in a class of sixty-four. Young had a more difficult time. He was turned back one year and, at the end of his first class year, was in serious academic trouble. One of Young's classmates, Charles D. Rhodes, was sympathetic. "Our colored classmate, Charles Young, whom we esteem highly for his patient perseverance in the face of discouraging conditions which have attended his cadetship for five years, did poorly in both engineering and ordnance, and was given a special written examination in each subject. . . . We are hoping that Young will get through." Young, however, was found deficient in engineering. But his engineering instructor, Lieutenant George Goethals, made a special plea on his behalf and the two men devoted hours that summer to preparing for a special reexamination. Young passed by a comfortable margin and was graduated in August 1889.

Major General John McAllister Schofield had replaced Ruger as Superintendent on September 1, 1876. It was "the mistake of my life," he later wrote. Sherman had advised him that his "rank and history [would] elevate [the Military Academy] and solve all trouble." But when Schofield arrived he found that Ruger had left the Academy in a very acceptable state and that there was little, if any, foundation to Sherman's assertion that the interests of the Military Academy required the assignment of such a senior officer as Superintendent. Sherman's motive in this is somewhat obscure, but Schofield was convinced that it was political.

To his dismay, Schofield discovered that despite his senior rank he stood in no different position, with respect to the powers of the academic board, than those who had preceded him. He bridled at the limitations placed upon him by the regulations governing the Military Academy; his direct authority was limited to those areas of cadet, Academy, and post life which dealt with military matters in the strictest and most limited sense. He could not influence the curriculum or other educational concerns except in his capacity as member of the academic board, where his was but one of many votes. Unlike his predecessors, however, Schofield could never accept a position subordinate in any manner to the board. Consequently, he battled the professors throughout his tenure in an effort to gain the upper hand.

The academic board of 1870 was a familiar assemblage—led by Mahan, Church, and Bartlett, who had assumed that leadership in the 1830s. The most recent addition to the board, John W. French, the chaplain and head of the Department of Geography, History, and Ethics, had held his appointment since 1856; four of the seven academic chiefs had taken over their departments in the 1830s.

But in 1871 the makeup of the board began to change: Bartlett retired, while both Mahan and Hyacinth R. Agnel, professor of French, died. The next year, 1872, John French, the chaplain, also died. In just two years, more than half the board was gone, and the balance departed within only a few years: Church died in 1878, and Weir and Kendrick retired—in 1876 and 1880 respectively.

The leading light on this new academic board was Peter Smith Michie, of the class of 1863. He had been an assistant professor of engineering from 1867 to 1871 and had, in 1871, been chosen professor of natural and experimental philosophy (a position he held until his death in 1901). Michie had a laugh that was natural and infectious, yet cadets thought him stuffy, even dour, and he was never popular with them. During his years at the Academy Michie wrote extensively: an elementary text on mechanics, a history of the Army of the Potomac in which he had fought, and biographies of George McClellan and Emory Upton. Michie was a deeply religious man and insisted that his explanation of the laws of matter and force proved the existence of "a Creator who set the hosts of the skies and determined their motions." He threatened to find deficient any cadet who did not agree.

Henry S. Kendrick, or "Old Hanks" as cadets called him. U.S.M.A. Library, Special Collections. Photo: Philip Pocock.

Charles W. Larned, class of 1870, who became the professor of drawing in 1876, was another of the new leadership. Larned, unlike his predecessors in the department, was not an artist. He had spent his years after graduation on frontier duty with the cavalry. Where Weir had concentrated on landscape painting, Larned emphasized mathematical drawing and topographical work. On the academic board, Larned was a steadying influence and an effective spokesman. "It is a very serious matter to tamper with the nice adjustment of so delicate and powerful an organism [as the Military Academy]," he would argue.

Other members of the new academic board included George L. Andrews, John Forsyth, and Junius Brutus Wheeler. Andrews had graduated first in his class in 1851. He was chosen professor of French in 1871, and in 1882, when the French and Spanish departments were merged, he was made professor of modern languages, serving in that capacity until his retirement in 1892. Forsyth, the chaplain and professor of ethics from 1871 to 1881, was a tall, portly, Falstaffian figure, who had a reputation for indifference to study—he "allowed ambition to seize other men," wrote one cadet. Still, cadets appreciated him for his short sermons and his pontification on the importance of ethics: "Every tub must stand on it own bottom," he would declare, grasping his lapels and rising on his toes. Wheeler, an 1855 graduate, was first assigned to the cavalry and then topographic engineers. He had been an assistant professor of mathematics from 1859 to 1863, and was selected professor of engineering in 1871. He retired in 1884.

The two longtime members of the faculty were Albert Church, who had been teaching mathematics at the Academy since 1828, and Henry Lane Kendrick, or "Old Hanks" as he was affectionately known to several generations of cadets. Kendrick, of the class of

1835, had joined the faculty upon graduation and had become professor of chemistry in 1857. A lifelong bachelor and for years the senior member of the officers' mess, he was popular with officers and cadets alike, and had the reputation of being exceptionally kind to new plebes.

Schofield spent the early months of his superintendency in a concerted effort to strengthen his position vis-à-vis the academic board. At his insistence, West Point was made a military department, a command more befitting his rank. He then set about drafting revisions to the regulations. First, he attacked the tenure of the professors. "It would be beneficial, both to the officer and the public service, although the officer be one of the most efficient, to allow him to return to his corps in the Army after a certain period of service at the Academy; his place there to be filled by a younger man." Then he attacked the powers of the academic board directly, proposing a permanent board of visitors, made up of the Superintendent, members of Congress, and representatives of the War Department. This entity would be able "to initiate all changes necessary to be made in the academic board"—usurping key powers of the academic board.

Although the War Department simply ignored these proposals, the two sides at West Point continued to snipe at each other. One example of this was the case of two cadets reported to the academic board in January 1880 as having received demerits in excess of the number allowed. The academic board declared the cadets deficient and recommended their dismissal. Schofield had not wanted to deal so harshly with the two, intending only to give them a stern warning. He appealed to the War Department and won the cadets a reprieve. In June, however, the academic board again declared them deficient—although their total number of demerits for the year were by then within allowable limits. Schofield angrily protested; he should have "sole jurisdiction to decide all individual questions of discipline," he argued. Both Sherman and the Secretary of War, Alexander Ramsey, agreed. At the next academic board meeting, Schofield read the opinion of the Secretary of War to this effect. To his chagrin, the professors simply ordered the communication held for consideration at a later meeting. Ultimately, a compromise was worked out. "It was decided after discussion," the board minutes reveal, "that the Superintendent withdraw his report of discipline" concerning the cadets. With no report of deficiency to act upon, the board's earlier dismissal was withdrawn. Schofield had won a very minor victory—the right to decide whether or not a deficiency in discipline should be reported to the board for its vote and recommendation—and no more.

In these contests, the Superintendent relied primarily on the support of the Army hierarchy in Washington—the Commanding General and the Secretary of War. The members of the academic board also wrote directly to these men, but in addition they used their own networks of connections in Washington and throughout the Army to press their cases. Most kept up a steady correspondence with both members of Congress and the Army's senior officers—many, in both categories, who had been former students or colleagues at West Point. As the conflict intensified in 1880, the academic board's supporters—using Schofield's inept handling of the Whittaker case as leverage—brought pressure to secure a replacement. Senator Augustus Hill Garland went so far as to propose that in the future "no officer above the rank of colonel" should be "assigned to duty at the Academy." President Rutherford B. Hayes, under attack by the Democrats who had regained control of the Congress, was sensitive to the charges that Schofield had mishandled affairs at West Point. In August 1880, he called Schofield to Washington and informed him that he would soon be replaced.

On January 21, 1881, Brigadier General Oliver Otis Howard, who is best known as commissioner of the Freedmen's Bureau (1865–1872) and for his work on behalf of the freed slaves, took up the reins as Superintendent of the Military Academy. Howard's reputation, it was hoped, would help deflect further criticism of the institution (and the

administration) while it was in the midst of the Whittaker investigation and trial. His assignment, however, seemed to promise even more. "It is an open secret," reported the *Army and Navy Journal*, that Howard was appointed because of "his disposition to effect a radical reform" that would "lower or break down the wall of caste separation" at West Point. Some reports noted that Howard, himself, had been ostracized by other cadets for his views on slavery and for treating a sergeant, who was a family friend, as a social equal. As Howard headed toward West Point, he was asked by reporters what he planned to do about the black cadets. "I think that Gen. Washington's 'hearty politeness' is about as good a thing as can be introduced anywhere," Howard answered, "or the golden rule, 'Do unto others as you would have them do to you'."

He applied a similar philosophy in his relations with the academic board. Shortly after assuming the superintendency, Howard raised one of the issues that had deadlocked Schofield and the board, asking "whether it would be preferable that the Superintendent should have sole power to declare a Cadet proficient or deficient in discipline or that this proficiency or deficiency should be declared by the Academic Board." Not surprisingly, the professors concluded that this role should fall to them and that they should "consider and act upon such a deficiency as in cases of deficiency in studies." The unanimous vote of the board on this issue indicates that Howard concurred. The academic board was a "body of able men," he noted, and "every interest of the Academy is carefully weighed" by them. "In my judgement," he continued, "it is the most powerful agent at work here. It is my earnest desire while Superintendent to work in harmony with the board as presently constituted."

Schofield's assignment to West Point had been marked by other difficulties as well. "Because the Superintendent is a General and has all his staff officers with him," wrote Lieutenant Tasker Bliss, "there are many more officers here than ever before. The consequence is that while the older ones are barely able to secure accommodation, the junior ones may as well go begging for a roof to cover them." Their arrival had created a good deal of turbulence. As a general rule, senior officers had the right to choose the quarters they preferred. In practice, this meant that an officer could select any set of quarters that were vacant or that were occupied by officers junior to him—although at West Point the Superintendent excluded from this process the quarters assigned to the permanent professors. Lieutenant Tully McCrea described the process thus: "Perhaps you have seen boys playing near a brick pile, by placing a long row of bricks on end, just close enough so that when you knock down the brick at the end, it knocks down its neighbor, and so on throughout the whole row. It happens that this is just the case with the officers here, who are the bricks, but instead of being knocked down, they are in turn turned out of their houses, to turn out someone else." The process was particularly hard on the wives. Although McCrea was a bachelor, he had compassion for the women on whom this policy fell most harshly. "I am very sorry," he wrote, "for one lady, for she has just moved this week, and she took it quite *manfully*, and was in a very good humor about it. But today another officer makes his appearance and chooses, which necessitates the removal of this lady again."

If the object had been to produce conflict and hard feelings, the process of assigning quarters could not have been better designed. Dissatisfaction with quarters was a constant. There were never enough and those available were often inadequate. Moreover, the turmoil created by the method of assigning quarters only added to hardship. In 1891, Superintendent John M. Wilson, observing that at West Point most of the officers arrived or departed in August of each year, established a new procedure. All the officers reporting for duty at the beginning of the new term, as well as those remaining on duty at the Academy who wished to change quarters, were to select quarters at a single drawing. There, they would each pick (with the most senior drawing first) from among the quarters vacated by the departing officers or from those thrown in by officers who hoped to better their situation. After each set of quarters had been selected, it was immediately assigned "and once assigned are not again subject to selection so long as occupied by assignee, no matter what may be the rank of any officer subsequently reporting for duty." Officers arriving at other times during the year were assigned quarters as they became available. No longer were officers at the Military Academy continually bumped and forced to move. This solution proved so satisfactory that it continues to be the policy at West Point to this day.

New quarters were added throughout the period, but there were never enough to satisfy the demand, for the number of officers brought to West Point also increased. The "embarrassment of doubling up families in unsuitable quarters," wrote Superintendent A. L.

The "House on the Rock," c. 1870, also served as housing for the officers. U.S.M.A. Archives.

Among the most venerable accommodations available to senior officers at West Point must be included this mid-nineteenth-century house—now the Dean's quarters.

Mills, in 1900, "will be bound to cause dissatisfaction." This, he concluded, would translate into an "impairment of the value of the services the officer would otherwise give." Neither the War Department nor the Congress was moved by his argument.

The situation for the unmarried officers was, if anything, even worse. Although a few sets of quarters for these officers were added, there was a great need by the end of the century for both bachelor officer quarters and a new officers' mess. The only substantial gain in housing was the long overdue construction, in the early 1890s, of some thirty sets of quarters for senior enlisted men with families.

Housing aside, most officers, wives, and families found their assignment at the Military Academy pleasant. "I never had a more agreeable tour of duty than my four years at West Point," wrote James Parker, who served as a tactical officer from 1894 to 1898. "Socially

Above:
Officers dined formally in the West Point Army Mess in Grant Hall. c. 1870s. U.S.M.A. Archives.

Lower left:
Brick duplex houses at West Point, constructed in the late nineteenth century for the married enlisted men. U.S.M.A. Archives.

Lower right:
These brick buildings provided quarters for the more fortunate bachelor officers at the Academy, c. 1871. U.S.M.A. Library, Special Collections. Photo: Philip Pocock.

it was delightful; we had many charming acquaintances there, and many visitors; my children went to good schools; the two eldest became young ladies, danced and rode with the cadets, with whom they were great favorites, and made among them many life-long friends."

The Hudson River provided a highway to the society and hospitality of families up and down the Hudson valley. New money and old was represented in the fine homes that had sprung up along the shores of the Hudson. At Garrison, there were the Hamilton and Stuyvesant Fishes and their cousins the Rogers and Benjamins, as well as many others, while at Cold Springs were the Haldanes, Fitzgeralds, and deRhams. On the west bank of the river, south of Highland Falls, lived a coterie of families, the John Bigelows, Clarence Pells, and Pierpont Morgans. The officers assigned to the Academy were frequent guests in their homes and, in turn, entertained these families at West Point. "One of our favorite visiting places was the John Bigelow villa near Highland Falls," recalled Hein, "where we were often most agreeably entertained by Mrs. Bigelow and Miss Grace Bigelow." "Sammy" Tillman, then an assistant professor of chemistry and later head of that department, took Grace Bigelow to her first officers' hop.

New York City also proved a magnet. Even before the West Shore Railroad linked West Point with New York City and points north in 1883, frequent river boats and the New York Central Railroad on the east shore of the Hudson (a ferry connected West Point's south dock with the train station at Garrison) provided convenient transportation to the city. Many of the officers were widely acquainted with New York's social elite. The city was a particularly attractive haunt for the bachelors. On weekend forays they mingled with old-line families, with literary, artistic, and theatrical celebrities, as well as with foreign dignitaries, government officials, and the new giants of American industry.

At West Point, novelty and invention rather than high society spiced the social life. One example was a Valentine party given in 1876 by Lieutenant Sam Mills, a tactical officer, and his wife. Before the party, each officer and lady who had been invited was required to compose a poem in honor of a guest of the opposite sex; the person to whom their endeavor was to be dedicated was determined by drawing slips from a hat. Some of the verse was highly complimentary and some contained witty ridicule—the end result, in any case, was an hilarious evening. The enterprising Mills were not finished, however. They gathered up these literary gems, published them, and provided each author with a copy.

At West Point, there were also Saturday-evening poker parties, moonlight excursions on the Hudson, and an occasional amateur theatrical performances. In 1879, some of the younger officers put on a performance of Gilbert and Sullivan's new "H.M.S. Pinafore," which had opened in New York earlier that year. All the parts, including the female roles, were played by the officers. The instrumental music was furnished by the band. They borrowed sailor costumes from naval friends at the Brooklyn Navy Yard, and the female apparel from the ladies of the garrison. Sam Mills, an obviously versatile talent, played the role of Little Buttercup; George Harrison, assistant professor of French, portrayed the pompous Sir Joseph Porter, K.C.B.; and John G. D. Knight, of the mathematics department, was Dick Deadeye. Ignorance of music was only a minor impediment; frequent rehearsals and much practice produced a "creditable amateur rendition" of the show which gained "the entire approval" of the audience.

Beginning in 1881, Samuel Clemens became a frequent visitor to West Point. He first came over from his home in Hartford at the request of Cadet Andrew Goodrich Hammond, class of 1881, of the same city. At West Point, however, Clemens befriended Lieutenant Charles E. S. Wood, an aide to General Howard, and later Wesley Merritt, and would visit them whenever the opportunity offered. Clemens loved to saunter around the post, chewing on a cigar and swapping stories with cadets, and he occasionally allowed him-

self to be coaxed into a formal speaking engagement. In 1887, he helped inaugurate the recently renovated cadet mess hall, where much to the delight of the cadets he read his "English as She is Taught." The next day he accompanied Merritt to review a parade. Here, too, he elicited much smothered laughter among the cadets, for he forgot to throw away his cigar before taking his place in line with the staff.

For more cerebral diversions there was still the officers' Napoleon Club, which had been guided by Mahan since he founded it years earlier. With his death in 1871 the group foundered, but its activities were soon absorbed by the new Thayer Club, organized in 1873 to honor the recently deceased "Father of the Military Academy," and to "promote professional, scientific and literary culture." In turn, in 1878, the Thayer Club was absorbed into the West Point branch of the new United States Military Service Institute.

In 1894, a group of the officers' wives formed the Ladies' Reading Club, which met weekly, November through May. At the first meetings, in November 1894, the topic was "Travel," but the members investigated and reported on a wide variety of subjects. Over the next few years topics included: "Modern Architecture in England and the United States"; "Landscape and Marine Painters of 19th Century America"; "Muscular Development in Women"; "Coxeyism and the Tyranny of Socialism"; "Home Rule for Ireland"; "The Right of Suffrage for Women"; "Evolution and Man's Place in Nature"; "The Dreyfus Case"; "Is it Womans' First Duty to be Attractive?"; "Historic Houses of Washington"; "[Edward Bellamy's] 'Looking Backwards'"; and the "Bi-centennial of Yale."

In September 1882, General Howard, having shepherded West Point through the Whittaker affair, was replaced by Colonel Wesley Merritt. Merritt, who had graduated in 1860, had commanded a cavalry division in the Civil War, and had been breveted for gallantry in every grade from major to major-general. Merritt brought the same dash to the affairs at West Point that he had displayed in the war—and in the south and west afterward. Among his continuing concerns was an aging physical plant. Little major construction had taken place at West Point since the mess hall and riding hall had been completed in the mid-1850s, although a new administration building had been completed in 1871. The latter was a grey stone structure with a mansard slate roof surmounted by wrought-iron grill work—somewhat resembling a French Renaissance château. It harmonized with none of the other buildings. The balance of the buildings dated from a much earlier period; the library and academic building dated from the late 1830s, and the barracks from the late 1840s and early 1850s. (A wing of two divisions and a second sally port were added to the barracks in 1882.)

Above left:
The social life at West Point included festive occasions such as this Christmas Hop of 1898, drawn by Howard Chandler Christy. U.S.M.A. Library, Special Collections. Photo: Philip Pocock.

Above right:
The cadet mess in Grant Hall. 1896. U.S.M.A. Library, Special Collections. Photo: Philip Pocock.

Samuel Clemens (Mark Twain) was a frequent, and welcome, visitor to West Point. The Bettmann Archive.

Under Colonel Merritt's superintendence, a new—although abbreviated—round of construction began at the Academy. A much needed new cadet hospital was constructed just south of the mess hall and completed in 1884. In 1887 the mess hall was renovated and re-dedicated as Grant Hall—the first formal memorialization of a building at West Point. Then came a gymnasium, completed in 1891, and a new academic building, conceived in 1885, approved in 1889, and finally occupied in 1895. Merritt, however, did not bring the high degree of conceptual power to the projects that had characterized Delafield's efforts a half century before. As a result, these structures lacked any central architectural theme. The hospital, on the one hand, had no discernible architectural style whatsoever. The gymnasium, on the other hand, resembled a medieval Norman castle and therefore clashed with the Tudor-Gothic style barracks beside which it stood.

The new academic building was designed and built by the firm of Richard Hunt, one of the leading architectural establishments in the nation at the time. The site was a difficult one. The structure was to be sandwiched between the conflicting styles of the classical chapel and château-like administration building on one side, and the Gothic barracks on the other. Hunt attempted to resolve this dilemma by blending a few of the characteristics of each of these into his design. The building's U-shaped plan naturally extended and complemented the quadrangle behind the barracks, and the sally port and battlements harmonized with the same features on the barracks. Small towers flanking the sally port were similar to the towers that were then a part of the old cadet mess hall. The use of various types of window openings on different floors reflected a Renaissance influence and was based on combining features of both the Greek and Roman styles. Finally, the use of prominent gargoyles on the building's towers was reminiscent of rainspouts in Gothic architecture. It was an excellent example of the Eclecticism that flourished during that period.

In August 1887, Merritt was succeeded by Colonel John G. Parke. Parke, a member of the class of 1849, was one of the Army's senior engineers, and the first of that branch to

be appointed Superintendent since that position had been opened to line officers in 1866. Parke introduced telephone service to the Academy in 1887, and considerably enlarged the post by purchasing the Kinsley estate, which lay to the south between the post and the town of Highland Falls.

The period of Parke's brief superintendency (1887–89) may be best remembered for the great blizzard of March 12, 1888. Snowdrifts stood so high that they covered the fronts of the stone houses of "Professors Row," and reached to the windows of the Dialectic Society Hall on the second floor of the barracks, closing both entrances to the sally port. Parke resigned from the Army in June 1889 in a fit of pique because he was not selected Chief of Engineers. He was succeeded by Lieutenant Colonel John M. Wilson.

Wilson, in turn, was succeeded, in 1893, by Major Oswald Herbert Ernst. In 1858, at the age of sixteen, Ernst had entered Harvard. Two years later he accepted an appointment to

Above left:
The old administration building, c. 1871, resembled a French château. U.S.M.A. Archives. Photo: Philip Pocock.

Above right:
The old hospital. 1870. U.S.M.A. Library, Special Collections. Photo: Philip Pocock.

The barracks and the old academic building in 1868. U.S.M.A. Archives.

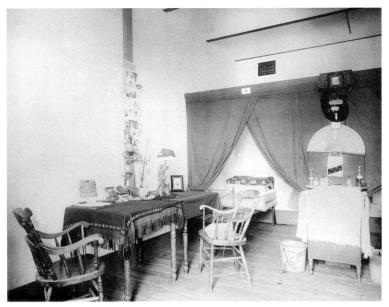

the Military Academy, graduating in 1864. The same year Ernst returned to West Point, the Academy received a bequest of $250,000 from the estate of former Superintendent George W. Cullum for the erection of a building to house trophies of war and "statues, busts, mural tablets and portraits of distinguished deceased officers and graduates of the Military Academy." After a limited competition, the trustees of the memorial hall selected the architectural firm of McKim, Mead, and White to design the building. Stanford White, who had earlier designed Battle Monument, undertook the project. Prominently located on the east edge of the plain, overlooking the river, this structure has a cold, austere quality about it. Its Classical style is emphasized on the principal front by the four colossal half-engaged Ionic columns, the Greek entablature, the pediment-capped entrance, and the ornamented decorations at the roof edge. Extending that influence, White was also chosen to design the West Point Army Mess, which was constructed next to the Cullum edifice, beginning in 1900. But, both the Cullum edifice and the mess were in stylistic conflict with everything that had been erected in the previous sixty years—blending only with the old chapel.

In the meantime, in May 1896, Ernst had appointed Professors Larned, Edgar Wales Bass, and Samuel Tillman to design a device, or coat-of-arms, for the United States Military Academy. The committee agreed that the design should typify: first, the national character of the institution; second, its military function; third, its educational function; and, finally, "its characteristic spirit and motive principle." In January 1898, after almost two years of effort, the three professors made their recommendation. The device was to be a shield bearing the arms of the United States, surmounted by a helmet of Pallas, the Greek goddess of wisdom and learning, over a Greek sword—the latter two symbolizing the double mission of the Academy. Above the shield was the American bald eagle, wings displayed, and a scroll bearing the words "West Point," the date 1802 in roman numerals, and the initials "U.S.M.A." The motto was also to be displayed on the scroll; it had simplicity, yet grandeur—"Duty, Honor, Country."

There was no time to incorporate the new design into the diplomas that were to be given to the class of 1898, for throughout the spring the United States had moved steadily toward war with Spain, and the class was to be graduated early. On April 22nd, the Congress authorized a volunteer force of 200,000 men. On April 26th, it approved an increase in the Regular Army to 60,000. At West Point, on the same day, Superintendent Ernst handed diplomas to the class of 1898, and then sent them off to the war.

Historians have variously characterized the period at West Point between the Civil War and the Spanish-American War as one of stagnation, isolation, or uncertainty—a time when the Military Academy was either unwilling or unable to consider the new ideas, new methods, and new organizational structures that had begun to characterize modern colleges and universities. For the same reasons, they conclude, West Point lost its scientific and engineering pre-eminence.

Without question, this was a period of unparalleled activity in American colleges. Henry Cabot Lodge entered Harvard in 1867 "under the old system," he recalled, "and came out under the new." He had entered the old college with its "narrow classical curriculum" and had come out the graduate of a modern, diverse university. The fundamental reason for the change was the accelerating advance in human knowledge. No longer could a person know everything worth knowing; no longer could the classically trained person hope to compete. Modern universities now prepared students for a variety of careers, but in making the transition from the classical to the modern curriculum they often found themselves unable to agree on what an educated individual needed to know. They solved the problem by adopting the elective, which threw onto the student the burden that the faculties would not accept.

At West Point, however, the process was very different. The decision to abandon the classical tradition had been made at the time of the Academy's founding. Political motives aside, Jefferson had created the school to provide select young men with the education necessary to prepare them to be army officers. Swift and Thayer had expanded on that foundation, establishing an institution that, in its time, was considered the finest engineering school in the country. But they did so because they concluded that a mathematical and scientific education would constitute the best preparation for future army officers. Despite the pressures from Congress and elsewhere that had precipitated an increased emphasis on civil engineering, the production of competent engineers was always secondary to the formation of sound officers.

The emphasis on mathematics and the sciences at West Point helped to develop mental discipline—the key to success no matter what sort of difficulties the future officer might encounter. At the same time, the Thayer system of daily recitation and grading produced habits of regularity and preparedness. Military discipline netted yet other benefits. "West Point had begotten habits of order, obedience and respect to authority," wrote Sherman, "which pass directly into the army, and thence to the country, and have borne fruits of infinite value to the Democratic country, if it has not been its actual salvation."

Below left:
West elevation of Cullum Hall, designed by McKim, Mead, and White in 1898. The main floor has an assembly hall where portraits of graduates, bronze cannons, and trophies from the Mexican, Civil, and Revolutionary Wars decorate the walls. The second floor has a ballroom that is used for hops and other social events. Courtesy The New-York Historical Society, New York City.

Below right:
The old cadet mess. c. 1907. U.S.M.A. Archives.

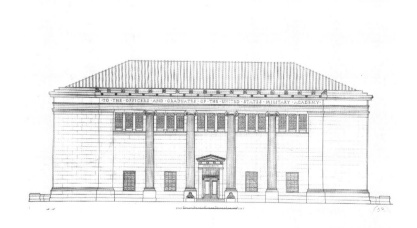

If the United States Military Academy seemed to be basking in the glory of the accomplishments of its graduates, however, it was not the result of any isolation from the world of education or any uncertainty of purpose, but rather the conscious and considered judgment of those in charge at West Point that they were already on the right course. Superintendent Thomas Ruger only echoed the sentiments of the majority of the faculty in 1872 when he reported that "the subjects of study at the Military Academy embrace all that is

Opposite:
The Battle of the Little Big Horn in 1876 is documented in these artifacts. The last message of George Custer (class of June 1861) is seen against a watercolor of the battle done twenty years later by White Bird, a Northern Cheyenne Indian, who had been at the battle. Arrows that were collected at the site are shown, together with a soldier's pistol. West Point Museum Collections, U.S.M.A.

Left:
The Battle Monument near Trophy Point, designed by Stanford White, was dedicated in 1897 to the men and officers of the Regular Army who lost their lives in the Civil War. There are 2,230 names inscribed on the various ornaments of the memorial, and a statue representing "Fame" at the top of the column.

The United States Military Academy Coat-of-Arms.

essential and nearly all that is necessary to the education of an officer of the Army." Still, West Point was not ignoring the changes in the world around it. Later that same year, the board sent Professors Michie and Kendrick to visit a number of colleges and universities in the United States and directed them to examine the newer schemes. "It is with pleasure," wrote Michie, "that I have to report that so far as the Military Academy is concerned, the character, scope and method of its instruction considering the end in view, is much superior to that of any institution either technical, special, or general." Even in a comparison of technical programs, he was convinced that the methods employed at West Point "display the best results." In conclusion, he said, "I think we may safely challenge any institution either in this country or in Europe to display results of study as favorable as those exhibited in the careers of our graduated cadets."

The instrument of change at the Military Academy was the academic board, but it was change of an evolutionary nature. When Albert Church died (1878) and Henry Kendrick retired (1880), the transformation of the academic board, which had begun ten years earlier, was complete. Church, who had been teaching mathematics at the Military Academy since 1828, was succeeded as professor of mathematics by Edgar Wales Bass. Bass, a graduate of the class of 1864, had served four years as an engineer officer before returning to West Point as an assistant professor of natural philosophy. Like Church, Bass was not particularly popular with the cadets. He was like "a piece of cold steel, with eyes like icicles, and a voice though soft, almost makes a fellow shudder from its cold-blooded softness," wrote one cadet. Bass continued as professor of mathematics until 1898 when failing eyesight caused him to retire. He, in turn, was succeeded by Wright Preston Edgerton, who had joined the department in 1882 as an assistant professor, and had been the associate professor since the creation of that position in 1893. Kendrick, who had served almost as many years in the chemistry department (beginning in 1835) as Church had in mathematics, was succeeded in 1880 by Samuel Tillman, class of 1869, who had served four and a half years as assistant professor of chemistry and a year as assistant professor of natural philosophy prior to this appointment. Tillman remained until 1911 when he retired, but he was called back to active duty as Superintendent from 1917 to 1919.

In 1883, Tillman, and G. L. Andrews, professor of modern languages, made a second tour of academic institutions to compare their methods of instruction with those at the Military Academy. Among others they visited the Massachusetts Institute of Technology, Harvard, Yale, and Dartmouth, where they observed recitations, laboratory exercises, and conferences. Andrews, upon his return to West Point, admitted that "the course at the Academy is susceptible of improvement," but added that "precisely what changes should be made, it is not easy to say." Still, he warned the academic board that "in this age of progress, not to advance is to retrograde."

Professor Tillman came back with more concrete measures in mind. He had long harbored concerns about the inadequacies of West Point's "physical teaching facilities" or laboratories, and upon returning from this junket he was more convinced than ever that West Point must begin to move its students out of the lecture hall and into the laboratory. In 1885, Tillman led the way in proposing a new academic building that would remedy this problem and also allow the Department of Natural Philosophy to move from the library building. A couple of years were spent in an unsuccessful attempt to remodel the old Academy building, but in 1889 appropriations were made for a new structure. The old academic hall was pulled down in 1891 to make room for the new structure. While the new building was taking shape, classes were held in the cadet barrack—in the ninth and tenth divisions and in the angle of the barrack, in the library, and in the administration building. The new academic building was occupied in 1895, finally making possible the laboratory method of teaching the sciences.

The years after 1871—reflecting the generational change that was taking place in the academic board—were years of revision, adjustment, and change in all the courses taught at the Military Academy. New knowledge dictated new texts. Michie introduced his first revisions of Bartlett's texts in 1874, and successively, in 1882, 1886, and 1887, replaced the older works on sound and light, analytical mechanics, and hydraulics. In engineering, Mahan's texts were revised repeatedly from 1882 to 1894 to reflect modern engineering practice and advances in the science and art of war. This work was begun by Wheeler,

The interior of the old library in 1886. The portrait of Thomas Jefferson by Sully can be seen at the top of the photograph, to the left. U.S.M.A. Library, Special Collections. Photo: Philip Pocock.

who had replaced Mahan in 1871, and was completed by James Mercur, who served until his death in 1896.

In mathematics, Bass had not only introduced new texts, but had completely restructured the curriculum. Surveying, which had for years been taught by that department, was changed from a theoretical to a practical course, and then transferred to the Department of Practical Engineering. Likewise, mathematical drawing was given over to the drawing department, which under Larned had also assumed a more utilitarian character.

But, the most dramatic changes in the Academy's curriculum came in the expansion of the humanities. Though there had been, since 1818, a Department of History, Geography, and Ethics, the professorial duties had been performed by the chaplain. For years the course consisted largely of the study of ethics and of the elements of constitutional or international law. Geography, history, and rhetoric had been introduced on several occasions, but had persisted only for brief periods. The expansion of the humanities beyond that taught by the chaplain began in 1874 with the creation of the Department of Law. Instruction in English was added in 1877 and the next year it was placed under the Department of French (later, Modern Languages). History was added in 1883 after the patient and persistent endeavors of Reverend Dr. William M. Postlethwaite, who had succeeded Forsyth in the chaplaincy and professorship of history, geography, and ethics in 1881. Upon Postlethwaite's death in 1896, history was transferred to the new Department of Law and History, and the chaplain's old department was dissolved. This increased emphasis upon the humanities proved to be a lasting development, although mathematics and the sciences continued to dominate the curriculum. And this was only the beginning of an evolution of the curriculum and an expansion of the humanities that would continue throughout the whole of the next century.

Neither these changes, nor any others, could have kept the Military Academy at the forefront of the institutions of science and engineering as it had been in the years before the Civil War. That earlier leadership had been largely serendipitous—falling to the Academy because its uniquely practical course in mathematics and military engineering positioned it advantageously just as the knowledge of basic engineering began to expand and as the demand for engineers began to grow. However, as soon as the growth in knowledge began to exceed that which was necessary for practical application in the military and civil realm, the Academy was displaced by institutions whose primary function was to extend the frontiers of knowledge—the universities with their expanding laboratory facilities and growing postgraduate programs. The absence of a graduate school of engineering at West Point—and there was no rationale for having one—meant the decline of the Academy relative to the nation's other technological institutions.

Although there were some who saw this as evidence of the demise of the Academy, the faculty that constituted the academic board was rightly unconcerned. The board members understood, better than their critics (both contemporary and modern), the purpose and role of the United States Military Academy. In 1900 they could point with pride to the most recent *Who's Who in America* that listed 5.6 percent of West Point's living graduates—a proportion higher than any other American college or university. Even if the academic board had seemed to stand in opposition to the tides of change that were affecting educational institutions all across the country, many of those who were champions of reform elsewhere agreed that the path West Point had chosen was correct for that institution. In 1893, the theories associated with mental discipline were reaffirmed in a National Education Association committee study: "To cultivate the habits of observation, the committee recommends the study of language and natural science; to train the reasoning faculties, mathematics; and to promote the invaluable mental power which we call judgment, history and its allied branches."

Few of the educators who commented on West Point criticized the Academy for failing to follow American colleges into elective programs and multiple specialties. Dr. William R. Harper, president of the University of Chicago, praised West Point's "concentration of effort." "The purpose had been a single one" with "no disposition . . . to dissipate the effort of instructor or student by undertaking to do things other than those directly and absolutely involved in the particular purpose for which the school was founded." He also praised "the degree of thoroughness demanded in the work"—a result of the small sections and daily recitations. "The spirit of accuracy developed under conditions which existed here at West Point, the high degree of thoroughness thus made possible are of inestimable value." Finally, he lauded "the spirit of subordination, of obedience, engendered in the student." It smacked of "pedagogical heterodoxy," he admitted, "to look with favor upon an educational policy which is not based upon the idea that the student must be allowed to follow his own sweet will in selecting his courses of study," but suggested that this trend may have "gone too far" and "been applied to fields of work in which it had no place."

In 1902, when Professors Tillman and Edgerton visited Yale, Harvard, and the Massachusetts Institute of Technology, they concluded that West Point cadets were receiving the same breadth of subject matter offered engineering students at these schools. The difference was that West Point spent nearly twice as much time as the rest on mathematics. Much of this excess was devoted to algebra and geometry, elementary subjects that should have been mastered in high school—the root cause being the low admission standards.

Admission standards was the one area in which the academic board had long sought reform—and here they had been repeatedly rebuffed. In 1866, the Congress had rigidly fixed admission standards calling for a knowledge of reading, writing, arithmetic, English grammar, and United States history. The oral examination had given way to a written one in 1870, and, as the general educational level of the country rose, the examinations had become more searching and demanding. Yet the standards of attainment required at

West Point continued to be more elementary than those of Harvard, Yale, the Massachusetts Institute of Technology, the Columbia School of Mines, the Rensselaer Polytechnic Institute, or even the United States Naval Academy. In addition, the high percentage of failures in the course and the crowded curriculum were attributed to the poor academic preparation of the candidates and the need to spend almost a year bringing a cadet up to the level of the average college freshman. But substantive change in the admission standards could come only if the law of 1866 were changed. Repeated recommendations to raise the standards had been made by the academic board and by the annual reports of the board of visitors, but Congress was not amenable to the idea.

For years, the calls for higher standards were met with essentially the same response. If West Point were to be "a perfectly republican, perfectly democratic institution" the standards of admission would have to allow "the son of the poorest" to enter "with the son of the richest." To ensure that, these young men would have to be allowed to enter the Academy if they were able to read and write and do simple mathematics.

It was not until the beginning of the twentieth century that Congress could be persuaded to act. In 1901, however, they changed the law and allowed the Secretary of War—in effect, the academic board—to establish the admission requirements. The new law specified only that "all appointees shall be examined under regulations to be framed by the Secretary of War" and that the examination should cover "such subjects as he may from time to time prescribe." In a few short years, the academic board raised the standards to an educational level commensurate with that common to the public and private high schools throughout the country.

By 1890, there was a well-established tradition of informal and intramural athletics at the Military Academy—field sports, baseball, sculling, tennis, and gymnastics. But nothing had prepared the institution for the upheaval that came in the wake of intercollegiate football or, more particularly, in the wake of the naval cadets from Annapolis when they were invited to West Point in November 1890 for a game. Navy had been fielding a football team for several years, but at West Point only two cadets, Dennis Mahan Michie and Leonard M. Prince, had ever played. Dennis Michie, son of Professor Peter Smith Michie, undertook to coach the team, but Superintendent John M. Wilson allowed the cadets to practice only on rainy Saturday afternoons when parades could not be held. Predictably, Navy proved too much for the inexperienced cadets—winning by a lopsided 24-to-0.

By the next year, 1891, Army was playing a full schedule of five home games: Rutgers, Tufts, Stevens Institute, Fordham and Princeton (winning only one). But even then, only the Navy game counted, and at Annapolis the cadets revenged the defeat of the year before by a score of 32-to-16.

The Army-Navy game immediately become a *cause célèbre* for the graduates of both academies. Contributions poured in from every regiment in the Army to hire a coach and buy uniforms for the team, and the Army Officers' Athletic Association was founded to support athletics at West Point. In 1892, the game returned to West Point, and in 1893 was played again at Annapolis; the midshipmen won both. Scores and play-by-play accounts of the games were printed in the *Army and Navy Journal,* and the game was the only topic of conversation at officers' clubs around the country for months before and after the encounter. The game in 1893 led to such a heated argument between an army brigadier general and a navy rear admiral at the Army-Navy Club in New York that there were threats of a duel. Superintendent Oswald H. Ernst, though amenable to football generally, was concerned about this growing rivalry. "The excitement attending it exceeds all reasonable limits," he reported after the game in 1893. He feared that the excitement would continue to grow and that the game would be marked by even more bitterness. He recommended that the series with Navy be discontinued. The Secretaries of War and Navy agreed and, in 1894, they canceled future games by the simple expedient of ruling that neither team could leave its grounds for a game.

Despite that setback, Army continued to expand its football program. They were soon scheduling the giants of the East—Harvard, Yale, and Princeton—and winning regularly. By 1897, the Army team was ranked fourth in the nation. In 1899, the Army-Navy game was revived—an annual series that has not been interrupted to this day. The game in 1899 produced Army's second victory over the Middies. Two more victories, in 1901 and 1902, brought the series to a 4-to-4 tie.

The year 1902 marked the completion of the first century in the life of the Military Academy. The close of the academic year was decided upon as the most suitable time for commemorating that anniversary. The four days of celebration began with Alumni Day on June 9th, when the oldest graduate present, General John S. McCalmont of the class of 1842, opened the celebration in Cullum Memorial Hall.

Centennial Day, June 11th, was marked by the arrival of President Theodore Roosevelt. Escorted by a detachment of cavalry, he rode up from the train station to the plain and received the salute of the Corps of Cadets while the cannon boomed a twenty-one gun salute. Then he rode on to the Superintendent's house, descended from the carriage, joined the assembled crowd of dignitaries, and led them across the plain to the reviewing stand. Later he spoke to the cadets and to the assembled guests. ''During [its first] century,'' the President told them, ''no other educational institution in the land has contributed as many names as West Point has contributed to the honor roll of the nation's greatest citizens. . . . And of all the institutions in the country, none is more absolutely American; none, in the proper sense of the word, more absolutely democratic than this. Here we care nothing for the boy's birthplace, nor his creed, nor his social standing. . . . Here you represent, with almost mathematical exactness, all the country geographically. You are drawn from every walk of life by a method of choice made to insure . . . that heed shall be paid to nothing save the boy's aptitude for the profession into which he seeks entrance. Here you come together as representatives of America in a higher and more peculiar sense than can possibly be true of any other institution in the land, save your sister college [the Naval Academy].''

That evening, West Point glittered. There was a graduation parade, a Centennial banquet, and a fireworks display. The next day the President handed each of the members

Below left:
Fencing class held in the gymnasium, c. 1901. U.S.M.A. Archives.

Below right:
The first Army-Navy football game took place in 1890. The more experienced Navy team won the game 24-0. U.S.M.A. Archives.

President Theodore Roosevelt is seen here (in top hat) on his way to the West Point Centennial Exercises. U.S.M.A. Library, Special Collections. Photo: Philip Pocock.

The West Point Centennial celebration in 1902 lasted four days and was attended by many celebrities, graduates of the Academy, and interested members of the general public. Culver Pictures.

of the class of 1902 their diplomas. With that, the Centennial celebration came to a close. Within hours, President Roosevelt had entrained, and the galaxy of ambassadors, university presidents, congressmen, and senior military officers had departed. Then West Point resumed the routine so long familiar to it. It "became again," wrote historian Roger Hurless Nye, "the eyrie of its duly-appointed oligarchs, the Superintendent, the Commandant, and the seven Professors of the Academic Board."

CHAPTER 8
THE NEW WEST POINT
1902-1930

In October 1902, invitations to participate in a limited architectural competition were mailed by Superintendent Albert L. Mills. The winner of the competition would create, in effect, a new West Point. It was to be the most massive construction effort yet undertaken there. Ten architectural firms were invited to compete: Cope and Stewardson; Hines and LaFarge; Carrete and Hastings; Peabody and Stearns; Armes and Young; Charles C. Haight; Daniel H. Burnham; Cram, Goodhue and Ferguson; McKim, Mead and White; and Frost and Granger. The work was to include a cadet barracks, an academic building, a post headquarters, a headquarters for the Corps of Cadets, a riding hall, an artillery barracks with stable and gun shed, a cavalry barracks and stable, a hotel, and quarters for the bachelor officers.

To the architects the project presented both an opportunity and a challenge. Few had ever undertaken the execution of such an impressive scheme—one that embraced not only the structures, but the related roads, utilities, and landscaping, as well. Moreover, their plan would have to both meet the practical requirements of the Military Academy, and "provide a treatment worthy of the historic associations and natural beauties of the site."

The seeds of this competition had been sown in June 1899 when the board of visitors, reflecting on the nation's unpreparedness for the war in which it was then engaged, insisted that the usefulness of the Academy should be increased. They called for a detailed report concerning present facilities and the additions necessary to expand the number of cadets to five hundred.

Charles W. Larned, professor of drawing, was asked to draw up this report, and he submitted it on August 10, 1899. It was a modest proposal recommending the enlargement of the chapel, cadet hospital, gymnasium, and mess hall, as well as provision for a new officers' mess, and more quarters for both the married and bachelor officers. He also pointed out the need for a new hotel and suggested a central heating plant, a new facility to generate electricity, and alterations and additions to the sewers. The overall cost of these improvements, he estimated, was just over $2,200,000.

The only item in Larned's proposal that stirred any immediate controversy was the site he had picked for the new cadet barracks. Larned suggested locating it on the west edge of the plain, north of and at a right angle to the existing barracks—although this would entail removing some of the professors' quarters. Mills preferred placing it behind the existing barrack, forming a quadrangle in the midst of the barracks and the academic building, and he won the academic board's approval of his plan.

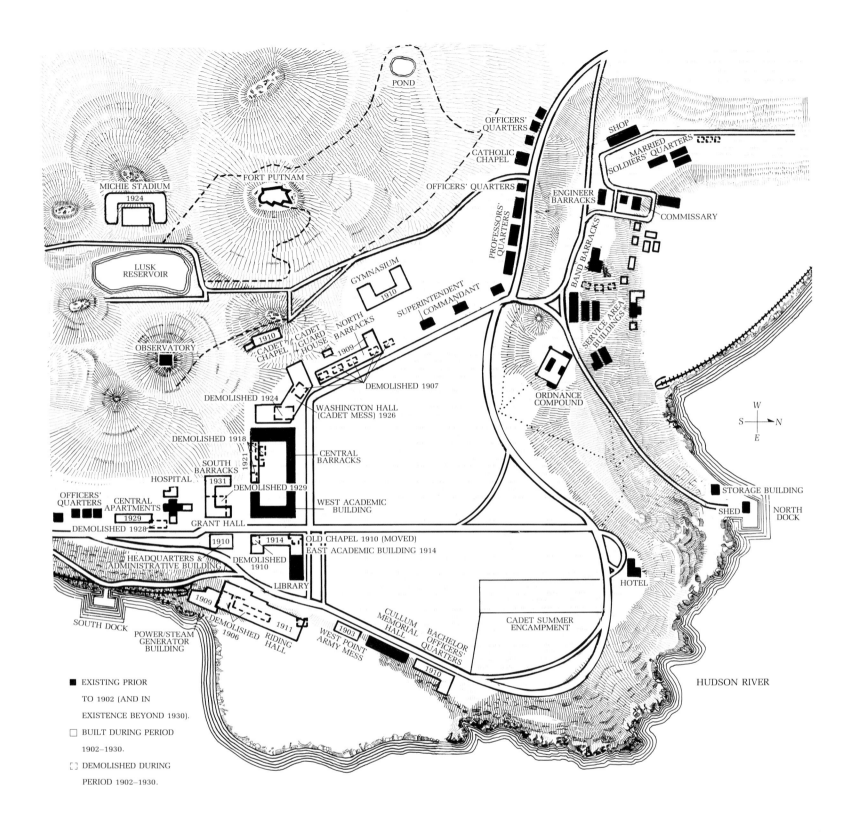

POND

OFFICERS' QUARTERS

CATHOLIC CHAPEL

OFFICERS' QUARTERS

SHOP

MARRIED SOLDIERS' QUARTERS

ENGINEER BARRACKS

COMMISSARY

PROFESSORS' QUARTERS

MICHIE STADIUM
1924

FORT PUTNAM

BAND BARRACKS

GYMNASIUM
1910

SERVICE AREA BUILDINGS

LUSK RESERVOIR

SUPERINTENDENT
COMMANDANT

OBSERVATORY

1910

CADET CHAPEL

NORTH BARRACKS

CADET GUARD HOUSE

1909

ORDNANCE COMPOUND

DEMOLISHED 1907

DEMOLISHED 1924

WASHINGTON HALL
(CADET MESS) 1926

W

S   N

E

DEMOLISHED 1918

CENTRAL BARRACKS

SOUTH BARRACKS

HOSPITAL

1921

DEMOLISHED 1929

STORAGE BUILDING

OFFICERS' QUARTERS

CENTRAL APARTMENTS
1929

GRANT HALL
1931

WEST ACADEMIC BUILDING

SHED

NORTH DOCK

DEMOLISHED 1928

1910

1914

OLD CHAPEL 1910 (MOVED)

HEADQUARTERS & ADMINISTRATIVE BUILDING

DEMOLISHED 1910

EAST ACADEMIC BUILDING 1914

LIBRARY

HOTEL

1909

SOUTH DOCK

DEMOLISHED 1906

DEMOLISHED 1911

RIDING HALL

WEST POINT ARMY MESS

1903

CULLUM MEMORIAL HALL

BACHELOR OFFICERS' QUARTERS

CADET SUMMER ENCAMPMENT

POWER/STEAM GENERATOR BUILDING

1910

HUDSON RIVER

■ EXISTING PRIOR TO 1902 (AND IN EXISTENCE BEYOND 1930).

□ BUILT DURING PERIOD 1902–1930.

⸦⸧ DEMOLISHED DURING PERIOD 1902–1930.

Map of West Point, 1902–1930.

In 1900, Congress acted on the recommendation of the board of visitors and increased the authorized number of cadets by one hundred, to 481, but they made no provision for enlarging the Academy's physical plant. The board of visitors, in 1900, acknowledged the increased number of cadets, but called attention to the need for additional barracks and for an enlargement of the mess hall. Mills endorsed their report, but warned against half-way or temporary measures. Not only would they be "destructive to the convenience and to the dignity and beauty of the institution as an architectural whole," but also "more wasteful and extravagant in the long run." With that, he set Larned to work again.

This time the professor produced a much more ambitious program. In addition to the new cadet barracks, he suggested a second academic building, a new chapel, a new riding hall, a new post headquarters, a new headquarters for the Corps of Cadets, and a new hotel—renewing, at the same time, his call for additional officers' quarters. The estimate for this work rose to approximately $6,500,000.

In 1901, the board of visitors restated their plea of the year before for an expansion of the Academy's facilities, but this time, led by Lieutenant General John M. Schofield, the former Superintendent and recently Commanding General of the Army, they went further. "It would be the part of wisdom and good business to place the Military Academy, with all its natural advantages and physical imperfections, in the hands of an architect of recognized ability," they reported adding that, "almost every dollar spent in the future for 'enlarging here and altering and patching there' is so much money thrown away."

Congress agreed and, in June 1902, appropriated $5,500,000 for the project. At West Point, Mills appointed a board to review Larned's work and specify requirements on which an architectural competition could be based. The board was composed of Larned, Samuel Tillman (professor of chemistry), Edward E. Wood (professor of modern languages), Gustav J. Fiebeger (professor of engineering), and Captain Frank E. Hobbs (instructor of ordnance and gunnery). Although there were some differences of opinion within the board, their report to the Superintendent on October 1st largely coincided with Larned's most recent proposal. But, since Congress had appropriated 5.5 million dollars, instead of the 6.6 million that Larned had deemed necessary, the board recommended against building a new hotel. Mills forwarded the report to Washington, but he had reservations about some of its recommendations. He was concerned that the report was not sufficiently forward looking. "In the scheme for the new improvements," he wrote, "the broadest view should be taken so that no work done now would have to be undone in the future." The architects, he added, should "be given the freest scope in making their studies without regard to the plans or to the particular locations recommended by the members of the Board."

The board's report was issued in early October 1902, and later that same month, at the direction of the Secretary of War, invitations inviting firms to participate in the architectural competition were issued. In February 1903, the formal rules governing the competition were circulated to the competing firms, and the jury was identified: Schofield, Mills, and three distinguished architects—George B. Post, Walter Cook, and Cass Gilbert.

Below left:
The Central Barracks in 1902. U.S.M.A. Archives.

Below right:
The view of Central Barracks from the plain in 1902. U.S.M.A. Archives.

This 1902 photograph shows the museum collection of cannons, weaponry, and flags. U.S.M.A. Archives.

The question of architectural style was ostensibly left to the firms participating in the competition, but there was a clear local predisposition toward the Gothic. In 1899, Larned had noted that the Tudor-Gothic style of the cadet barracks and library had, "to a certain extent, determined the character of some of the more important neighbors." In 1901, Larned had been even more direct. "It is not desirable," he wrote, "that any scheme should attempt to sweep the field clean and destroy architectural associations made honorable by generations of great men, while it is of the highest importance to preserve intact the structural sentiment which gives character and individuality to the Academy." In 1902, the board of officers, of which Larned was president, advised quite explicitly that "the design of the principal new public buildings should conform to the prevailing Gothic." Still, in his letter of invitation to the architects, Mills assured them all that the board's views "either as to location or character of buildings or as to the treatment of the subject" were not to be considered binding.

All of the firms that were known for their Gothic designs were invited to enter the competition, but since there were so few of these, other leading architects were also included. Still, when the Gothic designs of Cram, Goodhue and Ferguson, of Boston, seemed to meet all the requirements of the competition, and fit so masterfully the peculiarities of the site, the judges were unanimous in choosing their submission.

In most respects, the firm's plans followed the board's 1902 recommendations as to the location of structures. The riding hall was to sit on the ground then occupied by the stables, the old riding hall, and the cavalry barracks, while the new headquarters building was to be located across from the cadet mess. The new academic building was to occupy the site of the existing chapel and administration building, the new chapel was to be located on a hillside overlooking the parade ground, and the additional cadet barracks would create a quadrangle behind the current barracks. The architect's plan made only two important departures from the board's earlier recommendations. The first was the razing of the hotel and the construction of a new one on the hillside above the cadet hospital. Second, having cleared Trophy Point, the architects proposed to build there a massive residence for the Superintendent that would also contain reception rooms and suites of apartments for distinguished visitors. "We feel very strongly," wrote the architects, "that that main avenue as it prolongs itself across the Military Plain demands a focal point of considerable importance." The jury concurred in all of this except the location of the barracks. In that, the majority favored Larned's earlier proposal, and insisted on placing it on the west edge of the plain—to the north and west of the existing barracks.

In developing this new West Point it was the aim of the architects, both in their general plan and in the designs of individual buildings, to preserve the natural features that give such distinction to the site. They sought to make their style "harmonize with the majority of the existing buildings" and to make it "emphasize rather than antagonize the picturesque natural surroundings of rocks, cliffs, mountains, and forests." This was most evident in the design of the riding hall, chapel, and headquarters building. The natural appearance of these buildings was enhanced by using stone quarried from the hill immediately behind the Superintendent's quarters. The huge bulk of the riding hall made it impressive, yet it seemed to grow out of the granite cliff to which it clung. Although simple in conception, its steel arches were anchored in broad buttresses whose shallow vertical serrations gave it a distinctly Gothic character. Similarly, the new headquarters or administration building, with its buttressed granite walls and its tower rising 160 feet above the ground, stood like a Gothic castle.

The chapel, though, was the crown of the general plan. Situated high above the plain, its lofty spire seemingly seeking the heavens, it overlooked the barracks and dominated

Below left:
Drawing was an important part of the curriculum at the Academy. This is a class c. 1900. U.S.M.A. Archives.

Below right:
The billiard room in the officers' mess on the post in 1903. U.S.M.A. Archives.

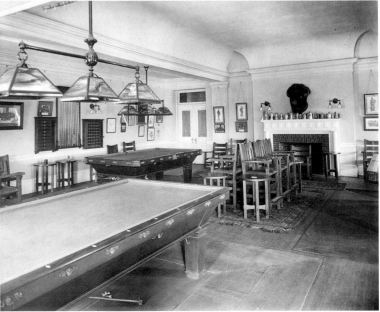

Cavalry training in the old riding hall. Drawn by R.F. Zogbaum. From Harper's Weekly. *U.S.M.A. Library, Special Collections. Photo: Philip Pocock.*

Cadets loading a mortar at the coast artillery in 1903. U.S.M.A. Archives.

the plain and academic area in a physical sense that suggested an even greater moral presence and purview.

Mills met privately with the architects at West Point in late June 1903. At this meeting, he presented the revisions that the jury had recommended and instructed the architects to consider in their plans the provisions necessary if the corps were to expand to 1,200 cadets. Mills did not include any of the permanent professors in the meetings—nor did he, at the time, solicit their views. "It did not seem advisable to authorize *ad libitum* conferences between the Advisory Board and the architects," he later wrote, adding, "it has seemed both wise and proper to require both parties to present their cases to the Superintendent."

A few months later, in September 1903, Mills reconvened the board of officers as an advisory board to consider the architects' plans. In their first session, the board applauded the work of the architects, suggesting only that in replacing the quarters lost to the barrack site, the architects should group "the houses of the professors and of the Commandant of Cadets in the [same] neighborhood, so as to keep the heads of departments in close contact with the Academy and barracks." Without comment, they approved the plan to construct new quarters for the Superintendent on Trophy Point.

In December, however, the board learned that the architects desired to increase the mass of the structures on Trophy Point and had proposed to group several additional

quarters near those of the Superintendent. The Superintendent, they were informed, had chosen to gather around himself his military staff—the Commandant of Cadets, the adjutant, the quartermaster, and the surgeon—rather than the academic staff. The advisory board immediately objected. This complex should house the Superintendent, the Commandant of Cadets, and "the permanent officers of the Academic Board," they argued. They would not be relegated to second importance. Mills ignored the board and forwarded the plan to Secretary of War Elihu Root, who approved it in late January 1904—one of his last official acts.

Mills's deliberate snub of the academic board in this matter was symptomatic of an underlying conflict with the permanent professors. When he had been appointed, in 1898, First Lieutenant Albert L. Mills, class of 1879, was the most junior officer ever to have been made Superintendent—although he immediately assumed the local rank of colonel. His appointment as Superintendent of the Military Academy had startled the West Point community and the Army. Mills was forty-four years old when appointed (several officers had been made Superintendent at a younger age), but he seemed young in comparison to his predecessor, who had graduated fifteen years ahead of him, and even younger in relation to many members of the faculty, several of whom had first arrived at West Point while he was but a young boy. Michie and Larned had been full professors, and Wood an instructor, while Mills was a cadet. His rank and his comparative youth seemed better to befit him for a more subordinate position. In fact, Major Otto L. Hein, the Commandant of Cadets, had suggested as much to him: "I wrote to . . . Mills of my regiment, who had been seriously wounded . . . expressing my sympathy, and offering to apply for his detail as Adjutant of the Military Academy." Imagine Hein's chagrin when, only weeks later, it was announced that Mills was to be made Superintendent.

This rather extraordinary appointment had come at the personal initiative of President William McKinley and had been advanced over the opposition of many in Washington. Mills had lost an eye when he was shot through the head in the battle for San Juan Hill. Barely a month later, while convalescing in Washington, Mills was introduced to the President. McKinley was quite affected by Mills and his ordeal, and was determined to reward him. Finding promotion impracticable, he sought an alternative. McKinley, at the time, had before him a slate of officers who had been recommended to replace the current Superintendent, Oswald Ernst. Instead of drawing from that list, he named Mills to be Superintendent of the Military Academy. Both Nelson A. Miles, the Commanding Gen-

Douglas C. MacArthur, as a cadet. He entered the Academy in 1899 and graduated at the head of his class in 1903. U.S.M.A. Library, Special Collections. Photo: Philip Pocock.

eral, and Secretary of War Russell Alger objected, but to no avail—the recent debacle in Cuba had diluted their influence and thus their ability to press the issue.

To the faculty, Mills soon came to be viewed as an *enfant terrible*—impertinent, abrasive, and vindictive—for in his zeal he often deliberately trod on turf the academics had long since staked out as their own. His snub regarding the new quarters became a *cause célèbre*. The fight it engendered illustrates both the nature and mode of the conflicts that periodically occurred between the permanent faculty and the transient, but reform-minded superintendents. Although, on the surface, these quarrels often seemed trivial and spiteful, they had a significance beyond the issues being debated. In fact, they often helped to decide the broader questions of province and prerogative—questions that determined who would define the essential nature of the institution.

The advisory board responded formally on May 5, 1904 to Mills's action. They now objected to removing the hotel from Trophy Point; that was only necessary as "a consequence of the carrying out of the proposed location of the Superintendent's quarters and other buildings at or near Trophy Point," they insisted. They urged that further consideration of a new hotel (and, by implication, the new Superintendent's quarters) should be postponed. Mills, again, simply dismissed their arguments and informed the board that he intended to erect all the principal buildings "under the present appropriation."

At that, the advisory board fired off a letter to the War Department complaining that Mills was ignoring their concerns that the plans, as they stood, could not be executed "within the limits of the appropriation." They also objected to the fact that they were not being shown all of the plans. "The issues involved," they insisted, "are such that if decided unwisely would detrimentally and permanently affect the efficiency of the institution and the comfort and welfare of its personnel." Appropriately, this letter was submitted first to Mills, but when he did not forward it to the War Department, one of the board members took the issue to the *Army and Navy Journal*, prompting an editorial critical of Mills's handling of the affair. "We have reason to believe that there is dissatisfaction with the plan of leaving so important a matter within the control of any one man [Mills]," wrote the editor, in June 1904. "Questions are being settled 'by authority,' which should be open to free discussion by those to whom the interests of the Military Academy are subjects of vital concern."

Thus prodded, Mills sent the letter on to the War Department, but he complained that the advisory board "wants power and authority over the work equal to that exercised by the Superintendent." This was, "but the first step in an attempt to upset the general plan," Mills insisted, and he recommended that the board's letter not even be shown to the new Secretary of War, William Howard Taft. He also solicited a statement from the War Department to the effect that "there is no intention to alter in any material respect the general plan" that had already been approved.

Fred Ainsworth, the military secretary in Washington, had no intention of getting entangled in this issue, and forwarded the whole package to the new secretary. Taft's response carved out something of a middle position. The plan approved by Root would be followed, he announced, but subject to those changes necessary "to bring the cost of the work within the amount appropriated therefor by Congress." Mills sent Taft's response to Larned and the board, but tried to stifle further dissent by ordering that the contents "not be made public."

Undaunted, the advisory board resumed their assault in October 1904—complaining this time that the architects seemed "exceedingly anxious to economize" in the construction of the academic building, "in order to preserve the integrity of plans of other buildings which the Board regards as of less vital importance to the institution than this one." The reference, of course, was to the complex of quarters for the Superintendent and his military staff.

Mills returned the board's communication, insisting that "no grounds exist to justify [the board's assertions]," and that the tone and wording of the report was both "unmilitary and unnecessary." In the future, he instructed the board, their views should "be expressed more effectively in less objectionable language." The advisory board answered him the same day. The letter had been properly respectful, they insisted, and—in any case—their remarks were directed at the architects and not the Superintendent. Moreover they wanted direct access to the architects, and wished to have their views made known to the Secretary of War. They were not opposed to the general plan, they said, and had raised only a few objections, including, of course, "the grouping of military rather than Academic Staff about the Superintendent."

After that salvo, the attention of all parties was diverted by the start of construction of the power plant and the administrative building. The issue of the Superintendent's quarters receded into the background for a time. Construction at the south end of the post began in 1905 with barracks and stables for the artillery and cavalry troops. These were completed in 1908. In the summer of 1906, work began on the new administration building (completed 1910) and on the heating and generating plant that was to be located adjacent to the riding hall (completed 1909).

In August 1906, Mills departed and Major Hugh L. Scott, class of 1876, became Superintendent. "One of the pressing questions found on my arrival," wrote Scott some years later, "was the location of the new chapel. One faction wanted it at the lower end of the post, while another demanded the northern end, where it would mask the view up the Hudson, one of the glories of West Point." Scott favored the hillside site that had been selected by the architects and approved by Mills. To settle the issue, he ordered Colonel J. M. Carlson, the quartermaster who supervised the construction, "to dig a hole where the chapel now stands, blast some rock, and what would still be more convincing, spend some money." This done, "it was generally recognized that the matter was settled, and the clamor ceased." The chapel was completed and dedicated in 1910.

The issue of the complex of quarters at Trophy Point was raised again in December 1906, this time by the architects—perhaps they believed that Scott would act in this case with the same resolve he had shown concerning the chapel. This "mass of buildings," they argued, "is imperative at the termination of the axis of the main Avenue . . . which is the principal and most important line of vision."

In the meantime, while this issue had lain dormant at West Point, opposition had been growing among the graduates and friends of the Academy who feared that these structures would block the north view of the river. This sentiment was voiced forcefully by the board of visitors in 1906, who made "a very earnest protest . . . against the construction of any buildings in this neighborhood."

New plans for the complex arrived from Cram, Goodhue and Ferguson in February 1907. But the advisory board now joined the chorus of opposition, insisting that "the intrusion upon the Plain of an extensive group of buildings . . . will necessarily intercept the view at this end of the Post and remove from the public use a large part of the most picturesque portion of the general parade." Letters from graduates that appeared in the *Army and Navy Journal* indicated the extent of the opposition. "To shut off the slightest portion of it would seem a useless act of vandalism and would cause more ill feeling among officers, professors and all graduates than anything that could happen," wrote Horace Porter, president of the Association of Graduates, to Secretary of War Taft.

The issue took on a new sense of urgency when President Roosevelt became involved. Letters to him from Mrs. Henry Cabot Lodge and Mrs. C. F. LaFarge asked that he intervene and save the renowned north view from West Point. "Indeed," wrote Scott to the architects, "the positive instructions of the President of the United States on this point are that this view shall in no manner or way be impaired."

The cadet chapel is cruciform in plan, with a huge central tower. Around the cornice are a series of figures representing the quest for the Holy Grail, and over the door is carved a great two-handed sword representing King Arthur's "Excalibur." The great chancel stained-glass window was installed in memory of departed graduates, and there is also a twenty-one panel window above the main door, as well as a fine range of clerestory windows. Pendor Natural Color.

A hasty meeting was arranged in early March 1907, between Scott and the architects. In advance of the meeting the architects asked that a pole be erected thirty feet high at the site that would be the southwest corner of the proposed structures. "This will enable us at once to see . . . just how much of the view is cut off from any portion of the Plain," they wrote. Scott and the architects came away from this meeting convinced that the buildings would neither obstruct the view nor encroach on the plain. The Superintendent took the report of this investigation personally to the President. Roosevelt was satisfied. "It shall be carried out exactly as recommended," he instructed.

With the President's personal approval of the project, the advisory board was informed that "the question . . . is therefore definitely settled." Two days later the advisory board forwarded to the Superintendent its study of the latest plans concerning the project. Dutifully they "recommend[ed] that the location of the buildings and their general arrangement be in conformity with the wishes of the architects." In the specifics, however, they raised new issues. They called attention to the areas devoted to official entertainment and functions, and two large suites of rooms—one for the President and another for the Secretary of War. These, they pointed out, would necessitate "a fully equipped kitchen," a "permanent staff" of domestics, and accommodations for all of them, despite the fact that "a large portion of the time there will be no use for [their] services." In addition, the board noted that the quarters proposed for the Superintendent's military staff were "considerably in excess of that designed elsewhere for officers of corresponding rank."

Based on the advisory board's latest report, Scott asked Cram, Goodhue and Ferguson to "restudy and replan this whole group." There should be a "material reduction" in the "official [guest] quarters," and he ordered a significant reduction in the size of the staff officers' quarters. The architects obliged and forwarded new plans to Scott for his approval. By this time, however, Scott had discovered that the opposition of the old grads had not been diminished by the President's approval, and he deferred final approval of the plans.

At that, the issue again receded into the background. For almost four years the attention of the Superintendent and the architects was occupied otherwise. North Barracks was

The old cadet chapel was moved to the post cemetery in 1910.

Typical cadet barracks room of 1912 as it is exhibited at the Academy today.

Cadets performing physical training under arms on the plain in 1903. U.S.M.A. Archives.

North Barracks, c. 1900s, had sally ports and corner towers that harmonized with the Tudor-Gothic style of Central Barracks. (During the expansion of the Academy in the late 1960s, North Barracks would be demolished.) U.S.M.A. Archives.

finished in 1909—the first building on the level of the plain to be completed. The new gymnasium was begun in 1908 and completed two years later. Work on the riding hall proper began in 1909 and was finished in 1911. In 1910, when the administration building and new chapel were occupied, the old chapel and headquarters were removed to make room for the east academic building, which was under construction from 1911 to 1914. In the summer of 1910, the old chapel was rebuilt—stone by stone—in the post cemetery where it stands today.

In 1911, Cram, Goodhue and Ferguson once again raised the issue of the quarters complex at Trophy Point but a new Superintendent, Major General Thomas H. Barry, of the class of 1877, was not sympathetic to the project. "This group of buildings has been a burning question from the beginning," he wrote, and then listed his objections: a separate set of quarters for distinguished visitors is not necessary; and the quarters for the Superintendent and military staff would be expensive and extravagant. Moreover, he added, "there is some sentiment connected with these old buildings," referring to the present quarters of the Superintendent and permanent professors. "I am satisfied," Barry wrote, that "the best interests of the Academy and economy do not warrant the construction of this group of buildings." And so the matter was finally resolved.

Superintendent Barry departed West Point in 1912 and left the completion of construction to his successor, Colonel Clarence Page Townsley, of the class of 1881. The work, which had begun in 1904, was finally completed in 1914. But, hardly had the last stone been laid, when Townsley began planning for still further construction to accommodate an enlarged corps of cadets. From 1900 to 1914 the total number of cadets authorized had grown from 481 to 748. In 1916, in response to America's growing commitment in the Caribbean and Pacific, and to the war in Europe, the number was almost doubled to 1,332. In 1918, when entry into the war made growth to the authorized level obligatory, construction was begun on facilities to accommodate the larger number of cadets. A new barrack completed the quadrangle behind the 1851 edifice, and followed the architectural lines of the Delafield barrack. It was completed in 1921. At about the same time, a new cadet hospital was begun, designed by Arnold W. Brunner; it was finished in 1923. The old (1884) hospital was converted to other purposes and was pulled down section by section (the last in 1959), as new buildings crowded in.

Above left:
The old library was next to the east academic building and is seen here as it appeared in 1914. U.S.M.A. Archives.

Above right:
The west academic building in 1914. U.S.M.A. Archives.

Dwight D. Eisenhower, class of 1915, as a cadet. U.S.M.A. Archives.

At West Point, football is played at Michie Stadium, which was dedicated in 1924 and expanded in 1969. Today, it can accommodate just over 41,000 spectators and is near the scenic Lusk Reservoir.

In 1920, with peace restored, a new Superintendent—Douglas MacArthur, class of 1903—called attention to the fact that while the recent reorganization of the Army had nearly doubled the pre-war size of the officer corps, the authorized strength of the corps of cadets at West Point had remained at 1,332. Noting that the size of the brigade of midshipmen at Annapolis had recently been increased to an authorized strength ceiling of over three thousand, MacArthur called for an expansion of the number of cadets at West Point to 2,500. The next year he submitted plans for construction to accommodate this number. Prominent in his plan was a sports stadium at Gee's Point and new quarters for the Superintendent at the edge of the plain at Trophy Point. MacArthur estimated the cost of the project to be six million dollars, including the construction of a new hotel. Although nothing came of the plan, piecemeal construction continued at West Point. A new stadium was constructed in 1924, but not at Gee's Point. Rather, it was nestled in a natural amphitheater just to the west of Lusk Reservoir—possibly the loveliest setting in

all of collegiate football. A new hotel was finally built in 1925 at the south end of the post, overlooking the river. The old hotel remained vacant for several years, filled only with its memories, until it was finally demolished in 1932.

The earlier construction of North Barracks on the western edge of the plain made a more centrally located cadet dining facility very desirable, and with the completion of the new gymnasium, the site of the old gym (1891)—directly between the two barracks areas—became available. In 1924, the older structure was pulled down and the next year a new mess hall was begun. Washington Hall, as it soon became known, was completed in 1926. William Gehron, with Arnold W. Brunner and Associates, was the architect, and his design, with its strongly built buttresses fronting the structure, conformed handsomely to the Gothic character of the barracks on either side.

The construction of Washington Hall, in turn, made possible the destruction of the old Grant Hall and the erection, in its place, of a new South Barracks—designed by Gehron

Cadets are shown here wearing the various uniforms in use during 1914. U.S.M.A. Archives.

and Sidney F. Ross. Begun in 1930, it was completed the following year; like the old mess hall that had previously occupied the site, it was called Grant Hall. The battlements, the rough-cut stone, and the entrances and windows of the cadet reception room on the first floor, allowed it to blend effectively with those buildings adjoining it.

Among the constants of life at West Point since the time of Thayer had been the summer encampment—traditionally established at the end of June on the plain just south of Fort Clinton, and closed on August 28 when the cadets would return to the barracks. During the summer, cadets lived under canvas and took a respite from their academic work. They spent the mornings training in artillery gun exercises, tactical movements, and drill. During summer afternoons they lounged about camp—resting and chatting, while the evenings were occasions for concerts and entertainments, with hops and balls on the weekends. Summer was the social season at West Point, and young ladies from the South and New York City traveled there to escape the heat (and possibly to meet a young man with prospects). The season began with a celebration on the Fourth of July and climaxed at the end of the encampment with a grand ball.

The summer encampment followed much the same routine until the late 1890s, when Major Otto L. Hein, the Commandant of Cadets, instituted a number of changes designed to better prepare cadets for actual field duty with troops. First, he issued the cadets field service uniforms and field equipment. Then, he expanded the course of practical military instruction, adding tactical exercises for the infantry and the cavalry, and practice marches for infantry, cavalry, and light artillery. Finally, he introduced the cadets to cavalry and artillery stable duties, and instituted a series of lectures on military hygiene.

In 1920, Douglas MacArthur abolished the summer encampment at Fort Clinton, saying that it was "a ludicrous caricature of life in the field." Instead, MacArthur ordered the cadets to report for summer training at Fort Dix, New Jersey.

This abrupt uprooting of the encampment—and with it the summer social season—engendered such resentment among the Academy's officers and their wives, and among the old graduates, that the traditional policy was reinstated by the War Department in 1922, even before MacArthur had left West Point for the Philippines. "The return to the traditional practice of establishing a summer camp at West Point proved an unqualified success," reported Brigadier General Fred W. Sladen, MacArthur's successor. Al-

The summer encampment provided the cadets with a welcome change of pace from their academic schedule, as can be seen in this 1905 photograph. U.S.M.A. Archives.

The cadet reception area in the new Grant Hall has a ceiling with exposed beams upon which appear the seals of the fifty states and the insignia from the military divisions of World War I. The portraits in the room are of famous senior generals.

though field training increased over the years, the cadets continued to encamp at Fort Clinton until 1942.

However much the life of cadets in the early years of the twentieth century may have resembled that of their predecessors, there were areas in which it had begun to change. One such was announced in the fall of 1919. "With this the first publication of 'THE BRAY', the Corps enters a new field—Journalism," announced the editors of a new weekly paper to be published by and for the corps of cadets.

The Bray first appeared in November of 1919 under the editorial direction of Cadet A. C. Spaulding, class of 1922, and was supervised by an officer who had personally been instructed by MacArthur that he would "be responsible, wholly and solely so, for every word that goes into this paper." Although it would be permitted "to set forth freely and unreservedly the Cadet viewpoint on all matters," wrote Robert M. Danford, the Commandant, the paper was expected to be "loyal always, as a good soldier, to official decisions rendered." It was to be "the organ of the entire corps" and to reflect "both the humorous and the serious side of cadet life."

All went well for about six months. Then, in the issue of May 11, 1920, an editorial complained that MacArthur's efforts to reshape the fourth class system was making the plebe year "a bed of roses." It opened bluntly: "We don't agree with the Superintendent's policies." When he was shown the article, MacArthur was furious. That edition was confiscated and destroyed. The publication was suspended immediately, and the officer-in-charge was summoned before the Superintendent and dismissed. "I am wiring Washington this very hour for your relief from the Academy," MacArthur told the officer curtly. "You will be off this Post without delay."

In the fall of 1923, after MacArthur had departed and after the class that had issued *The Bray* had graduated, the cadets again requested permission to begin their own publication. After some negotiation (during which the editorial staff finally agreed with an English department demand that at least half of each issue would be devoted to content of a literary nature) a bi-monthly magazine was approved by Superintendent Fred Sladen. *The Pointer*, as it was named, was an immediate and continuing success.

Debate over curriculum reform was virtually continuous at West Point from 1901 to 1911, for—by the beginning of that period—a consensus had developed among members of the academic board concerning the need for a number of changes. One clear need was for increased fluency in Spanish; the United States had only recently acquired important Spanish-speaking territories and, for a time, the Army was to administer them. In response, the academic board increased the regular Spanish course from seventy-eight to one-hundred-sixty lessons. The board also increased the number of lessons in English (to make a total of one-hundred-twenty–four) and in chemistry and electricity, and introduced instruction in military hygiene. This was to be accomplished by cuts in mathematics and natural philosophy, and by the elimination of one semester of French (from four to three).

Mills, who had encouraged the 1902 reforms—the "New Curriculum," as he called it—soon began to press for further changes. In a letter to the War Department in March 1904 he challenged two of the pillars of the Military Academy's academic program—the emphasis on mathematics and science, and the single curriculum for all cadets. The use of "scientific studies for the mental development of the students" had gone too far, he asserted. To remedy this, he suggested that "some of the courses taught might perhaps be omitted" and that the time thus gained could be allotted to other subjects and other departments. Next, he dismissed the argument that "every cadet who graduates from the Military Academy should pursue exactly the same course," and pointed out that "in more than one department of instruction Cadets in the upper portion of the class are now carried further in their studies than those in the lower portion." This brought him into almost immediate conflict with the academic board.

Larned answered him in an article that appeared in *The Churchman*, in August 1904. The cornerstone of the curriculum, he argued, was mathematics, and the bulk of the structure was necessarily made up of the sciences. West Point shunned "the liberty of *laisser-faire* in intellectual attainment" and offered instead a "well-balanced development of the mechanism of thinking based upon a thorough understanding of elementary princi-

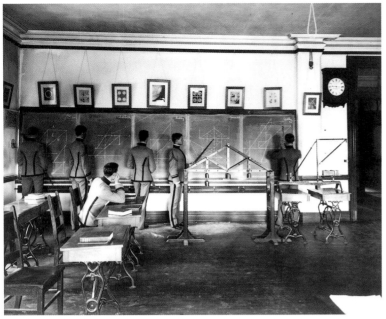 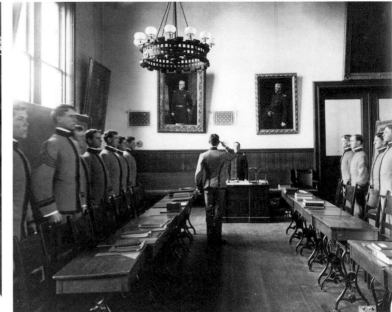

ples"—the stuff of "mental discipline." The "genius of West Point," Larned argued, lay in the "three fundamentals" on which its curriculum was based: "Every man in every subject—Every man proficient in everything—Every man every day." The West Point system required that every cadet take the whole program, there were no optional courses; that every cadet attain the required standard of proficiency in every subject (deficiency in one subject was deficiency in the course); and, that every cadet be prepared to recite each day in each class.

By September, the conflict had escalated to such an extent that even the *Army and Navy Journal* was reporting on the increasing "friction." An editorial charged that, at West Point, issues were too often settled by "a mere exercise of military authority." "Utmost weight" should be given to the permanent professors, the paper insisted, particularly "when questions of change" were considered. "Superintendents come and go," it continued, "but the academic staff remain as the inheritors and exponents of the ideas which have made the Academy what it is."

Mills, who was already at loggerheads with the professors over details of the construction and expansion underway at West Point, called a meeting of the board and demanded to know what "friction" existed. The members were polite, but explicit, in outlining their grievances. Mills was not moved. He brushed aside their complaints and ordered the board to undertake a new curriculum study which would provide instruction in French and Spanish throughout the cadets' last two years, and which would include physical education in each of the four years.

The committee's response, in February 1905, showed their exasperation quite clearly. They met Mills's demand for a new schedule in languages and physical education by abolishing the English course, but without touching the core of mathematics and sciences. Mills's displeasure at this result—in particular at the failure of the board to reduce or restructure the course in mathematics—was compounded when the new professor of mathematics, Charles P. Echols, declared forty percent of the third class deficient. Echols, who had graduated in 1891, had replaced Professor Wright Edgerton in 1904. Mills retaliated by ordering Echols away on a year's sabbatical to study European military schools. Echols protested, but without effect.

Although Mills had few allies at the Military Academy, he could usually count on support from the War Department—most significantly when he was given three votes in the academic board (following the precedent of the Naval Academy). Thus armed, he

returned to the curriculum issue in the late spring of 1905. This time he brought a directive from the Secretary of War to increase the number of hours of physical education. He instructed the academic board to reconsider the plan they had put forward in February. Mills cautioned them that if they were not more responsive this time, change would be prescribed from the outside "with results certainly less satisfactory to themselves and perhaps less prolific of good to the institution." From his perspective, however, their next report was only marginally better than the one before. Still, this plan was implemented on a one-year trial basis in the fall of 1905, while the board continued to explore other solutions.

By the end of 1905, however, Mills's base of support in Washington had begun to erode. His contest with the permanent faculty over construction issues was beginning to cost him backers, as was his open warfare with Echols. Not only had Mills sent the mathematics professor on an unwanted sabbatical, but he had written a critical report concerning the professor's conduct, questioning Echols's "attitude toward his immediate responsibilities," and charging that he had "taken a critical rather than helpful attitude" toward proposed reforms. These charges proved counterproductive. Echols protested, and won the support of then Acting Chief of Staff John C. Bates, and through him, the support of Secretary of War Taft. When Mills attacked Bates, saying that he had shown poor judgment and had improperly advised the Secretary, he further jeopardized his standing in Washington.

Discussion of various curriculum proposals filled the winter and spring of 1906. In all they produced "eight minor reports bearing upon special points of the curriculum" and "four full reports" with "proposed schedules." Finally, in the summer of 1906, two events helped move the board toward a compromise—the return of Professor Echols from his imposed sabbatical and the departure of Mills. Even then, the concessions the board made—the creation of a Department of English and History, and a Department of Military Hygiene—had little immediate impact. For example, the academic board refused to carve hours out of the old curriculum, and proposed instead to add courses by extending the four-year program by three months—requiring new cadets to enroll in March rather than June. Neither Hugh Scott, the new Superintendent, nor the board really approved of this plan, but the issue was taken out of their hands unexpectedly. George B. Davis, who had been professor of law a few years earlier and was now Judge Advocate General of the Army, had learned of the board's proposal and had taken it upon himself to promote it

George S. Patton, Jr., class of 1909, as a cadet. U.S.M.A. Archives.

in Washington. He discussed it with the Chief of Staff, the Secretary of War, and the Chairman of the House Committee on Military Affairs, and obtained the endorsement of each of these men. Finding the key actors already committed to the plan in Washington, Scott and the board had little choice but to send the proposal forward for approval.

In January 1908, just before this new program was put into effect, President Theodore Roosevelt threatened to undo the compromise. "It seems to me a very great misfortune," he wrote to his Secretary of War, William Taft, "to lay so much stress upon mathematics in the curriculum at West Point and fail to have languages taught in accordance with the best modern conversational methods. I have several times called attention to it, but nothing has been done." Now, he demanded "a full report on the matter." The curriculum committee responded immediately. They had spent considerable time studying just these problems, they reported, and a new curriculum addressing many of his concerns—the one just approved—was to be introduced for the class entering in March of that year. Still, they held fast to the view that mathematics was "basic in the curriculum of the Academy" and that "the habit of exact thought which has been developed by mathematical training" had utility, even for officers of the line. Although they might curtail "the ground to be covered in mathematical study," they insisted that the time gained be spent achieving "a more thorough mastery of the simple fundamental principles through further practical application and more detailed instruction." Concerning languages, they pointed out that a considerable addition had already been made to the time devoted to instruction in conversational Spanish, but they held the line on French. Attaining "mastery of the colloquial form" in French, they argued, was beyond the capability of the average student in the time that could be made available. The board ended its report by insisting that, while some changes might be necessary, there were "interests which cannot in justice be set aside." Pointing to the new curriculum that was about to be introduced, they "respectfully" asked "for a trial of [that] scheme."

The President agreed and the new curriculum was implemented in March 1908. Roosevelt left office a year later without any further inquiry into the subject. The new program, with its March entry date, soon proved unworkable. In 1911 the board voted unanimously to return to the regular four-year curriculum. At about the same time, another lingering symbol of the Mills reform era disappeared as quietly as had the recent curriculum changes. A committee established to revise the regulations of the Academy proposed restricting the Superintendent to one vote. Scott opposed this move but was about to depart, and left the matter to his successor—Major General Thomas H. Barry—who chose not to make an issue of it. The *Regulations, 1911* restored the equality of all board members in voting matters.

Discussions of curriculum change then lapsed for several years. In the meantime, the academic board underwent some significant changes. Edward Edgar Wood, who had served at West Point as a teacher of French almost continuously since 1872, and who had been professor of foreign languages since 1892, retired in 1910. Two other key members of the old guard departed in 1911: professor of drawing, Charles Larned, who died; and Samuel Tillman, professor of chemistry, who retired. Wood was replaced by Cornelius deWitt Willcox, class of 1885, who had been an assistant professor at West Point since 1892—first in natural philosophy and then in French. Larned was succeeded by Edwin R. Stuart, class of 1896, who had already spent nine of his fourteen years in service on the faculty. Wirt Robinson, who took Tillman's chair, was a member of the class of 1887 and had been assigned to West Point for eleven years. In most respects, Willcox, Stuart, and Robinson were more like the men they replaced than they were different. They were all military men, who had served the bulk of their careers at West Point and who were deeply imbued with the traditions of the Academy.

The Secretary of War presenting diplomas to the United States Military Academy graduates in 1917. U.S.M.A. Archives.

Another new member of the board, however, was not a military man at all. Lucius H. Holt, a Yale Ph.D. with no military experience, was hired in 1910 to head the Department of English and History. His predecessor, John C. Adams, also of Yale, had been hired just two years earlier, when the department was first created, but Adams had not been a propitious choice. He had stunned the other members of the faculty by dropping Thayer's system of instruction and lecturing to all the classes himself. Holt restored the instructor system and broadened the history curriculum by adding a textbook on political science.

With the departure of Larned, Tillman, and Wood, seniority on the academic board devolved to Gustave Joseph Fiebeger, professor of engineering, William Brandon Gordon, professor of natural philosophy, and Charles Patton Echols, professor of mathematics. Fiebeger, class of 1879, had been selected to succeed James Mercur when the latter died in 1896. He had served a number of years in the field as an engineer officer, but from 1883 to 1888 he had been an assistant professor of engineering at the Academy. Gordon, class of 1877, had assumed Michie's chair in natural philosophy when the latter died in 1901. In subsequent years, Gordon authored a number of texts that replaced those written by his predecessor. Echols, who had run afoul of Mills shortly after having been appointed professor of mathematics in 1904, weathered that trial only to cross swords in later years with another "youngster" appointed Superintendent—Douglas MacArthur.

The war that began in Europe in 1914 hardly touched West Point until 1917, but the two years that followed were to be a wrenching period. It began when Colonel John Biddle, who had just been appointed Superintendent in 1916, was ordered off to the war. To replace him, Colonel Samuel Tillman—who had retired as professor of chemistry in 1911—was recalled and made Superintendent.

As had often been the case in previous wars, the first class was graduated only days after war was declared on April 6, 1917. In May, the next class, which had entered the Academy in 1914, started an abbreviated version of the first-class course of studies. For them, intensive military training was added in June and ten weeks later they were graduated as the Class of August 1917. A second three-year emergency class was graduated in June 1918.

In July 1918, Tillman succeeded in obtaining War Department approval of a fixed three-year course for all cadets, but he soon found that what the War Department could give, they could also take away. Paradoxically, his most trying period was the weeks just before and after the fighting stopped in November 1918. "On the 3rd of October," Tillman recalled, "I got a telephone message from the Adjutant General at half past 10 o'clock at night telling me we were to graduate two classes on the 1st of November." Further, he was informed, for the balance of the wartime emergency the course of instruction at West Point would last just one year. "Why, this means there will be no upper classmen in the Corps," Tillman protested. "The regime and traditions, which have taken a century to develop, can never be restored." The next day the Superintendent was in Washington, but Chief of Staff Peyton C. March's mind was made up. In France, the Meuse-Argonne offensive, which had begun in September, was generating massive American casualties—many of them officers. There was now a critical shortage of trained officers and, to March, West Point cadets were one obvious source for the alleviation of that situation. Nothing could be done to change the order, Tillman was told.

The news numbed the post. There had been disruptions before, but now the long gray line seemed threatened. The "delicate, intangible impulses for conduct and honor, instilled and developed in hearts and minds over past decades" could only be handed down from one cadet class to another. But if there were only one class? The question went unanswered; the affair had a surreal character about it. By all accounts, the Germans were retreating and the war would soon be over. If that were true, they asked at West Point, why was Washington perpetrating this "absurd crime"? Tillman persevered, however, and extracted a promise from the Washington bureaucracy that, should the war end before January 1920, the members of the last class (which had been at West Point for less than sixteen months) would be returned to the Academy to complete their education.

On November 1, 1918 the classes that had entered in 1916 and 1917 were graduated. The next day, 360 new cadets were sworn in, all believing that they would be graduated the next year. Less than two weeks later, on November 11th, an armistice was signed, effectively ending the war. The recent graduates had not yet even been assigned to training camps. Barely four weeks after they had departed West Point, the more junior of the two recently graduated classes was ordered back to the Academy, but as student officers, not cadets.

With the end of the war, Tillman and the academic board faced an array of challenges. The first was how to deal with the unique structure of the classes then at the Academy. The class that had entered in 1917—and prematurely graduated in November 1918—were uniformed as officers, although not given the privileges. They proved so bitter at being returned to the Academy that they were quartered separately, and isolated from the rest of the corps at meals and at ceremonies. They were of no help in guiding the two classes that had been admitted in June and November of 1918—"fourth class A" and "fourth class B." As a result, tactical officers furnished the guidance and leadership usually provided by the more senior cadets. For several months, cadet gray uniforms were not available for fourth class B. Instead they were issued the olive drab enlisted uniform with a distinctive orange hat band that immediately earned them the nickname, "the Orioles."

The academic board, however, had to face a series of complex problems that extended far beyond any difference in uniforms. They had to devise unique academic programs for each class: a six-month program for the student officers; an additional eighteen months for fourth class A; and a thirty-month curriculum for fourth class B. The student officers were graduated again in June 1919, after six months additional schooling; the classes that had entered the Academy in June and November of 1918 were to be graduated in 1920 and 1921 respectively—after having completed courses of roughly twenty-four and thirty months duration. By the end of June 1919, with the admission of a new plebe class and the elevation of the two fourth classes to the upper classes—first and second classes respectively (there were only three classes until the four-year curriculum was restored)—some degree of normalcy had returned to the Academy.

Finally, the academic board was faced with the challenge of reestablishing a fixed curriculum. In November 1918, Peyton March, the Army's Chief of Staff, had directed the academic board to submit a three-year course of studies—it might be four years, he noted, only if it included a broader offering of "cultural subjects."

In mid-December, instead of the report that March had requested, the board forwarded an eight-page defense of the pre-war four-year course and of its emphasis on producing mental discipline. "The course of study at the Military Academy has been mathematical and scientific and it should continue so," the board insisted. "The power and habit of clear, exact and logical thought engendered by the proper study" of mathematics and science "are the best assets that can be provided our graduates." As far as the board was concerned, they could not condense the course; to them the only acceptable three-year solution was to require more mathematics, French, English, and history prior to matriculation—in effect, to eliminate the need for the subjects of the fourth class year. As to a broader offering of "cultural subjects," they insisted that "no Engineering school would think of substituting cultural for necessary scientific studies."

General March, however, was not receptive to the board's report, and in mid-May 1919, without consulting the Academy, he recommended to Secretary Baker that "the course of instruction at the United States Military Academy be fixed at three years." Baker approved this recommendation and the academic board was ordered to prepare a three-year curriculum. At the same time, March also selected a new Superintendent, Brigadier General Douglas MacArthur, and ordered him to West Point immediately.

Douglas MacArthur assumed command at West Point in June 1919, just after graduation ceremonies had been concluded. The thirty-nine-year-old officer was one of the youngest Superintendents since Thayer. The new Superintendent had not been there long before many on the board were convinced that their worst fears had been realized—they were being led by a boy Superintendent, inexperienced in educational matters, yet energetic and, above all else, ambitious. The older members could not help but draw parallels with the earlier *enfant terrible*—Mills.

MacArthur had been instructed by March to establish a three-year curriculum and to put it into place at West Point. But, on June 26th, at the first working meeting of the academic board, he found that the curriculum committee had already acted. Two curriculum reports were presented that day: the first, a math-heavy, engineering oriented program proposed by the curriculum committee; and the second, a two-tracked curriculum championed by Professor Lucius Holt. Holt's plan offered both an engineering track, and a track that put more emphasis on economics and civil government—with no engineering. To no one's surprise the board dismissed Holt's offering and approved the math-heavy, engineering-oriented curriculum. On June 28, 1919, MacArthur forwarded this recommendation to Washington. Secretary Baker approved and this curriculum was implemented in September 1919.

At the same time, the board began to lobby for the restoration of a four-year curriculum. They found a willing supporter in Congressman John M. Morin of Pennsylvania, who chaired the subcommittee on Military Academy appropriations, and who was president of the board of visitors in 1919. In February 1920, Morin opened the hearings on the Academy's appropriation by declaring his intent to reestablish the four-year course. Morin called on MacArthur to support his fight for the additional year, but the Superin-

Douglas C. MacArthur *by Arthur Dawson. c. 1922. West Point Museum Collections, U.S.M.A. This portrait was based upon one of MacArthur's favorite photographs.*

tendent demurred. It was Tillman, in retirement, who took up the standard, and, with Morin, persuaded Congress to restore the four-year program.

At that point, the curriculum committee began their deliberations again, but after an extended debate they had done little more than restore the courses of the old four-year curriculum, curtailing them only sufficiently to allow for a new course in economics and government. Holt, the professor of English and history, had been promoting such a course since 1911 and its adoption, a decade later, was a typical example of the working of the academic board. Although MacArthur backed Holt at this juncture and thus is often credited with this "liberalization" of the curriculum, his support was not instrumental in the outcome.

The process of achieving lasting, substantive change at West Point in the areas where the academic board had cognizance was one of consensus building, and it often took years. Tillman illustrated it thus: "In 1884, I submitted to the Academic Board [a new proposal]. This proposition involved the change of a long-established system; when first suggested, the Board simply referred it for 'further consideration.' Several times at intervals, I again submitted the plan, accompanied by results in its application in my own Department. In May, 1894, ten years after the new method had first been brought forward by me, the other Departments were directed to give it 'careful consideration.' In 1895, a committee appointed to 'test the method,' reported in favor of adopting it; in 1896, it was finally adopted." The process, at times, moved so slowly that outsiders—including Superintendents and non-permanent faculty—often failed to perceive any change at all. As slow as it was, however, the process did have significant advantages. It seldom permitted the implementation of poor ideas, for their disadvantages became apparent before sufficient support had been mustered to pass them. And, it kept curriculum turmoil to a minimum. "The Board," wrote Tillman, was "the continuing, developing and stabilizing factor of the Academy."

MacArthur forwarded the board's recommendation for a four-year program to the War Department on July 20, 1920, where it was approved and ordered into effect for all classes still at the Academy. This would finally end the turmoil that had engulfed them all. The class that had entered in November 1918 (fourth class B) had expected to be commissioned within a year—by late 1919. With the end of the war—just days after they had been admitted—their graduation had immediately been extended to June 1921. Now, they were told, they would not graduate until June 1922. To lessen the dissatisfaction among some members of this class and among the class that had joined the corps in 1919, both groups were offered the opportunity to choose between the three- and the four-year curriculums. Most opted for the longer course. Only seventeen of the November 1918 entrants chose the three-year program, and they became the class of 1921. The balance of that group, 102 cadets, were graduated as the class of 1922. A day later, thirty of the 1919 matriculants, who had opted for the three-year program, were graduated—becoming the class of June 14, 1922. The balance of that group chose the four-year path and were graduated the next year as the class of 1923.

MacArthur made no effort to woo the academic board. Although he could have reasonably written off most of the old guard, he might have been able to win support from some of the newer and younger members of the board. One possibility was Clifton Carroll Carter—a member of the class of 1899 who had taken William Gordon's chair of natural philosophy upon the latter's retirement in 1917. Robert Gorden Alexander, class of 1907, was an even more likely candidate. Alexander, who had become professor of drawing upon Edwin Stuart's death in 1920, had only recently returned from service in France with the American Expeditionary Force. But the Superintendent made no move to gain their backing.

Instead, he seemed to go out of his way to intrude on their domain. He quizzed professors concerning the courses taught by other departments, inspected their instructors in the classroom, and commandeered their officers for non-academic purposes. In time, he turned on the professors, charging that they were narrow, smug, and too satisfied with their traditional way of doing business. He told his adjutant, "they deliver the same schedule year after year with the blessed unction that they have reached the zenith in education."

Even when he was right, MacArthur's lack of tact and discretion further alienated the board. When Echols chose to protest the cuts made in his mathematics course by reporting 95 of 572 plebes deficient, MacArthur immediately (and quite correctly) appointed a committee of the board to investigate. They concluded that Echols's course was too "intensive" and "theoretical," that the assignments were too long, and that his instructors spent too much time grading recitations and too little time teaching. They proposed a whole new mathematics program. Echols was incensed, but his colleagues, who had little sympathy with his tactics, voted with the committee, although they did soften the report's criticism. Echols was humiliated. MacArthur, however, was not satisfied. He transformed the board's enjoinder into a military order: the board's resolutions "will be carried out by you"; the number of deficiencies among the "good potential officer material" were to be reduced by at least fifty percent; and the professor was to make periodic progress reports to the Superintendent. But this time, MacArthur had overreached himself. Not only had he further humiliated Echols, he had also injected himself into the internal affairs of a department—a privileged sanctum wherein, by regulation, the academic board, and not the Superintendent, had jurisdiction.

By now, the rumblings in the academic board room had begun to involve the alumni. The word of MacArthur's innovations reached them through faculty letters, the *Army and Navy Journal*, and the grapevine that naturally extends out from such an institution. They

The cadets are seen here marching to chapel in the 1920s. U.S.M.A. Archives.

resented his efforts at reform—both on the academic side, and in the area of cadet life. In his efforts to codify the fourth class system and in his more liberal pass policy, for example, they feared he was unduly pampering cadets. Hugh Scott seems to have been thinking of MacArthur (and also Mills) when he wrote in 1927: "West Point is not a subject for [drastic] reform. . . . It goes forward on its majestic course from year to year toward the fulfillment of its destiny, . . . improved from time to time to keep it abreast of the age, but without need of radical alteration."

"By the summer of 1921, MacArthur had so completely drained the faculty and alumni of good will that he could no longer innovate, and was instead waging a defense of all that he had changed," wrote Roger H. Nye, a latter-day professor of history at West Point. The disenchantment with MacArthur at West Point was matched by a similar mood in Washington. Secretary of War Newton Baker, who had supported him, was replaced by John W. Weeks when President Warren Harding assumed office. In July, Peyton March retired and was replaced as Chief of Staff by General John J. Pershing. Neither Weeks nor Pershing had any sympathy for MacArthur's plight. MacArthur had proven, in the words of biographer C. Clayton James, "a refractory individualist who created difficulties and embarrassments for the War Department in its relations with Congress, the White House, and the conservative alumni of West Point."

On November 22, 1921, Pershing informed MacArthur that he was to be replaced: "I am writing now to advise you that at the end of the present school year you will be available for a tour of service beyond the limits of the United States. The selection of your successor will be made shortly." At the end of January 1922, Pershing announced the appointment of Brigadier General Fred Winchester Sladen, who had earlier been Commandant of Cadets, as MacArthur's successor. "I fancy [that Sladen's appointment] means a reversal of many of the progressive policies which we inaugurated," was MacArthur's reaction. Within days after his departure, work was begun to restore the encampment area near Fort Clinton. Likewise, the academic board began a review of the curriculum, and soon restored Echols's mathematics course to its pre-war eminence.

Within eighteen months of MacArthur's departure the board had cut, by twenty percent, the time devoted to English, French, Spanish, history, law, economics, and government—but they only reduced these courses, they did not eliminate them. In fact, in 1926, the board sought and obtained congressional approval for the separation of English and history into two departments—the Department of Economics, Government, and History, and the Department of English—officially blessing an earlier *de facto* arrangement. These departmental shifts, along with normal retirements, meant changes on the academic board. Holt, the former professor of English and history, took over the Department of Economics, Government, and History, while Clayton E. "Buck" Wheat, who had been the Military Academy chaplain since 1918, was appointed professor of English. Earlier, in 1922, the scholarly William Augustus Mitchell, class of 1902, had replaced Gustave Fiebeger when he retired as professor of engineering. And, in 1925, William Eric Morrison, class of 1907, became Willcox's successor in the Department of Modern Languages.

By contrast to the MacArthur years, the balance of the decade was a period of quiet but steady movement forward. Shortly before he left West Point, Superintendent Fred Sladen petitioned for the Academy's admission into the Association of American Universities—a necessary step toward the granting of baccalaureate degrees. Full admission to the association was granted the next year, and in 1933 congressional action authorized the United States Military Academy to award the degree of Bachelor of Science. Sladen was replaced in 1926 by Brigadier General Merch Bradt Stewart, class of 1896, who had been Commandant of Cadets since 1923. Stewart, however, became ill and surrendered the superintendency late the next year. Major General William Ruthven Smith, class of 1892, was chosen to succeed Stewart, but was not immediately available. In the interim,

Major General Edwin Baruch Winans, class of 1891, assumed command of the post. Smith arrived just four months later, in February 1928. Neither Stewart nor Winans served long enough to make any significant mark on the Academy.

By the late thirties, Professor Charles Patton Echols had become the old man of the board—a lifelong bachelor and now in his early sixties, he was reminiscent of "Old Hanks" Kendrick of a half-century before. Like Kendrick, Echols lived alone in one of the large stone doubles along "Professors Row." Echols led a highly structured life and,

John J. Pershing, class of 1886, distinguished himself as a General in World War I. His quarters as a cadet have been recreated and are on exhibit at the Academy.

even when alone, dined formally, by candlelight. The old professor, who had repeatedly been in conflict with the various administrations at West Point, enjoyed catching a mistake emanating from headquarters. One day he emerged from his office waving the most recent communication. "Look at that," he exulted. "They have misspelled 'mispelled'."

After the expansion of the Academy in the first decade of the century, and the demolition of most of the old brick quarters along Jefferson Road, the three old stone doubles became the primary residences of the permanent professors. Then, as now, their social life was centered around their own small group. They might find occasional diversion in the great homes along the Hudson or among the city's elite, but at West Point they were an essentially closed society. At frequent dinners and parties they entertained one another, but few others from among the West Point community. Most had a maid and a gardener, some had cooks and other help, although the time was fast approaching when domestic help would become a rarity. The Ladies Reading Club may have sensed this change for their 1918–19 program included a discussion of the "Evolution of the Hired Girl" among their more traditional fare such as "The League of Nations" or "The Irish Question."

For the officers there were numerous amusements. The Thayer Club had become moribund in the late nineteenth century, but had been revived briefly during Scott's superintendency. An officers' polo club was formed and they played both civilian and military teams from up and down the East Coast. But polo was essentially a young man's sport and many of the professors preferred quieter diversions. Chess was a favorite and sometimes games went on evening after evening. After dinner, the professors would stroll in and out of each other's quarters by the back doors to take part, or kibitz. One night, it is said, Gustave Fiebeger, professor of engineering, tiring of the game, decided to withdraw. "Well, it's my bedtime. Goodnight, gentlemen," he said, and wandered out. Where he went was a bit of a mystery, for the game, that night, was being played at his house.

The location of Professors Row, just off the plain, was a mixed blessing. In the 1920s, as roads improved and as the American public took enthusiastically to automobiles, West Point became a major attraction. The resultant wholesale use of the reservation as a picnic ground so worried the administration in 1927 that traffic was restricted through the grounds. One Saturday, a group of visitors spread their blankets and picnic lunch on the broad porch of Professor Clifton Carter's quarters. That was more than Carter was willing to tolerate, but when he protested, they informed him that this was public property. "We are tax payers," they said, "and we intend to stay." Carter turned about and left without further comment, but reappeared shortly with a hose and started washing down the porch. When his unwanted guests objected, he rejoined: "I am charged with the maintenance of this property, and I always wash down the tax-payers' porch on Saturday."

Among their other duties, the permanent professors selected the instructors who would be detailed to them. In general, the selections were made on the basis of the academic record of the officer as a cadet, as well as what could be learned of his subsequent efficiency in the service. Each professor relied on his own method. Professor William Mitchel, head of the Department of Engineering from 1922 to 1938, kept a "little black book" in which he inscribed information on potential instructors and their wives. In it he recorded notes under four columns: "aim," "name," "dame," and "fame."

These instructors were usually detailed to the Academy for four years, but in 1912 Congress decided—against the advice of the War Department—that officers who had been away from their regiments for more than four of the previous six years must be reassigned to them immediately. Twelve of the twenty instructors in the Department of Mathematics departed in November and December of that year; in varying degrees such losses occurred in all the departments. The difficulty was that the officers West Point wanted were also

in demand elsewhere, outside their regiments, and often came to the Academy from other details. In 1913, Superintendent Clarence Townsley estimated that as a result of the so-called "Manchu Law" none of the officers they intended to request would be able to serve a four-year tour. Many would be allowed to stay just one year. The result, he added, "is that we are compelled to ask for officers as instructors who, without this detached service law, would not have been considered for such duty." Townsley's request that West Point be exempted from the impact of this law was denied. Relief did not come until after World War I, when the regimental system (and the assignment of officers by regiment) was abolished.

Over the years, instructors reported very similar experiences when they first joined the faculty—they were unprepared and had to work day and night just to stay ahead of the cadets. "On the first day of September as my cadets marched into the recitation room I was deeply conscious of my limitations as an instructor," reported Captain John McAuley Palmer, who joined the faculty in 1901. "During the whole of my first year I was hard put to it to keep ahead of my cadets," Palmer added. Tasker Bliss had found much the same thing in 1876: "I study a great deal harder than when I was a cadet, for now I feel as though I were in honor bound to know as much as I can." Tully McCrea had written in a similar vein in 1864: "I have three hours duty every day, hearing my sections. Nearly all the rest of the day, and a great deal of the night is taken up in hard study. I have to study harder now than I did when I was a cadet." John Schofield, who had taught natural philosophy in 1855 and 1856, likewise recalled that as an instructor he had "formed for the first time the habit of earnest, hard mental work to the limit of my capacity for endurance, and sometimes a little beyond." It required from one to two years' experience and hard work for even the best of the officers selected to become really proficient and effective instructors.

Beginning in 1911, in an effort to alleviate some of that difficulty, Professor Holt sent some of his officers to the summer session at Yale. In 1915, Professor Edward A. Kreger, of the law department, began sending an instructor each year to attend a summer session at the Columbia University School of Law. These experiments proved quite successful and in 1921 the academic board, with MacArthur's strong endorsement, recommended that, to prepare for their work at West Point, instructors should spend one year at a civilian university before reporting to the Academy.

MacArthur went even further, and attempted to persuade the academic board to take army officers who had graduated from civilian colleges as instructors. It was "a step back-

ward," a "dangerous" and "a problematical venture," the professors replied. MacArthur tried again to convince them, describing at length his rationale. In the midst of this presentation, one of the professors began to interrupt. Finally the interruptions became so intrusive that MacArthur banged his fist on the table and commanded, "Sit down sir. I am the Superintendent!" A hush followed and he added, "Even if I weren't, I should be treated in a gentlemanly manner." Although MacArthur sent lists of such officers with their qualifications to the departments, only Holt made any sustained effort to recruit these men. It was not until some years after World War II that any significant number of "non-graduates" were added to the faculty on anything other than an emergency basis.

For a brief period from about 1910 through the early-1920s there was a rare abundance of excellent quarters for officers at West Point. The bulk of these were built to the south

of the academic area along Wilson and Thayer Roads. The first had been the small frame cottages built in the 1850s just south of the hospital. More frame quarters were added in the 1870s. But, in the first decade of the twentieth century this area fairly exploded with new officers' quarters. The first were five brick duplexes built in 1901 to standardized designs from the office of the Quartermaster General. In August 1901, Captain John M. Palmer and his wife moved into one of these new buildings. They were immediately among friends. The other half of the house was assigned to a classmate, and two other classmates had quarters in the same row. Mrs. Palmer "was delighted with her brand new house," her husband wrote. Typical of army wives, she was settled "in a few days"—the "curtains were up," the "rugs down," the "furniture in place," and she had found an excellent cook.

In 1904, plans drawn by Cram, Goodhue and Ferguson were approved for additional quarters. Begun in 1905, their Gothic character and varied brick facades placed them among the most attractive quarters on post. The interior spaces of these quarters are also remarkable, for they embody some of the finest examples of Craftsman and American Art Nouveau designs. Seldom have officers' quarters been so elegantly and satisfactorily designed. They contained a parlor, dining room, library, and kitchen on the first floor, and on the second and third floors, four bedrooms and two baths, plus a suite of two bedrooms and a bath for servants. (Designed originally for married lieutenants who returned to teach only a few years after graduation, these quarters are now occupied by senior permanent professors.) Six sets of these triplexes were completed in 1908 after lengthy delays. A seventh set was added in the area in 1910. Four other similar sets were built in 1909 along Washington Road to the north of Professors Row and the Catholic Chapel, anticipating the direction of future growth in officer housing.

Slow, but steady expansion through the early years of the century had brought the authorized number of cadets to nearly 750 by 1915, although the actual number enrolled was always somewhat smaller. In 1916, the authorized number of cadets was nearly doubled. The number of cadets grew more rapidly after the increase in 1916, but still did not approach the new authorization level until the 1920s. More cadets, of course, meant more officers and the need for more officers' quarters. Two new apartment buildings—North and South Apartments—were begun in 1917 and completed in 1919. Although the plans

were drawn by the Quartermaster General's office, the designs followed closely those that had been prepared earlier by Cram, Goodhue and Ferguson.

By the mid-1920s, the growth of the Academy and the commensurate growth in the staff and faculty had led once again to a serious shortage of suitable officer quarters. By 1927, more than fifty junior officers and their families were forced to live in the neighboring towns of Highland Falls, Cornwall, and Newburgh. The next year, continued expansion increased that number. In 1929, a third apartment complex—Central Apartments—was constructed just south of the hospital, but this complex could accommodate only a fraction of those who needed quarters, and, in any case, the units were tiny two-bedroom apartments. As usual, the problem seemed to defy any easy solution.

Upon the death of Professor Wirt Robinson in 1928, Chauncey Lee Fenton, class of 1904, assumed the professorship of chemistry and electricity (as the department had been redesignated when Robinson had surrendered the courses in mineralogy and geology in 1917). Professor Lucius Holt, for some years second only to Echols in seniority on the academic board, retired in 1930 and left the Department of Economics, Government, and History to Herman Beukema, class of 1915. Beukema had served on the Mexican frontier, and had commanded an artillery battalion in France. He had attended the Field Artillery School and the Army Command and General Staff School, and had joined the West Point faculty as an assistant to Holt in 1928. Beukema was a soldier-scholar, who would remain as head of the department until 1954. He was archetypical of those who would lead the Academy through World War II, and beyond.

Above left:
The Thayer Hotel as it appeared in 1928. U.S.M.A. Archives.

Above right:
Cadets waiting for dinner in the Washington Hall cadet mess. Late 1920s. U.S.M.A. Archives.

This china, used in the cadet mess c. 1900 to 1930, was made expressly for the Academy by Shenango China in New Castle, Pennsylvania. U.S.M.A. Library, Special Collections.

CHAPTER 9
THE LONG GRAY LINE
1930-1960

In 1930, Superintendent William R. Smith proposed a restatement of the Military Academy's mission: "The mission of the Military Academy is to train a cadet to think clearly and logically and to do so habitually; to teach him discipline and the basic principles applicable to the various arms in the Military Service; to develop his physique and above all his character; and to teach him to approach all of his problems with an attitude of intellectual honesty, to be sensible to the rights of others, to be inspired by a high sense of duty and honor, and unhesitatingly to lay down his life in the service of his country should the occasion arise."

Smith's new delineation of the Academy's mission reignited a debate that had erupted on several earlier occasions concerning the relative emphasis to be accorded formal education on the one hand and military training on the other. One element in the Army held the position that the West Point graduate should be prepared to take over all the responsibilities of a second lieutenant immediately upon reporting for duty—including both technical proficiency and leadership skills. Douglas MacArthur's 1920 removal of the summer camp from the plain to Fort Dix, where the cadets would train with active Army forces, was an expression of this impulse. Another segment of the Army—including the Academy's academic board—felt that the Academy would best serve by providing a basic general and technical education that would ensure an adequate foundation for growth in the cadet's subsequent professional career. John P. Lovell, writing in the late 1970s, explained this recurring tension as "the contradictions between Athenian and Spartan goals." In many respects, the Academy has spent the major portion of the twentieth century trying to reconcile the demands of these divergent goals.

Superintendent Fred Sladen had pushed the Academy in the direction of academics in 1925, when he convinced the Association of American Universities to list the Military Academy as an "approved technological institution." Another step in the same direction was taken in 1927, with the admission of the Academy to membership in the Association of American Colleges.

In 1933, Superintendent William D. Connor, class of 1897 and Smith's successor, convinced Congress to confirm the emphasis on academics by authorizing the Academy to confer the degree of Bachelor of Science upon its graduates. President Franklin Delano Roosevelt had also endorsed that goal in 1934, when he proposed adding a year to the curriculum during which the cadets of the Military Academy would join with the mid-

Opposite:
The United States Military Academy at West Point, and the Hudson River. Pendor Natural Color.

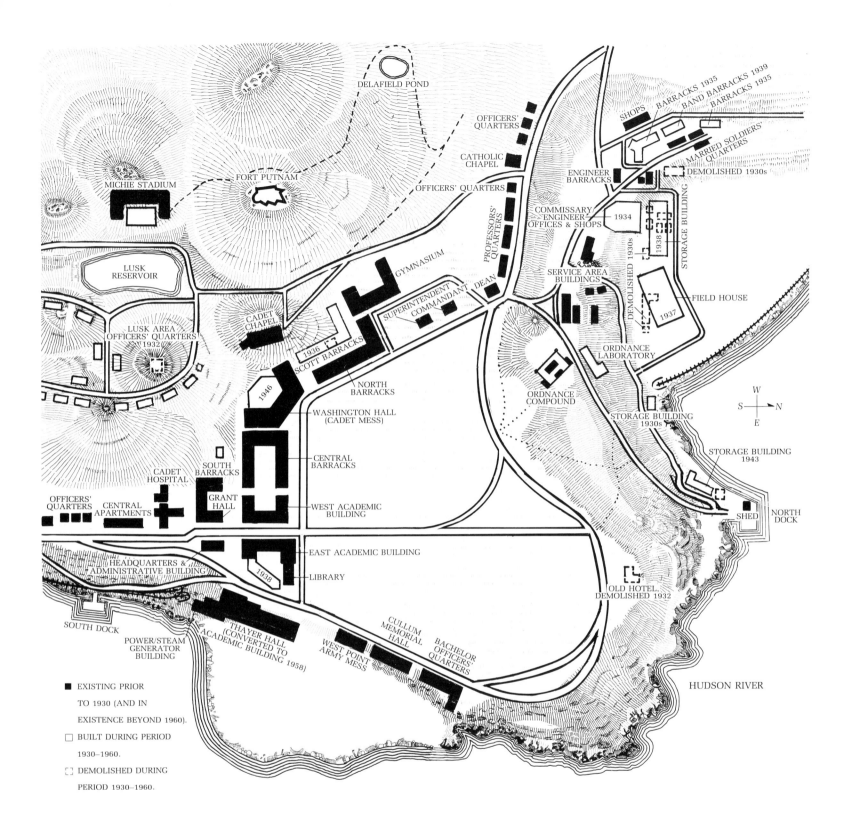

DELAFIELD POND

OFFICERS' QUARTERS

CATHOLIC CHAPEL

OFFICERS' QUARTERS

SHOPS

BARRACKS 1935
BAND BARRACKS 1939
BARRACKS 1935

MARRIED SOLDIERS' QUARTERS

ENGINEER BARRACKS

DEMOLISHED 1930s

COMMISSARY/ ENGINEER OFFICES & SHOPS

1934

1938

STORAGE BUILDING

MICHIE STADIUM

FORT PUTNAM

PROFESSORS' QUARTERS

DEMOLISHED 1930s

1937

FIELD HOUSE

LUSK RESERVOIR

GYMNASIUM

SUPERINTENDENT
COMMANDANT DEAN

SERVICE AREA BUILDINGS

LUSK AREA OFFICERS' QUARTERS 1932

CADET CHAPEL

1936

1946

SCOTT BARRACKS

NORTH BARRACKS

ORDNANCE LABORATORY

ORDNANCE COMPOUND

STORAGE BUILDING 1930s

W
S — N
E

WASHINGTON HALL (CADET MESS)

STORAGE BUILDING 1943

CADET HOSPITAL

SOUTH BARRACKS

CENTRAL BARRACKS

GRANT HALL

CENTRAL APARTMENTS

WEST ACADEMIC BUILDING

OFFICERS' QUARTERS

EAST ACADEMIC BUILDING

HEADQUARTERS & ADMINISTRATIVE BUILDING

1938

LIBRARY

SHED

NORTH DOCK

SOUTH DOCK

POWER/STEAM GENERATOR BUILDING

THAYER HALL (CONVERTED TO ACADEMIC BUILDING 1958)

WEST POINT ARMY MESS

CULLUM MEMORIAL HALL

BACHELOR OFFICERS' QUARTERS

OLD HOTEL, DEMOLISHED 1932

HUDSON RIVER

■ EXISTING PRIOR TO 1930 (AND IN EXISTENCE BEYOND 1960).

□ BUILT DURING PERIOD 1930–1960.

⸌⸍ DEMOLISHED DURING PERIOD 1930–1960.

Map of West Point, 1930–1960.

shipmen of the Naval Academy for a year long "finishing" cruise. In their floating academy they would visit all the key countries of the world. "The end in view should be to enable student officers, during their formative years, to develop a broad outlook, a cultural background and a sympathetic understanding of world conditions." When both academies proved cool to the idea, Roosevelt dropped it.

In 1939, a year after Brigadier General Jay L. Benedict, class of 1904, replaced William Connor, the new Superintendent proposed another statement of the Academy's mission: "The Mission of the United States Military Academy is to produce officers of the Army having the qualities and attributes essential to their progressive and continuing development, throughout their careers as officers and leaders." Smith's admonition that the Academy should teach "the basic principles applicable to the various arms in the Military Service" was deleted, and War Department approval seemed to resolve the issue in favor of the Academy's continually evolving academic program.

On one academic front, the social sciences and humanities were achieving a new maturity. Herman Beukema, professor of economics, government, and history, strove to integrate the study of geography, international relations, and the economics of national security. Building on a sub-course begun by Lucius Holt in 1929 entitled "Resources for War of the Great Powers," Beukema, by 1934, had created a full course in international relations. In history, he began to concentrate on the two areas of potential American involvement in war: Europe and the Far East. In 1938 he expanded the government course from one that dealt exclusively with the United States to one that compared the governments of the major powers. Beukema's courses expanded the horizons of the cadets. "I have seldom, if ever, encountered a group of students who struck me as having been better disciplined intellectually for the study of international relations," wrote Sir Alfred Zimmern of Oxford, after lecturing at West Point. "I am forced to confess that I had not expected to find in a military institution such intellectual keenness, such an open minded and critical interest in problems lying outside what used to be considered . . . the sphere of the professional soldier."

Likewise, the Department of English underwent a transformation under Clayton Wheat. Teaching methods became more liberal; classroom discussion and teaching began to supplant recitation. Cadets engaged in a healthy give-and-take among themselves and with the instructor. At the same time, an increased emphasis on literature began to balance an earlier concentration on verbal expression.

On another front, the science and engineering courses were also evolving. In 1931, physics instruction, which had been taught in various sub-courses by the Department of Natural and Experimental Philosophy and the Department of Chemistry, was incorporated into a new Department of Physics. Captain G. A. Counts, class of August 1917, was chosen to head the new department.

The academic board of 1932. From The 1932 Howitzer. *U.S.M.A. Archives. Copy Photo: Philip Pocock.*

In 1934, the Department of Natural and Experimental Philosophy, which over the years had given up control over most of the physical sciences, began to gather under its auspices the various components of the science of mechanics. Taught for years almost exclusively by analytical methods, Clifton Carter changed the emphasis to laboratory courses in hydraulics and thermodynamics, utilizing hydraulic pumps and turbines, internal combustion and steam engines, as well as a wind tunnel. This evolution was continued by Oscar J. Gatchell, class of 1912, who replaced Carter in 1940. Gatchell had a natural bent for scientific and engineering studies, but he understood that not all of his students shared that gift. Cadets insisted that he could simplify the most difficult problem, and had the ability to penetrate even the "goat mind."

With the transfer of work in mechanical engineering out of the Department of Civil and Military Engineering, William Mitchel and his successor (in 1938), Thomas D. Stamps, class of August 1917, were able to expand their course in the history of military art. By 1938 it was given more classroom hours than either civil engineering or military engineering. In 1942, in recognition of this development, the department was redesignated

General John J. Pershing with French Marshal Henri Petain, at West Point in 1931. U.S.M.A. Archives.

Toy cadets made by Britains Ltd. Toy Company. c. 1930. Anne S.K. Brown Military Collection, Brown University Library.

A cadet officer's uniform of 1930. The red sash, the chevrons, the sword, as well as the shako's feathered plume, distinguish the cadet officer from those of lesser rank. Watercolor by R. Wymer. Anne S.K. Brown Military Collection, Brown University Library.

the Department of Military Art and Engineering. The anomalous conjunction of these two subjects continued until 1969, when military history was shifted to a new Department of History.

Mathematics, now under Colonel Harris Jones, class of April 1917, who had replaced Charles Echols in 1931, continued to be the foundation of the curriculum. (Jones became Dean in 1947 and continued in that capacity until 1956.) Although the course changed little in this period, on at least one occasion the cadets were shown the practical benefits mathematics could bestow. In 1935, a department store in Newburgh offered a new Ford automobile to the person who came closest to guessing the number of pennies in a large glass bowl in their store window. Charles Nicholas, class of 1925, then an assistant professor, but later professor and head of the Department of Mathematics, measured the bowl from the sidewalk in front of the store using precision survey equipment. Later, at West Point, Nicholas translated the survey data into the internal volume of the bowl. Then, using calculus and statistical analysis (and a pile of copper pennies) he determined the statistical probability of distribution of pennies poured at random into the bowl. Combining this information he calculated the number of pennies in the container, submitted his "guess," and won the car.

In 1939, after having secured a revision of the mission statement, Benedict asked the academic board to review the curriculum once again. After a year-long study, the board recommended that no changes be made. "The curriculum of the Military Academy leads to a degree of Bachelor of Science and is framed for the purpose of giving the cadet a basic general education, but at the same time training him for one and only one purpose—for success in the military profession," wrote the committee. "Of necessity [the curriculum] must include the basic technical subjects essential to a general engineering education, certain professional subjects of special importance to all army officers, and cultural subjects of general educational value and sufficient in number to give proper balance to the curriculum." The curriculum committee had considered adding courses in

General George C. Marshall, United States Army Chief of Staff (right), Brigadier General Jay L. Benedict, Superintendent of the United States Military Academy (left), and Colonel Charles W. Ryder, Commandant of Cadets (center), reviewing the cadets in 1939. The Bettmann Archive.

logic, psychology, sociology, and philosophy but concluded that, despite the considerable value of these courses, they could not be introduced without displacing subjects currently being taught—courses which were "of more practical and cultural value to the army officers."

Benedict was not pleased, but departed for a new assignment before he could challenge the board. Still, in an exit report he called for an outside study board of civilian educators to report upon the Academy, "including its objectives, curriculum, procedure and methods." Wrote Benedict, "It is my belief that the pattern of the curriculum is still too much determined by the Engineer influence of former days."

The thirties had been a period of natural development in the curriculum and seemed to call for the evolution of all institutions at the Academy; the West Point Army Mess was one of these. It had continued through the twenties as a haven for the unmarried officers, but as the decade of the thirties wore on the number of bachelors on duty at the Academy began to decline. Still, they dined in formal elegance at a forty-foot-long table lined with massive silver pieces and candlesticks. Their meals were served by white-jacketed Filipino waiters and prepared by a chef who had been hired away from the old Astor Hotel. Although a small tea room at the north end of the building and a few rooms upstairs had been made available for the use of the wives of the married members, they were seldom allowed more than a peek at the splendor of the resident mess.

But that was about to change. It had become an increasingly common practice in the Army for commanders to expect officers, both married and single, to become members of the mess. The married officers and their wives soon began to argue that they received little benefit from their club membership and, in fact, were being required to support the bachelors. More than one wife at West Point thought that it was about time she had a right to use all the facilities of the mess. However, William Connor, the Superintendent, had little sympathy with this view. Perhaps Connor, a married man, valued the sanctity of that male bastion and its solitude. He had been known, for example, to shanghai the chaplain when going fishing and to insist that the cleric ride with Mrs. Connor—who would talk incessantly—while he and his aide escaped in another boat to the far side of the lake. The controversy came to a head almost immediately upon Connor's retirement in January 1938. Just a month later, a meeting was held in the old chemistry lecture hall in the east academic building to discuss changing the constitution of the mess. The married officers turned out in droves, but there were only a dozen or so bachelors—all that remained of their dwindling numbers. It had become common knowledge that Jay Benedict, the new Superintendent, was behind the married officers and that the bachelors were going to lose.

Chauncey Fenton, professor of chemistry and electricity, as well as president of the mess, allowed a brief debate and then put the question: "Shall the Mess be opened to everyone and not be restricted to the bachelors?" There was a thunderous "Yea" from the married side. The "nay" from the bachelors could scarcely be heard. Fenton drew himself up from his chair and announced: "The Nays have it. The meeting is adjourned." He put on his cap and started for the door. There was a moment of stunned silence, then, suddenly, a burst of laughter, whereupon Fenton returned to the chair and reversed the decision. Although the West Point Army Mess continued to restrict access during certain hours, thus allowing a mess to be maintained for the single officers, its fundamental character had been changed forever.

In contrast to the earlier mess arrangements for the officers, restaurant-style dining facilities would be provided in the early 1960s for faculty and staff members at the West Point Army Mess. Photo 1963 by Mr. Murphy. U.S.M.A. Archives. Copy photo: Philip Pocock.

Right:
Some members of the class of 1940. U.S.M.A. Archives.

Below:
The 1940 class crest. U.S.M.A. Archives.

Opposite above:
There are three cadet publications: The Howitzer, which is the West Point Yearbook, The Pointer, which is a bimonthly magazine, and Bugle Notes, which is a handbook. U.S.M.A. Archives.

Opposite below:
A selection of class rings, from 1940 to 1990. Each ring bears the Academy crest and the individual class crest. Before graduation, the ring is worn with the class crest toward the heart. After graduation, it is reversed, and the Academy crest is worn toward the heart. U.S.M.A. Library.

In 1946, the bachelors made a last ditch effort to maintain the traditional identity of the West Point Army Mess by proposing a separate officers' club, but they failed. The formal bachelor mess that had been established by Lieutenant Irwin McDowell more than a century before was soon thereafter abandoned. The long table disappeared in favor of restaurant style dining and the club was thrown open at all hours to the full membership and their families.

By late 1940, war clouds lay heavily on the horizon. Brigadier General Robert L. Eichelberger, class of 1909, who succeeded Jay Benedict as Superintendent, arrived in November 1940 committed to saving West Point from the fate it had met during World War I. To do so, he believed that he needed to increase the emphasis on military training. Eichelberger opened with a warning for the academic board. There were "many criticisms" being leveled at the young graduates, he advised the board, and some of the officers who had expressed "unfavorable opinions" were in a position "to influence or to take what appears to them corrective action" if they were inclined to do so. "We must recognize that time brings changes, therefore we cannot permit our curriculum to remain static," he warned. "The attitude which we take during this academic year may determine what harmful decisions will be made to govern the Military Academy next year." But that

alone was not enough: "We must keep the War Department, and through it, the people, informed that we are keenly aware of the existing state of flux in military matters, that we are meeting these changes as they occur, and that we shall continue to meet them."

Specifically, Eichelberger wanted to terminate the academic work of the first class in late April and give them some intensive military training in the branches they had chosen. In addition he suggested evening lectures "on leadership, soldier psychology, mess management, and kindred subjects which must be met by the young officer on joining his first command." The academic board concurred and, except for instruction in military law, course work ended for the first class on May 14, 1941. The period of intensive branch instruction that followed was so successful that Eichelberger made plans to repeat this training the following year.

At the same time, the approach of war caused the Academy to institute a number of changes in its military training program for all the cadets: an increase in the summer training time; an increase in branch instruction; an increase in the amount of physical training during the winter months; and an increase in motor vehicle instruction (at the expense of equitation).

For many years, summer training had been restricted to the morning, the afternoons usually being free time accorded to the cadets for relaxation and recreation. Beginning in

Cadets in training during World War II.
U.S.M.A. Archives. Copy Photo: Philip
Pocock.

Got him!

Waiting . . .

The bridge can tak

Engineers did it

Uncle Phil

160

Mediums of the 5th Armored

Reconnaissance . . .

We will attack at 1630

161

the summer of 1941, however, Eichelberger ordered two additional hours of training two afternoons each week, and added specialized branch instruction for the first classmen.

In its war mobilization planning during the decade of the thirties, West Point had insisted that "except for the early graduation of the then 1st Class, no change in the present four year curriculum is contemplated." They did suggest, however, that "tentative branch assignments" might be determined at the beginning of the first class year to allow additional branch training. When war did come, however, that plan was scrapped and new planning undertaken.

On January 12, 1942, Major General Francis B. Wilby, class of 1905, succeeded Eichelberger, who was soon sent to the South Pacific. Eichelberger wrote Wilby shortly after departing: "My major mission [was] to save West Point from its sad lot of World War I. All our publicity, the changes in the curriculum, the increase of hours for military training, the refresher course, etc., and particularly the new air program were based in no small part on my desire for the preservation of West Point." A week after taking over, Wilby initiated the first of a series of studies to determine the advantages and disadvantages of a curriculum of three years or less. The curriculum committee submitted its report on January 24th, recommending a three-year course of instruction if some shortening of the program was essential.

On January 27th, Wilby was summoned to Washington for a meeting with President Roosevelt. The President's instructions were simple and straightforward. He expected the Superintendent to minimize the discharge of cadets due to deficiencies in their studies, and to bring the Academy up to date in everything—particularly in air corps and tank instruction. The President also directed that they would continue intercollegiate football until instructed otherwise.

In March, the Army staff requested the views of the academic board on reducing the course of instruction. The board responded with a report that outlined one-, two-, and three-year plans, but that recommended retaining the four-year course. The War Department decided on the three-year option, and, in late August, asked Congress to authorize the President to effect the reduction for the duration of the wartime emergency. "We do not like to have West Point become subject to the criticism of being a place of refuge, where boys can go for four years and not be shot at," they told the lawmakers, "particularly when all the young men within that age group at other colleges are subject to the draft, and are going to be sent out after being trained and are going to be shot at." Congress obliged, although earlier in the summer they had increased the size of the corps of cadets from 1,960 to 2,496. On October 1, 1942, President Roosevelt ordered the course reduced to three years.

The original class of 1943 was thus graduated early, as the class of January 1943. The class then scheduled to graduate in 1944 received abbreviated versions of both the second class and first class courses and became the class of June 1943. The programs of subsequent classes were modified in order to permit their graduation after three years.

The war naturally gave a tremendous impetus to military training at the Academy. Summer furloughs were reduced so drastically that there was almost as much training time in the new three-year program as there had been in the pre-war four-year program. What is more, the new training area at Popolopen allowed vastly expanded military training.

The expansion of the training area had begun in the thirties. In 1931, Congress had authorized the purchase of some 15,135 acres to the west and south of West Point to ensure the post an adequate water supply. During the late twenties, the post had experienced several acute water shortages. By constructing a dam to control Popolopen Lake it was possible to store sufficient water to fully satisfy West Point's needs. The land would also provide room for needed facilities for military training—particularly small arms, machine gun, and artillery ranges. No money, however, was appropriated for the purchase until 1936 and then litigation so delayed the process that by mid-1939 only 528 acres had been acquired. The pace picked up in 1940 and 1941, and was even further accelerated in early 1942, when wartime condemnation procedures were employed wherever negotiations broke down. By late summer 1942, the government had acquired a tract of land comprising 10,300 acres. A new cadet camp was opened at Lake Popolopen in July of that same year and the summer encampment on the plain was abandoned for good. By the summer of 1943, the new training facility boasted twenty-four target ranges, a cleared artillery impact area, concrete pillboxes, two moving target ranges, a pontoon and amphibious training area, a 200-yard-long assault course, a mock freight train, and a highly realistic town in which cadets could train for combat within cities. The construction of facilities at Camp Popolopen made possible tactical training and instruction in the use of combat weapons far beyond anything that had ever been done before at West Point.

The most far-reaching change during World War II years at West Point, however, was the introduction of pilot training. As early as 1915, there had been attempts to add aviation observer training to the curriculum, but then the best that the limited facilities would permit was a lecture on air service organization and supply. In 1927, a seaplane hanger and ramp were completed on the Hudson, but no change was made in cadet instruction. Instead, the facility served only to allow flying officers stationed at West Point to maintain their flying proficiency. In 1931, after Congress had authorized the Popolopen purchase, plans were made to build an airfield, but the lack of appropriations and delays in acquiring land prevented any such construction. Again, lectures on aircraft, their construction, types, and capabilities were the only alternative. However, the Academy did begin to include (in the summer itinerary), visits to Langley, Wright, and Mitchell Fields, where cadets got a firsthand look at the Air Corps. Beginning in 1936, each cadet was given twenty hours of "air experience," but no flight training.

The first formal proposal that flight training be added to the curriculum was made in July 1941 by Oscar Gatchell, professor of natural philosophy, who suggested "a course in primary flying" for the first classmen who successfully passed the flight physical and who indicated a preference for the Air Corps. The facility at which such training could be conducted came into the Academy's hands just three months later when Stewart Field, on the outskirts of nearby Newburgh, became a part of West Point.

In January 1942, the War Department authorized the Military Academy to commission up to sixty percent of its graduates in the Air Corps. Cadets who were qualified for pilot training and who desired to enter the Air Corps were designated air cadets at the beginning of their second class year. These air cadets took their flight training at civilian facilities, although as facilities were completed at Stewart Field they began receiving their basic and advanced training there. Members of the class of January 1943 were the first to graduate with their "wings"—the class of 1946 the last. During this period, a total of 1,033 cadets were commissioned into the Air Corps from West Point.

Over the years, outside lecturers had become an important adjunct for many courses. In the thirties, a program of general lectures was instituted under the direction of an academic board lecture committee. Prior to the war, lecturers were chosen with an eye to broadening the cadets' knowledge of world affairs. As war became imminent, however, attention was focused on the world military situation, and—during the war—on the organization, training, and operations of the United States Army.

Academic training was hampered, but not halted, by the loss of regular officers in the early months of 1942. In fact, the exodus had begun in February 1941, when ten officers were relieved of duty and their places were taken by first classmen who taught half-time. Within weeks of Pearl Harbor, however, the process of recalling retired officers and

Range correct, fire for effect.

The impetus of supply.

Geronimo!!

Juggernaut in the attack.

Homeward bound.

commissioning civilian scholars was in full operation. By June 1944, more than two-thirds of the officers on duty at West Point were "non-graduates"—as West Pointers were inclined to call anyone who did not graduate from the United States Military Academy. The number of "non-graduates" grew so large that some, in jest, suggested forming an "Association of Non-Graduates." Although they had to be familiarized with the West Point system, these "non-grads" were often outstanding scholars and fine teachers. They demonstrated the advantage of specialized graduate training for officers detailed to duty in the academic departments. One of the civilians recruited in this era, Sumner Willard, later returned to West Point as professor and head of the Department of Foreign Languages.

Reducing the curriculum to three years meant a change in scope of many courses and the deletion of a number of sub-courses. In some departments, such as social sciences, it meant the elimination of entire courses. The Department of Foreign Languages was one of the few to add courses—German in 1941, and Portuguese (the language of Brazil, our principal ally in South America) in 1942. Russian was added in 1945. Still, the number of hours of language instruction was reduced. (For some time, cadets had spent three years in language training—two years in French and one year in Spanish. From 1945 onward, cadets would study a single language for two years, although they were allowed to choose from among the languages offered.) More significantly, under the guidance of Professor William Morrison, language training moved from the traditional concentration on formal grammar to an animated and predominantly oral approach.

The law that had established the wartime three-year course also mandated the return to the four-year course at the end of the war. In December 1943, to plan for that eventuality, Wilby directed the academic board to study the return to the longer course. In January 1944 the curriculum committee submitted its first report, recommending that the plebe class that had matriculated in 1943 (then scheduled for graduation in 1946, after three years) be designated the first four-year class. In effect, they were recommending an immediate return to the four-year program. Wilby sent this recommendation along to Washington, but the War Department replied that it was premature. In October 1944, buoyed by the Allies' successes in Europe, Wilby again raised the issue, but once more the War Department disapproved. This time, however, he was directed to resubmit the request upon the defeat of Germany or in July 1945, whichever date was earlier.

In May 1945, coinciding with the victory in Europe, the board again pressed for a return to a four-year curriculum. This time, the War Department agreed, but suggested that the class that was to enter in July 1945 should be the first four-year class. The academic board balked at such a slow transition. Instead, they proposed splitting the class that had entered in 1943—half to graduate in 1946, as originally scheduled, and half to be given a four-year course. The War Department, however, pointed out that retaining half the class at West Point for an additional year would limit the number of cadets that could be admitted in 1946. Because many Congressmen had already committed themselves to those appointments, it was decided instead to divide the class that had entered in 1944: half to continue in the three-year program, becoming the class of 1947; the other half to become the first post-war four-year class—the class of 1948. All subsequent classes would follow four-year programs. The plan was approved and put into effect in September 1945.

In the meantime, the curriculum committee had finished its work and made its report. The pre-war curriculum had been carefully and thoroughly revised and modernized. Chemistry and electricity were split, joining chemistry and physics under Captain Counts, and creating the Department of Electricity. Colonel Boyd W. Bartlett, class of 1919, became the first professor of the new Department of Electricity. Under his direction, and with the aid of the chief of the Signal Corps, laboratory equipment and facilities for

Opposite:
Photographs of cadet training during the war years. U.S.M.A. Archives. Copy Photo: Philip Pocock.

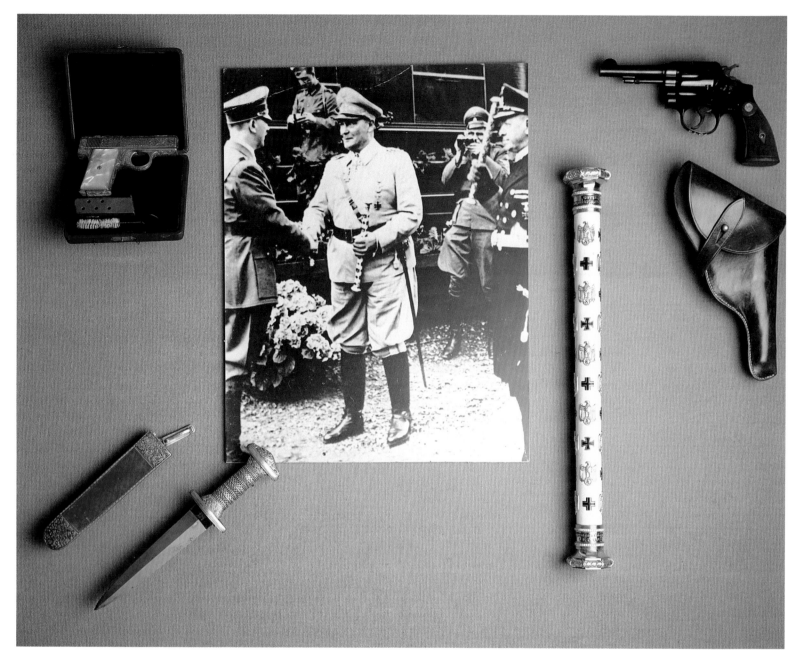

Above:
Trophies from World War II in the West Point Museum include side arms; the special "Lilliput" pistol presented to Adolf Hitler (which was found in the basement of Hitler's office building in Munich); a photograph of Hermann Goering with Adolf Hitler, as well as Field Marshal Goering's dagger and the baton (given to him by Hitler) that he surrendered when he gave himself up to the United States Army in 1945.

Opposite:
The pen and the sword. General Douglas C. MacArthur is shown signing the Japanese Instrument of Surrender on board the U.S.S. Missouri in 1945. The pen that was used to sign the document is next to the photograph; above is General Jonathan M. Wainright's sword

(which had been stolen in the Philippines and recovered in 1945); below is the sword of General Tomoyuki Yamashita, the "Tiger of Malaya," with a blade that was cast between 1640 and 1680. West Point Museum Collections, U.S.M.A. (Photo of Douglas MacArthur: The Bettmann Archive.)

the new department were much enlarged. At the same time, Beukema's Department of Economics, Government, and History was renamed the Department of Social Sciences.

The board also recommended that a Dean of the academic board be appointed, to be responsible for coordinating academic courses, schedules, and instructional facilities, and to serve as a representative of the academic departments, as well as an advisor to the Superintendent on academic matters. In addition, the board called for the appointment of a second permanent professor for each department, and suggested that all officers se-

lected for duty as instructors should be designated in advance and detailed to civilian universities for one year's post-graduate work. Finally, they recommended that special boards of consultants be appointed occasionally to examine the curriculum, the individual courses of study, and the methods of instruction at West Point.

On September 4, 1945, Major General Maxwell D. Taylor succeeded Wilby as Superintendent and immediately implemented the several recommendations of the board. Roger Alexander, professor of topography and graphics, was appointed Dean, and a number of the officers scheduled to join the faculty in 1946 were instead diverted to graduate school for a year's study before coming to West Point.

Meanwhile, at West Point, the academic board found that Taylor also had an agenda of his own. Shortly after his arrival, he gave the officers at West Point a preview of his plans and policies. "Many progressive additions and revisions in the academic program and organization are contemplated," they were informed. Like MacArthur, who had been the first Superintendent after World War I, Taylor was a brilliant young officer with a dazzling wartime record both as a commander and as a staff officer. And the similarities did not end there. Taylor, like MacArthur (and Mills and Schofield before him), soon earned the enmity of many of the senior members of the faculty. The transition from combat operations—where both the responsibility and authority assumed were absolute—to the more limited role of the superintendency seems always to have been a difficult one. But it is also worth noting that, as Superintendents, Mills, MacArthur, and Taylor had emulated the models they had known. Taylor's years as a cadet largely coincided with MacArthur's superintendency; similarly, MacArthur's cadet years were served under Mills; and Mills's under Schofield.

Taylor soon let it be known that, having created the office of Dean, he planned to limit his meetings with the academic board. Many matters of administration could now be handled without their formal input. "The Superintendent . . . will no longer have to deal with fourteen heads of departments over small details of academic administration either individually or through the Academic Board," his office reported. To members of the academic board this revealed Taylor's intention to reduce, if not usurp, their power and influence at West Point.

Though the ink had hardly dried on the academic board's new four-year curriculum study, Taylor immediately appointed a board of consultants to reexamine it. After careful scrutiny, that group expressed its approval. "The Board unanimously and most emphatically believes that the [Military Academy] should be an undergraduate institution on the collegiate level, giving a common four-year course to all cadets." The curriculum, they felt, provided a satisfactory balance between military and academic, as well as between scientific and liberal subjects. The consultants also endorsed the academic board's recommendation of the appointment of a Dean, and of additional permanent professors. In addition, they approved of graduate level training at civilian schools for prospective instructors. Although the consultants were somewhat critical of the inadequate leisure time afforded the cadets (they suggested cutting military instruction), they heartily commended the academic board's curriculum study.

Taylor, however, was not satisfied. Even before arriving at West Point, he had sent letters to many of the Army's senior officers requesting their advice. George Patton had replied immediately. "Nothing I learned in electricity or hydraulics or in higher mathematics or in drawing in any way contributed to my military career," Patton wrote. "Therefore, I would markedly reduce or wholly jettison the above subjects." He wanted more emphasis on history, and an overhaul of the system of determining class standing, giving half the weight to the tactical department. Dwight D. Eisenhower, as Supreme Allied Commander and then as Chief of Staff of the Army, recommended changes that he said were "more along the human than the technical side." He urged Taylor to insure "a profound respect for the Honor System," and strongly suggested that he include in the curriculum "a course in practical or applied psychology." Learning to handle human problems on a human basis would, Eisenhower suggested, "do much to improve leadership and personnel handling in the Army at large."

In response, Taylor sought to create a Department of Military Psychology and Leadership. The Dean and the academic board, however, were unsympathetic to this change. They had repeatedly considered additions to the curriculum, including psychology, and just as often they had concluded that all of them were less important to future officers than the material that already crowded the curriculum. They were not inclined to alter that position merely to accommodate the new Superintendent or even Eisenhower; no department head wished to give up hours he had fought time and again to win or protect. But Taylor would not be put off. If the academic board would not carve out hours for psychology in its portion of the curriculum, he would initiate the course under the auspices of the Commandant of Cadets. Under this arrangement, approximately ninety hours that had formerly been devoted to specialized branch training in the cadet's first class year were now devoted to the course in applied psychology. The academic board had been out-maneuvered; lacking any grounds to do otherwise, they gave their grudging approval to the new arrangement, but this outflanking action only fueled their determination to resist other inroads.

Taylor, however, remained critical of the curriculum; he felt that all offerings should be assessed "to verify their relevance to the whole officer corps." The curriculum, he insisted, retained an "engineering flavor" that was no longer appropriate, but his concern reached beyond the math, science, and engineering portion. He had a particular concern about the English instruction and "was determined to pay personal attention to the teaching of the subject." He particularly scrutinized the selection of the permanent professors of that department, and personally checked on instruction in the classroom. His invasion of this privileged preserve was no more welcome than had been MacArthur's. Nor did the academic board look kindly upon his efforts to eradicate "excessive inbreeding and homogeneity in the faculty" by hiring teachers from civilian life.

The academic board now felt compelled to respond. To some members, Taylor's efforts appeared nothing short of revolutionary. Others saw him as little more than a meddler, intruding in areas which were not his province. Three of the seven permanent heads of the academic departments had joined since 1945 and exercised little influence outside their own departments: Boyd Bartlett, in the Department of Electricity; Colonel Lawrence E. Schick, class of 1920, who had taken over the Department of Topography and Graphics from Alexander when the latter was made Dean in 1946; and George R. Stephens, a Princeton graduate with a Ph.D. from Pennsylvania, who had been selected to head the Department of English after ten years' service at the Naval Academy. Still, the board retained significant influence, particularly among its older members. Herman Beukema, the professor of social sciences, had sat on the board since 1930 and was a classmate and close personal friend of Dwight Eisenhower's, the new Chief of Staff of the Army. When other means proved inadequate, Beukema went to Ike. "You tame him," he is said to have told the future President concerning Taylor, "or we will."

Taylor, to the relief of the board, soon turned his attention to areas more traditionally reserved for the Superintendent—among them, the honor system and plebe training. Eisenhower had expressed concern to Taylor about the former, and the Superintendent worked closely on this issue with the Commandant and the honor committee. In 1948, he drafted an honor pamphlet for cadets and in it coined the phrase that soon became synonymous with the honor code—"a cadet will neither lie, cheat nor steal."

(continued on page 246)

THROUGH A GLASS, DARKLY

George S. Patton, Jr., 1922

The George S. Patton, Jr. Monument was "erected by his friends, officers and men of the units he commanded." The statue was unveiled by Mrs. Patton and dedicated in 1950. Melted into the bronze hands of the statue are four silver stars worn by the General and one gold cavalry insignia that Mrs. Patton had worn since their marriage. The textbook in front of the statue belonged to Patton when he was a cadet, and he scrawled at the bottom of the page shown: "End of last lesson in engineering. Last lesson as cadet—Thank God." (The book is from the U.S.M.A. Library.)

Through the travail of the ages,
Midst the pomp and toil of war
Have I fought and striven and perished
Countless times upon this star.

In the forms of many peoples
In all panoplies of time
Have I seen the luring vision
of the victory Maid, sublime.

I have battled for fresh mammoth
I have warred for pastures new,
I have listened to the whispers
When the race trek instinct grew.

I have known the call to battle
In each changeless changing shape
From the high-souled voice of conscience
To the beastly lust for rape.

I have sinned and I have suffered,
Played the hero and the knave;
Fought for belly, shame or country
And for each have found a grave.

I cannot name my battles
For the visions are not clear,
Yet I see the twisted faces
And I feel the rending spear.

Perhaps I stabbed our Savior
In His sacred helpless side.
Yet I've called His name in blessing
When in aftertimes I died.

In the dimness of the shadows
Where we hairy heathens warred,
I can taste in thought the lifeblood—
We used teeth before the sword.

While in later, clearer vision
I can sense the coppery sweat
Feel the pikes grow wet and slippery
When our phalanx Cyrus met.

Hear the rattle on the harness
Where the Persian darts bounced clear,
See their chariots wheel in panic
From the hoplite's leveled spear.

See the mole grow monthly longer,
Reaching for the walls of Tyre.
Hear the crash of tons of granite,
Smell the quenchless eastern fire.

Still more clearly as a Roman,
Can I see the Legion close,
As our third rank moved in forward
And the short sword found our foes.

Once again I feel the anguish
Of that blistering treeless plain
When the Parthians showered death bolts,
And our discipline was vain.

I remember all the suffering
Of those arrows in my neck.
Yet I stabbed a grinning savage
As I died upon my back.

Once again I smell the heat sparks
When my Flemish plate gave way
And the lance ripped through my entrails
As on Crécy's field I lay.

In the windless blinding stillness
Of the glittering tropic sea
I can see the bubbles rising
Where we set the captives free.

Midst the spume of half a tempest
I have heard the bulwarks go
When the crashing, point-blank round shot
Sent destruction to our foe.

I have fought with gun and cutlass
On the red and slippery deck
With all Hell aflame within me
And a rope around my neck.

And still later as a general
Have I galloped with Murat
When we laughed at death and numbers
Trusting in the Emperor's star.

Till at last our star had faded,
And we shouted to our doom
Where the sunken road of Ohein
Closed us in its quivering gloom.

Yet now with tanks a'clatter
Have I waddled on the foe
Belching death at twenty paces,
By the star shell's ghastly glow.

So as through a glass and darkly
The age-long strife I see
Where I fought in many guises,
Many names—but always me.

And I see not in my blindness
What the objects were I wrought.
But as God rules o'er our bickerings
It was through His will I fought.

So for ever in the future,
Shall I battle as of yore,
Dying to be born a fighter
But to die again once more.

(From "Selected Poems by George S. Patton, Jr.," in the Patton Collection, USMA Library,
Special Collections, West Point.)

He also undertook a complete review of the fourth class system, and appealed to the senior cadet officers in the same manner, he said, "as MacArthur had to my class twenty-five years before, to root out any practice which could not be directly related to making a better cadet out of the plebes undergoing training." He also found an affinity with Schofield on this subject. Quoting him, Taylor wrote: "The discipline which makes the soldiers of a free country reliable in battle is not to be gained by harsh or tyrannical treatment. On the contrary, such treatment is far more likely to destroy than to make an Army."

Over the years, West Point had come to participate in almost the entire range of intercollegiate sports, but football always remained pre-eminent and Army rose steadily in the ranks of the major teams. Through the twenties and the thirties it won many more games than it lost; in 1933, under the coaching of Lieutenant Garrison "Gar" Davidson, class of 1927, an otherwise perfect season was spoiled only by a single 13-to-12 loss to Notre Dame. By the early forties, however, Army's fortunes were in decline. The cadets failed to win a single game in 1940, so, the next year, Eichelberger hired a new head coach, Earl "Red" Blaik, class of 1920 (who had been at Dartmouth), and his entire coaching staff. By 1944, Blaik had assembled one of the finest college football teams of all time. Over the next three years Army went undefeated, although many opponents—particularly

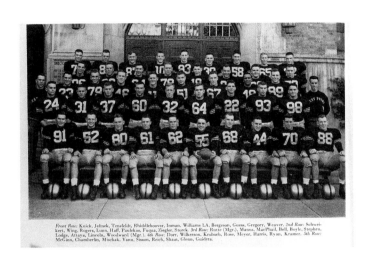

Front Row: Kuick, Jelinek, Tenafeldt, Rhiddlehoover, Inman, Williams I.A, Bergeson, Guess, Gregory, Weaver. *2nd Row:* Schweikert, Wing, Rogers, Lunn, Haff, Paulekas, Fuqua, Ziegler, Stuork. *3rd Row:* Lunn, Rowan, Gillette, Drury, Bullock, Lodge, Attaya, Lincoln, Woodward (Mgr.). *4th Row:* Dorr, Wilkerson, Kraboeh, Rose, Meyer, Harris, Ryan, Kramer. *5th Row:* McGinn, Chamberlin, Mischak, Vann, Sisson, Reich, Shaun, Glenn, Guidera.

The 1951 Army football team after the players involved in the cheating scandal had been dismissed. From The Howitzer. U.S.M.A. Archives. Copy Photo: Philip Pocock.

1st Row: Biles, Hayes, Ray, Fuson, Davis, G., Blanchard, Tucker, Poole, Enos, Tavzel. *2nd Row:* Galloway, Vinson, Routt, Bryant, Foldberg, Shelly, Steffy, Gerometta, Green, Cosentino. *3rd Row:* Lunn, Rowan, Gillette, Drury, Bullock, Anderson, Burckart, Irons, Mackmull, Lindeman. *4th Row:* Dobelstein, Fastucca, West, Livesay, Barnes, Davis, B., Scholtz, Feir, Yeomans. *5th Row:* Rogers *(Equipment Manager)*, Gustafson, Gabriel, Trent, Galiffa, Aton, Rawers, Scott, Summerhayes, Means, Scowcroft *(Manager)*

Twenty-eight straight games without defeat—so stood the amazing record of Coach Earl Blaik's Army Team as its third straight year of undefeated football drew to a close. Disparaged by many experts at the beginning of the year, the Black Knights waded through the toughest possible schedule against the nation's most powerful teams, each primed in its turn to topple the Cadets, and emerged unbeaten! Villanova, Oklahoma, Cornell, Michigan, Columbia,

Co-Captains
Davis and
Blanchard

FOOTBALL

The 1946 Army football team that played in the famous game with Notre Dame which ended in a tie. Coach Earl Blaik is shown in the photo insert above. From The Howitzer. U.S.M.A. Archives. Copy Photo: Philip Pocock.

Notre Dame—insisted that this was only because their own best players were in the service.

Possibly the most famous game in Army history was played against Notre Dame at New York's Yankee Stadium in 1946. Army's Black Knights had won the games in 1944 and 1945 by lopsided scores. In 1946, with their players now back from the service, Notre Dame was determined to turn the tables, but the game ended in an indecisive 0-to-0 tie. Billed as the "Game of the Century," the contest had become the subject of excessive hype—end-zone seats were being scalped for as much as $300, and huge amounts of money were being bet on the game. As a result, the two schools agreed to end the series after the 1947 season.

Army was finally defeated in 1947—by Columbia and Notre Dame, but otherwise continued to pile up victories and belie the claim that their wartime success had been a fluke. From 1944 through the end of 1950, "Red" Blaik's team had won seventy games and lost only three. By all indications, the Army team would be even better in 1951.

Then, in April 1951, the Commandant of Cadets learned of widespread cheating among a group of football players and cadets who were assisting them. In clear violation of the honor code, members of the ring who had taken written tests would pass on to their associates who had not, the questions that were being asked. The system worked because, in most classes, identical written examinations were given to successive groups, even though as many as half the cadets in the course might take the examination a full day after it was first given.

The Commandant's board of inquiry reported that approximately ninety cadets were guilty, and recommended their separation. The academic board concurred. Before making a final decision, however, the Secretary of the Army, Frank Pace, Jr., appointed a board to review the investigation and pass on the recommendations. The board, chaired by Judge Learned Hand, concurred in the finding that the cadets were violating the honor code, and unanimously supported the recommendations of the Academy. Ninety cadets were ultimately offered the opportunity to resign. Most did so; those who did not were administratively separated.

The cadet honor code is rooted in the earliest years of the Academy. It was derived from the code of honor of an officer and a gentleman—a code which required that his word be his bond and that his personal character and conduct would make him worthy of association with his brother officers. In 1807 the cadets attempted to punish one of their number for his ungentlemanly behavior toward a servant by enforcing "silence" toward him. Jonathan Williams, the first Superintendent, intervened—arguing that this case was cognizable under the law and therefore the "silence" (or the withholding of social intercourse, and conversing only in the line of duty) was inappropriate. Although Williams insisted that he would not allow these "self erected Censors" to prevail, and that "nothing of that kind shall ever be permitted on this Ground," the concept of a cadet enforced code of honor persisted.

Infractions and other breaches of gentlemanly conduct were usually settled by a confrontation between the accused and his accuser. In the early nineteenth century, many gentlemen still felt compelled by the code to fight a duel to answer personal affronts. In the Army, however, regulations strictly forbade that practice, so at West Point a fist fight between the two parties was usually considered sufficient to resolve such matters. Other violations, such as making a false statement, were referred to the Superintendent for administrative punishment—often dismissal. Four cadets were dismissed in 1816 by Superintendent Alden Partridge for lying as to their whereabouts.

The code continued for years as an unwritten prohibition against lying and ungentlemanly conduct. It was passed from class to class through informal mechanisms. Although

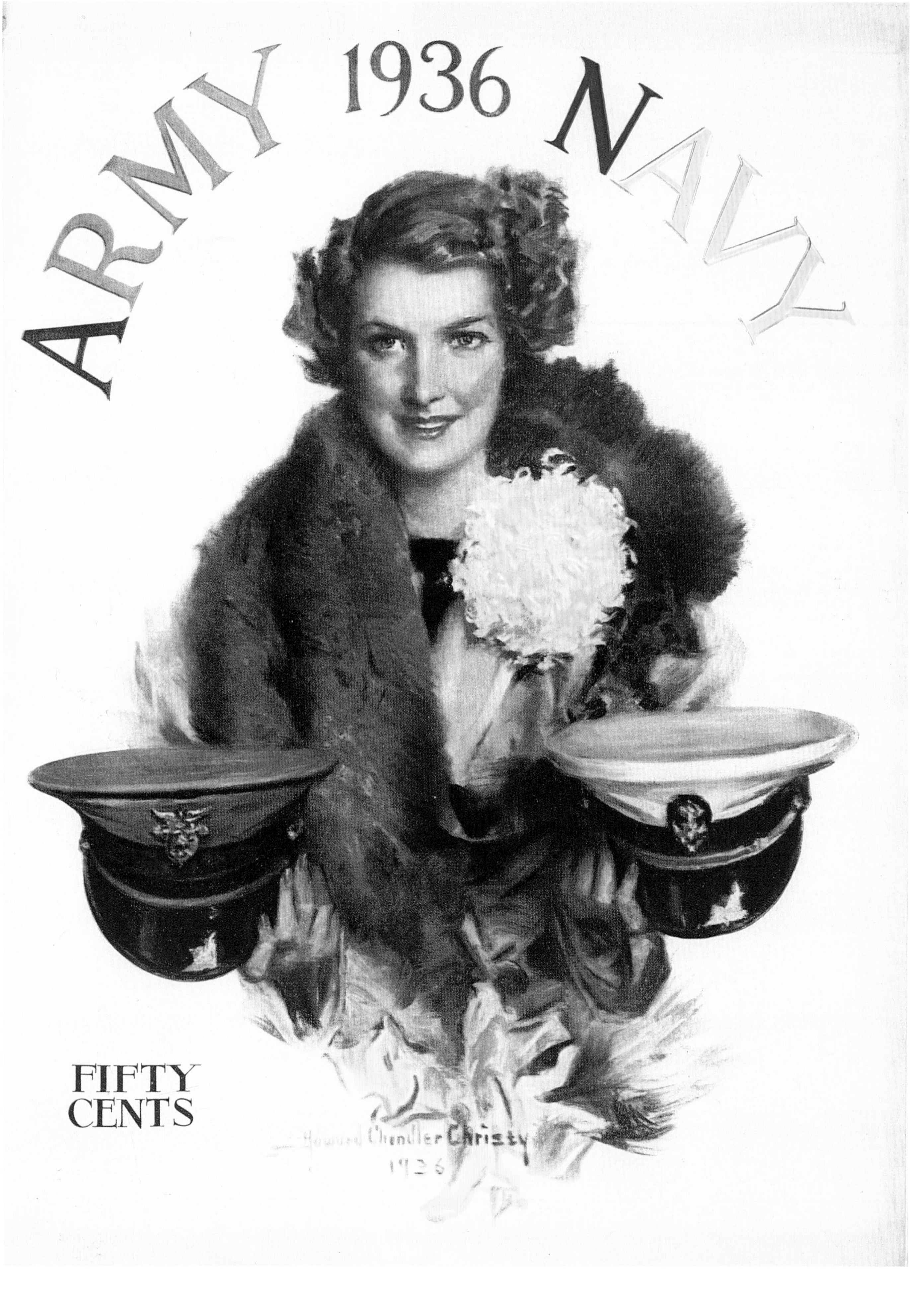
ARMY 1936 NAVY
FIFTY
CENTS
Chandler Christy
1936

Left:
A colorful program cover for the Pittsburgh-Army game of 1932. U.S.M.A. Library, Special Collections. Photo: Philip Pocock.

Opposite:
Program cover for the Army-Navy game of 1936, by Howard Chandler Christy. U.S.M.A. Library, Special Collections. Photo: Philip Pocock.

the inculcation of these values was sometimes considered to be a responsibility of the chaplain and the Commandant of Cadets, the maintenance of the code was largely the preserve of the corps of cadets.

In 1865, an informal cadet committee attempted to drum another cadet out of the corps for stealing. When Academy officials intervened and blocked their effort, the cadets again resorted to "silence." In this case, Academy officials made no objection. In 1871, when three fourth classmen broke regulations and then compounded their offenses by lying, a group of first classmen gave the trio some civilian clothes and money, and told them to leave the post. In the investigation that followed, the upperclassmen indicated that, although they had knowledge of only one other similar case, they believed such action to be traditional.

At first, such actions were organized by leaders of the corps whenever they were deemed necessary. As the years passed, however, more formalized mechanisms evolved. By the 1890s, *ad hoc* vigilance committees conducted organized, if unofficial, investigations of suspected honor violations. By 1911, the vigilance committee had become a permanent fixture whose membership included representatives from each class—although the group was still not officially recognized by Academy authorities.

The first effort to capture on paper the essence of the cadet honor code was undertaken in 1907 by Charles Larned, professor of drawing, whose brief essay "Corps Honor," appeared in the first edition of the *West Point Hand-Book*—a publication that soon became known as *Bugle Notes*. "Corps Honor is not and should not be different from the accepted standard of honor recognized by the ethics of Christian Nations—the code of a gentleman the world over," Larned wrote. He insisted that "Corps Honor is concerned with all questions affecting the integrity of personal action." By various illustrations Larned defined a code that encompassed a wide range of activities: a cadet would not steal, lie, cheat or slander; he should be physically brave, sober, and chaste; he should forswear indirection, evasion, sophistry, subtlety and guile; and he should neither "bootlick," nor take mean advantage, nor neglect his duty, nor betray a confidence. "A true code of honor," he wrote, "stands in its integrity for right doing all around." Still, there were "different degrees of culpability, and there are certain infractions regarding which the Corps is wholly intolerant." These, he indicated, were "theft, cowardice and deliberate falsehood."

Cheating—at least getting unauthorized advanced information about examinations—was not always considered an offense against honor. Thayer had attempted to treat it as such, but his successors generally had not. This began to change about the turn of the century. The first evidence of a shift in attitude came in 1899 when a vigilance committee indicted a cadet for stealing examination papers. Larned, in 1907, had similarly indicated that "cheating the instructor" was an honor offense, although only two years earlier the adjutant had indicated the opposite. To clear up any confusion concerning this point, Superintendent Hugh Scott followed up Larned's piece with a memorandum confirming that "hereafter in the section-room, either at oral recitation or at written recitation, all cadets shall be considered on honor to receive no information concerning their recitations or their lessons from any unauthorized source whatever."

By the end of World War I, the vigilance committee had become an elective body, with representatives from each of the twelve companies. Although it had no official standing, it had, for a number of years, constituted an informal court to consider honor violations. In 1920, MacArthur began to move the honor system more directly under the control of Academy officials. William Ganoe, MacArthur's adjutant during that period, suggests that his action was triggered by Secretary of War Newton Baker's testimony before Congress: West Point must insure "the inculcation of a set of virtues admirable always but indispensable in the soldier." As Baker pointed out: "Men may be inexact or even untruthful in ordinary matters, and suffer as a consequence only the disesteem of their associates, or the inconveniences of unfavorable litigation, but the inexact and untruthful soldier trifles with the lives of his fellow men; and it is therefore, no matter of idle pride, but stern disciplinary necessity that makes West Point require of her students a character of trustworthiness which knows no evasions." After discussing the problem with Robert Danford, the Commandant of Cadets, MacArthur decided to dissolve the vigilance committee. "Select a few cadets of the highest, all-round character, who are most respected and influential in the Corps," he told Danford. "Let them be called an Honor Committee." In 1922, he formally recognized the committee and charged it with the administration of the honor code.

In 1923, the new honor committee worked with the administration to define the "guiding principles" of the honor system. First, "no intentional breach of honor is excusable." Second, "everyone, offender or not, is honor bound to report any breach of honor which comes to his attention." Third, there will be no "second chance." Fourth, questions as to interpretation should be taken to a member of the honor committee. Fifth, "quibbling" and "evasive statements" to "shield guilt" would not be tolerated. And, sixth, if in doubt, one should err on the side of caution—"always be on the safe side." These basic principles were amplified by specific examples of their application to academic work, and everyday cadet life.

Soon, however, the honor committee had begun to overreach its authority—acting as if all infractions of discipline which involved questions of honor "could be handled by them without any reference to the military machinery provided for enforcing discipline." In 1924, Merch Stewart, then the Commandant of Cadets, reined them in by carefully delineating their duties. They were told they should: assure that cadets understood the system; guard against the birth of practices inconsistent with the stated principles; consult with the Commandant when the principles required interpretation; inquire into all suspected honor violations; and report the results of their investigations to the Commandant.

In 1926, the academic board reviewed the "general code of rules that has been evolved by the Cadet Honor Committee" and suggested a rewording of the portion dealing with academic work. "No cadet shall impart or receive any unauthorized assistance, either outside or inside the section room or examination room, which would tend to give any cadet an unfair advantage," they wrote, adding a number of examples to clarify specific cases.

A few years later, in 1931, Superintendent William Smith reduced the statement of the code to a single sentence. "Honor . . . is a fundamental principle of character—a virtue which implies loyalty and courage, truthfulness and self-respect, justice and generosity." Smith also further defined the operation of the honor system. Honor violations detected by cadets and reported to the honor committee, he directed, were to be investigated by the honor committee, but violations discovered by officers or otherwise reported to the Commandant of Cadets were to be investigated by the Commandant. In the aftermath of such investigations, a cadet found guilty of an honor violation could demand a court-martial, although few did. Most simply resigned. Even if acquitted or given a punishment short of dismissal by the court, cadets already found guilty by their peers were likely to be silenced.

In 1948, Maxwell Taylor subjected the honor code and system to a detailed review. MacArthur's recognition of the honor committee had soon led to the codification of the honor system. Taylor's reforms carried that process one step further, defining the process in legal terms. The honor committee was described "as a grand jury reporting possible violations to the Commandant of Cadets," and, from 1946 to 1953, at least, honor hearings were formalized and conducted essentially as court-martial proceedings.

One outcome of the codification of the honor system was the establishment of a close linkage between honor issues and Academy regulations—producing the oft-heard charge that the Academy was using honor to enforce regulations. That issue has been a continuing source of cadet frustration. In 1899, in an effort to stop hazing, Superintendent Albert Mills ordered cadet company commanders to sign statements "on their honor" that they were not permitting hazing in their units. Cadets so resented this and a chain of similar demands that, in 1901, they responded by towing the reveille cannon to the Superintendent's quarters and pointing it at Mills's front door. A similar directive in the 1920s demanded that the cadet officer of the day and the cadet officer of the guard sign statements that they had reported all violations of all regulations. This time, cadets responded with a campaign of evasion and passive resistance. Cadets exercising these duties loudly jangled key chains against their swords to warn other cadets of their approach and dined with their heads lowered lest they observe infractions in the dining hall.

In the 1930s and 1940s, the honor committees tried in vain to have the "poop sheets," which listed what was and was not an honor violation, deleted in favor of cadets obeying the simpler demands of the code itself. In an effort to defuse this argument and to better distinguish between honor and regulations, Taylor created the cadet duty committee in 1948, which was designed to aid the administration in dealing with issues of duties and regulations—separating them from honor issues. This attempt soon lapsed due to a lack of support within the corps. The poop sheets persisted, but individual items were subject to dramatic reversals. For example, the cadet practice of stuffing their bed with pillows

HONOR COMMITTEE

LEEVER; GEORGE; PALMER; DAVIS, J. H.; MYERS; EWELL; STUDER; CURTIN, R. D.
SMITH, M. C.; HOWARD; LITTLE; PULLIAM; CANTRELL

The honor committees are responsible for ensuring that cadets adhere to the code of honor. Shown here is the honor committee of 1939. From The Howitzer. U.S.M.A. Archives. Copy Photo: Philip Pocock.

to avoid detection during an unauthorized late-night absence was judged to be a violation of regulations in 1921, 1948, and 1963; on other occasions it was labeled an honor violation. Increasingly, cadets complained that the spirit of the honor code was being subordinated to a "laundry list of do's and don'ts."

In 1962, the cadet honor committee formally protested the use of honor to enforce regulations. In response, West Point made some significant changes during the 1963–64 academic year. The most important of these dealt with the "all right." Previously the response "all right" to a challenge signified that a cadet: (1) had been within authorized geographic limits, (2) was not hazing, (3) did not possess either liquor or drugs, and (4) was not gambling. The new policy changed the "all right" to mean simply that the cadet had not violated the authorized limits.

In the early 1970s the non-toleration clause was added to the statement of the code: "A cadet will not lie, cheat or steal nor tolerate those who do." This change, of course, was more apparent than real. Non-toleration had long been an implicit element of the code and, on occasion—as in 1923—it had been an explicit part. The significance of its inclusion in the code this time lay more in its symbology as an Academy effort to respond to a growing cadet frustration with the honor system (although not with the honor code itself) at the beginning of what was to prove a very troubled decade.

Given the expansion in the size of the corps of cadets in the thirties and forties, it seemed axiomatic that physical expansion would follow. As the corps inched toward its authorized size of 1,374 in the early thirties, many of the Academy's facilities were already insufficient. The further enlargement of the corps beginning in 1936—reaching toward a newly authorized strength of 1,960—necessitated added barracks and classroom space, as well as the expansion of the gymnasium. To plan this expansion the Academy chose one of America's foremost architects, Paul Cret. Beginning in 1936, he finished the work in two years. Cret's Scott Barracks, nestled against the hill behind North Barracks, was the first major structure at West Point to be built of reinforced concrete, although it was faced in gray stone. Cret gave this structure the clean simplicity of modern functionalism, yet its towers, battlements, and buttresses projected a definite sense of the Gothic. Cret's addition to the east academic building was even more remarkable than his design for Scott Barracks. Although sandwiched between three buildings, he produced a structure that matched the site and yet was remarkable for its individuality and visual impact. Its uneven outcroppings of gray stone, large pseudo-buttresses, and huge Gothic openings—achieved by massing the windows of several floors—assured its harmony with the surroundings, and yet endowed it with a distinct character.

In 1942, the Academy strength was once more increased—to a maximum of 2,496. The war soon filled the Academy to overflowing. This increase, coupled with needs that had been gradually accumulating over a period of many years, prompted Academy officials

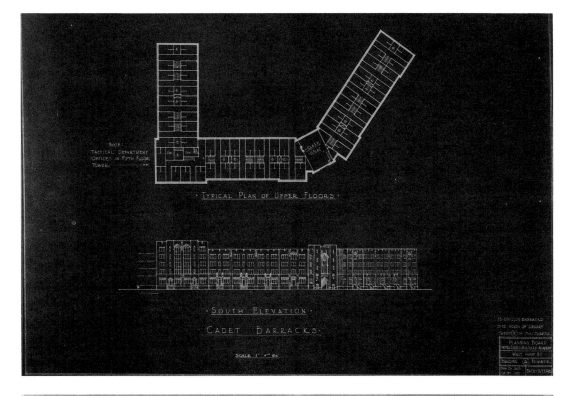

Floor plan and south elevation for proposed cadet barracks. 1943. U.S.M.A. Library, Special Collections. Photo: Philip Pocock.

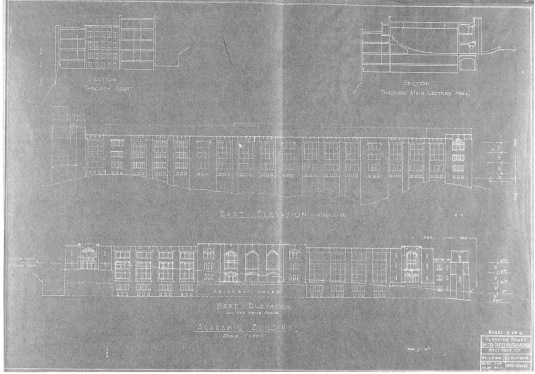

Plan showing the east and west elevation for a new academic building. c. 1943. U.S.M.A. Library, Special Collections. Photo: Philip Pocock.

to consider once again the massive sort of overhaul of facilities that had been undertaken forty years before.

A new competition was held in 1943. Design requirements included a new academic building within the walls of the existing riding hall, a new memorial hall supplementing the facilities of Cullum Hall, and an additional barracks. The winner was the firm of Delano and Aldrich of New York City, but competing wartime and post-war demands for funds doomed the project. In the end, the work was limited to additions to the gymnasium and mess hall, which were completed in 1946.

In 1955, continuing this piecemeal approach, the firm of Gehron and Seltzer were chosen to convert the riding hall into an academic building. The building was to be gutted and then rebuilt to house the Departments of Mathematics, Military Art and Engineering, Social Sciences, Law, Ordnance, Foreign Languages, English, and Military Psychology and Leadership, as well as the museum, bookstore, and computer center. Construction began in 1956 and was completed in 1958. In 1959, Gehron and Seltzer converted the old (1895) academic building into a modern barracks. Two additional barracks—named for Lee and Sherman—were begun on the site of the old hospital in 1960 and completed in 1962, under the direction of the architectural firm of O'Connor and Kilham.

The pressure on facilities caused by the growth of the Academy in the 1930s and 1940s was mirrored in the demand for faculty quarters. Already inadequate by the late 1920s, housing was a high priority item when the passage of the National Industrial Recovery Act made public-works funds available. Foremost among the projects undertaken were fifty sets of officers' quarters at the north end of the post. These quarters were especially designed for the young married officers and the area was soon tagged "Looeyville." (To-

Above:
The cadet mess in Washington Hall was built in 1929 to provide dining facilities for the expanding student body. The Gothic-style mess hall, with its ceiling of exposed beams, was built on the site of the old gymnasium. This photograph was taken in the 1930s. U.S.M.A. Archives. Copy photo: Philip Pocock.

Opposite:
The barracks quandrangle in the early 1930s. U.S.M.A. Archives. Photo: Philip Pocock.

day lieutenant colonels, not lieutenants, inhabit the neighborhood—now known as "Lee" area.) Economies of the depression era insured that these new quarters would not match the lavish sets built by Cram, Goodhue and Ferguson at the turn of the century. Still, these quartermaster-designed brick doubles possessed a dignity and graciousness that was enhanced by the thoughtful and attractive plan for the area as a whole. These units and some additional sets of new officers' quarters in tasteful brick row-houses, also in Lee area, were completed in 1935. It was anticipated that they would be sufficient to accommodate all the married officers assigned to the post. The new expansion of the corps of cadets that same year, of course, meant that quarters would soon be in short supply once again. This situation persisted throughout the war and into the late 1940s.

In 1946 and 1947, faced with a critical nationwide housing shortage, the Congress limited the cost and size of army-built family housing units. At West Point, however, the rough, rocky terrain meant inordinately high building costs. As a result, when Congress authorized 133 new sets to be built (less than half of what was needed), there were funds enough for only shoddily-built, clapboard row-houses that soon acquired the name "Grey Ghost."

Major General Bryant E. Moore, class of August 1917, who had succeeded Maxwell Taylor, and his successor, Major General Frederick A. Irving, class of April 1917, both reiterated West Point's requests, without effect. Moore asked specifically for eighty three-bedroom officers' quarters with 1,250 square feet of living area—tiny in comparison to the older quarters but in excess of the post-war allowance. He justified this exception by pointing out that West Point officers had a greater need for guest facilities, that instructors needed a study, and that "the type of officer selected for duty at the Military Academy would, almost without exception, occupy a dwelling with three or more bedrooms if he were doing similar work in a civilian institution."

Finally, in 1960, with no relief in sight, West Point authorities acquiesced to the proposition that even inadequate housing was better than none, and accepted a parcel of brick duplexes, providing roughly 130 sets of tiny (1,050 square feet) quarters, known as "New Brick." Tightly packed on the site, devoid of ornament, and without either basements or garages, these units have all the architectural charm of low-income tract-housing.

The officers and their wives, however, did not allow their surroundings to interfere with the active social life to which they were accustomed. The more senior, of course, drew the older, very pleasant quarters. Many of the new additional professors that each department was allowed at the end of World War II, settled in the turn-of-the-century quarters at the south end of the post. Among them were George Lincoln and Vincent Esposito. This group organized itself into the "South End Officers Protective Association," which was soon famous for its exclusive New Year's Eve party and springtime masquerade. The latter, the Magnolia Festival that celebrated the annual blooming of Esposito's magnolia tree, was a costumed affair at which the members were required to read verses they had composed for the occasion.

In the years immediately after Taylor's departure there were few significant programmatic reforms at West Point, although pressures were building for change by the mid-1950s. In 1954, Lieutenant General Blackshear M. Bryan, Class of June 14, 1922, succeeded Frederick Irving as Superintendent. Bryan faced a challenge that was novel to West Point—a threat to enrollments. In 1954, the Academy filled only 67 percent of available vacancies, continuing a downward trend that had begun in the first year of the Korean War, when only 82 percent of the vacancies had been filled. The opening of the Air Force Academy in 1955 compounded recruitment difficulties. In response, Bryan poured time, energy, and resources into the recruiting effort and into public relations. He promoted cadet

Opposite above:
Cadet barracks of the 1950s, as recreated, are on exhibition at the Academy.

Opposite below left:
West end of the Lee room in the Superintendent's quarters. 1936. U.S.M.A. Archives.

Opposite below right:
A view of West Point showing the Academy buildings as seen from the tower of the cadet chapel. 1949. The Bettmann Archive.

Graduates

H. Norman Schwarzkopf, 41 Maplewood avenue, Maplewood was graduated last week from the U. S. Military Academy at West Point. He was commissioned a second lieutenant in the infantry and received a BS degree. His father, Maj. Gen. (Ret.) H. Norman Schwarzkopf, was graduated from West Point in 1917. During his senior year, the new officer was a cadet captain.

* * *

News clipping announcing the 1956 graduation from West Point of H. Norman Schwarzkopf. Copyright News Record, Maplewood, N.J., June 14, 1956.

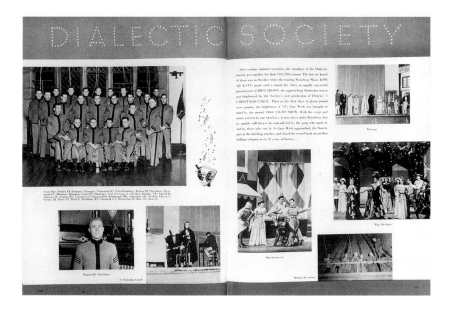

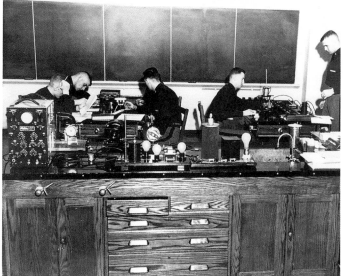

speaking tours, and expanded contacts with high school counselors, educators, and any group that might conceivably yield candidates—even the Boy Scouts. In the meantime, the Academy's public relations people redoubled their efforts. Colonel Russell "Red" Reeder, then employed by the Army Athletic Association, undertook his popular West Point series: *West Point Plebe* in 1955; *West Point Yearling* and *The West Point Story* in 1956; *West Point Second Classman* in 1957; and *West Point First Classman* in 1958. Frederick Todd penned his *Cadet Gray* in 1955, which was followed the next year by Jack Engeman's *West Point, The Life of a Cadet.*

Hollywood got into the act in 1955 with *The Long Gray Line,* starring Tyrone Power, Maureen O'Hara, and Ward Bond. And, in September 1956, CBS began a regular dramatic series entitled simply "The West Point Story," and produced a total of thirty-nine episodes. The Academy was a willing subject in this publicity barrage: cadets, faculties, and families were the eager extras, with the gray stone walls and rocky hills as a ready backdrop.

"Gar" Davidson, who twenty-some years earlier had coached the Academy's football team, replaced Bryan as Superintendent in 1956 and continued to expand the general recruitment effort. He organized a formal admissions division directly under his supervision and personally selected the director. He enlarged the pool of potentially acceptable candidates by shifting from exclusive reliance on the College Entrance Examination Board tests to a "whole man" selection procedure which supplemented academic achievement tests with evidence of character, leadership potential, and physical fitness. Davidson also attempted to persuade members of Congress to permit the academic board to arrange their candidates for them in an order of predicted probable success in the Army—in effect, to allow the Academy to designate their principal appointees. In 1957, only three congressmen availed themselves of this offer, but by 1960, 128 were doing so and that number continued to increase.

Recruitment, however, was but a sideshow to the new Superintendent's primary objective; Davidson had long sought the assignment to West Point and had already formulated a comprehensive scheme of reform. But, unlike most of his reform-oriented predecessors, Davidson was mindful of the politics and process of change at such an institution. In that sense, he had been well served by his prior tour as commandant at the Army's Command and General Staff College at Fort Leavenworth.

Davidson spent much of his first year at West Point considering his goals and carefully formulating a strategy for achieving them. That scheme provides insight into the institutional prerequisites for successful reform at West Point. In its simplest form, the strategy won the support of major constituencies by including them in the study process. An elaborate curriculum review, that encompassed an array of staff studies, harnessed the efforts (and ultimately the support) of many on the staff and faculty to the project, and a variety of opinion surveys tapped (and co-opted) other important groups. It disarmed numerous potential opponents of change by seeking their advice and by posing questions that encouraged them to consider problems from a perspective that Davidson himself had established.

Never in the history of the Military Academy had such a substantial portion of the staff, faculty, student body, and alumni been engaged in contributing to a critical review of the Academy's programs. And never, since Thayer, had a reforming Superintendent enjoyed such esteem among the many constituencies concerned with West Point—most particularly, his colleagues on the academic board.

Davidson could effect some reforms by decree, and did so. He announced that henceforth all officers who were appointed to permanent professorships were expected to obtain their doctorate; he established a program of sabbatical leaves; and he urged all the faculty to write articles for the professional and scholarly journals.

Curriculum reform, of course, required the assent of the academic board—that venerable institution which had managed to frustrate most reform-minded Superintendents. The complexion of the board, of course, had been changing. Colonel Charles West, class of 1920, had been named the first permanent professor of law in 1947, although he had served as head of that department since 1943. Colonel William W. Bessell, Jr., a classmate of West's, had succeeded Harris Jones as professor of mathematics when the latter was made Dean in 1947. Colonel Charles J. Barrett, class of 1922, had replaced William Morrison as professor and head of the Department of Foreign Languages in 1948. Colonel Elvin R. "Vald" Heiberg, class of 1926, had become professor of mechanics when Oscar Gatchell retired in 1953. Heiberg's selection was particularly important in changing the make-up of the board, for he was a strong advocate of electives—the first such on the mathematics-science-engineering side. His own prescription for academic reform—contained in an article, "A BS or BA Election for Cadets," published in 1953—had been soundly criticized by his colleagues, although in time, his views gained adherents.

In 1954, upon Herman Beukema's retirement, Colonel George A. Lincoln, class of 1929, became professor and head of the Department of Social Sciences. Two years later, Colonel Vincent "Mike" Esposito, class of 1925, succeeded Thomas Stamps in the Department of Military Art and Engineering. Both Lincoln and Esposito had enjoyed brilliant careers on George Marshall's staff in World War II. Lincoln had served in the Operations Division of the War Department General Staff and as a member of the Joint Planners Committee of the Combined Chiefs of Staff. Esposito had served with Lincoln in the Operations Division and had been a War Department representative at the Quebec, Malta, Yalta, and Potsdam Conferences. Both had been promoted to the rank of brigadier general in 1945. But both were scholars, and had surrendered their stars at war's end in order to return to West Point. Lincoln's *Economics of National Security* was an outstanding and widely adopted textbook. Esposito's two-volume *The West Point Atlas of American Wars* was based on numerous instructional atlases whose preparation he had overseen in the years just after the war. Said one critic, "These two volumes are at once a thing of art and a scholarly enlargement of our knowledge in the field of military affairs." Largely unheralded was the brilliant work of Esposito's cartographer, Edward J. Krasnoborski, whose handsome campaign maps had long been a fixture of West Point's classrooms and atlases. Krasnoborski, a man whose modesty only served to highlight his enormous talent, celebrated fifty years of service at West Point in 1985, but continued for many more years to preside over his studio in the Department of History.

Colonel Edward C. Gillette, Jr., another member of the class of 1920, was selected to head the Department of Physics and Chemistry in 1957, when Gerald Counts was promoted to brigadier general and made Dean. In 1959, when Counts retired from that office, William Bessell was selected to replace him. Bessell, in turn, surrendered the Department of Mathematics to Colonel Charles P. Nicholas, class of 1925.

Davidson asked the academic board for a thorough review of the curriculum. The study was completed in November 1958, but proved something of a disappointment to the Superintendent. Although it advanced the concept of electives which he desired, it suggested only a single elective—which was to be taken in the first class year. The study did nothing to alter the emphasis on mathematics, science, and engineering that had always characterized West Point curricula. To provide time for the one elective, the board proposed reducing the law course from two semesters to one.

Davidson passed the report to an outside curriculum review board in December, telling them that, in his view, the report's recommendations "had not gone far enough in proposing modifications to our curriculum." He then gave them his own "somewhat more radical" recommendations. In particular, he called for fifteen hours of electives, substantially more than the committee had envisioned—gaining time for those by converting some of the first class engineering and law courses to electives, and by shifting some tactics instruction to the summer.

The curriculum review board attempted to reconcile the two sets of recommendations. They concurred in the prescribed curriculum in general, but did call for six semester-hours of electives (two courses) for all first classmen, and an additional six semester-hours of electives for "particularly able cadets by accelerating their progress through the required courses of earlier years." To make room for the six hours of electives for all cadets they proposed reductions in engineering and law, as well as in tactics and military hygiene.

The struggle for academic reform now moved back into the arena of the academic board. In March 1959, Davidson appointed an *ad hoc* curriculum committee to consider the various studies that had been offered, and to make recommendations to the academic board. In April, when their report was completed, it was debated by the board as a whole. Those opposed to the elective program argued that "the only reason advanced for electives is that they will provide an opportunity in their final year for cadets to abandon studies which are distasteful to them and to concentrate to some extent in the fields of their primary interest or aptitude." Still, they conceded, "it appears that we must give it a trial." Even many favoring reform preferred a cautious approach, expressing concern over large-scale changes. Still others saw little alternative to slow progress. "We might as well recognize," wrote Lincoln, "that the Academic Board of the Military Academy on most issues and the General Committee overwhelmingly on all issues is abdominally as well as cerebrally committed to the overriding priority of mathematics and science."

However, in late April 1959, when the issues were formally presented to the board, the very first vote revealed the evolution of opinion that was taking place on the most fundamental issue. When asked whether or not the Academy should be under a single completely prescribed curriculum, the board voted only eight to seven in the affirmative—preserving that sacred tradition by only one vote. They then proceeded to approve elective courses for all first class cadets on a trial basis, making room for them by reducing the courses in civil and ordnance engineering, and law—these and other adjustments to the curriculum were to be made over a four year period beginning in academic year 1959–1960. Still, they refrained from making a formal recommendation concerning this curriculum change to the War Department.

Throughout the autumn of 1959, the academic board continued to agonize over the curriculum. At stake was not only the preservation of local "fiefdoms," but also, in the

minds of many, the preservation of the integrity of the Thayer system. It was, as one observer put it, the era of "the Great Debate." Said General Davidson, "The discussion in the Academic Board meetings were intense to say the least—but friendly. Blood was drawn but the wounded lived."

The board proposed to expand elective opportunities by allowing cadets with advanced preparation to validate introductory courses and accelerate their programs—allowing additional electives in their first class year. But Davidson pressed them to further increase the number of electives to four, once again recommending that the two semesters of civil engineering be moved out of the core curriculum, while preserving them as electives for those who wished to take them. Feeling ran high against the proposal until Professor Heiberg, of the Department of Mechanics, suggested a compromise which would retain one semester of civil engineering in the core curriculum and allow three electives. After considerable debate, Heiberg's compromise was adopted. Heiberg told Davidson, "You shouldn't feel bad; you're going to get 92 percent of what you want."

Davidson then forwarded the academic board's recommendation to General Lemnitzer, the Chief of Staff, but with it he enclosed a long minority report expressing his own preference for a fourth elective at the expense of the one remaining semester of civil engineering. Lemnitzer, however, sided with the board (which included four of his classmates from the class of 1920), and approved the three-elective program. Two years later the academic board restored the excised semester of civil engineering to the prescribed curriculum, and cut the number of electives to two. But, this setback was temporary; only a few years later the board again reversed itself.

As the sequel would prove, Davidson had initiated an extended era of curriculum consideration and revision. Never, since Thayer, had a Superintendent's efforts at academic reform produced such an enduring impact. The debate that followed was to become one of the important themes of the decades that lay ahead—decades that would reshape the Long Gray Line and its Alma Mater.

Above left:
Cadets receiving instruction in the proper method of pitching a tent. 1958. U.S.M.A. Archives.

Above right
A Cadet Hop in progress in Cullum Hall. 1958. On the wall to the right can be seen the portraits of graduates, each of whom attained the rank of general officer and commanded a unit in wartime. U.S.M.A. Archives.

CHAPTER 10
THE YEARS OF TURMOIL 1960-1990

Major General William C. Westmoreland, class of 1936, became Superintendent on July 1, 1960. "I was anxious to carry on the good work of my predecessor, Lieutenant General Garrison Davidson, in modernizing [the Academy]," wrote Westmoreland. "One of my goals as superintendent was to increase the size of the Corps from approximately 2,400 cadets to 4,400, roughly the strength of the Brigade of Midshipmen at the Naval Academy." Expansion was an issue he had considered while on the Army staff before coming to West Point, and it became the central focus of his superintendency.

In the early months of 1961, Westmoreland raised the question of expansion with the Department of the Army and secured permission "to plan for and make recommendations concerning an incremental expansion of existing facilities or provision of new facilities in proximity of existing ones to accommodate an increase in the size of the Corps to about 4,250 cadets."

"As I prepared to get the expansion bill started in the long trek through bureaucracy," wrote Westmoreland, "a discussion with President Kennedy at the Army-Navy football game in December 1962 gave me an opportunity to make my point in person to the Commander in Chief." During the second half, as Navy punished Army, President Kennedy turned to the Superintendent and asked, "General, why are there so many more midshipmen at the game than cadets?" Westmoreland pointed out that the two academies operated under separate statutes, and that the Naval Academy was allowed 2,000 more men—adding that that meant 2,000 more men to draw from for a football team. "That," he told the President with a smile, "is one of the reasons we are getting the hell kicked out of us today."

By that time, Westmoreland had already established a full-time expansion planning group under the chairmanship of Colonel Charles R. Broshous, class of 1933, professor and head of the Department of Earth, Space and Graphic Sciences. Broshous was an ideal choice for the post. He fussed over every detail of the construction from concept to completion, and he strongly resisted efforts to cut corners.

In the midst of this, a new library, approved prior to inception of expansion planning, was begun on the location of Delafield's 1841 library. The new structure was designed by the architectural firm of Gehron and Seltzer, and begun in 1962. Broad, pointed arch windows divided by delicate tracery, a massive tower, and the pseudo-buttresses maintained the Gothic motif. Adorning the face of the tower over the main entrance was an eighteen-foot-high relief statue of the patroness of the military Academy, Athena, mythological protectress of the brave and valorous, and symbol of supreme wisdom—both in the sciences of peace and in the arts of war. The new library was completed and occupied in 1964.

In February 1963, a preliminary expansion plan was approved by the post planning board and forwarded for approval to the Pentagon. At the same time, Westmoreland

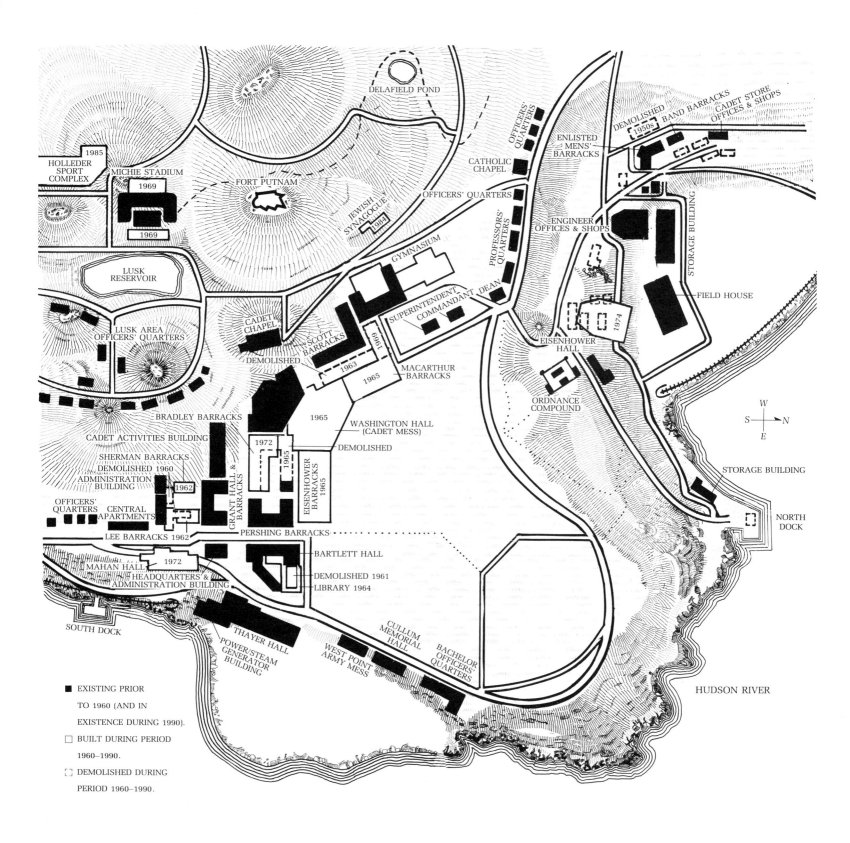

Map of West Point, 1960–1990.

briefed the former Superintendents and the leadership of the Association of Graduates on the plan; shortly thereafter he took the issue to a number of key graduates, including MacArthur, Eisenhower, and Lucius Clay (class of 1918).

Westmoreland and Broshous were determined that the new plan must provide a single integrated facility in the immediate vicinity of the existing structures on the plain, and they promised worried alumni that it would entail only a "minimal encroachment upon the Plain." Moreover, they believed it essential to adhere to West Point's traditional aesthetic and construction standards. The Academy would continue to be gray stone and Gothic. The new arrangements would preserve the scene across the plain long familiar to graduates and visitors—barracks extending along the southern and western boundaries of the plain, with the mess hall at their intersection.

Broshous's studies indicated that the existing mess hall could be expanded, but that the Central Barracks (completed in 1851 along lines laid out by Delafield, and added to in later years) and North Barracks (by Cram, Goodhue and Ferguson, in 1909) could not be renovated effectively. It was decided that they should be replaced with new construction similar to that of the Academy's more recently completed barracks—particularly Cret's Scott Barracks. By placing the first floor on the street level and reducing ceiling height, they were able to get six floors into the vertical space that four had previously occupied. The new plans would provide billets for over 2,550 cadets where only 824 were then housed. Broshous estimated that the projects would take some eight-and-a-half years to complete.

By June 1963, when the House Armed Services Committee began hearings on the expansion bill, Westmoreland and Broshous had built a strong base of support for the project. Even President Kennedy personally lobbied for its passage. Westmoreland, however, had new orders reassigning him to the growing military assistance command in Vietnam, and he left the further development of the project in the hands of Major General James B. Lampert, class of 1936, who replaced him.

In February 1964, Congress passed the legislation authorizing both the increase of the corps from 2,529 to 4,417 and the construction necessary to accommodate these cadets. The next month, the architect-engineering firm of O'Connor and Kilham of New York City was hired to design the Washington Hall-Barracks complex and to supervise the preliminary planning of the overall expansion program.

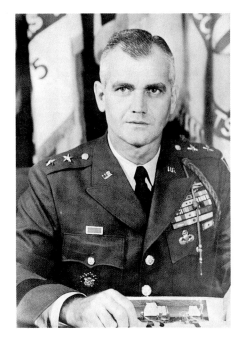

Major General William C. Westmoreland as Superintendent of the United States Military Academy. 1960. U.S.M.A. Archives. Copy Photo: Philip Pocock.

The Faulkner room in the library commemorates a teaching visit to the Academy by the Nobel Laureate in Literature, William Faulkner.

The fortress-like administration building, with its 160-foot tower, is the tallest all-stone masonry building in the world. Inside, a chamber of particular interest is the academic board room, a vaulted Gothic hall illuminated by stained-glass windows blazoned with the symbols of the arts and sciences.

West Point as seen from Highway 9-W.

The ground breaking for the expansion took place during graduation week in June 1965. Soon, in excavating for the eastern wing of the new complex (Eisenhower Barracks), workers discovered the foundations of the old Academy building that Swift had built in 1815 and that had been destroyed by fire in 1838. "It is interesting to note," wrote Lampert, "that the new building will represent a return to the general line on the plain" occupied by the earliest permanent Academy structures. In August 1967, Major General Donald V. Bennett, class of 1940, who had succeeded Lampert, opened the first new wing of the mess hall. A year later, his successor, Major General Samuel W. Koster, class of 1942, ordered the cadets into the newly completed Eisenhower Barracks.

The mess hall was completed later in the fall. The Gothic facade of the new Washington Hall designed by O'Connor and Kilham may have lacked some of the vitality of the older Gehron structure, but the similarities in design and exterior finish were striking, and its imposing mass made it the most prominent building on the plain. In its visual impression, the new Washington Hall was very much a part of the continuum of the architectural tradition at West Point that had begun with Richard Delafield and Frederick Diaper.

The mess hall now consisted of six rectangular dining areas radiating from a central "poop deck." The interior finishes of the new wings were made to match the old as closely as possible—in particular, the slate flooring and wood paneling of the old mess hall was repeated in the new. The 1926 facade was retained as the centerpiece of the new structure from which all the dining wings radiated. The grotesques depicting the

evolution of warfare, which had been removed from the Old North Barracks when it was demolished, were incorporated into the interior architectural treatment of the new wings. Carved into the granite and limestone facade of this massive structure was the coat of arms of Washington, and scenes depicting his genius. Surmounting all that was the Great Seal of the United States—known to the corps as "Foundation Eagle." Tradition states that any cadet who looks at it during parade will be "found deficient."

Construction on a new academic building, Mahan Hall, was begun in late 1968, after unexpectedly high bids forced the Academy to reexamine the project. "Rising construction costs are presenting a problem in initiating the construction of several key projects carefully programmed to meet the needs of our phased increase in Corps strength," reported Bennett in 1968. When construction did finally began, difficulties in pouring the foundation on the near vertical site further delayed the project. The building was not ready for occupancy until the spring of 1972, nearly two years behind schedule.

O'Connor and Kilham, the architects, followed the precedent established in all of the principal academic buildings and employed rockfaced granite set in random courses. While the Gothic details were less pronounced in Mahan Hall than in surrounding structures, the maintenance of strong Gothic massing complemented the earlier buildings, and, from all sides, the architects' sensitive design presented a strong, bold appearance. Situated as it was on the steep slopes that thrust up from the river, the building seemed to grow out of the hillside, much like nearby Thayer Hall.

The cadet chapel dominates this view from the plain. Washington Hall, in the foreground, had three new wings added to it from 1965 to 1967. During the course of this construction, the cadet dining hall was extended to the front onto the plain in a mirror image of the three existing wings, so that the entire corps of cadets could be seated and dine together three times a day. Washington Hall also accommodates various offices and academic facilities, as well as a post office and a barber shop. Pendor Natural Color.

Above left:
The statue of Athena, symbolic figure of the Academy, graces the tower of the library. It is eighteen feet high and was designed in 1963.

Above right:
Various "grotesques" decorate the top of Bartlett Hall.

Dwight D. Eisenhower had a barracks named after him in 1968 and, in the early 1970s, the new student activities center with its commanding view of the Hudson River was dedicated as Eisenhower Hall in his honor.

In April 1969, the north barracks wing (MacArthur Barracks) was completed and occupied. Shortly thereafter, to make room for the remaining three wings called for in the new plan, the old Central Barracks was pulled down—all, that is, except the venerable and historic first division, which was preserved in place. In addition to its special significance as the billet of many of the old corps' first captains and other illustrious graduates, it is a lasting link to West Point's architectural heritage. In the summer of 1972, the last of the new barracks wings were completed and occupied.

In January 1971, construction of Eisenhower Hall, a cadet activities center, was begun. The facility was completed and opened in 1974. Its 4,500-seat auditorium could seat the entire corps. It also contained a ballroom accommodating 1,000 persons, a snack bar to seat 1,000 cadets and their guests, a reception hall for 150 persons, and numerous activity rooms. Built below the level of the plain, the planners felt justified in allowing the building to be constructed of red brick rather than the gray stone so prominent in the other structures that define the cadet area.

Overleaf:
The cadet mess in Washington Hall can accommodate the more than 4,000 men and women who constitute the corps of cadets.

Left:
Pershing Barracks—the old (1895) west academic building.

Opposite:
Mahan Hall. Construction on this new academic building began in 1968, and the first classes were held there in 1972. The nine-story building bridges an elevated roadway that has been designed to carry through traffic around the cadet area and alleviate traffic congestion within the academic and barracks areas.

To round out the expansion program, a number of other projects were undertaken beyond the limits of the plain. Michie Stadium was expanded, beginning in 1969, to a capacity of 41,062. Keller Army Hospital, a four-story, sixty-five bed facility—a steel frame structure of precast concrete facade—was begun near Washington Gate in July 1974 and completed in November 1977. In the spring of 1983 construction began on the Holleder Multipurpose Sports Complex. Located next to Michie Stadium, it housed a 5,000-seat basketball arena, a 2,500-seat hockey rink, and various athletic offices. It was completed in October 1985. 1983 also marked the beginning of construction on a Jewish synagogue. This effort, a $5.6 million project which was built with private funds, was completed in 1984.

Athletics are an important component of cadet life. Here, we see members of the Army hockey team in a game against Yale University. Late 1980s.

As expeditiously as the construction of facilities would allow, the strength of the corps was incrementally increased from 2,529 to 4,417. Beginning with the class that entered the Academy in July 1964, the corps was enlarged by between 200 and 275 cadets per year until the new, authorized strength was achieved in 1972.

As the corps grew, so did the requirement for additional faculty. To meet that need the Academy sought an increasingly large number of faculty from among the officers who had done their undergraduate work somewhere other than at West Point. By 1966 almost one-fourth of the faculty were "non-graduates." In time that number reached (and has remained) approximately one-third—more, on average, in the humanities and public affairs and less in mathematics, science and engineering.

Bringing officers to West Point for a teaching assignment was planned well in advance, for by now it typically entailed two years at graduate school prior to the assignment at the Academy. The sudden demand for an increased number of faculty during the expansion (at the same moment the Academy was being forced to compete with increasing requirements for officers in Vietnam) impelled the Academy to draw upon a pool of reserve officers who had deferred their two-year active duty commitment in order to attend graduate school. Many of them now had doctorates, and a number were ordered to West Point. It was a marriage of convenience—a marriage in which neither party was com-

Cadets cross a bridge that leads to Thayer Hall. The granite-faced structures harmonize well with the winding river and rugged hills that form their background.

Above:
The reception area of Eisenhower Hall.
U.S.M.A. Archives.

Below:
The auditorium in Eisenhower Hall can accommodate 4,500 people. U.S.M.A. Archives.

Above left:
The Catholic chapel is an almost exact replica of a church in England erected by Carthusian monks. Pendor Natural Color.

Above right:
The Jewish synagogue was built in 1984. Like the Catholic chapel, many years before, its construction was privately funded. Pendor Natural Color.

pletely comfortable. On the one hand, the senior faculty often found these short-term officers less deferential and polished than the regular officers with whom they were accustomed to work. On the other hand, the new officers sometimes resented and resisted the discipline that West Point imposed on them, and they rebelled at the term "non-graduate" that was unthinkingly applied to them. They quickly resurrected the idea of an "Association of Non-Graduates," and suggested that their journal should be called *Disassembly*—mocking the Association of Graduates' *Assembly.* Still, the Academy profited from many of the skills they brought to their assignments.

Construction on what was to have been 200 new housing units in the Stony Lonesome area behind Michie Stadium began in 1968 and was completed two years later. Rising costs, however, had forced the Academy to reconsider these plans. Major General William A. Knowlton, class of January 1943, who had replaced Koster, chose to scale back the designs in order to build as many units as possible. As had been done repeatedly since World War II, they decided that even inadequate housing was preferable to none. When the Air Force's housing units at Stewart Air Force Base in nearby Newburgh were made available to the Academy, a second stage of construction (another 160 units) in Stony Lonesome was deferred indefinitely.

Faculty housing, however, continued to be an issue; in 1979 it topped the list of officers' complaints. Although sufficient quarters were now made available, the long and sometimes treacherous commute across Storm King Mountain from Stewart put a premium on housing at West Point itself. And there, the relative inadequacy of the post-World War II quarters made competition for the remaining older sets quite keen.

In 1978, when the housing office attempted to abandon the old quarters drawing policy and allow newly-arriving officers to draw on the basis of family size rather than seniority, a senior major appealed to the Superintendent. After noting how pleased he was to be returning for a second teaching tour, he added: "I am a bit perplexed, however, by the new housing assignment policy that seems likely to relegate us to quarters less desirable than those we occupied five years ago. I fear another perquisite of seniority, one both traditional and functional at West Point, has been stripped away." The Superintendent directed a review of the new policy, and then ordered revisions that essentially restored the old procedures. "This subject has received a thorough review," the officer was told in reply. "The net result is that you are now at the top of the Majors' list and will have the choice of . . . [available] quarters at West Point."

Above:
The sets of houses designed by Cram, Goodhue and Ferguson (which are among the best quarters available to the Academy staff) offer scenic views of the Hudson River.

Lower left:
These quarters on Professors Row were originally constructed in the 1820s. Known as "doubles," they are mainly of stone construction.

Lower right:
In order to accommodate the housing needs of the faculty and their families, there have been various additions to the quarters along Professors Row, as shown in this photograph of the back of number 107B.

This photograph was taken at the dedication of the Douglas C. MacArthur Memorial at West Point in 1969, which was attended by his wife. U.S.M.A. Archives.

GENERAL OF THE ARMY DOUGLAS MacARTHUR'S SPEECH, DELIVERED

AT HIS ACCEPTANCE OF THE THAYER AWARD. May 12, 1962.

"General Westmoreland, General Groves, distinguished guests, and gentlemen of the Corps:

As I was leaving the hotel this morning, a doorman asked me, 'Where are you bound for, General?' and when I replied, 'West Point,' he remarked, 'Beautiful place, have you ever been there before?'

No human being could fail to be deeply moved by such a tribute as this [Thayer Award]. Coming from a profession I have served so long, and a people I have loved so well, it fills me with an emotion I cannot express. But this award is not intended primarily to honor a personality, but to symbolize a great moral code—the code of conduct and chivalry of those who guard this beloved land of culture and ancient descent. That is the meaning of this medallion. For all eyes and for all time, it is an expression of the ethics of the American soldier. That I should be integrated in this way with so noble an ideal arouses a sense of pride and yet of humility which will be with me always.

Duty—Honor—Country. Those three hallowed words reverently dictate what you ought to be, what you can be, what you will be. They are your rallying points: to build courage when courage seems to fail; to regain faith when there seems to be little cause for faith; to create hope when hope becomes forlorn. Unhappily, I possess neither that eloquence of diction, that poetry of imagination, nor that brilliance of metaphor to tell you all that they mean. The unbelievers will say they are but words, but a slogan, but a flamboyant phrase. Every pedant, every demagogue, every cynic, every hypocrite, every troublemaker, and I am sorry to say, some others of an entirely different character, will try to downgrade

them even to the extent of mockery and ridicule, but these are some of the things they do. They build your basic character, they mold you for your future roles as the custodians of the nation's defense, they make you strong enough to know when you are weak, and brave enough to face yourself when you are afraid. They teach you to be proud and unbending in honest failure, but humble and gentle in success; not to substitute words for actions, not to seek the path of comfort, but to face the stress and spur of difficulty and challenge; to learn to stand up in the storm but to have compassion on those who fail; to master yourself before you seek to master others; to have a heart that is clean, a goal that is high; to learn to laugh yet never forget how to weep; to reach into the future yet never neglect the past; to be serious yet never to take yourself too seriously; to be modest so that you will remember the simplicity of true greatness, the open mind of true wisdom, the meekness of true strength. They give you a temper of the will, a quality of the imagination, a vigor of the emotions, a freshness of the deep springs of life, a temperamental predominance of courage over timidity, an appetite for adventure over love of ease. They create in your heart the sense of wonder, the unfailing hope of what next, and the joy and inspiration of life. They teach you in this way to be an officer and a gentleman.

And what sort of soldiers are those you are to lead? Are they reliable, are they brave, are they capable of victory? Their story is known to all of you; it is the story of the American man-at-arms. My estimate of him was formed on the battlefield many, many years ago, and has never changed. I regarded him then as I regard him now—as one of the world's noblest figures, not only as one of the finest military characters but also as one of the most stainless. His name and fame are the birthright of every American citizen. In his youth and strength, his love and loyalty he gave—all that mortality can give. He needs no eulogy from me or from any other man. He has written his own history and written it in red on his enemy's breast. But when I think of his patience under adversity, of his courage under fire, and of his modesty in victory, I am filled with an emotion of admiration I cannot put into words. He belongs to history as furnishing one of the greatest examples of successful patriotism; he belongs to posterity as the instructor of future generations in the principles of liberty and freedom; he belongs to the present, to us, by his virtues and by his achievements. In 20 campaigns, on a hundred battlefields, around a thousand campfires, I have witnessed that enduring fortitude, that patriotic self-abnegation, and that invincible determination which have carved his statue in the hearts of his people. From one end of the world to the other he has drained deep the chalice of courage.

As I listened to those songs of the glee club, in memory's eye I could see those staggering columns of the First World War, bending under soggy packs, on many a weary march from dripping dusk to drizzling dawn, slogging ankle-deep through the mire of shell-shocked roads, to form grimly for the attack, blue-lipped, covered with sludge and mud, chilled by the wind and rain; driving home to their objective, and, for many, to the judgement seat of God. I do not know the dignity of their birth but I do know the glory of their death. They died unquestioning, uncomplaining, with faith in their hearts, and on their lips the hope that we would go on to victory. Always for them—Duty—Honor—Country; always their blood and sweat and tears as we sought the way and the light and the truth.

And twenty years after, on the other side of the globe, again the filth of murky foxholes, the stench of ghostly trenches, the slime of dripping dugouts; those boiling suns of relentless heat, those torrential rains of devastating storms; the loneliness and utter desolation of jungle trails, the bitterness of long separation from those they loved and cherished, the deadly pestilence of tropical disease, the horror of stricken areas of war; their resolute and determined defense, their swift and sure attack, their indomitable purpose, their complete and decisive victory—always victory. Always through the bloody haze of their last reverberating shot, the vision of gaunt, ghastly men reverently following your password of Duty—Honor—Country.

The code which those words perpetuate embraces the highest moral laws and will stand the test of any ethics or philosophies ever promulgated for the uplift of mankind. Its requirements are for the things that are right, and its restraints are from the things that are wrong. The soldier, above all other men, is required to practice the greatest act of religious training—sacrifice. In battle and in the face of danger and death, he discloses those divine attributes which his Maker gave when He created man in His own image. No physical courage and no brute instinct can take the place of the Divine help which alone can sustain him. However horrible the incidents of war may be, the soldier who is called upon to offer and to give his life for his country, is the noblest development of mankind.

You now face a new world—a world of change. The thrust into outer space of the satellite, spheres and missiles marked the beginning of another epoch in the long story of mankind—the chapter of the space age. In the five or more billions of years the scientists tell us it has taken to form the earth, in the three or more billion years of development of the human race, there has never been a greater, a more abrupt or staggering evolution. We deal now not with things of this world alone, but with the illimitable distances and as yet unfathomed mysteries of the universe. We are reaching out for a new boundless frontier. We speak in strange terms: of harnessing the cosmic energy; of making winds and tides work for us; of creating unheard synthetic materials to supplement or even replace our old standard basics; of purifying sea water for our drink; of mining ocean floors for new fields of wealth and food; of disease preventatives to expand life into the hundred of years; of controlling the weather for a more equitable distribution of heat and cold, of rain and shine; of spaceships to the moon; of the primary target in war; no longer limited to the armed forces of an enemy, but instead to include his civil populations; of ultimate conflict between a united human race and the sinister forces of some other planetary galaxy; of such dreams and fantasies as to make life the most exciting of all time.

And through all this welter of change and development, your mission remains fixed, determined, inviolable—it is to win our wars. Everything else in your professional career is but corollary to this vital dedication. All other public purposes, all other public projects, all other public needs, great or small, will find others for their accomplishment; but you are the ones who are trained to fight; yours is the profession of arms—the will to win, the sure knowledge that in war there is no substitute for victory; that if you lose, the nation will be destroyed; that the very obsession of your public service must be Duty—Honor—Country. Others will debate the controversial issues, national and international, which divide men's minds; but serene, calm, aloof, you stand as the nation's war-guardian, as its lifeguard from the raging tides of international conflict, as its gladiator in the arena of battle. For a century and a half you have defended, guarded, and protected its hallowed traditions of liberty and freedom, of right and justice. Let civilian voices argue the merits or demerits of our processes of government; whether our strength is being sapped by deficit financing, indulged in too long, by federal paternalism grown too mighty, by power groups grown too arrogant, by politics grown too corrupt, by crime grown too rampant, by morals grown too low, by taxes grown too high, by extremists grown too violent; whether our personal liberties are as thorough and complete as they should be. These great national problems are not for your professional participation or military solution. Your guidepost stands out like a tenfold beacon in the night—Duty—Honor—Country.

You are the leaven which binds together the entire fabric of our national system of defense. From your ranks come the great captains who hold the nation's destiny in their hands the moment the war tocsin sounds. The Long Gray Line has never failed us. Were you to do so, a million ghosts in olive drab, in brown khaki, in blue and gray, would rise from their white crosses thundering those magic words—Duty—Honor—Country.

This does not mean that you are war mongers. On the contrary, the soldier, above all other people, prays for peace, for he must suffer and bear the deepest wounds and scars of war. But always in our ears ring the ominous words of Plato, that wisest of all philosophers, 'Only the dead have seen the end of war.'

The shadows are lengthening for me. The twilight is here. My days of old have vanished tone and tint; they have gone glimmering through the dreams of things that were. Their memory is one of wondrous beauty watered by tears, and coaxed and caressed by the smiles of yesterday. I listen vainly for the witching melody of faint bugles blowing reveille, of far drums beating the long roll. In my dreams I hear again the crash of guns, the rattle of musketry, the strange mournful mutter of the battlefield.

But in the evening of my memory, always I come back to West Point. Always there echoes and re-echoes Duty—Honor—Country.

Today marks my final roll call with you, but I want you to know that when I cross the river my last conscious thoughts will be of The Corps, and The Corps, and The Corps.

I bid you farewell."

Above left:
At the end of "Beast Barracks," the entire cadet training regiment moves out to the shores of Lake Frederick, an eighteen-mile march from the plain. Cadets wearing West Point T-Shirts are upper classmen. Late 1980s.

Above right:
New cadets being sworn in on July 1, 1968. U.S.M.A. Archives.

In 1969, Brigadier General Bernard W. Rogers, class of June 1943, the Commandant of Cadets, directed a major review of the fourth class system. That system, they found, was rooted in changes that had their origins in the years just before the turn of the twentieth century. Beginning in the late 1890s there had been a consistent effort made by the tactical department to have all cadet officers, especially the first class, exercise increased leadership responsibilities. Though not explicitly permitted, this soon led to their assumption of authority over new cadets. Although this sometimes produced complaints of unnecessary harassment of the new cadets, the tactical department was impressed by the soldierly results that were so quickly brought about by the sharp disciplinary control both in and out of ranks, and did little to change the practice.

In 1918, Samuel Tillman, who had been recalled from retirement to superintend the Academy during World War I, began to regularize the fourth class system. He officially authorized control of the new cadets by selected upperclassmen. Still, Tillman had reservations. "The success of the method now in operation," he wrote, "will depend upon whether men as young as our cadets can be given the authority outlined for them without abusing it themselves, or countenancing its abuse by their associates."

When Douglas MacArthur succeeded Tillman in 1919, he immediately began to build upon his predecessor's efforts. He ordered the first classmen—the class of 1920, who had matriculated in June 1918—to formulate and reduce to writing the "customs of service of the corps." After numerous conferences with the tactical department and after days of debate and argument, the class, on August 4th, proposed a set of regulations to govern "the relationship between the upper classes and the lower class." MacArthur praised "the response of the Class of 1920 to the wishes of the authorities," and added: "I regard this as the first and in some respects the greatest safeguard of the New West Point which we are mutually evolving in the Spirit of Old West Point." He approved the regulations which the class had proposed and had them published as "Traditions and Customs of the Corps of Cadets, 1920."

Subsequent studies of the fourth class system during the 1940s and 1950s made only minor changes in the system that had been formulated under Tillman and MacArthur. Still, the system had its critics. A curriculum review board appointed by Superintendent Davidson in 1958, spoke of the necessity of eliminating the abuses of the fourth class system, and John L. Throckmorton, Commandant of Cadets during that same period, reported that, "in spite of numerous efforts . . . to effect beneficial changes in the Fourth Class System . . . I do not believe, in the final analysis, that the System as now constituted serves the Military Academy and the Army as a whole to the best advantage." Amos Jordan, a professor of social science, agreed. "As it now operates at the Military Academy," he wrote in 1960, "the plebe system is probably detrimental to the development of intellectual interests and to academic achievement." These critics, however, had little impact. In 1963, Superintendent Westmoreland reported to the Academy's graduates that "Beast Barracks is little changed from what you experienced." The Academy had "studied this problem in detail," he added, and we have "reassured ourselves that it is a sound and effective training experience."

The study initiated by Brigadier General Rogers in 1969, however, responded to many of the earlier concerns. It took a much more critical look at the elements of the system than in the past and found many to be inconsistent with fundamental Academy goals and objectives. It was little more than "an initiation process designed to place the Fourth Classmen in a subservient and dependent position to all upper classes." If it was the Academy's mission to develop mature and independent officers, the study concluded, then the system, as it then existed, was counterproductive and in need of a major overhaul. The remedy Rogers applied emphasized positive leadership and mitigated, for a time, the harshness of plebe life.

In 1979, in the wake of other difficulties and changes, the Academy undertook yet another effort to ensure that the fourth class system—"which is intended to enhance the motivation, self-discipline, and sense of responsibility of cadets"—was a positive one. They reduced by one-third the total number of verbatim memorizations required of fourth class cadets, reduced the number of inspections to which plebes were subjected, and again attempted to delineate the responsibilities of upper classmen, placing more emphasis on professionalism and positive leadership. "I think we stripped out a great deal of the nonsense . . . that had grown up around the Plebe system," said Superintendent Andrew J. Goodpaster. But he had concerns, if not reservations, about a system that attempted both to shape fourth classmen in accordance with the West Point mold and to teach leadership to the upper classmen. Sounding much like Tillman six decades earlier,

Below left:
On the morning after "R" Day (Reception Day), the plebes begin their training exercises on the plain. Late 1980s.

Below right:
The first inspection of "Beast Barracks," the summer training session for plebes. Late 1980s.

Cadets of the fourth class are "recognized," as upperclassmen shake hands with them. Late 1980s.

he said: "They're adolescents growing to maturity, and they've got to learn how to handle authority, which is a very heady experience for them. To lord over somebody else is all very tempting to young people."

In 1988, the Academy's accreditation steering committee argued that the system did not develop essential leadership attributes, but instead "induces leader behavior in conflict with accepted practices in the Army." In their view, many of the objectives of the fourth class system were achieved early in the academic year. "Beyond that point, considerable time is devoted to repetitiveness," they said. The system could be made more efficient if cadets were involved sooner in leadership experiences, and that, they argued, would "provide for a smoother transition from Fourth to Third Class year." In 1990, in a move in that direction, Brigadier General David A. Bramlett, the Commandant of Cadets, advanced the date of "recognition"—the effective end of "plebe" status for the fourth class—to the middle of the second academic term.

In 1974, the Association of Graduates alumni magazine *Assembly* reported that less than a decade before "there were so few blacks at USMA that they were inconspicuous"—not so much that they blended in, but because "they were simply overshadowed." That had changed. "Now the black is conspicuous. He is 161-strong. He holds more rank. He's a varsity team captain. He's involved in every aspect of cadet life."

During the four decades after Charles Young graduated in 1889, only two black cadets had entered the Academy. Each stayed for less than six months. In 1932, however, another young black man arrived at West Point, Benjamin Oliver Davis, Jr., the son of Brigadier General Benjamin O. Davis, the Army's first black general. An excellent student, he had spent a year at Western Reserve University and two at the University of Chicago, before his father could convince Congressman Oscar DePriest of Illinois to nominate him to West Point.

Yet Davis's experiences were not remarkably different than those of Henry Flipper, the Academy's first black graduate more than a half-century earlier. The corps was still openly hostile and the social ostracism that had prevailed in the nineteenth century continued; during Davis's first year, none of the cadets spoke to him, although when he demonstrated that he could take the "silence," some began to treat him more kindly. Davis graduated in 1936, thirty-fifth in a class of 276, and ultimately joined the Air Corps and then the U.S. Air Force. In 1965 he became the first black to attain the rank of lieutenant general in the military service of the United States. James D. Fowler followed Davis to West Point in 1937. He too was silenced—a white cadet was forced out of the corps because of a rumor that he had "recognized" Fowler—but, like Davis, he persevered and graduated in 1941. From 1932 to 1947, twenty-one black cadets were admitted to the Academy and seventeen graduated. However, they continued to be poorly treated by the other cadets.

Beginning in 1948, the black experience at West Point began to change. For one thing, there were black cadets in every incoming class after that year. For another, there was a shift away from the open hostility that had characterized the black experience in earlier years, although there were still impediments to full participation in cadet life.

The decade of the sixties witnessed further changes—in particular, incidents of overt racism and discrimination began to disappear. Most important, however, was a new emphasis on recruiting. As late as 1968, there were only thirty blacks at the Military Academy. That year, however, a black officer was assigned to the admissions office and charged with the responsibility of identifying and attracting minority men who possessed the requisite intellectual and physical qualifications. Almost immediately, the number of black cadets began to increase. By the fall of 1970, there were almost one hundred. By 1988 minorities numbered almost one in every five applicants; 232 minority cadets (17

*Black graduates of the class of 1980.
U.S.M.A. Archives. Copy Photo: Philip
Pocock.*

percent) were admitted with the class that year. During that same period, black officers increased in number on the staff and faculty, and Brigadier General Fred A. Gorden, class of 1962, became the first black to be appointed Commandant of Cadets (1987–1989).

While blacks and other minorities were making notable strides at the Military Academy, another group was entirely excluded. Women at West Point was simply a notion that had never seemed to deserve serious consideration. The *Howitzer* staff in 1900 had depicted an unlikely looking female cadet of the year 2000—with the traditional tar bucket hat and tight-fitting, high-collared gray tunic, but with a bustle, and high-buttoned shoes. In 1964, Elvin R. "Vald" Heiberg, professor of mechanics, also took a tongue-in-cheek look ahead to the year 2000. He found the female element of the corps billeted, in isolation, on Constitution Island. These "trimly-clad, glamorous young ladies in gray skirts, blouses, and berets" were known as the "Codettes." Heiberg's year 2000 corps was divided into three separate brigades: engineering and science majors; public affairs majors; and physical education majors. The "Codettes" were members of the physical education brigade, and they provided the Rabble Rousers (the cheerleading squad) and "lovely-to-look-at" women's teams that were nicknamed "the Black Knighties."

In the sixties and early seventies, American women grew more vocal in their demands for equality, and soon such citadels of masculinity as Yale and Princeton were opening their doors to women. The service academies were warned that in refusing to admit women they were opposing the inevitable.

In 1973, Congressman Pierre Du Pont of Delaware introduced a bill in the House of Representatives designed to permit the admission of women to the service academies. Hearings on the bill began before the House Military Personnel Subcommittee the following spring. Secretary of the Army Martin R. Hoffmann and Superintendent William Knowlton testified against the bill. Their opposition was based foremost on two points. First, the Academy's mission was to train combat leaders. Because the American public would never accept women in combat leadership roles, and because only a limited number of cadets could be accommodated at the Military Academy, the available appointments should be reserved for men. Second, they argued, women would not be able to meet West Point's rigorous, demanding, highly-disciplined training standards, either physically or emotionally; their admission would lower standards and weaken discipline.

Those supporting the bill made a simple rebuttal: The academies were no longer educating just combat leaders. At West Point, in the branch drawings, cadets were regularly allowed to choose an assignment to engineer, signal, military intelligence, adjutant general, chemical, military police, medical service corps, ordnance, quartermaster, or transportation—as well as infantry, armor, and artillery. In fact, the lower reaches of the classes were regularly "ranked" into the combat arms just to fill the minimum quotas. In reality, they argued, the Academy was educating young men to be career military officers, not just combat leaders, and on that basis there was no rationale for discriminating against women. Furthermore, the proponents of the bill pointed out, women were already being admitted to the Merchant Marine Academy, and applications from women were being accepted by the Coast Guard Academy.

In May 1975, the House of Representatives passed—by better than a three-to-one margin—a bill mandating the admission of women to the nation's service academies. The Military Academy began immediately to plan for their admission in 1976. Senate approval came in June and President Gerald Ford signed the legislation into law in October. The Academy's Superintendent, Major General Sidney B. Berry, class of 1948, who had replaced Knowlton two years earlier, launched a series of studies to establish standards and procedures for everything from the folding of brassieres to dealing with menstrual periods in the field. Berry reserved to himself the approval of any policy that would establish different standards for women. Should female cadets be permitted to wear makeup or perfume? Yes, he said, but in "tasteful" moderation. Boxing and wrestling had long been mandatory physical education courses. Should female cadets be required to take them? No, because of possible breast injuries. Instead they would take a two-semester course in the martial arts. In November the Academy's plans were submitted to the Department of the Army, and approved.

"I think it is a disgrace for women to be here," remarked one male cadet, echoing the feelings of the majority of cadets—and of the majority of alumni. In an effort to lessen the hostility, West Point's three generals, Berry, Dean Frederick A. Smith, Jr., and Commandant Walter F. Ulmer, Jr. (class of 1952), met with large groups of the cadets in question-and-answer sessions that instantly became known as "Stump the Stars." Although the questions were often ludicrous—even taunting, the generals tried to respond in reasoned tones. But sometimes reason was not enough. Once, after Berry had explained that women would be allowed to wear their hair to the collar, a cadet asked why, if they were going to have the same standards for everyone, he could not wear his hair down to his collar? Before Berry could answer, Ulmer jumped up and shouted, "Because I say so!" The cadets applauded the Commandant's frank outburst, but these sessions did little to change cadet attitudes. "I feel it is my duty to the alumni and the entire Army," wrote one cadet, "to run out as many females as possible."

In June 1976, the first female cadets were admitted to the United States Military Academy. As soon as the bill authorizing women to attend the service academies had become law, the admissions office had sent letters to thousands of high school counselors, to hundreds of women who had applied for ROTC scholarships, and to others who had been identified in a student search conducted through a College Entrance Examination Board program. 631 women were among the 6,761 candidates ultimately nominated and examined for the class of 1980. Of these, 176 women were found qualified, 148 were offered admission, and 116 became members of the Class of 1980.

In cadet basic training—as the plebe summer had come to be called—these women were fully integrated into the new cadet organizational structure. After the summer training, groups of eight to ten women were assigned to twelve of the thirty-six cadet companies. By late the following year, as modifications to all the barracks were completed, and as the number of women increased, they were assigned to all of the thirty-six cadet companies. From the beginning, they were housed in rooms on the same corridors with their male counterparts.

Academy officials hoped that the presence of women in each of the cadet companies would remove some of the stereotypical attitudes many males held toward the female cadets, but they were disappointed. "Male cadets continued to be more influenced by the attitudes of their male peers, cadet leaders, and officers than by the presence of women," the Academy reported. The class of 1979—who reveled in the dubious distinction of being the last all-male class—was the most chauvinistic of all. It was not until after this class had graduated that the attitudes of male cadets began to shift.

Women's teams, at the club level, were organized immediately in a number of sports—and in some sports women successfully competed on men's club teams. The women's basketball team, known formally as the Lady Knights, but nicknamed the "Sugar Smacks" (not the "Black Knighties" as Heiberg had predicted), closed their first varsity season with a strong winning, 18–5, record. The team's first intercollegiate contest was against Skidmore, which it defeated handily, 73-to-48. The Skidmore coach said after-wards that it was a culture shock for her team to play Army's "group of Amazons." The Skidmore captain said, "Gee, they're rough!" In 1978, the Academy fielded nine women's intercollegiate teams—basketball, cross-country, gymnastics, softball, swimming, tennis, indoor track, outdoor track, and volleyball—and all nine turned in winning seasons.

Due to the senior-subordinate nature of the fourth class system, the Academy estab-lished a non-fraternization policy that prohibited upper classmen (male or female) from dating or socializing with plebes. Dating among cadets of the upper classes, or among cadets of the fourth class was permitted, and West Point soon drew up regulations to govern this behavior. At least one tactical officer used masking tape to mark just how far doors should be left open in cadet rooms when both men and woman were present.

When cadets ran afoul of these regulations, the Academy dealt with them in the same straight-faced manner with which it dealt with all infractions. One such report cited a male cadet for having a female cadet in his room (with the door closed) and in his bed—engaged in acts of affection prejudicial to discipline and good order in the corps. His partner in the escapade was not identified. The next item on the same "gig-sheet," however, was the report of a female cadet who had been caught in the room of a male cadet (with the door closed) and in his bed—likewise engaged in acts of affection prejudi-

The first female cadets to graduate from the Academy in 1980. U.S.M.A. Ar-chives. Copy Photo: Philip Pocock.

Cadets stand ready to march onto the plain for the Reception Day parade. Late 1980s.

cial to discipline and good order in the corps. Her partner was not identified either, but the juxtaposition of these reports was suggestive. Their indiscretion netted them demerits, confinement, and long hours "on the area." For reasons that were not immediately apparent, the young man spent more hours on the area than the young woman.

By 1990, women could look back with judicious pride at their accomplishments. Female cadets had led the corps at every level—from squad leader to cadet first captain, and they had produced both Rhodes Scholars and All-American athletes. In every echelon women had earned their places within the corps.

The dramatic arrival of women at West Point in the summer of 1976 was nearly overshadowed, however, by an honor crisis that had begun in mid-March. It plunged the Academy into an agonizing period of analysis and re-evaluation, both external and internal. The tip-off had been a statement acknowledging unauthorized assistance, jotted at the end of a cadet's solution to an Electrical Engineering 304 (EE304) computer problem—one part of a graded take-home assignment. "This computer project does not represent all my own work. Due to the fact that I was unable to complete it on my own I received help towards its completion. I am stating this so as to avoid an unfair advantage over my classmates," the cadet wrote. Written instructions issued with the assignment had specifically stated that collaboration was not permitted on that particular problem, although it had been permitted on earlier work and on two of the four problems on that same take-home assignment.

EE304 was a course required of all second classmen, but it was unpopular. Even engineering majors saw minimal utility in the course. Those with less interest in engineering tried to get by with as little effort as possible. The department knew of the cadet attitude toward the course and made allowances: collaboration on homework was actively encouraged as a means of assisting cadets. Unfortunately, as the investigations revealed, to some cadets collaboration had come to mean simply copying the homework of more industrious cadets. By the time of the assignment in question, the habit of collaboration, even plagiarism, had become ingrained.

A quick check by instructors of the work turned in for this assignment uncovered similarities, such as the same misspelled words and duplicate computation errors, on a number of papers. The department then cross-checked all the papers, checking in detail the papers of cadets assigned to the same companies. When that was completed, the electrical engineering department forwarded the papers of 117 cadets suspected of cheating to the cadet honor committee for investigation. On April 12, 1976, 102 of the 117 cases were placed before the full honor board. Fifty of these were found to have violated the honor code. Two cadets immediately resigned, but the remaining forty-eight requested that their cases be heard before a board of officers.

The EE304 scandal involved even more cadets than had the 1951 affair, although, unlike the earlier case, this was not the product of an organized ring. Rather, those who collaborated did so in small groups ranging from roommates to small circles of classmates and friends. On April 7th, even before the preliminary investigations were completed, the press carried its first stories on the alleged cheating—stories prompted by a cadet who called *The New York Times* with the message: "I don't cheat. Why should they?"

On May 3rd, the military counsels representing the accused cadets wrote to Secretary of the Army Hoffmann charging that upwards of 300 cadets were implicated by sworn affidavits—including members of the honor committee and captains of several athletic teams. They requested the convening of an external board of inquiry. Superintendent Berry endorsed their request, indicating that an independent board of inquiry might be useful. Although the request for a review board was denied at this time, Berry did direct a second review of all 821 EE304 papers. This effort identified another 150 collaborators. Eighteen of these cadets resigned and another 102 were found guilty by an officer board that had supplanted the honor committee during the course of the continuing investigation. In the end, a total of 152 cadets either resigned or were otherwise separated from the Academy in connection with the scandal.

In the meantime, pressure on the Academy and on the Secretary of the Army had begun to build. One cadet who had been implicated filed a suit in U. S. District Court in early June, seeking an injunction against the enforcement of the honor code and system. Although that injunction was denied, seven other similar suits were filed in the civil and military appeals courts.

On Capitol Hill, Senator Sam Nunn of Georgia announced that his Senate Armed Services subcommittee would hold hearings on the service academies, and Representative Thomas J. Downey of New York, convened an "informal public forum" to discuss the honor issue. A total of 173 congressmen joined to ask Secretary of the Army Hoffmann to intervene—stating their belief that "punishment should be something short of expulsion from the Academy."

By August, the issue was no longer "How would the crisis be resolved?" but "Who would resolve it?" Hoffmann settled both issues on August 23rd, when he testified before Nunn's subcommittee. First, he revealed that a special commission on the Academy would be empowered to make an in-depth assessment of the honor situation and its underlying causes. Second, bowing to pressure from Congress, he announced that the cadets involved in the EE304 affair who had resigned or had been found guilty of honor violations and expelled would be eligible for readmission the next year, and the affair would be expunged from their records. For those who had left the Academy and did not wish to return, the active duty service normally demanded of first and second classmen who leave West Point would be waived.

The Secretary's Committee on the United States Military Academy was appointed on September 9th. Former astronaut Frank Borman, a member of the class of 1950, headed the group, which soon became known as the Borman Commission. They swiftly set up offices in the Academy's library. There, they sifted through a mountain of materials that

The Chairman of the Joint Chiefs of Staff, General Colin Powell, stands with the first woman to become First Captain, Cadet Kristin Baker, at the graduation of the class of 1990. AP/Wide World Photos.

had been generated in the earlier investigations, and interviewed hundreds of officers and cadets. After several months of intensive work the commission released its report. There was, they said, a degree of disaffection with the honor code in the corps that bordered on contempt; "cool on honor" was the cadet expression. Further, they had heard allegations of corruption in the honor committee—one cadet, for example, supposedly had been acquitted eight times of various honor violations, always protected by friends on the committee who could stymie action with a single vote. Although West Point's leadership had been aware of major inadequacies in the honor system, the report alleged, "no decisive action was taken."

In January 1977, Hoffmann directed that the Academy's regulations be changed to read that a "cadet who violates the Cadet Honor Code shall normally be separated from the Military Academy"—adding the word "normally" and giving the Superintendent greater latitude in his dealings with honor cases. Of the 152 cadets who had left West Point as a result of the EE304 affair, 148 were found eligible for readmission. Of these, 105 completed their applications and were offered readmission. In June 1977, ninety-eight actually reentered the Academy—most as first classmen in the class of 1978; as penance they had lost a year's seniority on their former classmates.

In the years that followed the EE304 scandal, a number of procedural changes were made to the honor system, but little was done to solve the problem most often identified by cadets—the use of honor to enforce regulations. In 1988, Wesley W. Posvar, class of 1946, president of the University of Pittsburgh, was asked to head an outside examination of the honor system. The Posvar panel praised the honor code saying it "represents a standard of ethical behavior that functions effectively for cadets, to which all American professionals can aspire, and which all citizens should appreciate as a national asset." Still, they charged that the Academy was trivializing the code—a charge that echoed a number of earlier reports—by intermingling honor and regulations. They argued that matters such as rapid-fire or "pop-off" answers, bedstuffing, or the hiding of articles in a laundry bag ought not to be elevated to the status of breaches of personal integrity. "The serious issue," they wrote, "is that such misuse of the System has been a repeated source of antagonism, misunderstanding, grievous injustice to cadets, and harm to the repute and regard for the honor code itself." As usual, however, it proved easier to identify the problem than to effect meaningful change.

Many, in and out of uniform, feared that the EE304 scandal had shaken the nation's confidence in West Point. Critics in the press and in Congress multiplied. This came atop the growth of a troublesome, strongly antimilitary sentiment, which had become widespread beginning in 1968 as the war in Southeast Asia dragged on with mounting casualties and no end in sight. That had already resulted in increasing intrusion into the governance of the Academy—by the Congress, the courts, and by the Department of the Army.

Those intrusions had begun in the late sixties when Congress began to press for increased minority recruiting. In the early seventies, it was the courts. In 1972, three cadets, who had been dismissed from the Academy for "deficiencies in their military conduct," obtained American Civil Liberties Union help in securing an injunction against the Academy, arguing that the procedures employed to dismiss them had violated their right to due process.

1973 was a particularly difficult year. It was the year that the Supreme Court ruled that to require attendance at chapel violated the cadets' constitutional right to religious freedom. It was the year that the "silencing" of Cadet James Pelosi subjected the Military Academy to a barrage of criticism. It was the year that Simon and Schuster published *West Point, America's Power Fraternity* by K. Bruce Galloway and Robert B. Johnson, Jr.,—the most scathing critique of West Point since Partridge's attack in 1830. (Like Partridge's attack, the tone of this new critique was so bitter that many dismissed it.)

1973 also brought two major outside reviews of the Academy. The growing attention focused on West Point by the Congress, the Courts, and the media, prompted increased attention from both the Department of the Army and the Defense Department. In December 1973, Deputy Secretary of Defense William P. Clements established a Committee on Excellence in Education, whose membership included the service secretaries. It was tasked to investigate the programs of the various service schools, including the service academies. A more comprehensive study of the service academies by the GAO was also begun in 1973 and entailed a much more comprehensive review of Academy programs than the Clements Committee. It focused its inquiry on three issues: attrition, curriculum, and financial management. However, these three topics provided a rationale for probing into virtually all facets of the academic environment.

Honor violations usually entail expulsion. Punishments for lesser offenses can include several hours of "marching the area." Late 1980s.

On a company level, infractions of the rules are considered by a board of company officers. Significant honor code issues are referred to the higher levels of the cadet honor system. Late 1980s.

And, in 1973, the football team lost every game—amassing a record ten-game losing streak.

The EE304 crisis had focused renewed attention on the Academy and resulted in further intrusions into the Academy's affairs. Secretary of the Army Hoffmann spent much of his time during the spring and summer of 1976 seeking to diagnose and remedy the problems that had come to light in the wake of that scandal.

The findings of the Borman Commission, which were issued in December 1976, seemed to suggest that the foundations upon which the Academy stood had been badly undermined. "The Academy," they wrote, "must now acknowledge the causes of the breakdown and devote its full energies to rebuilding an improved and strengthened institution." The commission highlighted criticism it had heard from the junior members of the faculty that the academic board was "unduly resistant to change," and that some board members had "stacked arms" and were no longer effective. It recommended that the authority of the Superintendent be redefined—that "the Superintendent should have responsibility for all aspects of the internal administration of the academy," and the permanent professors should be forced to retire after thirty years of active service "unless requested to continue on a term basis by the Superintendent." The professors were incensed and offended. "I have been insulted personally, as has the Corps of Professors and the Academic Board as corporate bodies," wrote Colonel Charles H. Schilling, professor of military art and engineering, to Borman.

Secretary of the Army Hoffmann and Army Chief of Staff Bernard W. Rogers (the former Commandant of Cadets) were under pressure from the Academy's friends everywhere to protect the institution—to save it from itself, if necessary. Rogers immediately appointed a special action group on the Army staff to respond to the commission's recommendations. That group went even further than the Borman Commission, recommending that the authority of the Superintendent be significantly increased at the expense of the academic board.

"The scope and pace of these changes are unprecedented," the department heads protested. "Those initiatives which derogate the role of the academic board to matters purely academic, greatly reducing its influence over related aspects of the USMA program, are bound to lead to a progressive weakening of the cadet's education," they argued. This was certain "to have the most adverse long run consequences." They agreed, however, that "in the last decade there had been slippage in the priority accorded to academic excellence," but pointed out that there had been "a continual temptation" to pursue "more tangible short-term goals—a better athletic record, lower costs, lower attrition, [or] more technically qualified 2d lieutenants." But, attacking the academic board was not the solution, they argued: "If one agrees that academic excellence must be restored to first priority, it would seem appropriate to strengthen the voice of those elements of the organization with responsibility for and commitment to academic excellence. Yet the changes contemplated are in the opposite direction."

They objected to the "composition of the [Army staff] committee and the tone of its charter" and asserted that "the primacy of education" had never "been fully understood" by the Army staff. "This raises the issue of the extent to which USMA will govern its affairs and to what extent it will be governed by direction from Washington." Congress, the Department of Defense, and the Department of the Army all had the prerogative to establish rules of operation for the Academy, the board acknowledged. Nonetheless, they argued, there must be "a willingness to permit the institution to govern itself in a mode comparable to that which occurs in any reputable institution of higher learning." This included, they wrote, "the teacher in the classroom in his exercise of academic freedom" and "the Academic Board in deciding questions such as design of the curriculum."

Chief of Staff Rogers then appointed three new study committees to conduct an even more in-depth examination of the Academy: a military professional development committee; an academic committee; and an environment committee—known collectively as the West Point Study Group. The academic board's fears were hardly diminished by the focus of this new study group. "It became clear to me [at the first meeting]" Thomas E. Griess, West Point's liaison to the group, told his colleagues, "that the authority and role of the Academic Board will be a major area of study." Griess, class of January 1943 and professor and head of the Department of History, warned his colleagues that "the questions asked in the briefings reflected some skepticism about the functions of the Academic Board" and that at least two of the consultants to the board had "observed that the Board may be the major problem in the institution's ability to govern itself and accomplish reforms."

Charles H. Schilling, class of 1941, who had succeeded Vincent Esposito and was now professor of engineering, argued strongly for an academic board arrangement that would provide sufficient checks and balances to "preserve the stability required in an academic institution." "Individual Superintendents," he wrote, "should not be able to completely scrap an existing or initiate a new curriculum or policy based upon his own personal decision." Still, Schilling cautioned his colleagues against seeking "an exact 'status quo'."

He pointed particularly to the increased number of permanent faculty—both the "not Head" professors and the new permanent associate professors. The development of the elective program that had begun in 1960 under Superintendent Garrison Davidson, and the growth in the number of courses offered as electives that followed, carried with it the requirement for both greater breadth and greater depth of knowledge than the small permanent faculty then enjoyed. As a result, in 1963, the Academy had begun to appoint permanent associate professors who would serve the balance of their thirty-year Army careers at West Point. This program soon doubled and then tripled the size of the "tenured" faculty.

These officers had both "considerable service and talent," Schilling noted. In the past, the academic board had been collectively the memory of the Academy; now, he pointed out, "*all* tenured people comprise that body of institutional knowledge." Then he cautioned the board that these other tenured members would soon come to desire a voice in the governance of the institution. "Those who cannot input to or influence the decision making body are prone to call that body 'obstructionist'." But Schilling's warning had come too late; the frank views of a number of such tenured individuals (and other, non-tenured instructors) had already infected the Borman Commission and the committees of the West Point Study Group. The study group was particularly susceptible to such views; seven of the nine members of the academic committee had once been among the voiceless faculty at West Point and shared many of their convictions.

Meanwhile, on February 15th, Superintendent Berry had asked an internal study group to examine the governance structure of the Academy and to submit recommendations regarding the authority of the academic board. From that point forward, governance became a continuing topic of discussion, both internally and with the West Point Study Group. The internal study noted the charge of obstructionism but argued that "a more reasonable assessment" of the operation of the academic board "is that it is conservative" and that "there are compelling reasons for its conservatism." The academic board, it argued, was "firmly rooted in the history of the Military Academy." It insured stability. "Without the bulwark of the Academic Board," the report suggested, "each Superintendent could redesign the curriculum as he chose."

Berry's internal study group submitted its recommendations in early June. "Any institutional governance proposal," they noted, "must grapple with one central fact: West

Point's governance is essentially a collegial decision-making process imbedded in a military hierarchial authority structure." The study addressed the recent criticism of the academic board, but rejected the "radical surgery" approach. In fact, they suggested, it was the academic board "more than any other group or individual" that deserved credit for bringing the Academy through "the turbulent late sixties and early seventies." As to the EE304 scandal, they also found fault elsewhere: It had been developments in the honor system, the leadership evaluation system, the conduct system, and incursion upon cadet time by activities not directly related to academics (activities not within the purview of the board) that "fostered an impression that academic pursuits and academic excellence were secondary to other concerns, and in turn, contributed to the EE304 situation."

In opposing a strengthening of the superintendency at the expense of the academic board they quoted Sylvanus Thayer's 1865 advice: "Nor can the desired work [of curriculum reform] be done by the Superintendent alone for reasons too obvious to need pointing out, but, granting it could be done by him, the work would not be likely to endure[;] every new Superintendent would wish to ride his own hobby, not that of his predecessor. Besides, there could scarcely fail to result a deplorable antagonism between the Superintendent and Professors. The programs once fixed in the best manner should not be changed to suit the whims of anybody. Better to 'leave well enough alone' than to try hazardous experiments."

In the end, however, the internal study group acknowledged the realities of the situation: the Army staff and the West Point Study Group had already concluded that radical surgery was necessary. Moreover, they agreed with Schilling, who had suggested: "a Superintendent or a Commandant or a Chief of Staff would feel most comfortable operating in an environment that is similar to that of the military command structure from which he has just come." Traditional checks and balances, and the collegial decision-making process were surrendered as the internal study group recommended a new structure in which "board decisions would be clearly advisory and could be overturned at any time by the Superintendent."

In Washington, Bernard Rogers had already become convinced that dramatic action was necessary. Also convinced that the power of the Superintendent must be increased (and the power of the academic board decreased) was General Andrew Jackson Goodpaster, class of 1939, who had been an early consultant to the West Point Study Group. Many West Point graduates, whose association with the Academy had been limited to their cadet days or to a brief tour as instructor, believed that the academic board had played too dominant and too conservative a role—their number included former Superintendents and former Commandants, such as Rogers. In their view, the board seemed only to obstruct change. Few appreciated the importance of the board's stabilizing role in a military institution whose leadership was, by its very nature, autocratic. In resisting the sometimes over-zealous Superintendents (and occasional like-minded colleagues), the academic board had generally preserved stability and insured continuity. Still, over the years, they had gradually yielded ground to reasoned and measured change. Unmindful of this, the outsiders who dominated the West Point Study Group and the Army hierarchy were determined to reduce the power of the academic board. General Goodpaster shared the outsiders' view that the influence of the academic board over affairs at West Point was too extensive.

Goodpaster was one of the Army's foremost elder statesmen. He had retired in 1974 after five years as the Supreme Allied Commander of NATO's forces in Europe, but had remained active in Washington affairs. At Rogers's urging, he agreed to return to active duty and accept the post at West Point, although to do so meant giving up one star and reverting, for the time being, to the three-star rank of lieutenant general. In the Chief of

Staff's view, Goodpaster was the one man who could revitalize the Academy at West Point, and he was given free rein to do so. Goodpaster succeeded Sidney Berry in June 1977.

In July, after nearly seven months of study, the West Point Study Group's final report was completed and given to Rogers. He forwarded it to Goodpaster, saying only that the new Superintendent should take whatever action on its recommendations he deemed appropriate. Goodpaster, however, was in substantial agreement with the report and most of its recommendations. "From this day forward," he replied, "we will make the Report our own."

The new Superintendent established a number of committees to address the study group's recommendations. One of the most important of these was the committee on governance. The Borman Commission had highlighted the failure of the Military Academy's top officials and senior faculty members to remain abreast of changing values and attitudes, not only among cadets but also among junior faculty. The West Point Study Group had recommended a major restructuring of the Academy's governance. It was essential, they believed, to alter the power relationships at the Academy—in effect, to increase the power of the Superintendent in relation to the academic board.

The governance committee, after months of study and argument, recommended changes in the governance structure of the Academy along lines that had been proposed by the West Point Study Group. Goodpaster approved. Most significant was the creation of the "policy board," which was to be the Superintendent's main source of advice and counsel on all matters having general significance to the Academy. It supplanted the academic board in many of the latter's traditional advisory functions. The West Point Study Group had recommended that four tenured faculty members sit on the policy board, but Goodpaster opted for just two (in addition to the Dean), and the influence of the academic community was further reduced.

"Now, I know there was some mumbling that I was diminishing the role of the Academic Board," Goodpaster recalled. "I never saw it that way. I felt that in the academic area I was really strengthening their role through the process of making it very clear that they would be responsible for giving the academic direction needed at the Military Academy, and they would not be allowed to evade it. They would not be allowed to fail to see what was going on as it happened." Under Goodpaster, the primary responsibility of the academic board was to advise the Superintendent on all academic matters. No longer was the academic board independently responsible for determining the curriculum. And, no longer was the board the exclusive preserve of the academic heads; the Superintendent now had the authority to appoint other members to the academic board, as he wished.

The members of the academic board, quite naturally, took a dim view of these developments and, in the summer of 1977, five department heads opted to retire: Colonel Elliott C. Cutler, class of 1944, Department of Mechanics; Colonel David G. MacWilliams, class of 1944, Department of Chemistry; Colonel Edwin Van V. Sutherland, class of 1936, Department of English; Colonel Walter J. Renfroe, Jr., class of 1934, Department of Foreign Languages; and Colonel Frederick C. Lough, class of 1938, Department of Law. Never before in the history of the Academy had there been such a rush to retirement. Upon his departure, Sutherland commended the West Point community on its ability "to put a cheerful countenance in the face of what ever aggravation or adversity." But, he warned his colleagues who remained not to become too defensive—not to allow "our reasoned recognition of West Point's virtues and strengths to be translated into a defensive abatis, turning aside all criticism." Said Sutherland, "Ritual self approval leads to complacency and can end in disaster."

The power of the academic community was further eroded in 1984 when General John

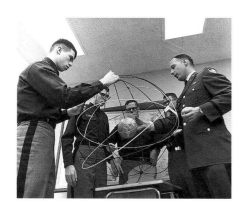

Astronomy class in 1970. U.S.M.A. Archives.

A. Wickham, the Army Chief of Staff, instructed Superintendent Willard W. Scott, Jr., class of 1948, who had succeeded Goodpaster, to implement a plan of "faculty development" that seemed intended to undermine the tenure of the permanent professors. Since World War II, professors had served beyond thirty years' active service (to age sixty-four) at the pleasure of the Secretary of the Army, but no one could recall a professor being forced out. The Borman Commission, in 1976, had recommended that permanent professors should be allowed to continue beyond thirty years of service only with the approval of the Superintendent, but that recommendation had never been acted upon.

Wickham, who had visited West Point in November 1983, had taken note of the poor turnout of officers—particularly the senior permanent faculty—at the lecture he delivered, and saw it as a sign that they had lost touch with the modern Army. The permanent faculty, he told Scott, needed to be "regreened," and he directed that they begin to participate in activities that would enhance their knowledge of the activities of the Army in the field. After some reflection, the Chief of Staff decided that even more needed to be done to ensure that the tenured faculty were not allowed to stagnate or become too isolated. In June 1984, Wickham summoned Scott to Washington, where the Superintendent was briefed on a new procedure to be used in the selection of permanent academic faculty, and for the periodic review of faculty tenure. Washington ensured its continued participation by including a representative of the Army staff on future selection boards.

Under Wickham's plan, the permanent faculty would be required to spend one summer of every three (or one year of every seven) with the Army in the field or at Army schools. In addition, the performance of the senior tenured faculty would be reviewed upon reaching thirty years' service and at five-year intervals thereafter. They would be "confirmed in the position or retired" based on the judgment of a panel made up of the Superintendent, the Army's Deputy Chief of Staff for personnel, and the director of the Army staff. Scott and the staff at West Point drew up plans to implement Wickham's new directive but deferred development of the "criteria for continuation" for the locally unpopular tenure review and—when they were not pressed—let that matter drop completely.

The issue of tenure reviews lay dormant until 1987 when Lieutenant General Dave R. Palmer, class of 1956, who succeeded Scott, resurrected the issue and presented his proposal to General Carl E. Vuono, class of 1957, Wickham's successor. Under Palmer's plan the first review—after thirty years' service—would be made by the Dean and the Superintendent, thereafter, at five-year intervals, the panel proposed earlier by Wickham (with the addition of the Dean) would determine the fate of the academicians. The criteria for the review of tenure included: consistent academic growth and a commitment to academic excellence; an "outstanding manner of performance of military duties;" and military bearing. In addition the professor must: "work constructively with colleagues in routine coordination and on committees and study groups," and "demonstrate a distinctively moral lifestyle characterized by integrity and intellectual honesty." Vuono approved the plan and, after final approval by the Secretary of the Army, the new policy was put into effect in January 1988. The professors were incensed, but they had nowhere to turn.

The turmoil that attended the governance issue was even more evident in two other critical areas—the curriculum and the faculty. As the academic board lost the power to govern the institution, it also seemed to lose the ability to resist or manage change. In the years from 1977 to 1988 the academic program underwent four major revisions—each of which remolded the core curriculum. The board seemed unable to make up its collective mind.

That may have stemmed, in part, from the increasingly rapid turnover among members of the board. Frustrated by their growing inability to influence events or to bring order, the permanent faculty (in particular the department heads) departed from the Academy earlier and earlier. By the latter years of the eighties the flood of retirements among the Academy's traditional leadership had reached epic proportions.

The Davidson reforms of the late fifties had brought the abolition of the totally prescribed curriculum and the introduction of electives (albeit a limited number). In 1965, room was made for additional electives (making a total of four) by trimming the courses in mechanics and electricity.

In 1967, Superintendent Donald Bennett began to press the academic community for a commitment to curriculum changes that would extend the Davidson reforms and allow "specialization in a chosen field." The majority of the academic board agreed. Led by Dean John Jannarone, class of 1938 (who had left physics and chemistry in 1965 to assume the deanship when Brigadier General William Bessell had retired), the proponents included: MacWilliams in chemistry; Charles Broshous in earth, space and graphic science; George Lincoln in social sciences; Lough, law; Heiberg, mechanics; Colonel Edward A. Saunders, class of 1946, physics; Renfroe in foreign languages; and Sutherland in English. (Sutherland had replaced the widely recognized Yeats scholar, Colonel Russell Alspach, in 1965.) Only three were opposed: Schilling in engineering; Cutler in electricity; and Colonel John S. B. Dick, class of 1935, in mathematics. In April 1968, the board approved the new curriculum—increasing the number of electives to six. In addition, cadets were allowed, if they wished, to choose their electives from a specific field within one of four areas of concentration—basic sciences, applied sciences and engineering, humanities, or national security and public affairs. Still, the curriculum continued to be a largely prescribed one, with only a limited potential for specialization.

History class in 1970. U.S.M.A. Archives.

To those opposed to the new curriculum, the Academy was poised "at a watershed on the trace of curriculum development." They predicted that: "Henceforth there will be three academic categories of cadets, . . . 'social science' cadets; 'engineering' cadets; and 'science' cadets. . . . The core will soon start to be differentiated for cadets pursuing the various major tracks. The elementary drive toward optimization will force this differentiation. . . . Cadets pursuing the public affairs concentration will hardly regard themselves as possible selectees for later graduate schooling in engineering . . . and will increasingly regard their already emasculated engineering component as a useless imposition. . . . The arguments in favor of free cadet choice which have brought the majority of the Academic Board this far will then apply with redoubled vigor to the further reduction in the core."

The growth in the number of courses offered as electives by the various departments seemed to confirm the fears of the critics. The elective program "contains powerful seeds of self-acceleration," they had warned—correctly, it proved. In fact, the growth of electives (from twenty in 1960 to over 150 in 1971 and over 380 in 1988) had become a force unto itself. Indeed, it changed the nature of the academic departments. Those once small fiefdoms, ruled by a usually benevolent head, in which all taught well defined segments of a well defined curriculum, were fast becoming polyglot empires with diverse and sometimes conflicting interests, and with increasingly independent and vocal subcultures championed by members of the growing permanent faculty.

Davidson's carefully managed reform, however, gave way to uncertainty and sometimes self-serving compromise. That was illustrated in the curriculum debates of 1972–73. In 1972, Superintendent William Knowlton asked an outside review board to examine the curriculum. Although they found the academic program to be essentially sound and properly oriented, they did recommend a reduction in the overall course load and a reduction in plebe mathematics. The cadets, they said, were over-scheduled.

What followed bore little resemblance to the reform debates of a dozen years earlier, but, by the early seventies, the academic board of the Davidson era had been wholly supplanted. The departure of many of that old guard has already been noted. Of the balance, Heiberg, in the Department of Mechanics, retired in 1968, and was replaced by Colonel Frederick A. Smith, Jr., class of 1944. In 1969, Lincoln left the social science department and was succeeded by Colonel Amos A. Jordan, class of 1946. Jordan's highly regarded *Foreign Aid in the Defense of Southeast Asia* had marked him as another in a respected line of soldier-scholars in the social science department. Also in 1969, Broshous, the last academic member of the Davidson era board, retired as head of the Department of Earth, Space and Graphic Sciences. He was succeeded by Colonel Gilbert W. Kirby, class of 1949.

There were also changes among the newer members of the board. Jordan, who had only recently taken the reins of social science, surrendered them in 1972 to Colonel Lee Donne Olvey, class of 1955. Dick in mathematics retired in 1973 and was replaced by Colonel Jack M. Pollin, class of 1944. Also in 1973, Frederick Smith was chosen as Dean, succeeding Brigadier General John Jannarone, and Colonel Robert M. Wilson, class of 1950, became head of the mathematics department in Smith's stead.

In late 1973, after a lengthy and often heated debate, the academic board voted to reduce the number of class attendances, but they could not agree on which course or courses should be dropped. In the end, compromise born of paralysis yielded a "lesson drop plan" which levied an across-the-board ten percent cut in almost every department's core course hours. It was a solution that all recognized as unsatisfactory, and one that caused many to question the ability of the academic board to govern responsibly. The academic board of the earlier debates—men whose long service on the board had welded them into an effective body—had moved on. In their place was a new generation whose increasingly rapid turnover on the board seemed to make it difficult for them to find their way along a path that was not of their choosing and not wholly to their liking.

Further changes followed in the wake of the 1976 EE304 affair. A proposal of a 1976 curriculum study group (that would have reduced the number of required courses from forty-eight to forty-two) was held in abeyance until the recommendations of the Borman Commission and then the West Point Study Group could be considered. Both groups concluded that West Point needed increased emphasis upon academic excellence. To many that meant cutting the number of required core courses in order to allow cadets to better focus the use of their time. In response, in 1977, the academic board approved a curriculum that set the number of required courses at forty—thirty core courses and ten electives, plus military science and physical education. Once again, however, as had become the general case, change came largely at the expense of the math-science-engineering sector.

The five resignations that followed the EE304 affair (more than a third of the board) further unsettled matters. To replace them, four new department heads were named in 1977; the selection of the fifth (law) was deferred. Colonel William J. Hoff, Jr., replaced MacWilliams in chemistry; Colonel Stanley E. Reinhart, class of 1950, replaced Cutler in mechanics; Colonel Sumner Willard, who had pioneered the use of language laboratories at the Academy, took Renfroe's place in foreign languages; and Sutherland in English was succeeded by Colonel Jack L. Capps, class of 1948. Capps had already achieved a reputation as a scholar with his *Emily Dickinson's Reader,* and continued to augment it as general editor of the William Faulkner Concordance Project.

Also in 1977, in response to a recommendation from the West Point Study Group, the Department of Behavioral Sciences and Leadership was created from the office of military leadership, which had remained under the Commandant since it had been created by Maxwell Taylor. In 1978, Lieutenant Colonel Howard T. Prince, II, class of 1962, was selected to head the new department. He replaced Colonel Harry A. Buckley, class of 1948, who had led the earlier organization and who had managed its transition to departmental status under the Dean.

At this juncture, the science and engineering faculty began to move to the forefront of curriculum reform—particularly Saunders in physics, Wilson in mechanics, and Schilling in the engineering department (and, in 1981, Schilling's successor Lieutenant Colonel Allen F. Grum, Jr., class of 1953). Their motivation was twofold. First, in recent years it had been the science and engineering curriculum that had given ground to make room for electives. They were concerned that they had given up too much. Schilling argued strongly that "the engineering design process [was] a paradigm of the rational decision process" and that this way of conceptualizing problems was essential in a military career. Second, they were beginning to experience resistance, from some of the better engineering schools, to the admission of West Point graduates to advanced degree programs; the candidates from West Point were being told that their undergraduate program had not sufficiently prepared them for graduate-level studies in engineering.

In the late winter of 1981, a new curriculum committee, under Saunders's chairmanship proposed a fundamental change in the Academy's academic program. Under this plan cadets would be required to select one of two academic tracks at the end of their plebe year: a mathematics-science-engineering track or a humanities-public affairs track. That decision would determine the core curriculum the cadet would take. This change would allow the math-science-engineering community to strengthen their core curriculum as a preliminary to seeking accreditation in some engineering fields by the Accreditation Board of Engineering and Technology (ABET)—a move that would vastly enhance future graduates' engineering credentials.

The key feature of this tracking scheme was the addition of required "area courses" to strengthen the programs in both tracks. Following the board's favorable action, Superintendent Goodpaster approved the new program in May 1981.

In July, Army Chief of Staff Edward C. Meyer, class of 1951, told Willard Scott, who had just arrived to replace Goodpaster, that "the time may be right to move forward with the 'majors' concept." In August, Scott directed the Dean to proceed with the development of a program of optional majors.

In September 1982, after a sometimes rancorous debate, the academic board approved an optional majors program—eight majors in the math-science-engineering disciplines and eight in the humanities-public affairs area. Two arguments proved most persuasive. First, as a result of the earlier decision to allow cadets to concentrate upon a particular field of study, and the recent move toward ABET-accredited engineering programs, the Academy was already offering majors in all but name. Second, virtually all of the reputable American colleges and universities, as well as the other service academies, were offering majors—including ABET accredited engineering majors. That impacted on recruiting. If the Military Academy was to continue to attract high quality students, it had little option. In October, Superintendent Scott forwarded the proposal to Meyer, together with a minority report representing the view of four dissenting members of the academic board.

As the Academy had moved toward the majors program and ABET accreditation, the membership of the academic board had continued to shift, as had its alignment on various issues. In 1979, Colonel Robert Berry was chosen to head the Department of Law. In 1980, Colonel John J. Costa, class of 1949, succeeded Willard as head of the Department of Foreign Languages, and in 1981, Colonel Roy K. Flint replaced Griess in the Department of History. Griess had headed that department since its creation in 1969, and had shepherded the production of an impressive collection of texts used in the History of Military Art—known collectively as the "gray books."

It is interesting that two of the newest members of the academic board—Berry (law) and Flint (history)—were among those opposed to majors. And, it is noteworthy that all three of the members of the academic board who were not West Point graduates—Flint, Berry, and Hoff (chemistry)—were opposed. Perhaps these "non-graduates" were better able to appreciate West Point's uniqueness than the Academy's own sons. In their minority report, these three and Jack Pollin, in mathematics, expressed two general reserva-

Above left:

A cadet's speech is videotaped and then analyzed by his speech instructor and his tactical officer, as part of the skill development necessary for effective command. Late 1980s.

Above upper right:

A class in calculus in the late 1980s.

Above lower right:

A class in chemistry. Late 1980s.

tions: first, that West Point's majors—which were fitted around a still substantial core of required courses, for the most part mathematics and science—were very different from majors programs in other schools and might be troublesome to accreditation committees; and second, that the cadets' focus on a specific discipline might detract from their general preparation for officership. Their concerns, however, were not shared by their colleagues or by Meyer in Washington.

In early 1983, with Department of the Army approval, the Academy proceeded with the introduction of the sixteen academic majors—chemistry, civil engineering, computer science, electrical engineering, engineering management, engineering physics, mathematical science, mechanical engineering, behavioral science, economics, foreign language (five choices), geography, history, literature, management, and political science. But majors were made optional; cadets could choose either to concentrate in a field of study or declare a major. Final ABET accreditation for civil, electrical, and mechanical engineering, and for engineering management followed in 1985.

Satisfaction with the new program, however, was short lived. Soon, many of the professors outside the engineering departments came to believe that the cadets who had not chosen engineering majors were not getting adequate career preparation in engineering. In 1986, in what now seemed a turnaround, they began to object that the engineering elements of the core curriculum (for non-engineer majors) were no longer adequate. In 1988, the curriculum committee recommended yet another revision of the core curriculum, a fundamentally different approach—one built around what was called "the engineering thought process." Rather than the general engineering core that cadets then took, they proposed that, beginning with the class of 1991, all cadets should enroll in one of six thirteen-course core sequences in mathematics, basic science, and engineering. Regardless of their majors, cadets would choose a carefully structured sequence in either civil, electrical, mechanical, systems, computer, or nuclear engineering. In each sequence, the capstone experience would be an engineering design program that would integrate the whole: for example, the civil engineering sequence would lead to courses in structural analysis and the design of steel structures; and the electrical engineering sequence would be capped with courses in electronic design and electrical systems. The object, explained

Superintendent Palmer to Army Chief of Staff Vuono, was to allow every cadet "the opportunity to experience the engineering thought process in depth." But, after three decades of wrenching curriculum changes, cadets and faculty alike could have been justified in wondering if the academic board had the ability or the will to resist further change. It seemingly no longer acted as a buffer against novelty and experimentation.

The little opposition there had been to this last change had come from some of those departments that had taught the traditional core engineering courses. The road to agreement seemingly had been aided by the increasingly rapid turnover among the heads; from 1984 through 1988 ten had left their departments. Two new heads were named in 1984: Colonel Wendell Childs succeeded Saunders as head of the Department of Physics; and Colonel William Carroll, class of 1957, succeeded Wilson as head of the Department of Mechanics. Carroll was in turn succeeded, just a year later, by Colonel Peter D. Heimdahl, class of 1961. Two more new department heads were named in 1985. Colonel David H. Cameron, class of 1950, succeeded Pollin in mathematics. The Dean, Brigadier General Frederick Smith, retired and was replaced by Roy Flint (the first "non-grad" selected as Dean). Lieutenant Colonel Robert A. Doughty, class of 1965, became head of the history department. Doughty, an active scholar, published two books in his first five years: *The Seeds of Disaster: The Development of French Army Doctrine, 1919–1939*; and *The Breaking Point: Sedan and the Fall of France, 1940*. Allen Grum, in engineering, retired in 1986 but a successor was not immediately named. In 1987, there were two more changes: Childs left the Department of Physics and was replaced by Lieutenant Colonel Raymond J. Winkel, Jr., class of 1967: and Colonel Dennis Hunt replaced Berry in the Department of Law.

Three more department heads retired in 1988, as the issue of the new curriculum came to a head—Hoff in chemistry, Capps in English, and Cameron in mathematics. They were replaced by Colonels James H. Ramsden, class of 1958, Peter L. Stromberg, class of 1959, and Frank R. Giordano, class of 1964, respectively. Various articles, books, and scholarly papers marked each of these three new department heads as mature educators. Of particular note was Stromberg's *Teaching Ethics in the Military* (co-authored) and Giordano's *A First Course in Mathematics Modeling* (co-authored).

Above upper left:
Second classmen in an electrical engineering class. Late 1980s.

Above lower left:
Cadets in conference with a member of the computer science department. Late 1980s.

Above right:
Third classmen receiving instruction in military science and tactics. Late 1980s.

The Army boxing team. From The Howitzer. U.S.M.A. Archives. Copy Photo: Philip Pocock.

A swimming meet at the gymnasium's fifty-meter pool, which has eight lanes and was opened for intercollegiate competition in 1970.

An intramural basketball game between companies A1 and G1 in the late 1980s.

Lieutenant General Dave Palmer with his staff in front of the Superintendent's quarters. Late 1980s.

The Dean and the 1989 academic board gather in the academic board room of the administration building. Behind them is the massive stone mantel designed by Lee Lawrie, which features statues of great leaders, including Alexander the Great, Hector, and King Arthur.

In July 1989 a number of structural changes (driven largely by the recent ABET accreditation) were made in the engineering departments. Geography and computer science and electrical engineering were reorganized as the Department of Electrical Engineering and Computer Science, and the Department of Geography. Similarly, the engineering and mechanics departments were restructured into the Department of Systems Engineering and the Department of Civil and Mechanical Engineering. Colonel James L. Kays, class of 1962, was chosen to head the new Department of Systems Engineering. Later that same year the new Department of Geography was redesignated the Department of Geography and Environmental Engineering.

Meanwhile, the turbulence among the permanent faculty continued to increase; three department heads left in 1989. Costa in foreign languages was succeeded by Colonel Edward J. F. Thomas. Kirby, in geography and computer science, was replaced by Gerald E. Galloway, Jr., class of 1957. And Olvey in social sciences was succeeded by Colonel James R. Golden, class of 1965. Olvey and Golden, both economists, had jointly authored (with Robert C. Kelly) *Economics of National Security*. But Golden's *NATO Burden Sharing* and *Dynamics of Change in NATO* also marked him as a scholar in international affairs.

Three more faculty members retired in 1990—Reinhart in electrical engineering and computer science, Prince in behavioral sciences and leadership, and Ramsden in chemistry. In addition, Brigadier General Flint, the Dean, departed and was succeeded by Galloway, who had only recently been appointed head of the geography department. In all, four new department heads would join the academic board that year. Never had the Academy experienced such turmoil in its faculty as had been witnessed since 1976.

Bob Hope entertaining the cadets at West Point in 1970. U.S.M.A. Archives.

Cadets, although hardly oblivious to the changes whirling about them—particularly the curriculum reforms—were less caught up in the events than the staff and faculty. In addition to the demands of academics and military training, a myriad of well-organized extracurricular activities and recreational facilities competed for their attention. By 1962, there were fifty-eight authorized extracurricular activities—academic clubs, such as the debate council, the mathematics forum, or the German language club; competitive groups, such as the fencing club, the rugby club, and the ski team; entertainment groups, such as the Glee Club, and station KDET; hobby groups, such as the chess, model, and rifle clubs; religious groups, such as the several cadet choirs; numerous cadet committees, such as the class ring and crest committees, as well as the hop committee; and the staffs of *Bugle Notes*, *Howitzer*, and *The Pointer*.

By 1990, the number of activities had grown to 110. Among the new ones were: the mountaineering club, the scuba club (which soon established the tradition of diving off the Florida coast during spring break), the cadet pipes and drums (with their own registered tartan), the gospel choir, and the computer electronics forum. In the midst of all this growth and change, however, some traditions survived; the "100th Night Show" was still written, produced, directed, and performed by cadets, and sponsored by the venerable Dialectic Society.

Not all cadet extracurricular activities, however, were condoned by the Academy; consider the "great goat caper" of the class of 1966. The weekend before the Army-Navy game, a small band of conspirators drove to Annapolis determined to kidnap Navy's Billy XV. To their dismay, they learned that the goat had been moved from the Naval Academy's dairy farm to a high security Atlantic Fleet communications center across the Severn River. Still, they didn't give up. They made a reconnaissance run past the installation, and found a ten-foot chain-link fence crowned with barbed wire surrounding the facility and two marine guards manning the gate. Just beyond the guards, in a twenty-foot pen

A selection of class rings and pins. U.S.M.A. Library.

Below left:
On the day of the 1989 Graduation Parade, the plebes of company A1 observe the tradition of "knocking brass," as the brass buckles they have been "dinged" for not polishing are now "donged" by the upperclassmen. This dented and scarred brass will become a cherished memento of their fourth class experience.

Below right:
The "100th Night Show" in the late 1980s.

topped with more barbed wire, stood the prize. Despite these obstacles, however, they concluded it could be done.

That night they returned, wearing black turtlenecks, their faces darkened with burned cork. While four girls, who had been recruited as accomplices, flirted with the marine guards, the cadets entered the compound through an unlocked pedestrian gate they had discovered during their reconnaissance and made their way to the goat's pen. There, using a crowbar wrapped in a black towel, they broke the padlock, opened the gate and made off with the cooperative Billy. Days later, when the affair had played itself out and Billy had been returned to an embarrassed and angry Naval Academy, the culprits were called before the Commandant. "We've got to give you some punishment, so I'm going to remove your first-class privileges for two months," he told them. "But I want you to know I'd be proud to have you serve under me in the Army. Well done."

Cadets have often proved to be an impish lot. In the early 1970s, they took up the newest collegiate rage—"the streak." One cold winter night, as the officer-in-charge left the guardhouse on his after taps inspection, a yell thundered from the south area barracks and a multitude of naked bodies issued forth into the cold night air. But before the officer could reach the area it became still and quiet—no movement anywhere. As he stood in the center of south area, however, a shout rose up in central area and streakers rushed back and forth across that area. Into central area strode the officer, only to find it as deserted as the area he had just left. Then, another shout: south, new south, and north areas were suddenly filled with naked bodies. The officer headed for north area, but once again, all was silent. Just then, another shout went up from central area and another wave of streakers emerged. The officer-in-charge weighed the magnitude of his task, returned to the guardhouse, called out the cadet chain of command and turned the problem over to the cadet officers.

In some cases cadet antics went beyond impishness, however. One fall evening in 1963, a mess hall rally ran amuck. It began with the firing of a cannon, which cued the plebes who had been primed to respond. They leaped onto their chairs, peeled off their uniform tunics and whirled them over their heads, shouting, "Rally! Rally! Rally!" Then in came the Rabble Rousers, and the corps took up the chant.

For reasons still not fully understood, the rally almost immediately turned into a food riot. Cadets tilted their tables on end, sending china and silver crashing to the floor. "Stack tables!" someone commanded, and throughout the mess hall, cadets lifted the heavy oak tables one atop another until they were stacked three, four, five, even six tables high. Then cadets leaped onto the chandeliers and began swinging like gray-clad apes.

Opened half-pint milk cartons sailed across the room, leaving in their wake a white liquid trail, followed by ketchup bottles and then globs of honey. Nothing since the "Egg-Nog Riot" of 1826 could match this frenzy. For twenty minutes they persisted, the officer-in-charge all the while yelling, "Halt! This has got to stop." Then, as quickly as it had started, it was over, and the cadets surveyed the scene. Even they were shocked and alarmed by what they had done, and all of them scurried back to their barracks to await the inevitable reaction.

West Point's senior officials were justifiably outraged, but they could not identify any ringleaders; besides, following that rally, Army had upset Penn State, 10-to-7, spoiling, for a second year in a row, the Pennsylvania school's hopes for a national championship. When it finally came, the official reaction was surprisingly mild. Every cadet was docked $1.27 each month until the damage had been paid for. Some said, "If that was a $1.27 rally, let's have a $5.00 rally." Most cadets, however, were perfectly satisfied to have gotten off so lightly, and had no intention of trying their luck again.

Cadets also seem to have an instinct for getting to the heart of a matter. In 1977, the West Point Study Group's final report remarked that, "a relatively humorless atmosphere seems to prevail" at the Academy. When *The New York Times* duly reported this finding, the cadets responded: "How can a newspaper with no comics call us 'humorless'?"

The culmination of the entire cadet year lies in graduation week. It is a milestone for everyone in the corps. For the plebe there is advancement into the ranks of the upper classes. For the yearlings, there is the longed-for summer furlough. For the second class-men—the cows—there is the elevation to the first class. And for the firstie, of course, it marks the culmination of the four year experience—graduation.

Members of the class of 1940 prepare to march in the graduation ceremonies of 1990, as they celebrate the fiftieth anniversary of their graduation from the United States Military Academy.

First Captain Kristin Baker at the graduation ceremonies of the class of 1990.

Above:
Cadets are seen through this sally port, an important architectural feature at the Academy. Late 1980s (The World War II Battle of Leyte Gulf is commemorated in the inscription above the arch.)

Opposite:
Buffalo Barracks, used for housing some of the enlisted members of the West Point garrison.

But graduation week is also a special time for former graduates, for it is impossible to spend four years at West Point without being touched by the pervasive influence of all its traditions. For the "old grads" it is a time to renew friendships and strengthen the class ties and spirit that so distinguishes members of the Long Gray Line. May 1990 was such an occasion for the class of 1940 who had come to celebrate their fiftieth reunion. They were joined by other classes celebrating other special reunions—almost 1,000 graduates in all.

Then came the day of the graduation parade and the sequence of music not used in any other ceremony. The battalions marched onto the plain to the tune of "Stars and Stripes Forever," then "The Dashing White Sergeant" as the units began to form on line. The band trooped the line to the "Graduation March"—consisting of the first eight bars of "Home, Sweet Home," followed by parts of "100 Days Till June," "The Wedding March," "The Girl I Left Behind Me," "Auld Lang Syne," and then concluding with the whole of "Home, Sweet Home." The first class was formed "front and center" to the tune of "Army Blue," and then moved to the reviewing line to strains of "Alma Mater." As the corps passed in review the band struck up the "Official West Point March." Each company, as it passed the graduating class, executed "eyes right" and held that salute until it had passed the end of the line of the graduating class.

The following day, 895 members of the class of 1990 performed their final rite of passage at the United States Military Academy. Diplomas in hand, there was an exchange of the "Long Corps" yell between those cadets remaining and those departing, a last "dismissed!" and then a blur of white as caps were tossed high into the air, to remain where they fell—trophies for enthusiastic children who might themselves someday say:

From these, these gray and ancient halls of ours
An hundred martial heroes once have sprung;
An hundred mighty men well known to fame
And countless others by all TIME unsung.

They thronged these halls and clattered on the stair
They danced and jested while soft music low
Once played for the silver swinging shadows
That, like life and beauty swiftly go.

Here they lived, and saw too clearly life's lasting dream;
Here they strove for strength with distaff and with bar,
Here they saw the mighty Hudson's majesty
Stark white beneath a vault of moon and star.

We did it too, and found our life like theirs,
These buildings meant to us a little more.
This heritage is ours to carry on . . .
Our memories, like theirs, our golden store.

Take this and carry on.
What matter outward marks or Rings?
We carry with us an affection that
Transcends the glow of earthly things.

"Glimpses of West Point," 1928
R. M. Wohlforth (Class of 1927)

YOUR MISSION REMAINS FIXED, DETERMINED, INVIOLABLE — IT IS TO WIN OUR WARS. ALL OTHER PUBLIC PURPOSES WILL FIND OTHERS FOR THEIR ACCOMPLISHMENT. YOURS IS THE PROFESSION OF ARMS — THE WILL TO WIN, THE SURE KNOWLEDGE THAT IN WAR THERE IS NO SUBSTITUTE FOR VICTORY; THAT THE VERY OBSESSION OF YOUR PUBLIC SERVICE MUST BE DUTY · HONOR · COUNTRY

The Long Gray Line marches past the Superintendent's quarters in formation. Duty • Honor • Country •

BIBLIOGRAPHICAL NOTES ON SOURCES

General

Among the many works dealing with West Point, there are a small number that I found so helpful that I will mention them at be beginning of this essay, with the reader's understanding that I have consulted and drawn on them throughout—or, at least, across the time span that they cover.

The first of these is Edward C. Boynton's *History of West Point and its Military Importance During the American Revolution: and the Origin and Progress of the United States Military Academy* (New York: 1863). Boynton's work is the first widely used history of West Point. Though often inaccurate in the details of the narrative, Boynton's work is nonetheless indispensable, particularly in his description of the physical facilities at West Point in the mid-nineteenth century. A second work is the *The Centennial of the United States Military Academy At West Point, New York*—often referred to simply as the *Centennial History*. In addition to individual essays covering a number of topics, including a history of each academic department, this two-volume work contains a detailed chronological listing of events relating to the Military Academy. Although there are serious errors in that chronology, the listing is nonetheless invaluable.

Two more modern works also require general citation. Sidney Forman's *West Point, A History of the United States Military Academy* (New York: 1950) is one of these. Though short on analysis, Forman's work provides a most useful and accurate narrative of events. The second work is Stephen E. Ambrose's *Duty, Honor, Country, A History of West Point* (Baltimore: 1966). Ambrose's work is more interpretative than Forman's, but is less accurate in narrative detail. In addition, Ambrose's later chapters are flawed by an excessive reliance on William Ganoe's near hagiographic *MacArthur Close-Up* (New York: 1962). Still, Ambrose's work remains a useful account.

Chapter 1

The opening Mansfield quote comes from "The United States Military Academy at West Point," *The American Journal of Education* (March 1863). The discussion of the region's geological history was informed by Jeffrey P. LaMoe and Rick W. Mills, *Field Guide to the Geology of West Point* (West Point: 1988). The Washington Irving quote comes from *A Book of the Hudson*.

In dealing with the colonial era—both Dutch and English—I found two works most useful: Maud Wilder Goodwin, *Dutch and English on the Hudson. A Chronicle of Colonial New York* (New Haven: 1919) and Carl Carmer, *The Hudson* (New York: 1939). My understanding of the history of the West Point environs was aided by E. M. Ruttenber's *History of the County of Orange* (Newburgh: 1875), by Leonara Cross's unpublished essay "The Moores of West Point" (USMA Library), and by J. M. Carson's *Information Relating to the Lands Comprising the Military Reservation at West Point, NY* (West Point: 1891).

Chapter 2

The most readable account of West Point in the Revolutionary War is Dave R. Palmer's *The River and the Rock* (New York: 1969). More accurate in the minute details of its fortifications is *Highland Fortress: The Fortification of West Point During the American Revolution* (West Point: 1988) by Charles E. Miller, Jr., Donald V. Lockey, and Joseph Visconti.

Chapter 3

The discussion of the Moores and the purchase, by the government, of the West Point lands is drawn from Cross's "The Moores of West Point" (cited above) and the *Journals of the Continental Congress*. The Rochefontaine episode is described in letters from Rochefontaine to Timothy Pickering and Alexander Hamilton, and in garrison orders. See the Pickering Papers (Massachusetts Historical Society) and the Stephen Rochefontaine Papers (USMA Library).

On the early efforts to establish a Military Academy at West Point see the correspondence of Alexander Hamilton, John Adams, James McHenry and Samuel Dexter in the *Hamilton Papers*, the *Works of John Adams*, the *American State Papers; Military Affairs*, and the Jonathan Williams Papers (Lilly Library, Indiana University).

The elaboration of Thomas Jefferson's founding of the Military Academy was drawn from my own earlier works: "The Founding of West Point: Jefferson and the Politics of Security," *Armed Forces and Society* (Summer 1981); and *Mr. Jefferson's Army, Political and Social Reform of the Military Establishment, 1801–1809* (New York: 1987).

Two Ph.D. dissertations deserve particular mention: Edgar Denton, III, "The Formative Years of the United States Military Academy, 1775–1823" (Syracuse University, 1964); and Thomas Elliott Shaughnessy, "Beginnings of National Professional Military Education in America, 1775–1825" (Johns Hopkins University, 1965). Of the two, Shaughnessy's work is the more insightful, though both must be consulted.

Also useful were: *The Memoirs of Gen. Joseph Swift* (Worcester: 1890); and Augusta Blanche Bernard, *Reminiscences of West Point* (East Saginaw, MI: 1886).

Chapter 4

Much of the material in this chapter draws on my own earlier works (cited above), particularly *Mr. Jefferson's Army*. Also helpful were the Shaughnessy and Denton dissertations (cited above).

This chapter also draws heavily on: *The Memoirs of Gen. Joseph Swift*: Jonathan Williams Papers (Lilly Library and USMA Library); Jared Mansfield Papers (USMA Library and Yale Library); Elizabeth Mansfield Papers (USMA Library); *Thayer Papers* (USMA Library); and "Letters Sent, Chief of Engineers, Relating to Military Academy" (M91), (Record Group 94, National Archives).

Chapter 5

The interpretation of Sylvanus Thayer draws on Thomas J. Flemming's *West Point, The Men and Times of the United States Military Academy* (New York: 1965), and also on the Shaughnessy and Denton dissertations (cited above). The memoir literature for this period is also helpful, particularly Albert E. Church's *Personal Reminiscences of the Military Academy from 1824 to 1831* (West Point: 1879).

Primary sources consulted included: *Thayer Papers* (USMA Library); George Washington Cullum Papers (USMA Library); "Correspondence Relating to the Military Academy, 1819–1866," (Record Group 94, National Archives); and "Staff Records" (USMA Archives).

Chapter 6

Three particularly important secondary works dealing with this period are: James L. Morrison, Jr., *The Best School in the World, West Point, The Pre-Civil War Years, 1833–1866* (Kent, OH: 1986); Mary Elizabeth Sergent, *They Lie Forgotten, The United States Military Academy, 1856–1861* (Middletown, NY: 1986); and Thomas Everett Griess, "Dennis Hart Mahan: West Point Professor and Advocate of Professionalism, 1830–1871," Ph.D. dissertation (Duke University, 1969).

The discussion of Delafield's selection of the Tudor-Gothic is drawn largely from materials in "Correspondence Relating to the Military Academy, 1819–1866" (Record Group 94, National Archives) and from the Superintendent's Letterbooks (USMA Archives). Also important were the West Point architectural drawings and other items in the "Fortifications File" (Record Group 77, Architectural and Topographic Branch, National Archives).

Concerning the history of the West Point Army Mess see the Irwin McDowell letter (1881) in "WPAM Minutes of Meetings" (USMA Archives). "A Sonnet to 'Analytical'— was found in Oliver E. Wood, *West Point Scrap Book* (New York: 1871).

Chapter 7

The billiard-table story came from *West Point Scrap Book*; on the origins of the New Year's Eve celebrations see Edgar W. Howe, *The History of the Class of 'Seventy-Eight at the U. S. Military Academy* (New York: 1881).

The most helpful secondary source dealing specifically with this period is W. Scott Dillard, "United States Military Academy, 1865–1900," Ph.D. dissertation (University of Washington, 1971). Also useful was the rich memoir literature of the period, particularly: John McAllister Schofield, *Forty-Six Years in the Army* (New York: 1897); O. L. Hein, *Memories of Long Ago* (New York: 1925); Henry O. Flipper, *The Colored Cadet at West Point* (New York: 1969); and Williston Fish, "Memories of West Point, 1877–1881" (USMA Library).

Important primary sources included the *Annual Reports* of the Superintendents (USMA Archives) and the records of the academic board (USMA Archives).

Chapter 8

The documents relating to the conflict between Mills and the advisory board are contained in the Samuel Tillman Papers (USMA Library) and, particularly, "Document File, USMA Headquarters, Correspondence, 1904–1917, File No. 2333" (USMA Archives).

The most useful secondary source for this period was Roger Hurless Nye, "The United States Military Academy in an Era of Educational Reform, 1900–1925." Ph.D. dissertation (Columbia University, 1968). Also helpful was William Addleman Ganoe's *MacArthur Close-Up* (New York: 1962) although it must be used with caution, for it is a wholly uncritical view of MacArthur's superintendency.

Concerning the social life of the professors of this era see Mrs. E. R. Heiberg's unpublished essay "Professors' Row" (USMA Library).

Chapter 9

Two secondary sources proved particularly useful. The first is "Wartime History of the United States Military Academy," a typescript which was prepared by the Department of Social Science immediately after the war (USMA Archives). The second is John P. Lovell's *Neither Athens Nor Sparta, The American Service Academies in Transition* (Bloomington: 1979).

Also helpful were the memoirs of Superintendents Maxwell D. Taylor and Garrison H. Davidson: Taylor—*Swords and Plowshares* (New York: 1972); Davidson—*Grandpa Gar, The Saga of One Soldier As Told To His Grandchildren* (1974).

The discussion of honor draws heavily on Vance O. Mitchel, "A Brief History of the West Point and Air Force Academy Honor Code" (Office of Air Force History, 1984). Primary sources which supplemented Mitchel included: the annual *Bugle Notes*; and numerous USMA pamphlets and fact sheets dealing with honor.

Other important primary sources were: Herman Beukema Papers (USMA Library); George A. Lincoln Papers (USMA Library); and the "Honor System" and "Honor Committee" files (USMA Archives).

Chapter 10

The most useful sources for this most recent period were the *Annual Reports*. Also helpful were occasional articles in *Assembly*, the publication of the Association of Graduates, and the *Interim Report of the Middle States Accreditation Steering Committee* (West Point: 1988).

The discussion of expansion planning and new construction draws on both The *Annual Reports* and *Assembly* articles, as well as on the memoirs of William C. Westmoreland, *A Soldier Reports* (Garden City: 1976).

On the issue of governance the final reports of the Borman Commission and the West Point Study Group were indispensable, as were the Charles H. Schilling Papers (USMA Library), and "File 1011-14. School Study File, Committee on Governance" (USMA Archives).

On curriculum changes the critical sources were again the *Annual Reports, Assembly* articles, and the Schilling Papers.

Also helpful in providing color was Rick Atkinson's *The Long Gray Line* (Boston, 1989) which chronicled the USMA class of 1966—covering, among other things, their lives both as cadets and as junior members of the faculty. The story of the food fight in 1962 and the cadet rebuttal to *The New York Times* in 1977 were drawn from it.

The concluding poem by Wohlforth was taken from the 1928 *Howitzer*.

INDEX

A page number in **boldface**
refers to an illustration.

THE UNITED STATES MILITARY

EDWARD HAMILTON KYLE

GEORGE JOSEPH LaBRECHE

HARRY BERT LANE

GEORGE THOMAS LARKIN

RAYMOND JOHN LaROSE

WALTER WELLMAN LAVELL

OSMUND ALFRED LEAHY

MILTON DAVID LEDERMAN

JOE WILBUR LEEDOM, JR.

LAURENCE JOSEPH LEGERE

KENNETH McRAE LEMLEY

WILLIAM FIELDING LEWIS

WILLIS FRANKLIN LEWIS

EVERETT DeWITT LIGHT

WILLIAM POWELL LITTON

JAMES DAVID LOEWUS

PHILIP COURTNEY LOOFBOURROW

JAMES ANTHONY LOTOZO

EDWARD DEMING LUCAS, JR.

EDISON ALBERT LYNN, JR.

RICHARD WARE MABEE

ROBERT NEVILLE MACKIN, III

JAMES RICHARD MAEDLER

ARTHUR GORDON MALONE

FRANK CHITTENDEN MANDELL

THOMAS FRANKLIN MANSFIELD

RUSSELL JOSEPH MANZOLILLO

WILLIAM EVERETT MARLING

CLARENCE TALMAGE MARSH, JR.

MORRILL ELWOOD MARSTON

JOSEPH LEE MASTRAN

ARTHUR DUDLEY MAXWELL

ROBERT EDWIN MAXWELL

GEORGE MAYO, JR.

JAMES BYINGTON McAFEE

ARTHUR AUSTIN McCARTAN

JOSEPH LEE McCROSKEY

EUGENE ORVILLE McDONALD

EARL McFARLAND, JR.

JAMES EDWARD McGINITY

STEWART LAWRENCE McKENNEY

BURTON ELMO McKENZIE

JOHN ROBERT McLEAN

MONTGOMERY CUNNINGHAM MEIGS

LOUIS GONZAGA MENDEZ, JR.

MARVIN HATFIELD MERCHANT

FRANK MESZAR

HENRY AUGUSTINE MILEY, JR.

RAYMOND WEIR MILLICAN

JAMES WILBOURNE MILNER

THEODORE ROSS MILTON

JOHN EDWARD MINAHAN

RALPH EDWARD MINER

THOMAS HUNTINGTON MONROE, JR.

BIDWELL MOORE

CRAIG LOWE MOORE

JAMES MONTGOMERY MOORE

PHILIP JOHN MOORE, III

STEPHEN BERNARD MORRISSEY

GEORGE HANS MUELLER

THOMAS HENRY MULLER

WILLIAM HENRY HARRISON MULLIN

DELBERT EARLE MUNSON

CORNELIUS ARTHUR MURPHY

EDWARD ALOYSIUS MURPHY, JR.

JOHN JOSEPH MURPHY, JR.

ARTHUR HAROLD NELSON

ROY WILLARD NELSON, JR.

CHARLES CARMIN NOBLE

HENRY HUDSON NORMAN, JR.

ROBINSON RILEY NORRIS

JOHN WILLIAM NORVELL

THADDEUS MICHAEL NOSEK

JOHN ANDREW O'BRIEN

ROBERT ANTHONY O'BRIEN, JR.

CAREY LAW O'BRYAN, JR.

ROBERT FRANCIS O'DONNELL

MELVILLE OFFERS

CHARLES EUGENE OGLESBY

JOHN THOMAS O'KEEFE

PAUL FRANCIS O'NEIL

LEONARD MILTON ORMAN

JAMES LAWSON ORR

RALPH ANDERSON OSBORN, JR.

FREDERIC WATSON OSETH

HERBERT EDWARD PACE, JR.

DAVID STUART PARKER

MAURICE EARLE PARKER

SAMUEL MERRICK PATTEN

MICHAEL PAULICK

HOWARD WILSON PENNEY

MANLEY CALBRAITH PERRY

HOWARD LEWIS PETER

SAMUEL RICHARD PETERSON

ROBERT CARTER PFEIL

PAUL DAVID PHILLIPS

JOHN JOSEPH PIDGEON

HOBART BURNSIDE PILLSBURY

JAMES HAROLD PITMAN

JAMES ARTHUR PLANT

EDWARD THOMAS PODUFALY

WILLIAM LYON PORTE

BRADLEY FOOTE PRANN

JOHN FINZER PRESNELL, JR.

THOMAS DUVALL QUAID

ROBERT CHARLES RALEIGH

JAMES HOLLAND STEPHEN RASMUSSEN

KARL TWEETEN RAUK

PAUL SORG REINECKE, JR.

RAYMOND RENOLA

ROWLAND HERMAN RENWANZ